D0387358

NATIONAL UNIVERSITY LIBRARY
ORANGE CO.

ORANGE COUNTY

Also by Robin Clarke
THE SECRET WEAPONS

The Science
of War
and Peace

ROBIN CLARKE

McGRAW-HILL BOOK COMPANY
New York • St. Louis • San Francisco
Dusseldorf • London
Mexico • Panama • Sydney

LIBRARY
NATIONAL UNIVERSITY LIBRARY
SOUTHWESTERN
ORANGE CO. ORANGE COUNTY

MAR 1 3 1972

Copyright © 1972 by Robin Clarke.
All rights reserved. Printed in the United
States of America. No part of this publication may be reproduced, stored in a re-
trieval system, or transmitted, in any form
or by any means, electronic, mechanical,
photocopying, recording, or otherwise, without the prior written permission of the
publisher.
Library of Congress
Catalog Card Number: 71-169016
Design by Stephanie Tevonian
First Edition
07-011239-8

Acknowledgments

As this is not a scholarly book, I have not observed the scholarly ritual of indicating the sources of my information in the normal way. I have, however, tried to include much of the relevant factual information and to indicate at the end of each chapter where the information came from. I hope this will enable those who wish to consult the sources to do so and at the same time provide the general reader with a text unencumbered by either footnotes or references.

I must express an enormous debt of gratitude to many people who took it on themselves to guide both my reading and my writing—in particular Frank Barnaby, Tony de Reuck, Dan Greenberg, Bill Gunston, Gordon Hilton, Geoffrey Hindley, Mary Lee, Milton Leitenberg, Tony Loftas, Jacques Richardson, Bryan Silcock, and Anthony Storr. Equally important was the help of the Conflict Research Society's Peace Research Centre in London, which provided me with a desk, a library and a stimulating environment.

Robin Clarke

Contents

The Science
of War
and Peace

The War Explosion

In the next half hour about 7,000 children will be born. Rather less than 3,000 people will die. And this gap between the birth rate and the death rate will saddle the planet earth within the next year with an extra 65 million people—roughly the combined population of Spain, Poland, and Yugoslavia.

The process is expected to continue well into the future. The earth's population, now around 3,500 million people, seems bound to double by the end of the century, now only 30 years away.

These facts are known to be more or less true; they are based on extrapolations from the past and on measurements of what is going on now. These are the figures with which our population experts must wrestle if they are to prevent the earth's population from growing insufferably large. Yet they pose an almost insignificant problem compared with one much less widely discussed.

A precisely similar line of reasoning leads us to expect that in the second half of this century more than 400 million people will be killed in war. In this period there will be about 120 wars. Together they will eliminate about 10 per cent of the earth's population. One of these wars will claim ten times as many victims as did World Wars I and II. In this war some 360 million people—more than now live in the whole of Africa—will be swept off the face of the earth.

If we look further ahead, to the first half of the next century, the picture is even more depressing. Again there will be about 120 wars, but they will claim ten times as many deaths—more than 4,000 million, which is larger than the world population today. The largest war of all will again leap up in size by an order of magnitude. This war alone will claim about 3,600 million victims—almost precisely the present world population. But by then there may be as many as 10,000 million people alive; war will eliminate 40 per cent of them between A.D. 2000 and 2050.

The population explosion—reckoned by many of our wisest forecasters as our biggest problem—dwindles into comparative

3

insignificance when compared to the war explosion. As the following table shows, every half century the percentage of the world population killed in war goes up by four or five times. On this basis, there will be no population explosion to worry about in the second half of the next century: sometime in the next 80 to 130 years virtually 100 per cent of the world population will be killed

TABLE 1

Casualties per war	1820–1859	1860–1899	1900–1949	1950–1999	2000–2050
500–5,000	100,000 killed in 63 wars	100,000 killed in 75 wars	100,000 killed in 71 wars	100,000 killed in 64 wars	100,000 killed in 57 wars
5,000–50,000	300,000 killed in 25 wars	200,000 killed in 21 wars	300,000 killed in 25 wars	300,000 killed in 25 wars	300,000 killed in 25 wars
50,000–1 million	400,000 killed in 4 wars	700,000 killed in 7 wars	1.5 million killed in 15 wars	2.2 million killed in 22 wars	2.5 million killed in 25 wars
1 million– 5 million	—	3.6 million killed in 3 wars	4.6 million killed in 4 wars	5 million killed in 5 wars	6 million killed in 6 wars
5 million– 50 million	—	—	36 million killed in 2 wars	38 million killed in 3 wars	40 million killed in 4 wars
50 million– 500 million	—	—	—	360 million killed in 1 war	400 million killed in 2 wars
500 million– 5,000 million	—	—	—	—	3,600 million killed in 1 war
TOTAL	800,000 killed in 92 wars	4.6 million killed in 106 wars	42 million killed in 117 wars	406 million killed in 120 wars	4,050 million killed in 120 wars
World Population	1,000 million	1,300 million	2,000 million	4,000 million	10,000 million
Per Cent Population Killed in War	0.1	0.4	2.1	10.1	40.5

After Ivan A. Getting, "Halting the Inflationary Spiral of Death," in *Air Force/Space Digest* (April 1963).

in war, leaving only Desmond Morris's famous Bushmen to survey the wreckage.

From all this a cynic might conclude that we should abandon our halting attempts at population control, issue directives to encourage faster breeding, and thus hope to delay the evil effects of the war explosion by a few more decades.

Of course, no such extravagant generalization is warranted. Apart from the fact that the figures in the table are probably grossly inaccurate, the predictions it contains are only extrapolations from the past into the future. They are valid only if we continue to behave as we have in the past. As the human species is the only one of millions to have been endowed with intelligence, we should at the very least be able to improve on our past performance.

The war explosion, then, is best regarded as a convenient thermometer against which to measure our progress toward international health. And if we try to map out our likely behavior over say the next 50 years, we should be able to see just how we are going to avoid the 120 wars that might be expected; in particular, we should have a very clear idea indeed of how to prevent the four biggest wars—which might otherwise claim 400 million victims.

But when we do this, no such startling insights are apparent. On the contrary, it is my belief that we are doing our utmost to ensure that the horrific extrapolations of the war explosion will be fulfilled ahead of time. I can see few arguments to contradict this, but I can see a great many reasons for believing that we will indeed bring about the fate which history predicts we shall suffer.

The first and most obvious reason is that a nuclear holocaust may yet occur. If the nuclear war which is now being planned and perfected by our strategists actually takes place, there is no question but that the war explosion will continue on its smooth upward curve.

The second reason is less obvious. It is that there may be some subtle connection between war deaths and deaths from the complex barrage of problems which now appears to be engulfing the human race. These problems include the population explosion, the poverty gap between the rich and poor countries, the hunger gap, and the prospect of worldwide pollution (blame for which, as we shall see in Chapter 4, should properly be laid at the military's doorstep). I see no prospect of our being able to disentangle the vast amount of human misery and suffering which these are already creating from the superficially more clear-cut effects of war.

The prospect for the next 50 years is that population pressure, poverty, hunger, and even pollution will give rise to wars; and wars will give rise to poverty, hunger, and pollution as well as to local population problems arising from the millions made homeless and nationless.

Finally, there is the yet more awful prospect that reasons one and two may be combined—that our growing social problems may actually precipitate a global nuclear holocaust. Should that occur, then I think it would be safe to conclude that the dire predictions of the war explosion are actually wildly optimistic.

These are serious and gloomy matters. And to be quite sure what we are talking about, it will be necessary to examine each of the three issues in more detail.

World War III: The East-West Problem

The nuclear warfare experts tell us that past wars no longer contain any lessons for the future. With the invention of nuclear weapons, they argue, the whole course of history was changed. The paths we tread on our new radioactive soil are blazing a trail into a future as different from anything that went before as can be imagined. Nuclear weapons, at last, have given us the means to bring the war explosion to a grinding halt.

Yet the numbers of predicted deaths over the next three half centuries are so huge that they should give us pause. Physically, it would be very difficult to kill 400 million people with high explosives in 50 years; it would be nearly impossible to kill 4,000 million.

If one looks back at the table, it is not difficult to see that the trend after 1950 could not possibly continue without the invention of some radically new weapon. Anyone who chose to ponder the war explosion in, say, 1900 would have been led to conclude that some incredible new military discovery would be made about 1950. And he would have been right. The first thermonuclear device was exploded in the Pacific on November 1, 1952.

But the use to which we put it was of our own choosing. Less than four years after the first H-bomb, the U.S. Armed Services Committee sought elucidation on the possible effects of World War

III. Senator Duff put the problem to Lt. Gen. James Gavin, then chief of U.S. Army research and development. "I would like to ask you, sir," the senator said, "if we got into a nuclear war and our strategic air force made an assault in force against Russia with nuclear weapons . . . what would be the effect in the way of death over there under those circumstances? . . ."

The general's reply was to the point:

> I will give you an answer to this and I will give you a specific one, sir. . . . Current planning estimates run on the order of several hundred million deaths. . . .

Six years into the second half of the twentieth century, then, a war was being planned which would account almost precisely for the 360 million deaths predicted by the war explosion. If those deaths occurred in the West and not the East, every human being from the Amazon River to the Arctic would be killed—the entire population of Canada, the United States, Mexico, Central America, and some of South America too.

Yet the apologists for nuclear strategy still argue that nuclear weapons should—with a little luck and much good judgment—prevent the holocaust which their very existence makes possible. Historically, their optimism is less than justified. In 1866 Alfred Nobel coined the name dynamite for his latest discovery of destruction. "Perhaps my factories," he later told the Baroness von Suttner, "will put an end to war even sooner than your congresses: on the day that two army corps can mutually annihilate each other in a second, all civilized nations will surely recoil with horror and disband their troops." The first shots of World War I rang out just 22 years later.

Incredibly we have once again reverted to a Nobel-type logic. We have chosen the nuclear weapon as both the means of preventing big wars and as the means of causing the Armageddon which history predicts for us. To both these ends, we now devote an immense proportion of our wealth, our scientific talent, and our global resources. Today, nearly one-fifth of the world's scientists are working on projects connected with the strategy of deterrence. The world's weapons bill now approaches $200,000 million a year or one-third of a million dollars a minute. Nearly all this money is spent in the name of a ritual designed to prevent war.

There are reasons why it is important to understand the nature of this ritual. The first is that it is unlikely to work indefinitely.

And when it breaks down it will develop into the most barbaric and insane slaughter ever to be recorded in the pages of history. The gap between deterrence and genocide is a slim one, and the first is actually no more than a cleverly disguised commitment to practice the second.

The other reason is that the ritual may eventually prove too costly to be supportable. Today the world's military expenditure is equal to the total income of everyone living in Latin America, southern Asia, and the Near East. By the end of the century, it is predicted, we may be spending as much on arms and soldiers as the whole of the world's economic output today. As two-thirds of the world is already in dire economic need, it is no exaggeration to suggest that this mighty straw could well break the camel's back. If it does, it will not be for the first time in the history of evolution that the cost of ritual weapons has led to the extinction of a species.

In the Pleistocene epoch, which began some two million years ago, there lived a deer known as the Irish elk (*Megaceros giganteus*). Standing 6 feet high, it devoted most of its energy to growing a massive pair of antlers, spanning up to 11 feet and weighing nearly 112 pounds. Every year this enormous burden was shed and a replacement grown. Deer never use their antlers for attacking prey or for defending themselves against predators. They use them in ritual combat with their own species and they never use them to kill. They are in every sense a true deterrent weapon, and the Irish elk sought to give its own deterrent maximum power and credibility. But the burden which this crippling defense budget inflicted on the animal's metabolism proved too great. It left the elk unable to cope with changing conditions. And in Ireland, Britain, Europe, and western Asia it lay down and died—leaving behind only the fossilized remains of its symbolic strength.

World War IV:
The North-South Problem

The demise of the Irish elk has too many parallels with the history of mankind for complacency on man's part. Changing conditions are now sweeping the globe for a second time. This time, however, they are not changes in climate but changes in the social environment. And the most important of all these changes is the pending population crisis.

The immediate danger comes not so much from a general population increase as from one of its special features. For every 100 children born today, 85 will live in the developing countries of Asia, Africa, and Latin America. These are the countries of the Third World, the countries that support two-thirds of the world population now. By the end of the century they will contain three-quarters of the human race. The population explosion, in other words, is happening in those very regions where its effects are likely to be most catastrophic.

Consider, first, the food situation. Today about 450 million people—mostly living in Europe and North America—eat well. Another 650 million—including the population of the Soviet Union—eat adequately. That leaves 2,400 million who are underfed. Of these some 1,000 million are never far from starvation level. And of those, from 10 to 50 million die every year simply because they are unable to fill their bellies with the right kinds of food.

The situation has been getting progressively worse since 1945. Since then the average intake of animal protein for every member of the luxury food club has gone up from 36 to 44 grams a day. For most of the world it has gone down—from about 11 grams to a mere 8. A recent survey has shown that the per capita food production of the peoples of Latin America dropped by 6 per cent between 1961 and 1965.

To make matters worse, the net flow of food is not from the well-fed to the hungry but from the hungry to the well-fed. Every year the rich people of the Northern Hemisphere exchange grain for oilseed products (certain forms of plant protein, such as soybeans, peanuts, and coconuts) from the poor people of the Southern Hemisphere. The balance of this transaction is such that the well-fed end up with a million more tons of protein than they started with.

As a result about one-third of the world now eats two-thirds of all the food produced. One-quarter of the world uses three-quarters of all the fertilizer manufactured. And as every year goes by, the well-fed are better-fed and the starving die more frequently.

All this is reflected in the statistics of death. The death rate in the Third World is two or three times higher than it is in the rich countries. Between 50 and 150 of every 1,000 children born south of the equator die before the age of one. Life expectancy, too, is much shorter—in India it has only just reached forty years of age. If you live in the Third World, it is more likely than not that one of your four children will die before he or she grows up. If you are a male living in Gabon, you cannot expect to celebrate even a thirtieth birthday.

And if we consider the distribution of wealth, the situation is much, much worse. Today one-fourth of the population spends nine-tenths of the world's wealth. Ninety of the world's 137 countries can command only one-tenth of the world's riches.

In the Third World the average income per capita is about $150 a year. In the 27 richest countries it is $2,500 a year—seventeen times as much. As a result the world today consists of rich pockets of well-fed people surrounded by vast wastes of poverty and starvation. Only two figures are needed to show just how large those wastes will have grown by the end of the century. In tropical Latin America, with a certain amount of success with fertility control, the population will soar from 180 million to 578 million. In Africa it will rise from 273 million to 768 million.

It would be absurd to suppose that most of the world's population will allow themselves to be exploited in this way for very much longer. "The gap is widening," writes Peter Worsley in his book *The Third World,* "and out of this particular alienation of the majority of men from the rich minority will be generated a veritable Pandora's box of endemic human misery, frustration and violence." The result will be World War IV, the fight of the underprivileged South against the overprivileged North.

What form this war will take is not clear, except that it probably will not resemble any of the wars of the past. The first blows have already been exchanged, in the form of the kidnapping of Western diplomats by discontented minorities in poor countries. And before we condemn too roundly the technique of hostage holding, we should not forget it is practiced on a far larger scale by the "civilized nations." Every member of the population of the two superpowers is held hostage for the good actions of his government by a nuclear missile aimed at his home.

The Nigerian civil war has also given us a taste of the future. When that war stopped, famine became quickly and progressively more serious. And whether similar wars in the future are followed by hunger, accompanied by it, or caused by it, the result in human suffering will be little different. The borderline between military action and human disaster has always been fuzzy; in World War IV it will be obliterated. Viewed in this light, the extrapolations of the war explosion take on a new significance which it would be unwise for anyone to dismiss as the idle speculations of the prophets of Doomsday.

But the equation of violence is still not complete. One more factor has to be added—the nuclear weapon. Hasan Ozbekhan, director of future planning for Systems Development Corporation, is one of the very few people to have looked even superficially at what might happen when poverty, hunger, and the power of the atom are mixed together. He writes:

> Within the next 20 years all the main
> underdeveloped nations will be in possession
> of (nuclear) weapons and of limited, but
> perhaps sufficient, delivery capabilities.
> Thus, by the year 2000, the underdeveloped
> portion of the world will have a population
> of some five billion, they will still be poor,
> they will be hungrier than today, they will
> be angry—and they will be sufficiently
> armed to hurt.

With this in mind, we can at least outline some of the dangers of the nuclear journey that lies ahead. By definition, it must be a journey not just between east and west or between north and south. It is a journey that involves all four corners of the globe.

The Nuclear Journey

Let us compare man's recent progress to that of several cars being driven very fast along a bumpy road. At the dawn of the nuclear age, it was argued that a collision (a nuclear holocaust) between two of them could be avoided by obeying a few simple traffic laws. The advocates of nuclear weapons even claimed that a collision would not be fatal to all—that the occupants of at least one of the cars would eventually recuperate. It would then be their privilege to buy a second, more powerful car and repeat the journey.

To illustrate how the problem of nuclear war, hunger, overpopulation, poverty, and pollution might interact, it may be worth pushing this analogy to its limits. In doing so I shall sketch out many of the issues raised in this book. They are all concerned with the nature of the cars, their drivers and passengers, and the countryside through which they are traveling.

In the past decade many things have happened to these cars. We all know that they have become more dangerous. But their components have also become cheaper and easier to manufacture. As a result future collisions have become physically more dangerous and statistically more likely.

We have also discovered some new facts about the drivers. Not only have they doubled in number but what they can see through their windshields turns out to be very blurred. As a result they have a distorted view of other vehicles on the road. Nor are all the drivers as psychologically balanced as we would wish. Paranoiacs and schizophrenics, as we shall see, are especially prone to seek the driving wheel and to be asked to sit behind it. Alarmingly, the strain of driving itself aggravates the problem.

Changes in the countryside are also having a disturbing effect. The affluent society has lined the roadside with garbage, making nuclear punctures more likely. The cars carry more screaming children, and the drivers drink and smoke a great deal more. The chance of a car surviving a puncture if the driver is drunk, has dropped his cigarette on the floor, and has a child screaming in the back is almost nil. But the chance that some or all these events will occur simultaneously is not zero and is rising fast.

In certain cars most of the more technically minded passengers have become mechanics. They are well-paid and have invented interesting new ways of designing the cars of the future. They have made elaborate plans for extending the nuclear journey into space and into the oceans. But in their preoccupation with their technological future, they have forgotten the plight of the passengers of the other cars on the road.

Most of these are hungry, short of money, and tired of the drive. They are fighting to overpower their drivers and get their hands on the wheel; together they have the strength to do so. To let them or to stop them may be equally disastrous. The only solution may be to drive the cars into the scrapyard.

The passengers in all the cars have also become much more numerous. Of this the drivers have been vaguely aware for quite some time but do not seem disposed to take much notice. And although it may seem obvious, scientists are warning that there is a maximum to the number of people that can be safely stuffed into one vehicle. If the maximum is exceeded, they argue, the passengers' behavior is likely to become extremely violent.

Finally, there is one quite new aspect of the journey. When the spires of their destination come into view, the passengers have been found to become extremely restive, to threaten a backseat revolution. To delay this process, the drivers have taken to masking the windshields—making their own progress very erratic, particularly on tourist trips to Southeast Asia, Africa, and Latin America. But once the spires have been sighted, it seems, there is no turning back. For all their experience, the aging and disturbed drivers must hand over the wheel. They are not doing so with much grace or confidence.

Analogies can be carried too far. Whether this one is illuminating can best be judged from the more specific discussion that follows. I should add that much of our new knowledge of road behavior comes from the young field of study known as peace and conflict research. The only comfort to be found in this book is that these new sciences do suggest a few ways by which the nuclear journey might be made safer.

CHAPTER I

The Nuclear Future

Nuclear Catastrophe–The Nature of
the Beast–The Cost of Membership
–The Reactor Problem–Accident,
Miscalculation, and Madness–Strategy and Superkill–Dangers from the
Labs

Jornada del Muerto means "Journey of Death." It
is the name given to a region of desert lying within the U.S. Air
Force Alamogordo Base in New Mexico near the village of Oscuro
—which means "dark." But its reputation for darkness and death
depends on more than geographical accident, for it was here—at
0530 on July 16, 1945—that the world's first atomic bomb was
exploded.

Few of those present on that summer morning could have foretold the enormity of the chain of events which they set in motion.
If they had, they would hardly have chosen the word "Trinity"
for the code name of the test. Citizens of New York might well
have been unhappy about calling the whole atomic bomb program
the "Manhattan Project." And even the most macabre imagination
would have had second thoughts about the code signal for success
which was subsequently flashed to American and British leaders.
"Babies satisfactorily born."

Just three weeks later, on August 6, what had been a scientific
experiment was turned into a military triumph and a human disaster. The United States aircraft *Enola Gay* dropped the bomb
"Little Boy" on what *Encyclopaedia Britannica* once described as
"a city seaport . . . very beautifully situated on a small plain surrounded by hills, the bay being studded with islands." The seaport
was Hiroshima; "Little Boy" was the world's first uranium bomb;
and *Enola Gay's* payload was the cause of 75,000 or more deaths.

Nuclear Catastrophe

What death was like at Hiroshima on August 6, 1945, has been described many times. I make no apology for quoting again one eyewitness account. This chapter is concerned with our nuclear future, and the arguments and the predictions can be couched only in the flat terms of numbers and probabilities. It is too easy to lose sight of what a nuclear weapon actually does. Even the following account, by Dr. Hanaoka, a senior Japanese medical officer, is perhaps less emotive than if it had been written by one less used to the sight of injury and death:

> Between the Red Cross Hospital and the centre
> of the city I saw nothing that wasn't burned to a
> crisp. Streetcars were standing at Kawaya-cho and
> Kamiya-cho, and inside were dozens of bodies,
> blackened beyond recognition. I saw fire reservoirs
> filled to the brim with dead people who looked as
> though they had been boiled alive. In one reser-
> voir I saw a man, horribly burned, crouching beside
> another man who was dead. He was drinking
> blood-stained water out of the reservoir. Even if
> I had tried to stop him, it wouldn't have done any
> good; he was completely out of his head. In one
> reservoir there were so many dead people there
> wasn't enough room for them to fall over: they
> must have died sitting in the water.
>   Even the swimming pool at the Prefectural
> First Middle School was filled with dead people.
> They must have suffocated while they sat in the
> water trying to escape the fire because they didn't
> appear to be burned. . . .
>   That pool wasn't big enough to accommodate
> everybody who tried to get in. You could tell that
> by looking around the sides. I don't know how
> many were caught by death with their heads
> hanging over the edge. In one pool I saw people
> who were still alive, sitting in the water with dead
> all around them. They were too weak to get out.

Three days later, on August 9, a second atomic bomb was dropped on Nagasaki. This one, like the Trinity test, used plutonium as the fission material. These two bombs together killed more than 100,000 people and injured 200,000 or more. Each bomb released the equivalent of about 20,000 tons of TNT; each had the power of about 2,000 of the largest TNT bombs used in the war.

At Hiroshima a firestorm was created which lasted for six hours. It completely burned out an area of 4.5 square miles. The blast from the bomb, and the fires it created, destroyed 62,000 out of the 90,000 buildings in the city. These figures indicate the futility of organizing city defense against nuclear attack. And the bombs that fell on these two Japanese cities were puny compared with those that were to follow.

On November 1, 1952, man achieved the distinction of eliminating from the Pacific a complete island—leaving in its place a hole 175 feet deep and 1 mile in diameter. This explosion was the prelude to the first real hydrogen bomb test, which took place at Bikini on March 1, 1954. This explosion, equivalent to 15 million tons of TNT, was 750 times more powerful than either of the Japanese bombs and exceeded in power all the bombs dropped in World War II, including atomic bombs. The event was a disaster in more ways than one, for a sudden change of wind blew a snowy curtain of fallout onto nearby inhabited islands and onto the deck of a Japanese fishing vessel, the *Lucky Dragon*. The islanders suffered radiation sickness and thyroid growths, and one of the fishermen died. Displaying their customary lack of taste, the authorities had christened the test "Bravo."

By 1957 similar tests had signaled to the world that both Britain and the Soviet Union were also thermonuclear powers. By this time the rapidly mounting score of nuclear weapons had reached epidemic proportions. For the first time in its history the world could blow itself up. Little by little public pressure—often led by the very scientists who had developed the weapons—forced governments to reveal what the existence of this nuclear stockpile promised for the future. The prospect was not rosy.

By current standards a 20-megaton bomb is not the biggest that can be made. One American B-52 bomber can carry at least two of them, and the United States now operates about 500 of these bombers. Let us look, then, at what half the load of one such bomber might achieve if dropped on the middle of Manhattan.

Tom Stonier, an associate professor of biology at Manhattan College, studied this particular problem in detail in the early 1960s. He wrote: "The number of deaths that could result from the detonation of just one 20-megaton bomb on New York City could exceed tenfold the total number of fatalities that America has suffered in all its battlefields throughout all its history." He estimated that such a bomb would endanger the lives of people living in a 4,000 square mile area. It would probably kill 6 million out of New York City's total population (which was then 8 million) and produce an additional million deaths outside the city.

A bomb of this type could ignite the clothing of a man standing 20 miles away if the weather was clear. Within half an hour, Professor Stonier estimated, more than one million fires would be raging in New York City. The 4½-mile-diameter fireball would ignite an area of more than 1,000 square miles. Danger from the blinding flash of the explosion would extend over much greater distances. (After a high-altitude test over Johnson Island, the retinas of rabbits 350 miles away were subsequently found to be burned.)

If effects like these could be expected from one bomb, what could result from an all-out nuclear attack? In the United States two special committees presided over by Congressman Chet Holifield undertook to find out. During 1958, 1960, and again in 1961 they questioned expert witnesses as to the whole range of effects that nuclear war might bring. To do this, they specified the actual, hypothetical attack in some detail.

Their first assumption was that the attack took place on October 17, 1958, a day when west-southwest winds were blowing at 40 miles an hour over New York City. Two 10-megaton bombs were assumed to fall on New York, 275 megatons were delivered on the area running between Washington and Boston, and in all 1,446 megatons were showered on the United States. First calculations, which later evidence showed would have to be increased, were that 31 per cent of the United States population would be killed and 12.5 per cent would survive injured. In round figures, there would be 47 million deaths and 19 million surviving casualties.

About 21 million of the country's 46 million houses would be moderately or severely damaged. A further half million would be so badly affected by fallout that they would have to be evacuated for at least a year. At most one-quarter of all United States houses would be habitable in the two months immediately following the attack. Lack of medical services would also take a heavy toll. In the Boston area, for instance, the attack would leave one doctor to treat every 1,700 injured people. Even taking the figures for Massachusetts as a whole, there would be 1,000 injured for every surviving doctor to attend. On the most optimistic assumptions it would be up to a fortnight before all the injured in Boston received even 10 minutes of qualified diagnosis and treatment. After that, according to three Boston specialists, Drs. V. W. Sidel, H. J. Geiger and B. Lown, the situation would be improved because "when physicians emerge from their shelters . . . large numbers of the injured will have died in the interim."

With this as background, it seems unnecessary to specify precisely what other effects a large nuclear attack might bring. Suffice it to say that nearly all fuel services would be brought to a halt and transportation services would be wrecked; in addition, the proportion of surviving electricity networks that would be useful rather than hazardous is open to doubt. Furthermore, as Professor Stonier points out, if the country were not resilient enough to cope with the ensuing chaos, "the degenerating economy [would] have famine as one of its inevitable consequences." All this would be compounded by man-made weather changes, hopefully lasting a few hours, probably lasting some days, and possibly even becoming a permanent feature. Profound ecological changes, with insects— the most radiation-resistant animals—becoming dominant for a period, would be inevitable and essentially unpredictable.

In spite of all this, there are still those who argue that nuclear war is survivable; that the economy would not be ruined for more than a few years at least; and that the human spirit is resilient enough to rise again, perhaps even to fight another war. I do not intend to indulge in any of these fantasies. The evidence from Hiroshima, as retold by Dr. M. Hachiya in *Hiroshima Diary,* points the other way. Within two weeks of the explosion:

> . . . the ruthless and greedy were ruling the city.
> . . . People with evil faces and foul tongues were
> wearing the best clothes . . . the country was in
> the hands of the mean and the unintelligent. . . .
> A scarcity of sentries made looting easy. . . . The
> city was infested with burglars. . . . Vandals even
> came with carts and hauled away everything
> they could carry. . . . Hiroshima was becoming a
> wicked town. Without police I was not surprised,
> but I was ashamed.
>
> In the ruins of Hiroshima, money was valueless
> and cigarettes took over as a medium of exchange.

It is not surprising that Sir Solly Zuckerman writes:

> It is totally beyond my capacity to understand
> what some American writers on nuclear strategy
> think they are saying when they talk about a
> "nuclear exchange" in which the United States
> alone would suffer something like 100 million fa-

tal casualties in a single strike, and when they
then go on to imply, by the use of words unrelated to any experience, that the survivors could
reconstitute a great and thriving civilization.

The United Nations, to whom one might look for an authoritative statement on the effects of nuclear war, did not get around to
studying the question until much too late. However, a special committee did report to the UN Secretary-General in 1967. They saw
little hope of the postnuclear recovery in which the military opti-
mists would have us believe:

> . . . the nuclear armouries which are in being al-
> ready contain large megaton weapons, every one
> of which has a destructive power greater than that
> of all the conventional explosive that has ever
> been used in warfare since the day gunpowder
> was discovered. Were such weapons ever to be
> used in numbers, hundreds of millions of people
> might be killed, and civilization as we know it, as
> well as organized life, would inevitably come to an
> end in the countries involved in the conflict.

The Nature of the Beast

It might be thought that little more need be said about our nuclear
future, that our prospects cannot be worse than they have been
for the past 15 years, and that the situation is not likely to change
drastically. None of these suppositions now appears true.

A whole new range of scientific and technological developments
are on the horizon. For the most part they threaten to make nuclear war more likely than it previously was. The most immediate
and most appalling fact is that new countries are already beginning
to get their hands on the bomb. When they do, the risk of nuclear
war must go up. The technology of the bomb is also changing.
Cheaper ways of making nuclear weapons are beginning to be developed by the laboratories, sometimes in the guise of pure research. Nuclear reactors are spreading, carrying with them the raw
material from which the inspired maniac or dictator might fashion
his own version of Trinity or Nagasaki. And the great powers
themselves are wrestling with new developments that promise to
upset the precarious peace they have striven to maintain.

For these reasons it is important to look more closely at the nature of the atomic beast—first at the technical requirements of nuclear weapons and second at the cost of achieving them. With this information in mind, the horizon looks darker than it has for a long time.

Nuclear weapons are made either from very heavy elements or from very light ones. The reason is not hard to understand. Many of the heavy elements have a tendency to split or fission into smaller fragments. When they do, they release enormous amounts of energy. The light elements, by contrast, can literally be forced together to make heavier elements. Light elements which are fused in this way also release large amounts of energy. These two processes are the bases of the atomic or fission weapon and of the hydrogen or fusion weapon.

Two heavy elements are used in the manufacture of atomic weapons. One is plutonium, the power source of the first atomic explosion in New Mexico. The other is uranium, which was used in the first bomb ever dropped in anger, on Hiroshima. As we shall see, technical developments threaten to make both types of bomb more accessible to more countries.

Plutonium does not occur naturally. But it is normally formed as a by-product in a nuclear reactor. One of the first problems for the wartime Manhattan Project, then, was to build a self-sustaining nuclear reactor which converted its uranium fuel into plutonium, incidentally liberating energy in the form of heat. This was first done in 1942, in a squash court in Chicago, under the direction of the famous Italian-born physicist Enrico Fermi.

The process is not an efficient one and the minute quantities of plutonium formed have to be carefully separated from all other elements. These include a form of plutonium known as Pu-240, which is of little use as a fission material, as well as the unconverted natural uranium. But in theory just one pound of plutonium-239, the useful isotope, can liberate the energy of 8,000 tons of TNT. About 10 pounds of plutonium are needed to make a bomb, and so the smallest bomb could in theory produce an explosion of 80 kilotons. In fact the first bombs produced less than one-fourth of this energy.

A plutonium weapon is made by purifying the 10-pound "critical mass" of plutonium, forming the metal into two hemispheres and surrounding them with a carefully designed system of TNT wedges. Nothing will happen until the two halves are exploded together by the TNT. But then the material undergoes a violent explosion; the two halves affect one another in such a way that a self-sustaining reaction sets in, in which much of the plutonium fissions in a tiny fraction of a second.

The uranium bomb works on precisely the same principle. Here, however, more than 30 pounds of the required uranium isotope, U-235, are needed to make a bomb. But the problem is enormously complicated by the fact that, although uranium does occur naturally, the right isotope is in very short supply. The uranium dug out of the ground contains 99.3 per cent U-238—an isotope which is useless for making atomic bombs. The remaining 0.7 per cent therefore has to be laboriously separated out. And the process is laborious, for the two isotopes are chemically identical. They differ only in that one is slightly lighter and much more fissile than the other. During the war, huge resources were put into separating the isotopes for one simple reason: a single pound of the fissile isotope contains the energy equivalent to 1,500 tons of coal or 300,000 gallons of high-grade petrol.

The Manhattan Project investigated several methods for separating the isotopes. The one that was eventually adopted, at a cost of millions of dollars, was the gaseous diffusion process. The uranium was first converted into an extremely corrosive compound known as uranium hexafluoride. This was then allowed to diffuse through a fine membrane which acted as a filter, allowing one isotope to pass through slightly more easily than the other. Each passage through the membrane produced only a tiny enrichment of U-235, so the gas had to be continuously recycled through the plant. Some 4,000 membranes were needed, and hundreds of miles of special noncorrosive tubing had to be installed. The wartime plant, at Oak Ridge in Tennessee, occupied an enormous tract of ground and consumed the energy of a large city. Gaseous diffusion is by far the most expensive process involved in making nuclear weapons.

The hydrogen bomb did not come until much later, and in any case could never have been invented without the existence of the atomic bomb. Hydrogen, with an atomic weight of 1, is the lightest element known to man. Two of its isotopes, H-2 and H-3, known as deuterium and tritium respectively, are used in the hydrogen bomb. Deuterium occurs naturally in sea water but tritium is an artificial isotope which has to be specially made. This can be done either by exposing the element called lithium in an atomic reactor or by incorporating lithium in the hydrogen bomb itself. In either case neutrons from uranium undergoing fission strike the lithium atoms and release tritium.

What then happens can be observed at any time of day by looking at the sun. The deuterium and tritium atoms fuse together, forming an isotope of hydrogen of atomic weight 4. At the same time prodigious amounts of energy are released. For instance, the fusion of a 1-pound mixture of deuterium and tritium theoretically provides the same energy as the burning of 9½ million pounds of coal. In practice the hydrogen bomb is less efficient. Even so, a pound of the fusion material produces the energy of about 5,000 tons of TNT.

The difficulty in all this is providing the right conditions for fusion. They are the conditions found in the heart of the sun, whose energy derives almost entirely from fusion reactions. On earth, more modest goals must obtain and the fusion mixture must be heated to above 100 million degrees centigrade. The only way man has so far found of doing this is to set the hydrogen bomb off by an atomic bomb. TNT sets off the A-bomb, the temperature mushrooms, and the hydrogen bomb detonates.

This means that thermonuclear or H-bombs obtain their energy from both fission and fusion. The ingenuity of military science is such, however, that a further refinement is possible. The package I have just described can itself be wrapped in a blanket of uranium-238—the relatively nonfissile isotope which up to this point has found little military use. However, the intensity of the H-bomb explosion is sufficient to make even this isotope fission. This not only adds greatly to the overall power of the bomb but also makes it extremely "dirty"—the outer uranium cloak produces a great deal of long-lived radioactive compounds which float slowly down to earth. This multiple type of bomb is known as a fission-fusion-fission device.

The largest nuclear bang ever made by man, the 57-megaton explosion detonated by the Russians on October 30, 1961, did not include an outercasing of uranium. This made it very clean but it also detracted considerably from its total power. Had a uranium casing been used, the bomb would have released more than 100 megatons of energy. A railway train loaded with the equivalent amount of TNT would stretch nearly the whole way round the globe. If it could be properly harnessed, 100 megatons would be sufficient energy to put into orbit a space station weighing about 10 million tons.

There is one other point that is important to bear in mind about the hydrogen bomb. It is thought that so far the only kind of atomic trigger that can be used to set off a thermonuclear weapon is a uranium bomb. A plutonium bomb, though perhaps effective in theory and more easily available from reactors, is probably not used as a trigger in any existing stockpile. This so far limits the ease with which new nations can get their hands on hydrogen bombs. But as we shall see the situation might change.

The Cost of Membership

What is the cost of membership in the nuclear club? The wartime Manhattan Project cost about $2,000 million and produced only three bombs. But of course the cost included a massive research and development program, and after the war, the equipment was still there to continue bomb manufacture.

Today, the first cost of any nation wanting to become a fully paid-up member of the club would be to build a gas-diffusion plant. The French have recently acquired such a plant, at Pierrelatte in southern France, at a cost of some $1,000 million. This seems not untypical, for the three huge diffusion plants in the United States, at Oak Ridge, Paducah, and Portsmouth, cost together about $2,500 million. The much smaller British plant at Capenhurst seems to have been somewhat cheaper at about $250 million, but no costs are available for the plants in the Soviet Union or for the new Chinese one at Lanchow on the Yellow River.

Large though these figures may be, they are in the long run small compared with the cost of electricity consumed. Enormous amounts of power are required to operate the pumps that drive the uranium mixture through the diffusion membrands. Together the United States plants used, at full stream, about 6,000 megawatts of electrical energy—enough to supply several very large cities or one-tenth of the total United States demand for electricity. Supplying power for a large diffusion plant can easily cost $250 million a year. To this one must add, of course, the further cost of building the generators able to supply such a vast amount of energy.

The United States plants are together capable of turning out something like 75 tons of weapons-grade uranium-235 every year. This gives the Americans the capability of producing a staggering 5,000 atomic weapons every year. In fact, of course, these plants are no longer operating at full capacity and some of their products go to fuel nuclear reactors, which require enriched uranium. Even so, it does mean that because of economies of scale, the production cost for a small atomic bomb could in theory fall as low as $150,000 per bomb, although a more realistic figure would be two or three times as much.

No detailed figures on the costs of using an atomic trigger to set off an H-bomb are available. The thermonuclear components themselves are not expensive—as these things go—and hence the Atomic Energy Commission (AEC) is able to offer for civilian purposes a 2-megaton explosion for as little as $600,000. Hence it is clear that diffusion is the biggest component of the nuclear weapons bill. What is even larger is the cost of delivering these weapons in a sophisticated way. A single missile is likely to cost at least 10 times its warhead, and sometimes much more. The British V-bomber force, for instance, set the British taxpayer back at least $1,400 million before becoming obsolete. The Polaris submarine fleet will run to a total bill of well over $1,000 million. In all the cost to Britain and to France of becoming major nuclear powers is estimated at $8,400 million for each country. And for 1966–67 the British Institute of Strategic Studies estimated that Britain paid about £100 million a year to maintain her nuclear strategic forces.

The reason why cost concerns us so much now is the possibility of other nations, perhaps those that can least afford it, trying to attain nuclear status. To throw some more light on this, a recent United Nations report tried to itemize the expenditure that would be involved. Cumbersomely entitled "Effects of the Possible Use of Nuclear Weapons and the Security and Economic Implication for States of the Acquisition and Further Development of These Weapons," the report stated that there were only seven of the lesser powers that could currently afford nuclear status: Canada, the German Federal Republic, Japan, Italy, India, Poland, and Sweden.

The overall cost was given as $5,600 million spread over a 10-year period. For this, the nation would acquire within five years from 10 to 15 bombers and from 15 to 20 nuclear weapons. During the second five years the force would include 20 to 30 thermonuclear weapons, 100 intermediate-range missiles and two missile-launching submarines. The annual cost of maintaining bomb production would be about $5 million a bomb.

When estimating the costs of nuclear weapons, we should not forget indirect costs. If a nation spends this kind of money on weapons, it incurs a further penalty—very real though less easily calculated —in not having spent that money on other, perhaps more immediate needs. Thus the United Nations report claimed that to build the nuclear warheads would require 1,300 engineers and 500 scientists. If 50 missiles are added to the bill,

> a peak labour force directly applied of 19,000 men would be needed, over 5,000 of them scientists and engineers with access to high speed electronic computers. Skilled personnel would include physicists, aerodynamic, mechanical, and other engineers and large numbers of production workers, including machine operators and welders. The suggested fleet of 50 bombers would require a minimum of from 1 to 2 million man-hours of skilled and unskilled labour just to assemble. The design and development stage would absorb an additional 2 million or more engineering man-hours, which would involve highly skilled efforts in aerodynamics, stress analysis, design work and flight testing.

The diversion of such an enormous and skilled task force to military matters would cost a nation as dearly as its real monetary expenditure. "Who knows," asks the American physicist Ralph Lapp, questioning his own government's expenditure on weapons, "what constructive works of science and technology might have been achieved for the benefit of mankind if the arrow of our effort had been directed toward peaceful goals?"

Yet in one sense the high cost in men and money of nuclear weapons is reassuring. It acts as its own deterrent to nuclear proliferation. There can be no doubt that a cheap nuclear weapon is much more dangerous than an expensive one. Unhappily, the cheap weapon is nearly with us.

The fate of Hiroshima shows that no nation need go as far as thermonuclear weapons to become a nuclear menace. And if atomic weapons suffice, the cheapest is the plutonium bomb of the kind dropped on Nagasaki. No expensive diffusion plant, no costly submarine force would be required. Instead the purchase of a nuclear reactor, from one of a number of countries, will start the atomic ball rolling. Shortly before his death, the late Sir John Cockcroft, one of the pioneers of the British nuclear program, wrote: "$100 million will buy reactor capacity for the production of plutonium for several bombs a year." Also required would be a reprocessing plant capable of separating out the useful plutonium. India has built such a plant for a cost of $8 million at Trombay. To this must also be added the cost of designing the weapon, setting up a laboratory, testing the bomb, and providing it with built-in safeguards. Cockcroft put the cost of this at another $300 million. Thus for little more than $400 million a nation could make a token show of nuclear strength.

Of course, this begs the question of delivery. If a nation really wanted to wave its nuclear fist, to make a threat of the Hiroshima type, an expensive force of bombers or submarines is not essential. Some of Nigeria's planes could easily have dropped a small atomic weapon on Biafra. Any nation operating a civil airline could deliver a bomb against an underdeveloped country. It could even resort to the use of a ship sailing into a foreign harbor, docking, and setting a time fuse to go off. This may not be what we currently understand by actual nuclear power but it is a real enough threat. That threat is made possible by the explosive growth of nuclear reactors throughout the world—a growth which is just beginning and which will reach enormous proportions by the 1980s.

The Reactor Problem

The danger caused by the spread of nuclear reactors is that for every megawatt of electrical energy installed, a reactor can also produce more than a pound of plutonium a year. When the new breeder reactors come into widespread use, late in the 1970s, worldwide plutonium production from reactors will reach staggering amounts. The fast breeder reactors will use a mixture of natural uranium and plutonium as fuel. And by what may turn out to be an extremely unfortunate quirk of nature, every pound of plutonium used as fuel will produce nearly a pound and a half of plutonium as a by-product.

A look at the future predictions of world nuclear power shows how alarming the future could be. By 1975 the world's nuclear energy output could be producing enough plutonium to make at least 5,000 bombs a year; by 1980 as many as 20,000 to 30,000 bombs a year will be possible. Writing in *Science Journal,* Leonard Beaton has found the prospect far from hopeful:

> This vision has been made broader and more
> fearsome by the coincidence of the nuclear age
> with a period in which sovereignty has spread far
> and wide, with the number of countries in the
> world rising from about 65 to double that num-
> ber. . . . Ultimately, are 130 governments really

going to have the means of mass destruction in
their hands? Are we going to have a new and startling kind of international blackmail emerging in
the form of an atomic arms ring? This horrifying
vision has been slowly forming in the sunny atmosphere of rising living standards and self-
government.

Alarmist though Mr. Beaton's views may sound, they are based
on solid fact.

As long ago as 1965 no less than 43 countries were already
producing some plutonium—though few of them had enough to
make a bomb. But by 1970 a total of 17 countries were producing large amounts of plutonium, and this figure is expected to rise
to 23 by 1975. Apart from the five existing nuclear powers, they
will include: Argentina, Belgium, Bulgaria, Canada, Czechoslovakia,
East Germany, Formosa, Hungary, India, Italy, Japan, Netherlands,
Pakistan, South Korea, Spain, Sweden, Switzerland, and West Germany. Eventually, perhaps in little more than a decade, to this list
will have to be added Austria, Australia, Brazil, Denmark, Finland,
Mexico, Greece, Portugal, Romania, Thailand, Norway, and South
Africa.

The Soviet scientist V. S. Emelyanov claims that nonnuclear
countries "will be able to produce enough plutonium by 1980 to be
able to make between 12,500 and 15,000 warheads annually. Included are eight countries which, while at present possessing no
nuclear weapons, could make, by 1980, some 8,000 to 10,000 nuclear weapons from the plutonium produced by their nuclear reactors."

To give just one instance, in 1961 India was producing more
than 20 pounds of plutonium a year—enough for two 20-kiloton
plutonium bombs. By 1969 her plutonium production had risen to
more than 400 pounds a year—enough for 40 such weapons.

Some degree of sanity is restored to this situation both by the
international safeguards systems which have been set up to prevent
proliferation and by the technology needed to make the weapon itself. If military-type plutonium is to be produced from a reactor,
the reactor must be run in a different way from one simply producing power. The fuel rods must be taken out much earlier than
otherwise, or the plutonium will be further converted to militarily
useless isotopes. And the plutonium in the rods has to be converted
and purified. As I have mentioned, this does require a special re-
processing plant. Such plants are already possessed by India, Italy,

Japan, and West Germany (as well as the existing nuclear powers) and by Eurochemic, a European consortium of 13 nations.

This does reduce greatly the number of countries that could easily produce weapons. It also reduces greatly the total number of weapons that could be made without it being quickly noticed by the international inspection community. However, the potential is so vast that the Swedish nuclear chemist J. Prawitz has stated, "Within a decade many non-nuclear countries will annually produce enough plutonium for the production of several hundred bombs. Diversion of less than 1 per cent will then make the difference between nuclear and non-nuclear status." Prawitz goes on to say that this calls for a new assessment of safeguard techniques designed to prevent countries misusing their reactors in this way. But the diversion of 1 per cent of several thousand pounds of plutonium spread over a score or more of countries will not be easy to detect.

Leonard Beaton, again, is not optimistic:

> In our time the size of the proliferation problem will be determined by the conditions laid down by those who provide "atoms for peace." Most governments will have no access to the necessary materials unless they are presented with a plutonium stockpile. The plans for doing this are now being actively laid throughout the advanced countries with a totally irresponsible disdain for the implications.

The vision of even a dozen new nations becoming nuclear powers is not one that can be contemplated with equanimity. It is important to distinguish, however, between major nuclear powers such as the United States, the Soviet Union, and soon China; between medium powers such as Britain and France; and between small powers such as Israel, South Africa, or even Portugal. The latter are unlikely to get enmeshed in the strategic deterrent nightmare on the same scale as other powers. But they could make a good deal of mischief, and in general their attitudes to nuclear weapons might well turn out to be less responsible than those of the great powers. And whether or not they ever use their weapons in anger, any new nuclear power will inevitably create two new worries. The first is that it will have to test its weapons and hence open up once again the whole business of just how harmful fallout from tests can be. And, secondly, it will increase, perhaps quite sharply, the chances of accidental nuclear explosion or even war.

Accident, Miscalculation, and Madness

While the partial test-ban treaty signed in 1963 may deter nations from experimentally exploding nuclear devices, international law is powerless in the face of accident or madness. Extreme care and great sanity are the only weapons on which we can rely if one or more nuclear weapons are not to be exploded by mistake in the near future. At no time in the history of nuclear weapons can we be sure that either the requisite amount of care or of sanity has been taken. President Kennedy said as much on September 25, 1961. "Today," he told the United Nations, "every inhabitant of this planet must contemplate the day when this planet may no longer be habitable. Every man, woman, and child lives under a nuclear sword of Damocles, hanging by the slenderest of threads, capable of being cut at any moment by accident or miscalculation or by madness."

A year earlier a research team at Ohio State University had made a special report of the chances of accidental nuclear war. The team, led by J. B. Phelps, identified five possible causes:

1. Accidents to defense systems
2. Human aberrations
3. Spread of limited war
4. Catalytic war
5. Diplomatic or military miscalculation

A poll of distinguished and militarily knowledgeable experts suggested that the spread of limited war and diplomatic miscalculation were the two most important possibilities, in that order. And one senior military analyst "rated the joint probability of war from these two at 50 per cent in the next ten years."

Taking into account the number of nuclear weapons in the United States, and factors such as the distance they travel in 10 years, the military crash rate, and estimates of reliability, the team came up with a startling conclusion: "The chances are of the order of 1 in 100 that a U.S. nuclear weapon will explode some time in the next ten years." Compare with this the following probabilities. On January, 1939, Lloyds of London was giving 32 to 1 odds against war breaking out in 1939. And in 1964, William Hill was taking bets at 1,000 to 1 that a man would not land on the moon in 1969 (an indiscretion which cost that British bookmaker £10,000). By comparison, 100 to 1 in 10 years looks too likely for comfort. What were the factors which led the team to quote such a high probability?

The high rate of crashes involving nuclear weapons was certainly one such factor. The team estimated that up to the time of their report there had been 10 major accidents of this kind, and perhaps 50 "minor" ones. Nuclear weapons had twice been jettisoned over water. An intercontinental ballistic missile (ICBM) had burned itself out on its pad. In New Jersey, a nuclear-tipped Bomarc missile went up in flames. Four planes carrying nuclear weapons had crashed in the United States, and a B-47 bomber had exploded in Louisiana. In North Carolina a B-47 accidentally dropped a nuclear weapon, and there was a chemical—though not a nuclear—explosion. A false radar signal had shown a fleet of aircraft traveling at 2,000 miles an hour over the Atlantic toward the United States. And according to a report of a conversation between Premier Khrushchev and Richard Nixon, an erratic Soviet missile had had to be blown up while on its way to Alaska.

The research team would perhaps have increased the probability of accidental explosion had they known what was to follow their report. In 1961 a B-52 bomber exploded on its way to Utah. And according to Ralph Lapp another United States B-52 carrying two 24-megaton nuclear weapons crashed in flames on January 24, 1961. One bomb was parachuted to earth, and the other crashed with the aircraft. Examination showed that all but one of the safety mechanisms on one of the bombs had been thrown.

Representative Sidney Yates, concerned about the possible accidental explosion of an ABM, took Lapp's allegation to the Senate Appropriations Committee, which took it to the U.S. Air Force. The official answer came back that the story was untrue—not one, but two, of the safety switches remained untriggered. This means that four had been thrown by the crash.

And "broken arrows"—as the U.S. Air Force calls all nuclear weapons accidents—continued throughout the 1960s. Nuclear weapons were crash-landed in Spain and in Greenland. Radioactive hazards were spread, and then contained, and one bomb was lost for weeks in the warm blue waters of the Mediterranean.

Potentially serious though these events were, another set of strategic changes was itself far more important in the 1960s. The bomber was giving way to the missile. And while bombers could be sent lumbering on their way to the Soviet Union and called back before it was too late, missiles couldn't. Once the button had been pushed, nothing could be done to prevent nuclear war. And no United States missile has a built-in "self-destroy" mechanism that could be used in the event of miscalculation or madness for the simple reason that the enemy might learn the code for it. The bomber-to-missile changeover was marked by a rapid rise in the probability of accidental war.

In fact the United States authorities took great pains to improve reliability and to eliminate all chances of erroneous button-pushing. Not only was the system technically improved, but the great powers realized it might be beneficial to discuss the situation with one another in the event of emergencies. The result was the hot line—perhaps the greatest contribution to nuclear safety ever made.

But we should return to the Phelps report. The probability of accidental war quoted earlier was assessed on the basis of only a United States weapon exploding, and it did not take into account the possibility of human error. If these and other factors were also weighed, the report said, "The accidental explosion of one or more nuclear weapons in the next 10 years is not improbable."

Currently, most worry centers on the human problem.

The Phelps report raised important questions about the mental stability of those entrusted with nuclear responsibilities. It pointed out that since World War II no less than 43 per cent of all discharges from U.S. forces were made for neuropsychiatric reasons. At that time, too, there was no special psychiatric or psychological screening for bomber or missile crews. "The probability of a few breakdowns in positions of high responsibility," the report concluded, "is high."

One result has been the introduction of better screening techniques. But how effective are they? Two of the men responsible for the Navy's selection and testing program, Captain R. L. Christy and Commander J. E. Rasmussen, wrote:

> . . . it is unrealistic to expect any examiner to identify a reasonably well integrated individual's Achilles' heel and the unique combination of emotional and situational factors which could render him ineffective in the foreseeable future. . . .
> Isolated instances exist . . . where obviously unfit individuals have been assigned to nuclear-weapons systems and subsequently have been responsible for potentially disastrous situations. There is no question that the majority of these individuals would have been disqualified for such an assignment if they had undergone psychiatric assessment prior to assuming their duties in a nuclear-weapons system. However, it has been the authors' experience

> that the most potentially dangerous situations in
> the Navy have involved personnel who demon-
> strated no evidence of psychiatric disturbance at
> the time of their initial assignment to militarily
> sensitive duties.

The problem has been actively studied for a good many years now. In the United States the Human Resources Committee was given an assignment by the U.S. high command which read: "Our bombs are increasingly numerous, they are deployed widely because of the cold war, and they have quick reaction times because of the short warning times that obtain in the cold war. We begin to perceive they may not always be in safe hands." One of the committee's members, Dr. Paul Eggertson, has described the deliberations that ensued. But the conclusion was that neither that committee nor any other group could ensure that only "safe" people could deal with nuclear weapons.

Professor John R. Raser has also concerned himself with the problem. He states that the two basic assumptions on which the fate of the world may rest are that carefully selected men will retain cool judgment in an intense crisis and that even if one man fails, others will act as a "fail-safe" device. "Behavioral science research shows," he writes, "that both assumptions are almost certainly false."

Professor Raser also analyzed man's relations with his weapons through history, concluding that a new situation was reached with the advent of nuclear stockpiles. His words have a poetic ring but carry a macabre message.

> Coupling the individual human being to
> the power of the suns has meant that
> man's physiological response to crisis may
> no longer be functional—it may be a
> tragic flaw. He has become an unwitting
> victim of his own clever machinations.
> Now that we have attached our brains to
> intricate machines of near limitless power,
> and swaddled our tumescent bodies in
> frustrating physical inaction, even in the
> thick of warfare, man may become a self-
> destroying misfit.

But, it may be argued, the ultimate decision to press the button does still rest with the President of the United States—and with the leaders of the other nuclear powers, as far as is known. Is not this sufficient guarantee that the hand of madness will not send mankind to his doom? The British psychiatrist Anthony Storr is not so sure.

> Even countries such as our own have not solved the problem of getting rid of leaders who become senile or mentally ill. One of the most disastrous political decisions of recent years was made by a prime minister who was under such tension that he was taking amphetamine, a drug which notoriously impairs judgement.

The point can be made even more simply. "If only one of the major nations were led now by a man like Hitler," writes the ethologist Dr. N. Tinbergen, "life on Earth would be wiped out."

Perhaps we can still afford to brush aside such implications when there are only five nuclear powers. But when there are 10 or even 15? "How much compounded will the chance [of nuclear accidents] be," asks Professor Raser, "when Indonesia, Egypt, Israel or South Africa have their own primitive nuclear complexes to reinforce their local quarrels? And we may be sure that the experience and technology of every other country will not match the expertise that provides the safeguards incorporated into a Polaris."

Strategy and Superkill

By 1961 the world had stockpiled about 30,000 megatons of nuclear weapons. Since then production facilities in the United States and Britain have been slowed down, while those in France, the Soviet Union, and China have speeded up. What the total now comes out at is anybody's guess, but it must lie between 50,000 and 100,000 megatons of TNT equivalent—in other words, more than 20 tons of TNT for every man, woman, and child alive on the earth. One pound of TNT is more than sufficient to kill a human being; so the human race has now accumulated sufficient nuclear explosive to eliminate itself 50,000 times over.

But collective madness is one thing and national security another. So let us look at the conventional justification of the current U.S. nuclear force as outlined, for instance, in the journal *Science and Technology* by Daniel F. Fink, at one time Deputy Director of Defense Research and Engineering in the United States.

Currently, the U.S. forces include 1,000 Minuteman missiles, composed of a changing number of the Mark I model (carrying an average of slightly more than 1 megaton of nuclear explosive) and the Mark II model, which carries an average of 2 megatons. In addition there are 656 Polaris missiles capable of being launched by submarine, each carrying 700 kilotons of nuclear explosive. Finally, there are 54 Titan II missiles, each capable of delivering 5 or more megatons. The maximum "megatonnage equivalent" that is deliverable by these weapons, according to Mr. Fink, is 2,260 megatons.

Now for many years the damage which the United States needs to be able to inflict on the Soviet Union, should that country initiate a nuclear war, has been accurately quantified. The requirement is to "destroy" some 80 million Russians (about 30 per cent of the population) together with 70 per cent of Soviet industry. In Pentagonese, this is known as the "assured destruction of the U.S.S.R." It can be achieved, according to calculations, by delivering 400-megaton equivalents. In fact the calculations indicate that increasing the payload to even as much as 1,500 megatons has little additional effect; the percentage of industry knocked out stays at 70 per cent and the proportion of the population killed rises only to a little above 50 per cent. So 400 megatons is seen to be all that is required.

Why, then, are more than 2,000 megatons stockpiled in missiles? The answer runs as follows: Taking the most pessimistic assumptions, only four-fifths of the total missiles will be "available," only four-fifths of those will be "ready," only four-fifths of those will be successfully launched, and only four-fifths of those will behave as they ought to in flight. This leaves only two-fifths of the total. It must be assumed that the Soviet first strike eliminates one-third of these. But the missiles may still have to penetrate a Soviet ABM system not yet in existence but which may be by 1972. This eliminates another third of the remaining missiles, leaving less than one-fifth of the original number to do the work of destruction. One-fifth of 2,000 megatons, by a remarkable coincidence, turns out to be 400 megatons. From this, Mr. Fink concludes that "the actual 1967 stockpiled equivalent megatonnage closely matches the requirements that have been established to ensure a high confidence that our strategic policy of assured destruction will deter the U.S.S.R."

In fact it does nothing of the kind. There are many loose threads in the argument just quoted, but they can be ignored. However, Mr. Fink has omitted the small matter of a further 500 long-range bombers, together capable of delivering a further 1,853 nuclear warheads. And of course the United States stockpile of strategic weapons is far above 2,260 megatons—probably between 10 and 30 times more, not counting nuclear material in storage ready for package into weapons.

No one is better qualified to argue this matter than the U.S. Secretary of Defense. And on September 18, 1967, Robert Mc-Namara told a meeting of editors and publishers, "Our current numerical superiority over the Soviet Union in reliable, accurate and effective warheads is both greater than we had originally planned and is in fact more than we require."

How did this state of affairs come about? In 1945 it seemed inevitable that bombs would continue to be delivered by bombers. But by the early 1950s, thanks partly to the help of 170 German rocket engineers working in seclusion in Alabama, the idea of the rocket had taken root. At first this was conceived as only a short-range weapon. The weight of an H-bomb and the accuracy that would be required to deliver it on target several thousand miles away appeared to make the intercontinental ballistic missile a technical impossibility. But by 1957 the first Atlas of the U.S. Air Force had flown and more were on order; its function was to deliver a thermonuclear warhead to within a radius of 5 miles of the target at a distance of 6,000 miles. By 1960 the weapon had been proved. It now took just 30 minutes to send a hydrogen bomb a quarter of a way around the globe and land it with high precision on an enemy target.

In the meantime, of course, grand nuclear strategy had come into being, the doctrine of deterrence had been officially adopted, and nuclear weapon manufacture had gone full steam ahead. By 1961 there were in existence in the United States some 1,700 intercontinental bombers, consisting mainly of 630 B-52s and 1,000 B-47s. This alone was a strike force capable of carrying out the most insane destruction. Just one B-52, as I have said, could carry 50 megatons.

This enormous force had been built up on the strength of a "bomber gap"—a supposed gap between the number of bombers possessed by the Soviet Union and the number possessed by the United States. It was later revealed that the gap was the other way around—the Soviet Union in 1961 had only about 150 intercontinental bombers and a total of perhaps 1,000 megatons.

But even this was not the full extent of the United States nuclear armory. In addition there were 1,300 shorter-range bombers carrying nuclear warheads, a few score intercontinental missiles, 80 intermediate-range missiles, 80 Polaris missiles, and other tactical delivery systems. In short the changeover from bomber to missile was getting under way, and soon a "missile gap" replaced the bomber gap. One set of much-publicized figures estimated that by 1964 the Soviet Union would have 1,000 ICBMs compared to the United States figure of 130.

The missile gap turned out to be as nonexistent as the bomber gap. Only now is the Soviet Union's missile strength approaching that of the United States, and even the reason for that, again according to McNamara, "is in part a reaction to our own build-up since the beginning of this decade."

The detailed story of this quagmire of political confusion and interservice rivalry has been retold in lucid detail by Ralph Lapp in his book *The Weapons Culture*. Its consequences have been explored by many scientists, including Professor Seymour Melman of Columbia University. In 1964, he estimated, the United States could knock out Soviet cities of 100,000 people or more 231 times over, even assuming that 95 per cent of major U.S. aircraft were lost and 75 per cent of the major missiles were destroyed or did not reach their target. Professor Melman's calculations, though hotly challenged by many of the authorities, took overkill into the range of superkill. It took strategy from the ridiculous to the absurd. And it left the United States with the biggest destructive capability the world has ever known.

This enormous force had been built up in the name of defense. Earlier, in 1962, Sir Solly Zuckerman, who is now chief scientific adviser to the British Cabinet, had questioned this curious nomenclature. "We must avoid the conceptual framework derived from the military terminology of pre-nuclear warfare," he said. "One may fairly ask what meaning there is to the idea of using nuclear weapons 'to defend our territories and our peoples.' One can deter with nuclear weapons. Can one defend?"

The answer, certainly at that time, must have been no. The U.S. Department of Defense would have been better known as the "Department of Deterrence." But the biggest danger of all is that a department of deterrence can so easily turn into a department of offense.

The reason for this depends on the basic United States strategic mission "to deter aggression at any level and, should deterrence fail, to terminate hostilities in concert with our allies under conditions of relative advantage while limiting damage to the U.S. and allied interests." Thus the concept is first to deter and second to emerge from a nuclear exchange suffering the minimum possible damage. It now seems that these two aims are basically incompatible. It is not possible to put into effect a doctrine which seeks to minimize the chances of a nuclear war as well as to minimize its consequences.

Currently, there is little advantage to be gained on either side by striking first; mutual annihilation on a roughly equal scale is guaranteed. Repellent though such a situation may be, it is deterrence working as planned. However, it is possible to change the balance in a number of ways, one of which is currently being developed in both the United States and the Soviet Union. This is the plan to equip each missile with multiple warheads, known as MIRVs (Multiple Independent Reentry Vehicles), each capable of being landed on a separate target, such as an enemy missile base. This greatly increases damaging power without increasing the number of actual missiles deployed. The situation then arises of the United States being able to knock out a much greater number of Soviet missiles, thus limiting damage to itself, providing the United States strikes first.

Both the Americans and the Russians have often claimed they will never start a nuclear war. But another enigma of deterrence strategy is that the side to start such a war aims his missiles at the missile bases of his enemy, rather than at his cities. This is known as counterforce strategy. The side that retaliates aims his missiles—in one sense, less humanely—at the enemy's cities, because by this time there is no point in hitting empty missile silos. If we are to translate strategy into moral terms, as I believe we should, who is to judge the relative evils of being the first to start a nuclear war or being the only side to eliminate population centers in a nuclear holocaust?

In any event there are signs that strategic requirements may soon dictate a first-strike policy. Robert McNamara gave some indication of this when he outlined future United States strategy in 1967. He gave figures which showed that by 1975 the number of United States casualties from a nuclear war would be about three times greater if the Soviet Union made the first strike than if the United States did. There were in fact four sets of figures quoted which depended on such things as the strength of the Soviet forces and the number of MIRVs made operational. In the event of a Soviet first strike, United States casualties varied from about

50 million deaths to about 110 million. But if the United States struck first, casualties could vary only between 20 and 50 million deaths. Under such conditions, and in times of emergency, the pressure for the United States to strike first might be sufficiently high for nuclear war to be started. This situation arises in spite of the fact that, in theory, the side to strike first aims at missile bases and the side to strike second at cities. Wherever a first strike is aimed it will certainly cause substantial civilian damage and leave some missiles unharmed. A MIRVed first strike thus increases the number of missiles that can be eliminated, and so greatly reduces the effects of the retaliatory blow from the other side.

This situation is a classic example of the dilemma of deterrence. In fact, all the figures just quoted depended on the very basic assumption that the Russians did nothing to counteract the threat from the new MIRVs. This, of course, is unlikely; the Russians would probably increase their nuclear strength so that they could still inflict the same damage on the United States even after the MIRVs had knocked out a proportion of their missile force. This removes the advantage of first strike but it takes us into another round of the arms race: the Americans deploy MIRVs and the Russians retaliate by increasing their missile strength. Either way the doctrine of deterrence has unfortunate results. In the first case, nuclear war is made more likely, and in the second, more nuclear weapons are stockpiled to maintain equilibrium.

It is often thought that all nuclear weapons are coupled to the doctrine of strategic deterrence. This is not so. Much the greater part of the United States nuclear armory is in the form of so-called tactical weapons for which elaborate plans have been drawn up in the event of battlefield warfare ever occurring again. These tactical explosives have been much underpublicized and they pose a threat nearly as alarming as the strategic weapons.

First, they are not really tactical at all. A conservative estimate puts their total number in the region of tens of thousands. And according to McNamara, in 1964 their average yield was about 100 kilotons. The Hiroshima bomb, it will be recalled, was at the most 20 kilotons, and so the average tactical weapon is five times as powerful. Actually, we should define "powerful" rather more carefully. The fallout from a 100-kiloton bomb would cover an area about five times as large as a 20-kiloton bomb, other things being equal. But the blast and heat effects, which spread out in the shape of a sphere, would cover an area only three times as large. Even so, there was nothing tactical about the Hiroshima explosion. Not only were its effects devastating, far worse than the strategic bombing effects on German cities in the last world war, but the weapon was used in a strategic sense—to bring the war to a close. So why should we now think of a weapon five or even three times more powerful as "tactical"? The only real reason is that it is much smaller than the megaton strategic weapons. Here again we see a danger of using old terminology to describe new weapons and new strategies.

The tactical armory contains a vast array of weapons. They include huge numbers of air-to-ground missiles carried by aircraft, the ground-to-air missiles operated by the Army, and the ground-to-ground missiles such as the Pershing, with a range of up to 400 miles, and the Sergeant (range 75 miles). The 155-mm howitzer can fire a 2-kiloton nuclear warhead. Smaller missiles include the guided Lance, and the unguided Little John and Honest John with warheads of from 5 to 10 kilotons. The smallest nuclear weapon is the bazooka-launched Davy Crockett with a yield of from one-quarter to one-half a kiloton. The U.S. Navy's 15 attack carriers all have a nuclear capability, and each carries two fighter squadrons capable of delivering nuclear weapons. Not included in all this are the ground-to-air missiles, including Hawk, Nike, and Bomarc, which may be used strategically or tactically.

It is apparently believed that these weapons could be used on the battlefield without an all-out nuclear strategic exchange taking place soon afterwards. At best, this seems a dubious proposition. In spite of this, the use of tactical nuclear weapons has been threatened more than once. It occurred during the Korean war and later in an attempt to dissuade the Chinese from attacking South Korea in 1965. Similar warnings to China were reported during the Vietnam war, and new types of atomic weapons were apparently offered to the Pentagon as a means of clearing occupied Vietcong tunnels. Defense sources subsequently denied these threats were made. Whether they were examples of alarmist press reporting or deliberately leaked and deliberately denied threats we may never know. But they made few of us sleep easier at night. And though atomic weapons may never have entered Vietnamese territory, they were certainly available close by on U.S. aircraft carriers. Some of the more extreme senators even called for nuclear retaliation when the spy ship *Pueblo* was captured by the North Koreans.

But perhaps the most advanced plans for tactical nuclear warfare exist for Europe if NATO should ever be threatened by an invading Soviet or East European force through Germany. Sir Solly Zuckerman has described a war game known as Spearpoint which took place in northern Germany in October 1961. In this game involving

> . . . just three NATO Corps, nuclear weapons
> were used against military targets only, in an area
> of 10,000 square miles which contained no large
> towns or cities. In this "battle," lasting only a few
> days, it was assumed that the two sides together
> used a total of between 20 and 25 megatons in not
> fewer than 500 and not more than 1000 strikes.
> It turned out that 3.5 million people would
> have had their homes destroyed if the weapons
> were air-burst, and 1.5 million if ground-burst. In
> the former case, at least half the people concerned
> would have been fatally or seriously injured (i.e.,
> 1.75 million). In the case of ground-burst
> weapons, all 1.5 million would have been exposed
> to a lethal radiological hazard, and a further 5
> million to serious danger from radiation.

Sir Solly went on to question whether a tactical nuclear exchange of this kind could be controlled by military commanders
in the chaos likely to take place. But whether or not such an
exchange would bring about the third world war, we should not
be deceived about the results for Europe. The United Nations report of 1967 claimed that if nuclear weapons were used in this
way in Europe, "They could lead to the devastation of the whole
battle zone. Almost everything would be destroyed; forests would
be razed to the ground and only the strongest buildings would
escape total destruction."

More than 7,000 tactical nuclear warheads are already stationed
in Europe for use by NATO forces. A total of some 15,000 could
quickly be made available. Exactly to what use NATO intends to
put them remains obscure. During the 1960s, in the face of
mounting evidence of the catastrophic effect that tactical nuclear
war would have on Europe, policies were revised. Tactical nuclear
war was taken off the agenda of absurdities and a new piece of
insanity, unique to NATO, was added on. It went by the gentle-
sounding term of "initial use of nuclear weapons."

NATO is the only alliance in the world today that actually advocates starting a nuclear war. This, it claims, is the only way Europe
can be protected from the "potential invader," which is NATOese
for the Soviet Union. And as soon as that invader puts his foot
across the Iron Curtain, NATO promises to release a barrage of

nuclear warheads. Exactly how far the foot must go, however, has not been publicly specified. NATO's exact nuclear policy remains a secret. As a deterrent it is therefore presumably valueless.

This particular charade of policy making also involves the active participation of the United States President. He must give his assent to the first use of nuclear weapons as soon as the invader makes his forbidden move. And this, as a *Times* leader writer has put, not only makes the policy immoral but also unrealistic.

In the event, of course, the United States would be likely to disassociate herself from any such suicidal and genocidal activity. Unhappily, the danger does not end there. For there are in Europe two other nuclear powers—Britain and France.

Britain's nuclear force was based initially on V-bombers but now also includes four submarines capable of firing ballistic missiles. Each is equipped with 16 Polaris missiles, some of which carry a single warhead of 700 kilotons and some of which carry three smaller warheads. Together they can deliver some 45 megatons. In addition there are still 80 Victor 2 and Vulcan 2 medium bombers, some equipped with Blue Steel nuclear missiles, which belong to Strike Command. Some of the 70 Canberras belonging to RAF Germany carry nuclear payloads, as do the 50 Vulcan and Canberra bombers stationed in Cyprus and assigned to CENTO. The fleet Air Arm includes 80 Buccaneer light jets, some of which have a nuclear capacity. And, finally, the British Army on the Rhine has available to it tactical nuclear weapons in the form of three regiments with Honest John and 203-mm howitzers.

The French nuclear force is currently based on the Mirage IV A-bomber, which delivers 80-kiloton atomic bombs. There are 45 of these bombers, and a brigade of 27 intermediate-range ballistic missiles is being installed in Provence. The latter will carry thermonuclear warheads which are still not currently in service due to technical and economic problems. In addition four ballistic missile submarines, due to go into service by 1975, will also carry thermonuclear warheads. These submarines are a long way behind schedule; a further complication is that France, unlike Britain, did not accept the U.S. offer made in 1962 to use Polaris missiles.

The similarity of the French and British submarine deterrent has, however, led to suggestions that a Franco-British deterrent may yet emerge. There are grave political difficulties over this, but there is a set of circumstances in which it might yet come to be. They depend on the United States cutting down its contribution to NATO substantially in the future and France deciding to become a NATO member. If this were to happen, there might be some foundation for a European nuclear deterrent within NATO. The Germans would no doubt object, but this may have been one of the items on the agenda in the 1969 British-German discussions.

Finally, we turn to China—the third country that promises to become a major nuclear power in the near future. China's entry into the nuclear world was spectacular for the brevity of its development. Her first nuclear test took place on October 16, 1964, and was of a small atomic bomb, probably fabricated from enriched uranium supplied by the Russians. A second test followed in 1965 and another, of some 20 kilotons, in 1966. Later in 1966 an atomic weapon was detonated from a Chinese-built missile. On December 28, 1966, a thermonuclear device of some kind was exploded and on June 17, 1967, China's first 3-megaton H-bomb was detonated. In little more than 2½ years the Chinese went from primitive A-bomb to powerful H-bomb—a feat which took seven years in France and much longer for the other powers who had to develop the technology from the unknown. But the Chinese have also apparently been able to keep their devices small enough to be delivered by aircraft and missile—something which plagued the French program for many years.

Information about the Chinese nuclear program is, of course, hard to come by. And much of our knowledge is due to a piece of remarkable reporting by the Australian religious journalist Francis James. By some apparently obscure chain of events, James was actually allowed to visit some of China's nuclear centers and was given a great deal of information about progress. According to this information, the Chinese now have production capacity to make several hundred atomic bombs a year—but instead the material is being diverted to thermonuclear ends. This material comes from the Chinese gas-diffusion plant 10 miles out of Lanchow on the Yellow River.

The most extraordinary thing about the whole program is that this plant is now being closed down because the Chinese have managed to produce enriched uranium from a gas centrifuge plant—a device which I shall describe in the next section and which no other country in the world had succeeded in developing by 1969. This plant is situated in the Al Shan Mountains north of Lanchow.

In addition, a reactor complex at Yumen in Kansu produces some 650 pounds a year of plutonium which could be turned into atomic weapons. Another 65 pounds of plutonium a year comes from Paotow in Inner Mongolia.

According to James, China's first H-bomb factory is "in Tsinghai province, west of Lanchow, and weapons for testing are assembled

northwest of Lanchow and shipped up to the test site at Lop Nor."
In fact Lop Nor is a large lake 150 miles southwest of the program's
administrative center at Ha-mi, which lies between Lanchow and
Dzungaria. Exactly where the Lop Nor test site is situated is not
publicly known, and the Chinese have apparently built several dum-
mies which are indistinguishable from the real thing from the air.

The speed of all this activity leaves little doubt that the Chinese
will be a major nuclear power by the mid-1970s. What does remain
in doubt is whether China will adopt similar strategies to the other
powers. Both Morton Halperin and Michael B. Yahuda have argued
that the Chinese have great respect for nuclear power and will not
adopt a first-strike doctrine. Yahuda actually goes further than this
and argues that the emergence of China as a nuclear power may
well bring her at last into real dialogue with the other nations, from
whom she has remained isolated for many years. So far that dialogue has been limited to a one-way transmission of the tune "The
East Is Red" from China's first satellite, put up in April 1970, and
a table tennis match with the United States.

Dangers from the Labs

"The disease of which the hydrogen bomb is a symptom," wrote
Professor Freeman J. Dyson of the Institute of Advanced Study,
Princeton, N.J., in 1961, "is the continuous and apparently irresist-
ible march of technology which makes all kinds of weapons progress
more simple, more versatile and more lethal." This disease has not
been cured since 1961—if anything it has shown itself to be more
virulent than was once predicted. Work in the military labs continues, and in the advanced countries most of the civilian labs—
wittingly or not—play their part as well.

The main result is that the technology of the bomb has not stood
still. If it progressed slowly in the early 1960s it has gone forward
much faster recently. And if we are to be prepared for the results
it may bring, we should ask what the research now in hand promises for our nuclear future.

The first answer is reassuring. Fission and fusion have already
been invented, and no similar but so far undiscovered forces await
to be unleashed. The other forces that nature still has up her sleeve
are strictly for the devotees of science fiction. If an antimatter bomb
is ever built, it will be in a solar system other than our own.

That leaves two basic alternatives for the existing fission and fusion weapons—make them bigger or make them smaller. The latter aim was the subject of intense research in the late 1950s and early 1960s. It too has now reached a logical impasse with the development of the Davy Crockett—a weapon with a range of only a mile or two, according to some an accuracy not much greater, and a nuclear warhead of one-quarter of a kiloton (250 tons) of TNT. Not until after it was deployed was there a full assessment of the disadvantages of exploding a nuclear weapon—however small—a mile or so in front of your own troops. As a result of this assessment, the weapon is now being phased out.

Bigger bombs are quite another matter. There is no theoretical upper limit to the size that a fission-fusion-fission device can be made. However, as the 10-megaton weapon is large enough to destroy the better part of any city, there seems little strategic point in making it much bigger. But one of the unfortunate tendencies of today's research and development is that what is possible tends to get done. The rationale is evolved afterwards.

For this reason, it would be unwise to dismiss too quickly the possibility of the G-bomb, with an explosive power of 1,000 megatons or even more. Such a device would weigh several hundred tons, and so there is currently no missile, aircraft, or submarine that could deliver it. It might be delivered by boat and detonated in the port of a foreign country or simply stationed there and used as a nuclear "pistol" to point at the head of a foreign power. If a bigger space booster materializes, there is even the possibility—as Ralph Lapp has suggested—of assembling it in space "as a veritable Damoclean sword hovering over a nation's head."

Just as there are bigger and smaller bombs, there are also cleaner and dirtier ones. In fact, the ones already developed tend to be too dirty. If one subscribes to the theory that a nuclear war is winnable, one requirement is to enter the devastated territory soon after a nuclear attack. Today's bombs produce so much fallout that this cannot be done quickly. Understandably, then, the search for cleaner bombs has been a focus of nuclear weapons research for many years.

Public knowledge of this dates back to 1957. In that year the press first began to carry reports of a successor to the hydrogen bomb, known as the neutron bomb. This was claimed to be a bomb that produced so little blast and heat that it could not knock over a tree. Neither did it produce any fallout. But what it did do was shower the surrounding area with intense beams of neutrons and gamma rays. Both are lethal to man in large enough doses, and both can be produced at will in the laboratory.

The military importance of this was that, like chemical and biological weapons, the neutron bomb would destroy people but not buildings or bridges. Unlike chemical weapons, it would not contaminate the attacked area, which could therefore be occupied soon after the explosion. By 1961, it was claimed, both the Russians and the Americans were on the verge of testing their first neutron weapons. But those tests have never taken place.

The reason is simple enough—neither side had a clue as to how to make a neutron bomb. There were in fact only two means of doing so, and both were theoretically impossible. The first depends on the fact that neutrons are produced when atoms fission. But so is heat, and to produce enough neutrons to cause a lethal dose over any real range would also produce so much heat that the bomb would melt before it could carry out its function. If elaborate cooling systems were installed, the bomb would end up the size of a very large nuclear power station, posing acute problems in logistics for its users. The only conceivable application for such a device would be on or in the sea, which would act as a heat sink. The only targets for a seaborne bomb that can kill people but not sink ships are ships' crews. And even the most ardent devotees of military research did not see this as a goal worth a huge research program.

Neutrons are also produced during fusion reactions, and at first glance a neutron fusion device seems more hopeful. "The reaction of one gram of hydrogen would yield (in a fusion reaction) 7×10^{17} ergs of energy in the form of fast neutrons," wrote Professor Freeman Dyson. "This means that one gram of hydrogen could in principle give five times the lethal dose of radiation to anybody within one kilometre radius if neutrons were not absorbed in the atmosphere." It happens that neutrons are absorbed in the atmosphere, but it was not this that made the fusion neutron bomb unworkable. It was that to produce the reaction, an atomic weapon had to be used to get the fusion started. As there is no such thing as a clean atomic weapon—they all produce substantial fallout—there was no way of setting off a "clean" fusion neutron bomb once it had been built.

Why, then, did the neutron bomb get so much publicity? It seems clear now that it was but a fictitious weapon in the hands of those who opposed the United States voluntary moratorium on testing which was still in existence until late in 1961. In that year Thomas E. Murray, a former AEC commissioner, said of the neutron bomb, "The possibility of this development is more realistic than was that of the hydrogen bomb a year before its detonation. In fact, these weapons would already have been tested were it not for the moratorium." If this statement helped sway public opinion toward breaking the moratorium we shall never know; it was the Soviet Union that broke the unofficial ban—with a series of megaton tests—late in 1961. Though the Americans soon followed suit, no neutron bomb was detonated.

After that the affair died down but not out. It was widely thought that the whole neutron bomb scare had been fabricated by test devotees until 1967. But in that year the authorities saw fit to make their first official comment on the scene. A joint statement by the AEC and the Department of Defense said that they were pressing on with research into a neutron bomb. Once bitten, twice shy: the statement attracted a minimum of attention.

But this was the time to listen. For it now seems that a technical advance between 1961 and 1967 had made the fusion neutron bomb a distinct possibility. That advance was the invention, in a civil laboratory, of the laser—a source of incredibly bright and powerful radiation.

During the period from 1959 to 1965 the U.S. Department of Defense spent in the region of $100 million on various forms of laser research. They saw in the laser a new means of range finding, a device for illuminating military targets, and all sorts of new surveillance techniques, some from space. But the first indication that the laser also had nuclear weapon implications came from another source, the AEC.

On May 2, 1967, the AEC issued a statement which claimed sweeping new controls over "restricted data." The AEC had always had control over the data generated by AEC laboratories and personnel, but it now claimed that some research topics also fell into the restricted category, even if the research was carried out by private individuals in private laboratories. Under the AEC controls, those individuals would be forbidden by United States law to publish their results.

There were strong objections from the atomic energy industry and the scientific community. Dr. Margaret Mead, the chairman of the Committee on Science in the Promotion of Human Welfare, castigated the new proposals as "an unprecedented infringement of academic freedom and free scientific enquiry." And it was far from clear how the new system would work. Researchers without security clearance had no means of knowing precisely what it was that the AEC regarded as restricted data. The AEC had a list of such subjects, but the list itself was classified and could not be inspected by anyone without security clearance.

In the light of these criticisms the AEC modified its proposals and on December 28 published them in revised form. One section, paragraph 26, immediately caught the physicist's eye. The AEC had extended its security classification to cover

> All Restricted Data . . . concerning: (a) Atomic weapons and nuclear explosive devices or compo-nents thereof, including lasers and laser systems designed to produce or capable of producing in deuterium, tritium, or mixtures containing these materials, a one per cent rise in absolute tempera-ture . . . as a result of thermonuclear reactions.

What this paragraph implied was that a thermonuclear fusion re-action might be set off by a laser. The implications of this were enormous. As we have seen, all the hydrogen bombs in stockpiles rely on an atomic trigger, based on uranium-235, for detonation. This uranium isotope is both extremely expensive and difficult to ob-tain. And it is this which has so far restricted membership of the nuclear club to five nations.

But if the H-bomb could now be detonated by laser—a device that can be bought from hundreds of manufacturers for a few thou-sand dollars or less—the route to nuclear power would be opened up in an unprecedented way. So, too, would the route to a neutron bomb—or at least the route to a cleaner fusion bomb with little fallout.

The reason for all this is the several-hundred-million-degree tem-perature that must be obtained to make fusion start. Lasers them-selves are not generators of energy, but they can condense energy in an incredible fashion. The most powerful are capable, for a tiny fraction of a second, of emitting almost as much power as courses through the whole of the British electricity grid. And so if this power could be focused onto an already heated mixture of tritium and deuterium, the necessary temperature might well be generated.

Proof of this lies in the fact that laboratories in many countries are experimenting with lasers to see if they can produce thermo-nuclear fusion. Their object is not the production of hydrogen bombs but of a fusion reactor—a controlled means of producing fusion which liberates its energy without an explosion. If they ever succeed, they will produce an energy source for man far more important, far cheaper, and far longer-lasting than the fission reactor.

But their success would also spell other advances. If a laser could be used as a trigger for a fusion reactor, it could also be used as a trigger for a fusion bomb. The latter could then be manufactured in an ordinary laboratory. And it could be done in secret. While the enormous gas-diffusion plants now required for H-bomb manufacture are impossible to conceal—and hence give warning of a nation trying to go nuclear—the laser H-bomb could be made underground. And its cost might not deter even the smallest nation.

However, the laser bomb is not with us yet. There are theoretical reasons for thinking that the problem of making it may turn out to be intractable. A great deal more research is still required before we can know the answer. But it is clear that this new development has brought the cheap H-bomb nearer than any other single advance since 1945.

The laser H-bomb illustrates how quickly a discovery in a civilian laboratory can be developed as a military concept of great importance. One of the other current dangers from the labs illustrates the opposite: how difficult is the switch from the military laboratory to civilian application? And the device in question—already mentioned in connection with China—is the gas centrifuge.

Early in the 1940s several possible ways of enriching uranium for the first bomb were explored, and gas diffusion won through. A simpler idea, which had to be abandoned then because the technology was not available, has since shown itself to be eminently practical. The idea is that the two isotopes of uranium are separated by spinning them at high speed in a centrifuge. As a result the heavier, unwanted isotope moves to the outside, and the lighter collects nearer the inside. One centrifuge, like one membrane, produces only a tiny enrichment, and hundreds of thousands may be needed to make an enrichment plant. And each centrifuge must be spun at enormous speed—upwards of 60,000 revolutions a minute. The difficulty of doing this, and of continuously feeding in the corrosive uranium compounds and then extracting them, proved too great until recently. One of the principal results of early experiments was what the technologists rather charmingly called "catastrophic self-disassembly."

But because the technique held a theoretical promise of cheaper bombs, gas centrifuge technology was kept under strict security in both the United States and Britain. In one sense, this was unfortunate, for a distant relation of the gas centrifuge—the liquid zonal centrifuge—has shown itself to have very important biological and medical applications. These devices are now being used, for instance, in the preparation of vaccines. But their civilian applications were delayed for at least a decade because of the fear that they would spread with them valuable nuclear weapons technology.

This fear seems to have been justified, for early in 1968 both Japan and the Netherlands announced that the problems of using gas centrifuge for uranium enrichment had been largely solved.

What followed could have been easily anticipated. By November 1968 Britain, the Netherlands, and West Germany announced that they would jointly develop the concept still further. Two experimental plants are to be built, in Holland and England, at a cost of about £26 million. These plants will provide enriched uranium for nuclear reactors. They could also provide the same material for atomic weapons, or atomic triggers for H-bombs.

A gas centrifuge plant is a costly project—perhaps as costly as gas diffusion. Where it scores over the latter, however, is that it consumes much less electricity—between one-tenth and one-fifth the amount of a diffusion plant. So in the long run it produces enriched uranium a good deal more cheaply.

The gas centrifuge is not a development that brings nuclear weapons easily within the grasp of any country that wants them. The technology involved is difficult and the cost considerable. Nevertheless, it is a simpler and a cheaper method than diffusion. Thus, like the laser itself, the existence of gas centrifuge plants may open up a new route to nuclear weapons power. The tricks of centrifuge separation are likely to become widely known. Such a risk might be worth taking if there were sound economic arguments for developing centrifuge separators. But those that have been publicly advanced so far are not that persuasive. "In view of this," writes Dr. C. F. Barnaby, "one wonders why the British, the Dutch and the West Germans are so keen to go ahead with the development of gas centrifuges and why their governments do not make the clear decision that, because of the potential dangers involved, this development should be stopped, or at least slowed down, until steps are taken to reduce its consequences."

Dr. Barnaby supplied his own answer. "A possible reason may be connected with the momentum of technological development itself," he suggests. "By the time a development arrives at a stage where political decisions have to be made, there may be so many secondary interests involved that a positive decision may be politically irreversible." This self-perpetuating character of today's technology can be seen in almost every field. But nowhere is it stronger than in military development, which is largely secure from the self-correct-ing mechanism of scientific criticism and where large new programs can be easily justified through the use of the magic words "national security."

Justifications of this kind lie at the heart of today's technological progress. In broad terms the thrust of our technical efforts during 1960–80 have a common rationale: to drive us away from the habitable part of the earth which we find so difficult to manage. This philosophy has taken us first into space and secondly into the ocean depths, which cover two-thirds of the earth's surface.

Both these programs—the characteristic technical features of our times—have been spearheaded by military curiosity and paid for largely by the implications of national security. Though rarely acknowledged as such, the possibilities of nuclear space war and of nuclear ocean war will be seen by future historians—if there are any—to have served as the cutting edge of technology for more than two decades.

CHAPTER II

Missiles and the Moon

The Ballistic Bomber–The Bomb in Orbit–The "Civilian" Space Program–Astronauts for the Military –Satellites for the Military–ABM: The Great Debate–ASM: The Next Debate?–The Future in Space

"We didn't go to the war with one ship,
we went with a whole fleet of ships.
We must envisage the same sort of thing
for a possible war in space."
>   Dr. Walter Dornberger
>   *Air Force/Space Digest*
>   October 1965

The route from Peenemünde—the German rocket center which Dr. Dornberger directed during World War II—to the moon has been traced many times. As usually told, it makes a classic story of how Nazi know-how was directed away from war toward the great adventure of the human spirit known as the moon program.

In this chapter we will follow a different route. It will take us not through Cape Kennedy but through Vandenberg Air Force Base in California. On the way we will look not at the communication satellites used to bounce television pictures across the oceans but at the military communications, navigation, and reconnaissance satellites which are launched in far greater numbers from the Vandenberg base. We will look at the struggles of the U.S. Army, Navy, and Air Force to get their troops into space to fight battles of which they cannot begin to see the significance. And we will look at the subtle way in which the missile and the satellite are once again being linked together to form a weapon of greatly increased destructive power.

This route, unlike the other, ends not at the moon but much

closer home. Its culmination is a new and vicious twist in the spiraling cost of strategic arms. The end products of this particular space race are two new weapons systems likely to characterize the 1970s. What they promise for the future was described by George W. Rathjens, a visiting professor of political science at Massachusetts Institute of Technology, in the April 1969 issue of *Scientific American*. They portend, he wrote,

> . . . a decade of greatly increased military budgets, with all the concomitant social and political costs these entail for both countries. Moreover, it appears virtually certain that at the end of all this effort and all this spending neither nation will have significantly advanced its own security. On the contrary, it seems likely that another upward spiral in the arms race would simply make a nuclear exchange more probable, more damaging, or both.

The developments to which Professor Rathjens was referring were the antiballistic missile and the decision to equip American missiles with not one but several nuclear warheads. The technology for both developments depends in part on the much vaunted "spin-off" from the space race—a kind of spin-off rarely used to justify the moon program.

How this came to be is a complex story. It cannot be told as a simple chronological narrative, for the rival claims and vested interests in exploring the space frontier interacted in a complex series of moves which spanned two decades. What we should bear in mind is that it was the rocket which led to the current concept of strategic war. It was also the rocket which opened up the space frontier, and now the moon, to man and his equipment. And although these ideas have sometimes followed a separate development, it is not surprising to learn that the one followed the other in close company through four American administrations. Today, space and war are closer together than ever before—except perhaps in the days of the Peenemünde research station which produced the wartime V-2 rocket.

The Ballistic Bomber

On October 3, 1942, German engineers on the Baltic coast at Peenemünde ushered in the missile age. Their rocket, the V-2 that was later to terrorize London and Antwerp, had a range of more than 200 miles and could carry a payload of 1 ton of high explosive. Ten tons of fuel—alcohol and liquid oxygen—were needed to accelerate the rocket to its speed of 3,600 miles an hour. And on its way the 5-foot engine developed a power of some half a million horsepower and pushed the rocket forward with a thrust of 28 tons. But what most interested the technical director of the project, Dr. Wernher von Braun, was that his rocket could fly nearly to the edge of the atmosphere.

It soon became clear that von Braun would get no chance to develop his ideas in Nazi Germany. As the war dragged to its close, Peenemünde was destroyed and its scientists evacuated. Back in Washington, the Pentagon launched Project Paperclip—a scheme for recruiting German scientists to work in the United States. Though this was apparently not known by some of the U.S. intelligence forces in Germany, von Braun and "Paperclip" did eventually meet up. Together with 126 of his rocket colleagues and more than a ton of secret documents, he found his way to the United States and to the White Sands Proving Ground in New Mexico that the U.S. Secretary of War had set up in 1945.

There he was later joined by 300 railway wagons of V-2 parts, which had been discovered at a factory in Germany's Harz Mountains. Although the earlier Potsdam agreement had cited the area of this factory as one which was to be given to the Russians, and had stipulated that no factories there were to be stripped, the U.S. Army chose to ignore or forget an agreement which would have given Russian rocketry a substantial boost. As a result the Americans finished up not only with most of the know-how of the German rocket program, but with most of its hardware, too.

The reason, of course, was that rockets had not gone unnoticed in the United States. A small program had already been started, and both the Army and the Navy had begun their own highly secret studies of what space could mean to the military. Even earlier, before the end of the war, an Air Force study had concluded there were many applications for the missile and even for the orbiting satellites that they predicted would eventually come to be. One study, Project RAND (the name later given to the famous think tank), concluded that space satellites would produce "repercussions in the world comparable to the explosion of the atomic bomb."

In this the Army, the Navy, and the Air Force, as three separate units, were in complete disagreement with their master, the Pentagon. And in 1948 the Pentagon dared to make public the military's plans for space, to restrict them to a single program, and to cut them back to design studies. The reason was that there was then no missile in sight which could lift the weighty atomic bomb and deliver it a substantial distance with any accuracy. The missile program might have died a natural death had it not been for the forces' insistence on keeping the rocket option open.

Deprived of any ambitious military program, the military sought science as an ally. At White Sands some 70 V-2s had been refitted and flown. Furthermore, a means had been found of getting the rockets to radio back to earth details of what conditions were like near the edge of the atmosphere. This information was of great interest to scientists, who flocked to White Sands to be initiated in the fledgling art of rocketry. Soon other research rockets joined the V-2s, such as the previously developed Aerobee, Viking, and MX-744. For three or four years the forces played a waiting game, claiming their paramount interest in space was now scientific research.

The Korean war broke out in 1950. Von Braun was moved to the Redstone Arsenal in Alabama and told to develop a 500-mile-range rocket for the Army. Two years later the hydrogen bomb was born, giving rise to what Arthur C. Clarke has called "the single most important influence on the U.S. space program." The H-bomb provided an enormously greater explosive power, and research soon drastically lowered the weight of the bomb. The mathematician John von Neumann was called on to head the famous "Teapot" committee investigating the whole concept of the intercontinental ballistic missile designed to deliver a thermonuclear warhead.

His conclusions—that H-bombs were sufficiently small and powerful to be delivered with enough accuracy by a ballistic missile and that this program should be given top priority—finally gave birth to the unmanned "ballistic bomber." It took the form of the Atlas missile with a range of 5,500 nautical miles. And the forces' earlier use of science as an ally paid off, for they were able to develop the Atlas largely from the MX-774 rocket. By 1962 a total of 126 operational Atlas missiles had been installed, at a cost of $2 million per rocket. In addition each silo cost a further $16 million. When all the costs were added up, it turned out that more than $30 million had been used to install each Atlas.

The Air Force had won the battle for long-range missiles, greatly aided by the 1960 presidential election. Alarmist talk about a fictitious missile gap soon enabled the Air Force to expand its existing plans for new and improved missiles. The first was the giant Titan, the rocket which was also used to put the Gemini astronauts into orbit. After that came the quicker-reacting and more versatile Minuteman. The Navy squeezed itself into the act by arguing that land-based missiles were vulnerable to attack, and that missiles should really be hidden under the sea. In the mid-1960s the total missile force was planned to include 54 Titans, 1,200 Minutemen, and 41 submarines, each carrying 16 shorter-range Polaris missiles. With this incredible striking force, it seemed, the authorities would be satisfied for some time to come.

This was not to be. In 1964 came the first public reports of a new idea in rocketry—that of using one missile to deliver several warheads, each of which could be used to strike different targets hundreds of miles apart. The name of this macabre concept was MIRV—standing for multiple independently targeted reentry vehicle.

Gradually it was revealed that plans were far advanced for implementing this new phase of the arms race. Some 510 of the Minutemen were to be replaced by the Minuteman III—each of which could carry three 200-kiloton warheads. And 31 of the 41 submarines were to be reequipped with 16 Poseidon missiles each. Each of these would carry 10 to 14 separate warheads. The new Minutemen would cost about $8 million apiece, and the whole program would absorb a total of $10,000 million over a five-year period. The number of United States missiles would stay constant, but the number of nuclear warheads that could be delivered by them would rise from 2,382 to between 7,000 and 10,000.

The speed and apparent finality of this program took most people who were not in the know by surprise. It was not until 1968 that it leaked out that the Atomic Energy Commission had already been voted $32.5 million for the manufacture of the first of the new warheads. And in the same year it was widely rumored that the first tests of the new missile complex were about to be conducted at Cape Kennedy. Even the *New York Times* called on the Pentagon to halt the tests in case they should prejudice the impending missile disarmament talks with the Soviet Union.

But on August 16, 1968, both the Poseidon and the Minuteman III were tested at Cape Kennedy. "It was a good day for the country," a U.S. Air Force spokesman was widely quoted as saying. The *New York Times* was not so sure. "Future generations," it thundered, "undoubtedly will look back with disbelief at the way the United States again has invented, publicized, and tested a deadly new weapon which, instead of improving American security, creates an added threat to it by putting the Soviet Union under pressure to produce the same weapon and aim it at the United States."

The Pentagon did not reply until April 23 of the next year. Then it announced that five days previously the Soviet Union had indeed tested its own MIRV—and one which was much more powerful than the American model. The test, it said, had been made with the giant Soviet SS-9 rocket, which could deliver either one 25-megaton warhead or three 5-megaton heads. The Pentagon statement, however, did not specify whether the Soviet test had used three warheads, each of which could be separately aimed, or whether they were just carried to different distances. Other high-level government officials denied that the Pentagon had any information at all about Soviet tests of a MIRV system. But the United States left no one in doubt about its own MIRV intentions. It started a continuous MIRV testing program at the rate of three a month. In 1968–69 no less than $1,433 million was allocated for the development and production of nuclear warheads alone. And the first MIRV missiles were actually deployed in June 1970.

The Bomb in Orbit

When President Eisenhower announced in 1955 that the United States would launch a scientific satellite for the International Geophysical Year in 1957–58, there were three choices. Not surprisingly, they came from the overlapping space efforts of the three forces. The Air Force, of course, offered its new Atlas missile. The Army offered von Braun's Redstone missile topped off by a second and third stage to make the Jupiter C. And the Navy offered, successfully, the Vanguard.

It turned out to be the wrong choice, for von Braun's Redstone-Jupiter flew in September 1956—and could have put a satellite into orbit had the Pentagon not forbidden it and forced von Braun to fill his dummy third stage with sand.

In fact, the Pentagon had told the Army to forget satellites in 1955. But von Braun and his senior officer found an excuse to continue their testing, and they kept Redstone missiles in a hangar ready for whatever might turn up. Officially, it was ordered that the upper stages of these rockets be destroyed, but the Alabama base hit on the delightful idea of testing them for destruction by aging—they simply left them on the shelf. On October 4, 1957, when the first Sputnik was orbited, the Redstone was still there without a program. America's response with the Vanguard was due two months later. On December 6 the slender rocket ignited at Cape Canaveral (now Cape Kennedy) and toppled flaming to the ground—a crashing failure. Five days later von Braun was given just 90 days to get a satellite into orbit. He did it in 84, thanks to a certain amount of unofficial preparedness.

As the satellite age came into being, the Air Force began to imagine new roles for itself in space. If missiles used to deliver warheads could also be used to orbit satellites, why shouldn't the nuclear weapons themselves be orbited? What would come out of the strategic equation, they asked themselves, if missiles, satellites, and bombs were combined into one package?

The answer, in Pentagonese, was NABS—nuclear-armed bombardment satellites. And at one time it seemed as though NABS might put the ICBM out of business, just as the ICBM had begun to put winged bombers out of business in 1956.

The Air Force and the Pentagon began to chart the military potential of orbiting bombs. Several studies were carried out, but they all seemed to indicate that the orbiting bomb was a nonstarter. The trouble was that nuclear space weapons were all right while they were in orbit, but to bring them down on an enemy target with the accuracy of an ICBM was impossible. To provide a space deterrent of the ICBM force, it was calculated, would require 5 to 10 times as many satellites carrying nuclear weapons as ICBMs. As each would be much more costly than an ICBM, the whole system would be 10 to 20 times as expensive, costing the taxpayer an estimated $100–200 billion.

There were other disadvantages. With so many more nuclear weapons deployed, the chance of accidental explosion, and perhaps war, would be more likely. If upwards of 5,000 nuclear-armed satellites were to be blasted off to space, some of the launches would inevitably go wrong. Even if the nuclear warheads did not explode, there was the unpleasant thought of what might happen to any country that lobbed a megaton weapon by accident onto someone else's territory. And finally, not all these satellites could be kept up together and indefinitely. Some would have to be brought down unused and others would have to be hurriedly put up in times of crisis. The element of surprise would be lost to the art of nuclear attack.

At a time when the military juice had been squeezed out of any and every technological stone, these conclusions were refreshing. Almost for the first time since the war, a major technical advance had been made which did not appear to provide new military momentum. Credit for this must be given to the Americans' hardheaded approach to the cost-effectiveness of new weapons.

On Nikita Khrushchev must fall the blame for rudely shattering this short-lived triumph of reason. For in 1962 he warned the Americans that "while they bolt their front door, we shall come in at the back window." This military metaphor was not lost on the Pentagon. The whole of the United States early warning system pointed north, over the Arctic, toward the bases from which Soviet ICBMs would be launched. The back door, the route over the Antarctic from the south, had been neglected, for it was too long a journey for even the most powerful missile. If that was the route the Soviets were looking at, they must have some other trick up their sleeve than the simple missile.

A ballistic missile travels like a baseball—it is projected on a ballistic flight to a height of 700 or 800 miles and then drops out of space onto its target. In the 1960s the maximum range for this type of flight was about 9,000 miles. The back-door route to the United States was twice as long. If any nuclear weapon were to follow that route, it would have to be put into orbit round the earth, like a satellite.

The previous year, the world knew well, the Soviet Union had conducted a massive series of megaton tests at very high altitudes —some as high as 100 miles. The significance of this was not lost on the Pentagon, either. A first analysis suggested that Khrushchev planned to put nuclear weapons into orbit and detonate them at high altitude above the United States. The space war looked as though it had finally arrived.

But there were some puzzling features. First, if a weapon of this kind was to do any damage it would have to rely on heat effects alone. The most conservative estimates showed that the bomb would have to be at least 150 megatons to do any real damage below. And the Russians were not known to have any rocket that could put such an enormous payload into orbit. It was thought that even their 50-megaton bomb weighed some 20,000 pounds. That this might be orbited was just possible, for the Soviet Union had launched two Proton satellites, each weighing 27,000 pounds. Even the 150-megaton worry was later removed by Dr. Eugene Fubini, the Assistant Secretary for Defense, who calculated that a bomb aimed to explode above New York City and obliterate it from a height of 150 miles would have to pack a punch of at least 800 megatons. This was beyond the bounds of even the most alarmist assessment of Soviet rocket power, though the later Proton-4 satellite did weigh 37,500 pounds.

But that something funny really was in the wind was revealed by Marshal Biryuzov, the commander-in-chief of Soviet strategic rocket forces, on February 21, 1963. The Soviet Union, he claimed, could "launch rockets from satellites at command from Earth." This at least made one thing clear. If nuclear weapons were to be orbited, they would be exploded not in space but would be targeted from the satellite onto the ground below. This meant the space package had to carry an extra rocket system and that the warheads would have to be much smaller. By June the Air Force had reacted, announcing a four-point program to improve satellite detection, to develop a means of inspecting hostile space devices and of disabling them, and to seek the knowledge required so that military men could operate in space. In December Robert McNamara announced studies would go ahead for the Air Force's Manned Orbiting Laboratory (MOL)—the first scheme to put military men on military missions in military satellites.

The remorseless rhythm of move and countermove was not resumed until 1965. And then, on May Day and again on November 7, the Russians displayed an enormous new missile, which NATO christened "Scrag." And an announcement from Tass, the Soviet news agency, said that the missile "could deliver a surprise blow on the first or any other orbit round the Earth." A Soviet general was quick to point out that this new weapon was a defensive retaliation against the Air Force's MOL project which, he claimed, was intended solely to bombard the Soviet Union with nuclear weapons. Actually, MOL's objectives were highly classified, no doubt partly because President Kennedy had built into the Pentagon a powerful inhibition against ever mentioning space in a military context. But semiofficially, MOL's function was primarily reconnaissance and, again semiofficially, it might have a secondary objective for research into bombardment from space.

The Pentagon itself still saw no good strategic reasons for nuclear bombardment satellites. Indeed, since President Kennedy's historic 1961 announcement of the American man-on-the-moon program, powerful pressures were at work to preserve space for only peaceful activities. And on January 27, 1967, after much delay and double-talk, a space treaty was signed, in Washington, Moscow, and London, by 60 nations. Among many other things, the treaty forbade the placing in orbit about the earth of any object carrying a nuclear weapon or any other weapon of mass destruction. A similar UN resolution had been in quasi-legal force since 1963.

The Russians apparently made their first test of an orbital bomb system just two days earlier, on January 25, 1967. It consisted of a missile which placed a satellite into very low orbit, only 100 miles high, and a recovery system which brought the satellite down again somewhat before it had completed its first full orbit. Legally, anything that failed to make a complete orbit did not contravene the treaty, however many nuclear warheads it carried. Presumably the Soviet Union had delayed their tests of this device until they were sure of the exact wording of the space treaty.

Knowledge of these tests was not conveyed to the world until November 3, 1967, when Robert McNamara issued a public statement about the new system. The Soviet Union has carried out tests, he said, which relate "to the possible deployment by the Soviet Union of a FOBS." The *New York Times,* calling this a "ludicrous acronym for an unholy device," explained to its readers the next day that FOBS stood for "fractional orbital bombardment system"—a nuclear satellite that orbited but didn't orbit because it descended onto its target before making a full swing round the earth.

McNamara said 11 tests had been made in the U.S.S.R.—9 successfully—up to October 28. The system had one military advantage, which was that the warhead would give the United States much less warning of nuclear attack. In fact, it was not possible to determine the target of the satellite weapon until the retro-rocket was fired, perhaps three minutes and only 500 miles before impact. Nevertheless, McNamara reassured the nation that this did not represent a new level of threat or one which the United States wished to copy.

It was thought that FOBS would carry a 1- to 3-megaton warhead and would be aimed at bomber bases in the hope that the shortened warning time would be insufficient to give bomber crews time to get off the ground. And it was later revealed that the launching missile was not the ponderous Scrag but the SS-9. Scrag itself was thought to be able to deliver a warhead of 30 or even 50 megatons. There were five more tests of FOBS in 1968.

The truth about FOBS remains obscure. The Russians have denied their intention of ever deploying a weapon system of this kind—but not as often as they have boasted of their orbital bombers. Strategically, a decision to build a FOBS—inevitably less accurate than an ICBM—is difficult to understand except in purely psychological terms. Could it then be a figment of the United States military imagination? One theory holds that FOBS are nothing more than reconnaissance satellites flown at low altitude to inspect U.S. antimissile and antisatellite bases in the Pacific. And it is true that all the supposed flight tests of FOBS have taken the "satellite" directly over the U.S. antimissile base at Kwajalein in the Pacific.

A more depressing view is that FOBS is the Soviet equivalent of the American man on the moon program. The cost of a strategically effective FOBS, this argument runs, would be so enormous that it would have to be the principal goal of the Soviet space effort. As the Russians have never distinguished between their civil and military space program, there is currently no way of telling. The FOBS tests were all carried out in experiments designated "Cosmos," just as have been hundreds of other purely scientific space shots.

If this argument is correct, it is likely that FOBS may eventually be related to the MIRV system the Soviet Union is also said to be developing. A suborbital weapon carrying a shower of small nuclear warheads giving a warning time of perhaps three minutes is certainly a force that would command respect—whatever theoretical disadvantages it might have.

In all this the Soviet Union has certainly played the devil's advocate. Their actions have perhaps shown more clearly than any that wherever new technology and the military rub shoulders the result is a new weapon. In this, as in so many cases, it seems to be a weapon without a function. The pattern is closely paralleled by the U.S. Air Force's fight to put military men into space for reasons which as well as being classified seem also to be nonexistent.

The "Civilian" Space Program

The only real space race ever to have been run was held not in the 1960s but in the late 1950s; it was held not between two contestants—the United States and the Soviet Union—but among four. And none of those four had exactly the same goal.

The two favorites were the U.S. Air Force and the U.S. Army. The Pentagon and President Eisenhower joined the race but ran in the opposite direction. And the winner was apparently NASA, the civilian space agency, which was created between the starting line and the finishing tape. Even today, the real winner is still in doubt. If a manned landing on the moon is considered the final goal, then NASA has won. But if the real race is to stay in space longest, we should not underestimate the staying power of the U.S. Air Force. By the late 1970s the Air Force could well have overtaken NASA as the prime mover.

The starting gun for this race was the ignominious explosion that resulted from America's first effort to get into space. When the Navy's Vanguard blew up in December 1957 after a flight of a few inches, hundreds of reporters were there to witness the catastrophe. The next day their headlines offered several new names for the rocket—such as Kaputnik, Flopnik, and Stayputnik—and brought self-criticism to a new fever pitch. Only the White House remained cool, saying that America's intentions were not to win "an outer space basketball game." Eisenhower himself described Sputnik as "one small ball in the air . . . something which does not raise my apprehension, not one iota."

And Eisenhower knew just what he was contending with. The power of the military-industrial complex was already on his mind, and he viewed the passionate declarations for military space programs put out by the Air Force and the Army with great coolness. His object, as he later wrote, was "to find ways of affording perspective to our people and so relieve the current wave of near hysteria." To do this, he steadfastly dismissed as fiction every new military angle to space which the forces could dream up. And they were not lacking in imagination.

In the late 1950s there was much talk of space war. Nuclear-armed missile space stations tucked away behind the moon were claimed as the strategic mainstays of the future. Lunar nuclear artillery raised their ugly gun barrels in congressional discussion.

To the military, the moon was "high ground," traditionally a military vantage point. And, like the chemical corps only a few years later, the Air Force even offered a war without death in which remote controlled satellites attempted to blast each other out of space while life on earth continued its serenely peaceful existence. A "Project Bambi" studied the idea of filling the skies with anti-missile satellites which would identify and destroy Soviet missiles almost before they had time to get off their launching pads.

Even at this time all this had something vaguely—and never precisely specified—to do with getting a man on the moon. The Air Force claimed to be able to do it for $1,500 million by 1965 in a program called "Man in Space Soonest." As part of its plan to reserve space for itself, the Air Force even set up a new Directorate of Astronautics—a department which the Pentagon closed down three days after it was set up, thus setting a record for bureaucratic brevity. But the Air Force's big worry was von Braun, who belonged to the Army and who was quietly drawing up plans for an enormous space booster at the Army Ballistic Missile Agency in Huntsville. In retaliation, the Air Force countered with a new rocket called Titan III-C which they claimed would fulfil military functions better and more cheaply than von Braun's embryonic Saturn (an ancestor of the vehicle that ultimately put Armstrong and Aldrin on the Moon).

It turned out that the Air Force's claims were largely imaginary, and von Braun's project was only just saved from cancellation. Meanwhile the Army itself produced its own moon program: cost, $17,000 million; arrival time, April 1965. This particular project called for 149 launches of a Saturn rocket, at a rate of five a month. By the time NASA finally achieved a moon landing, it had cost nearly $30,000 million.

From this incredible barrage, Eisenhower saw only one escape route—to turn space over to a civilian agency devoted to peaceful purposes. In 1958 NASA was created and the forces told to keep their hands off space. While the peaceful intentions of NASA have always been outwardly preserved, its functions and purposes, at least as originally conceived, have never been crystal clear. While space was considered too important to be left to the generals, NASA's existence as set forth in the congressional act that created it was due to three factors. The first was national security; the second was to keep the United States on the leading edge of space exploration; and the third was to preserve space for peaceful and scientific activities. However neat its political footwork, NASA could never hope to fulfill these incompatible objectives. And it never has. While ostensibly aiming at lunar exploration, it has—as we shall see—proved of real military worth.

If Eisenhower approved of civilian space more than military space, he still could not be described as an advocate. NASA prepared its Project Mercury to get the first American astronaut into space and won its funds. But one of the last things Eisenhower did before stepping down early in 1961 was to refuse approval for NASA's Apollo program designed to get men on the moon.

Eisenhower's dead hand on space was an obvious electoral issue for the two incoming presidential candidates to seize on in 1960. And they did—Richard Nixon taking up the military tune of the forces and John Kennedy extracting poetic mileage from visions of peaceful space research—liberally mixed, it should be added, with some disastrously ill-informed talk of the missile gap. "If man orbits the Earth this year," Kennedy declared, criticizing Eisenhower's space blind spot, "his name will be Ivan." In fact his name was Yuri (Gagarin), but the point was well-made.

As Kennedy moved to the White House, NASA sprang to the attack. James Webb, the NASA administrator, used the Soviet military and political space threats to berate Kennedy for Eisenhower's Apollo decision. And scarcely had he done so when Gagarin made his historic flight on April 12, 1961. Washington went into convulsions, and Kennedy designated Lyndon B. Johnson to extricate America from the space mess. One of Johnson's first reactions was to tell the Air Force to reopen its analyses of space ventures.

Johnson's brief at this stage was quite clear. "Do we have a chance of beating the Soviets," Kennedy had asked him, "by putting a laboratory in space, or by a trip around the moon, or by a rocket to land on the moon, or by a rocket to go to the moon and back with a man?" When Johnson put the question to NASA, the space agency was able to report almost instantaneously that it could put a man on the moon in 1967, before the Russians.

The details of the hectic comings and goings during April and May of that year do not really concern us here. Two points are worth making, however. The first is a memorandum prepared by James Webb and Robert McNamara during a meeting between NASA and the Pentagon. It establishes quite clearly the political importance of the moon decision. The key passage reads:

> Our attainments in space are a major element in
> the international competition between the Soviet
> system and our own. The non-military, non-com-
> mercial and non-scientific but "civilian" projects
> such as lunar and planetary exploration are, in
> this sense, part of the battle along the fluid front
> of the cold war.

If this was the objective of the "civilian" part of the program, its military role was equally clear. William H. Shapley, at that time in charge of space and defense at the Bureau of the Budget, was quoted by the *Sunday Times* (July 20, 1969) as having summed it up thus:

> Both military leaders and military statesmen in
> Congress believed they had to find some good
> reason for developing a new class of booster
> rocket, even though they could not prove exactly
> why it was needed. The moon program was their
> golden chance to get it in the fastest possible
> time. . . . There was great concern for the aero-
> space industry. Could we afford the economic

consequences of a decline in defense procurement? The moon was as good a way as any of
buying off the industry and its Air Force patrons,
who were always demanding something more.
. . . By keeping the missile makers busy on space
boosters you were also keeping them ready to
return to missiles. You were maintaining preparedness without escalating the arms race.

The burden of what Dr. Shapley says is now being amply borne
out. In 1970, with the moon program nearly over and NASA's
funds fast dwindling, arms escalation started again. The missile
makers are again busy—this time preparing an antimissile defense
system and new warheads for new missiles.

But in 1961 little of this was generally appreciated. On May 25
Kennedy made his famous announcement of going to the moon
within the decade, and according to a Gallup poll, almost immediately afterward 58 per cent of Americans opposed it. In the
Senate few bothered to turn up to attend the hearings; those that
did seemed unclear of the relevance of the moon decision. Thus
Senator Robert Kerr, who stressed the practical aspects of space—
including "military spin-off"—said: "I say to the 183 million
Americans of today—that in my judgment, one of the benefits that
will come from the program will be an increased average life span
of at least 10 years for each one under 50 years of age today."

Senator Kerr's vision of what space meant—incredible though
it may sound now—was no further removed from reality than the
Air Force's vision of what space war might involve. And that, unlike Senator Kerr's vision, was much longer-lived. For while the
Air Force lost out on the moon program, it did not give up.

To get to the moon, NASA had to devise a bridging program
between the Mercury flights and the final Apollo program. The
result was the Gemini program, involving the orbiting of two astronauts at a time, which was to depend on the Air Force's modified Titan rocket. In 1962 NASA and the Air Force met to discuss
the question of manned military spacecraft—a crucial point because Gemini was of direct relevance to the Air Force's own program. Hence what should have been an entirely civilian project
was soon seen to be playing a double role. And in January 1963
an agreement was signed between NASA and the Department of
Defense to ensure that the "experiments undertaken as part of the
Gemini program are directed at the objectives and requirements
both of the Department of Defense and the NASA manned space

flight programs." To avoid duplication of effort, the document added, the Department of Defense will help fund the program. This it did, and the first openly acknowledged military experiments —16 in all—were carried out on a civilian space flight. Gemini astronauts made infrared observations of objects in space, photographed the launching of Minutemen missiles, and tried to identify from space the hidden locations of missile silos and other objects. The technique of orbital rendezvous was also developed. It was essential to the moon landing and also to the development of techniques by which one satellite might intercept another, hostile one.

That Gemini had real military value was revealed two months later by Robert McNamara. During testimony before the House Armed Services Committee, McNamara was asked to compare the Air Force manned space project known as "Dyna-Soar" with the Gemini project. McNamara favored the "civilian" Gemini because, he said, it had "greater military potential." Subsequently all contractors were asked by the Department of Defense to study the military missions of both Dyna-Soar and Gemini. They were to include possible roles in making a rendezvous with enemy satellites, inspecting them and "killing" them.

The Gemini story is only one example of the interdependence of the civilian and military space programs; more than 100 formal agreements of cooperation have been signed between NASA and the Pentagon. C. V. Glines, associate editor of *Armed Forces Management,* has called the Department of Defense "NASA's silent partner." He writes:

> Besides the continuing liaison that takes place on more earthly aeronautical matters, NASA has full-time military personnel assigned throughout its organization to provide specialized scientific expertise and management know-how. Approximately 280 DoD personnel are currently assigned for regular tours. Ranking officer detailed to NASA is Air Force Lieutenant General Samuel C. Phillips, Director of the Apollo program. Army, Navy and Air Force officers of lower ranks are assigned to the Washington headquarters, John F. Kennedy Space Center in Florida; Manned Spacecraft Center at Houston, Texas; George C. Marshall Spaceflight Center at Huntsville, Ala., and the half dozen NASA aeronautical research centers at other locations.

In addition, of course, nearly all the early astronauts were military personnel; none of them could have been recovered after splashdown without the elaborate tracking and pickup service organized by the Department of Defense. Until Saturn was developed, all the boosters used in the manned space program were military. And all NASA launches have been made from bases built largely from defense funds.

None of this is really surprising in view of the now obvious functions of the space program. Details of how the program began show clearly that it was conceived primarily as a military insurance policy—a civilian means of keeping space know-how abreast of whatever military space threats might emerge. Throughout the program, there has been the tacit understanding that if events warranted it, the program itself could be quickly stopped and turned to military purposes—just as was the sounding rocket program at White Sands in the 1940s. Elaborate plans are said to exist for turning Cape Kennedy into a military missile base should the international situation deteriorate. NASA's former administrator, James Webb, said as much—and more—in a television interview in April 1967:

> We wanted a complex that included Huntsville,
> the assembly plant at New Orleans, the Mississippi
> test [site], the Houston spacecraft [center] and
> the Cape for the launching site. We wanted this
> complex so that if we ever had to fly big military
> payloads on these big boosters here was an inte-
> grated system and the industrial system in the
> country could flow the materials toward this
> system.

To say that the civilian space program has been a military insurance policy is actually to understate the case. At times NASA has played an active and creative role in helping the military solve its problems. NASA-launched weather satellites have guided bombing missions in North Vietnam. And it was NASA in 1966 that got the Department of Defense excited about Project Able—the plan to hang a huge mirror in space over North Vietnam to light up the jungle at night and make infiltration more difficult. Angry yells from astronomers were one reason why the project was never implemented. Had it been, the space war would have been truly upon us. Inevitably, the Russians would have shot it down, and arms escalation in space might have started in earnest.

NASA has made other contributions to the art of limited warfare. Thus Thomas O'Toole wrote in the *Washington Post* on December 4, 1967, of "the growing role of the civilian space agency in the Vietnam war" and claimed that NASA was spending $4–5 million a year directing "the efforts of 100 scientists and engineers to tasks vital to the Vietnam war."

Three months later, on March 11, 1968, *Aviation Week* announced: "NASA is planning to establish a special projects branch within its Office of Advanced Research and Technology to aid in identifying and utilizing aerospace technology concepts applicable to limited warfare." Two of these concepts were later identified. One was to produce a bomber with a quieter engine that would give less warning of its pending arrival. Another was an acoustic device to help troops pinpoint more accurately the position of hostile mortars.

The congressional act that created NASA claimed that it was United States policy that "activities in space should be devoted to peaceful purposes for the benefit of all mankind." Cynics have claimed that the phrase now needs an addendum: "with the exception of the people of North Vietnam."

With the moon program nearly complete, it seems likely that space will in the future be more openly geared to the military. Two recent signs of this have been the resignation of NASA's Deputy Administrator, Robert Seamans, eventually to become Secretary of the Air Force, and the appointment of Dr. Eugene Fubini—already mentioned in connection with orbital bombs—to a new post as director of DoD and NASA military space liaison. NASA's administrator in 1969, Dr. Thomas O. Paine, described the merging of the program thus: "As we press forward to increase our knowledge and mastery of the aerospace environment, the goals of NASA and the DoD, though separate, are complementary . . . we are fitting our individual programs into a far greater common goal: to build and maintain a position of pre-eminence as a space-faring nation."

What that position of pre-eminence means in military terms we shall examine in the next section. But the civilian program should not be left without bringing it down to size. There is a popular misconception that NASA commands nearly all the money devoted to space in the United States. This is far from true, as C. V. Glines explains:

> U.S. military space programs make up about 35
> per cent of the total national space budget of $6
> billion. When the reimbursements to DoD from

NASA are added this year (1969), the percentage will be much nearer a 40–60 ratio. The military contribution to the national space program has been much greater than the money figures will show. There is no doubt that the knowledge gained by supporting NASA has been valuable to the various DoD space efforts.

These various DoD space efforts fall into two categories: manned and unmanned. The manned effort has been costly and, so far, quite abortive. The unmanned effort has been costly and terrifyingly successful.

Astronauts for the Military

The dinosaur, someone once remarked, was an evolutionary experiment in power politics. Its pin-sized brain and excessive brawn led it to inevitable extinction at a time in evolution when more intelligent experiments were first getting under way. Viewed in this light, Dyna-Soar was an extraordinarily appropriate name for the U.S. Air Force to choose for its first manned military space program.

Like a satellite, Dyna-Soar was to be launched by rocket into space. Once there, it would be guided by its pilot in a suborbital flight nearly around the earth and landed on an airstrip. First plans called for it to be launched from Cape Canaveral and brought down, having nearly circled the globe, at the Edwards Air Force Base on the other side of the United States. The point of this exercise was never made entirely clear. Much was made, however, of the idea that conventional flying should extend naturally out of the atmosphere and into space. Future Air Force missions, it was argued, would have to regard the atmosphere and space as one continuous military backdrop. And Dyna-Soar was a purely experimental program to prove the feasibility of flying aircraft in space and spacecraft in the air.

Dyna-Soar was the brainchild of Dr. Walter Dornberger, the former director of the Peenemünde research station and at one time von Braun's boss. Dr. Dornberger had little time for the Air Force–Pentagon battle on who was to do what in space. Between 1951 and 1958 he claimed to have made 678 "presentations" of the Dyna-Soar concept to various defense officials. At every stage he was questioned closely about the military functions of the craft. He later admitted to considerable impatience with this analytical approach. "The questions are being challenged while the defences of the free world hang in the balance," he said. "I cannot understand this saying, that we have no military mission in space. Is the protection of the free world not a mission?"

By 1957 the dogmatic Dornberger had won his battle, and the first Dyna-Soar contract was let two years later. It then emerged that the Dyna-Soar was not quite so purely experimental as it had first appeared. It was to be used to investigate such concepts as carrying nuclear bombs in orbit around the earth and shooting at enemy missiles or satellites. As we have seen, such military space ideas had been avidly put forward by space enthusiasts only to be debunked by those who saw no strategic advantage in them.

For this reason some spokesmen for the project saw this as a dangerous line of argument. Instead, they said, Dyna-Soar's purpose was as a ferry to service a manned military orbital space station—but no such space station was then planned. Dyna-Soar's true functions never did become clear. *Interavia,* the aviation journal, perhaps got nearest the truth when it said in an editorial in December 1962 that Dyna-Soar's "specific military applications . . . will emerge as research goes forward." Dyna-Soar was, in short, another military insurance policy.

It was a costly policy, for by 1963 some $400 million had been spent on it without a flight ever having taken place. Nor was it the only cost incurred at that time in the name of military insurance. Since 1959 the Pentagon had been looking at the even more advanced concept of an aerospace plane—a craft which could take off on its own, go into orbit, and be landed on an airstrip, all under the control of its pilot. Some $66 million had been spent on paper plans for this by 1963. Even in Britain it was announced in 1962 that the famous inventor, Dr. Barnes Wallis, was working with the Ministry of Aviation on a British manned military space vehicle to do the same thing. That project has never been heard of since. And then in 1964 the Russians said they were up to the same tricks. The chief of the Soviet Air Force, Chief Air Marshal Konstatin Veshinin, announced on August 17, "It is now regarded as technically feasible to design a plane which would combine the qualities of an aircraft and spacecraft. Advanced scientific and engineering thought is concentrating, and not without success, on this problem." The success seems to have been slowly achieved, for the Russian project has not been heard of since, either.

Serious worries about Dyna-Soar began to be voiced in 1963. The Gemini project was imminent, and McNamara, as we have seen, said Gemini was of more military use. The military functions of Dyna-Soar and Gemini were restudied. Meanwhile one obvious move had had to be made. While Dyna-Soar was only suborbital, Gemini—due for flight much earlier—was fully orbital. If Dyna-Soar was not to be evolutionarily extinct before it ever got off the ground, it had to be up-rated. This was done and the project made fully orbital from the first flight. And that, as one commentator put it, "had the effect of putting the Air Force squarely into the manned space flight business on about equal research terms with the civilian space agency."

It was clear that things had got out of hand. The leading edge of space research was intended to be explored peacefully by a civilian agency. But the pace of events had forced a decision which would give the military equal priority on a project with no specific aims other than to duplicate the research value of a more advanced civilian project. And on December 10, 1963, McNamara extinguished the abortive project. By doing so, he saved $400 out of the $800 million which it would have cost.

Dyna-Soar never made a flight. How much it accelerated the space arms race is difficult to tell. But one cannot help comparing the early suborbital Dyna-Soar, in one of its roles as a bombardment satellite, with the much later Soviet FOBS. They differ only in name and in that one is manned, the other not. Otherwise, their hypothetical functions seem similar.

Unhappily, the Dyna-Soar charade was only made worse by McNamara's statement. For instead of just canceling the project, he started—presumably as a sop to the Air Force—work on a yet more expensive military project in space. Design studies, he said, would now be begun on the Air Force Manned Orbital Laboratory, to be known as MOL. This exercise proved later to cost four times as much as Dyna-Soar; like it, it was never to come to fruition. And also like it, it duplicated NASA's plans but had no real military purpose. The *Guardian* science correspondent in England was quick to point out why he thought the project had been started. "Most probably," he wrote, "MOL owes its existence to the need to find some use for the Titan III rocket developed for the launching of devices such as Dyna-Soar."

The functions of MOL were also obscure. They were said at the time to be solely connected with proving that military man could operate usefully in space—but what was he to operate at?

Some clue is given by an agreement dating from the summer of 1963 in which the Department of Defense and the Air Force outlined the possible objectives of a manned space flight program. These were:

1. Reconnaissance of the earth
2. Inspection of space objects
3. Command and control of air, ground, or sea forces
4. Exploration of feasibility of bombardment from space

The reconnaissance applications were said to be so important that the Central Intelligence Agency had fought hard to have control of MOL as a successor to its ill-fated U-2 aircraft. The bombardment mission was never mentioned in public by any official connected with the program. And the need for inspection of potentially hostile satellites—doing what?—had been studied in countless programs but had never been given the go ahead. Had it been, a maneuverable craft like Dyna-Soar would have been more effective.

The riddle of MOL's functions, like those of Dyna-Soar, is best explained in terms of military insurance. The Air Force had spent $10 million since 1959 in trying to demonstrate that it had military tasks to perform in space. Its efforts proved none too successful, and in May 1963 the special assistant to the Director of Defense Research and Engineering, Dr. Lawrence L. Kavanau, was reduced to this argument: "History strongly suggests that opportunities must be provided for the military uses of space to mature even though the presently conceived military space missions are not all persuasive ones."

At this stage MOL's future still hung in the balance, and the search for real military missions continued. Those who heard the Secretary of the Air Force, Dr. Harold Brown, testify at a congressional hearing in August 1965 must have thought the project doomed to stay earthbound. "We do not see," said Dr. Brown, "any new use for military man in space than we did when we originally studied the MOL concept." Yet on August 25 of the same month President Johnson instructed the Air Force to proceed with the development of MOL.

NASA's James Webb was quick to point out the important role the civilian space agency had played in getting this military project off the ground. "The DoD/MOL program has been made possible," he said, "by the forward thrust of NASA's own earth orbital projects, Gemini and Apollo. The MOL will use, directly or indirectly, the systems and experience developed by NASA." To some, this decision—like the Dyna-Soar one—dwarfed in magnitude all previous space decisions. The *Air Force/Space Digest* described it in October 1965 as "one of the most significant of the space age— more important than the Apollo Moon-landing program—because it expresses the determination of the United States to explore military man's potential contribution to national security."

But this determination was short-lived. The Air Force's "beachhead in space" was abruptly canceled on June 10, 1969. MOL had never flown except in a dummy form, and the cancellation brought the total cost of aborted military projects since 1951 to some $11,000 million. The cost of MOL itself had risen from $1,500 to more than $3,000 million, of which more than half had already disappeared down the waste pipe. This was not all, for the cost of the Titan III-C, including the III-M model due to launch MOL, was itself estimated at about $2,000 million. But not all of this was lost, for the Titan III-C was used for other purposes, such as the launching of Vela satellites (see next section).

The cancellation surprised few people. MOL's program had slipped so far that its first flights had had to be postponed from 1967 to 1972. Technically, it was based on Gemini hardware, and by 1972 not only Gemini but also the later Apollo systems would be out of date. As everyone was careful to point out, what was canceled was an out-of-date space station. Although this left the Air Force with no major manned mission, few expected that things would stay that way for long.

In an editorial for *Aviation Week and Space Technology* (June 30, 1969), Robert Hotz explained why there need be "no tears for MOL." His argument was that

> the cancellation of MOL paves the way to end the
> uselessly expensive dichotomy between military
> and civil space programs . . . an inheritance from
> the confused and fuzzy reaction of the Eisenhower
> Administration to the stunning technical surprise
> of the first Soviet Sputniks. . . . Unless we are
> grossly in error in sniffing the Pentagon winds,
> this nation should see a well-integrated develop-
> ment program emerge for creating the space
> vehicles of the post-Apollo era.

One of these vehicles was the NASA equivalent of MOL, the Orbital Workshop. MOL's cancellation means that this space station will almost certainly carry a larger military payload than originally planned. Indeed, it is even possible that the Workshop might be launched not from Cape Kennedy but from Vandenberg Air Force Base on the West Coast. To the military, the advantage of this is that the station can then be put into an orbit which covers both poles. With the station orbiting in a north-south direction, and the earth rotating in an east-west direction below, military reconnaissance becomes much more effective, for every portion of the earth is revealed to the astronauts twice every 24 hours. A launch from Cape Kennedy means that the astronauts never see some parts of the earth at all.

MOL's cancellation deprived the Air Force of its main manned mission. It did not, however, remove for all time any possibility of the Air Force getting into space. For in the convoluted way in which these things happen, the program that had been canceled to make way for MOL was restarted under a different name and in a different guise. Dyna-Soar gave way to Project Start—a plan to build a space ferry to take equipment and crew into space and return to land on earth at a conventional airport. The first phase, known as "Asset," was completed by 1965 and successfully evaluated the materials that would be required. The two second phases—called "PRIME" and "PILOT"—are designed to show that unmanned and manned vehicles can maneuver during reentry into the earth's atmosphere. Both have flown, and the PILOT program is being conducted jointly with NASA. By 1966 the cost had reached $120 million, but severe financial restrictions were soon applied. Eventually, of course, the object of the exercise was to produce the aerospace plane—a craft which would prove for the Air Force that the atmosphere and space were nothing more than one continuous backdrop for military operations.

A few months after MOL was canceled, NASA announced its own plans for a space shuttle—a craft that could take off from land, go into orbit, mate with a space station, and steer its way back to earth. One configuration for it envisaged that the shuttle would be as big as a Boeing 747, much larger than the original Dyna-Soar concept. But, like the Dyna-Soar, the craft would carry unspecified military implications. According to a report in *Aviation Week and Space Technology*, "Minimum cargo compartment size planned is a cylinder 15 ft long, capable of carrying 50,000 lb. But some studies now are based on 25,000 lb. The large cargo bay, which would open to eject payloads, is a NASA/Defense Department requirement. . . ."

Thus does this extraordinary story of cancellation and go-ahead end up where it started—with a Dyna-Soar–type vehicle capable of carrying large payloads that can be ejected during flight. Thus does the development of military rockets carrying several nuclear warheads merge with a pseudocivilian plan to develop a space plane. Never far apart, the military and civil programs—as predicted—are now once again drawing closer together.

Satellites for the Military

Between 1957 and early 1969 the United States launched some 458 satellites that have been publicly recorded. Of these 284 were military and 174 civilian. The Russians' estimated score was 170 civilian, 162 military. As not all military launchings are openly acknowledged, the actual military proportion is somewhat higher.

In the five-year period of 1963 through 1967 the Department of Defense space budget varied between about $1,550 and $1,700 million a year. NASA's budget at this time was about twice as much, but things began to change in 1966. In 1968 NASA's budget had $500 million lopped off, and the DoD space budget increased by $400 million to top $2,000 million for the first time. How accurate a measure of the military space effort even that figure was remained in doubt. Not all the money allocated appears in the DoD budget figures. The CIA, for example, also spends substantial sums on the analysis of space reconnaissance data. As a result some commentators estimated the worth of the military space effort at nearer $4,000 million—almost as much as NASA's budget.

Most of this money is now used to provide the Pentagon with better communications, navigation, and reconnaissance. In each case the new space technologies being created are double-edged swords. On one hand they can be argued to improve our security a good deal since they make the subsidiary operations of warfare more efficient—and hence reduce the risk of major military mistakes. But they also enable the forces to perform tasks that were previously impossible and so extend the range of possible military operations. It is well to remember that the first military application of the aircraft was reconnaissance—and according to some generals, that would be their only application. What subsequently happened to the aircraft cannot be said to have increased the security of any of us. If history is a good guide, we can expect similar developments in the military space programs.

First attempts to investigate the military potential of space communications resulted in two major scandals. "Project Advent" was the name given to the initial plan to use satellites to relay military messages round the world. The system was estimated to cost $140 million, but the project was apparently grossly mismanaged from the start. Like both Dyna-Soar and MOL, it ended up by being canceled—by which time $170 million had been spent and the total cost estimate had risen to $350 million.

The second scandal concerned a plan, Project West Ford, to orbit round the earth 350 million tiny copper needles. The experiment was to provide an alternative system of communication to those that depended on bouncing radio signals off the atmospheric layer known as the ionosphere. Earlier high-level nuclear explosions such as Argus and Starfish had shown that worldwide communications could be disrupted by nuclear weapons—provided they were set off at the right height. The copper needles were to act as an artificial ionosphere. They also acted as an intense source of irritation to astronomers throughout the world, who claimed that their study of the heavens would be interfered with by this space junk. Pleas were made to halt the experiment, but to no avail. The needles were launched and failed to go into orbit. The whole affair started again, but this time more care was taken to consult astronomers—some of whom were prepared to admit that the plan would not really make their studies much more difficult. This infuriated other astronomers even more. "A major intellectual crime has been perpetrated," said Professor Fred Hoyle. "The astronomers are being used as a façade of respectability for an essentially military project." Nevertheless, the needles were eventually successfully orbited.

By the mid-1960s all this had been more or less forgotten, and plans were far advanced to put a semiexperimental, semioperational military system into orbit. Known as the "Defense Satellite Communication System," it consists of 17 satellites put into a high orbit so that they drift only slowly relative to the ground below. This system is due to be extended or replaced in the 1970s, when four very large satellites—one over the Atlantic, one over the Indian Ocean, and two over the Pacific—will be launched. For this, the Titan III-C booster will be used and the system is expected to cost from 100 to 200 million dollars. Each satellite will carry up to 1,000 voice channels simultaneously.

Agreements have now also been signed between four countries—the United States, the United Kingdom, Canada, and Australia—for a system known as Project Mallard that will bring satellite communication down to the tactical level. When in operation, this will be a very advanced system; the research and development costs alone are estimated at more than $120 million and the complete system may cost over $500 million.

NATO's strategic satellite communication system is due to become operational in the mid-1970s. The ground stations are being built, at a cost of £11 million, and two satellites costing £9 million each are already in orbit. Britain's own $70 million Skynet system uses almost identical satellites, one in the sky and one kept in reserve on the ground. Skynet can be hooked in to the American and NATO systems, as well.

These military communications networks may sound on paper simple and cheap affairs. They are not. They have to be supported by complex systems of ground stations which span the whole globe. They use the most advanced electronics available and are considerably ahead of civilian communications systems. The latter, incidentally, are not always quite as civilian as they might appear. The Syncom II satellite, for instance, was used by the Department of Defense for communications between Washington and Vietnam; Syncom III was used for military communications to Japan. Both satellites were subsequently handed over by NASA to the Department of Defense.

Satellite navigation is equally complex. The U.S. Army and U.S. Navy operate separate systems which have become of great strategic importance. Polaris submarines, for instance, use what are called inertial navigation systems to provide accurate "dead reckoning"— an essential if nuclear missiles are to be fired with accuracy onto an enemy target. Some Polaris submarines—and most U.S. Navy vessels—also rely on the Navy's Transit navigational satellites. The extent to which they do so is not public knowledge but does introduce a worrying factor. Any nation which perfected an antisatellite system would have an important advantage. If well-placed nuclear explosions, or maneuverable satellites, could knock out the navigation or communication satellites of its enemy, it might seriously reduce the latter's ability to wage nuclear war. That the danger is real is apparent from statements that United States antisatellite systems would be designed not to eliminate foreign bombardment satellites but to protect the United States operational satellites.

A special kind of navigational satellite is also used by the military to explore the dimensions of the earth in fine detail. Surprisingly, conventional mapping techniques can locate a city such as Moscow with respect to New York to an accuracy of at best 100 meters and sometimes only 1,000 meters or more. Early in the space program it was realized that satellites could be used to improve this accuracy, reducing the error to from 10 to 15 meters. NASA was the first to plan to exploit geodesic satellites, but the project became militarily so important that it was made a joint investigation between NASA and the three services—hence the name "ANNA," with one initial for each participant. As part of this program many satellites were flown with names like Secor, Surcal, Geos, and Pageos. Captain Robert Freitag, who worked with the U.S. Bureau of Naval Weapons, which directed Project ANNA, summarizes some of the implications of these satellites thus:

> The Defense Department is also considering applications of navigational satellites on land, particularly in limited war situations. Dr. Harold Brown, Director of Defense Research and Engineering, has said that such roles could include: air and surface target co-ordination between multiple units; the spotting in local map co-ordinates of landing and artillery units; over-the-horizon shore and tactical ballistic missile bombardment; determination of land and sea target co-ordinates to fire-control accuracies; . . . and rendez-vous at sea under radar and radio silence.

"The dynamic pace of modern space technology and the adaptation of space sciences to human welfare," Captain Freitag continues in the same article, "is little short of awesome." Few would quarrel with the adjective, but many might well question Captain Freitag's definition of human welfare.

It is difficult to overestimate the importance of communication and navigation satellites in modern strategy. They are now an integral part of the complex plans that have been made by both major powers for waging both nuclear and limited wars. As much was revealed when the costly MOL project was canceled before a flight was made. The cancellation was partly due, Deputy Defense Secretary David Packard claimed, "to advances in automated techniques for unmanned satellite systems including research, communications, navigation and meteorology." His reference to meteorology was particularly interesting, as this had been regarded as one of the important spin-offs from the space program for human welfare. But welfare has a double meaning in this context as well. When NASA launched the weather satellites Nimbus and Essa, they provided valuable information about the patterns of storms on the globe below them. They also provided vital information for United States bombing missions in North Vietnam.

Similar problems are raised by reconnaissance satellites—the first real military application of space ever to be taken seriously. In the United States the program began with the 36 Discoverer satellites launched between 1959 and 1961. Their purpose was to take photographs of the earth below, and a system was devised of recovering the film. Each satellite ejected an 84-pound cannister as it passed over Alaska. The cannister was slowed by a parachute system as it entered the atmosphere and was picked up from the sea or in the air by an aircraft equipped with recovery booms.

The experimental Discoverers were followed by two semioperational and interdependent systems. The first was MIDAS—the Missile Defense Alarm System—which carried an infrared sensor. It was hoped that this would pick up the heat from any missile being launched before or soon after it left its launching pad. Its importance is shown by the fact that the program was allocated $107 million in 1961 and nearly twice as much—$201 million—in 1962. The system promised to increase the warning time of nuclear attack from the 15 minutes that early warning radars provided to almost 30 minutes—hence the program's enormous funds. Britain was to be tuned in to the system with a new receiving station at Kirkbride in Cumberland. But in 1963 it became apparent that the system did not work too well. Different missiles produced different amounts of different kinds of heat, and MIDAS's sensors got thoroughly confused about the whole thing. They even began to confuse reflections from the sun with ICBMs. When the program was stopped late in 1963, it had absorbed $423 million.

MIDAS's partner in reconnaissance was SAMOS—Satellite and Missile Observation System. A much heavier satellite, it was used to inspect more carefully by photography and TV pictures anything MIDAS showed up as suspicious; its film was recovered by the Discoverer techniques. In 1969 its budget was running at $261 million a year.

How much these three systems cost altogether has not been revealed, but it is known that Discoverer, SAMOS, and MIDAS had cost $1,000 million by as early as mid-1960. Shortly afterward a strict security classification was applied to all reconnaissance satellites. SAMOS was replaced by Advanced Samos and was given anonymity by the code number 720A. MIDAS and its successors became Program 461. And on August 5, 1967, the first of their operational successors—known as "Spook Bird"—was launched from

Cape Kennedy. Part of the Integrated Satellite Program 266, it was placed in a high orbit from which it drifted slowly over the ground below. As it did so it turned a whole battery of radars, cameras, and sensors onto South China, North Vietnam, Saigon, the Indian Ocean, and Malaysia.

This program is due to be replaced by the Multipurpose Satellite System, which will carry every conceivable spying device—short of man himself—into space. Included in this will be devices for detecting nuclear explosions in space or the atmosphere. This job has previously been performed by 10 Vela satellites launched in pairs by the Titan III-C between October 1, 1963, and 1969—a program which itself has cost $200 million.

Much less detail is available on Soviet reconnaissance satellites. It is clear, however, that the Soviet program is on a similar scale. Between 1962 and 1968 no less than 102 Cosmos satellites had been identified from details of their orbits as reconnaissance vehicles of one kind or another. And in his time Khrushchev made great play of offering to show President Johnson space photos of U.S. missile bases.

What reconnaissance satellites can detect from space is truly astonishing. Technically, it is probably possible for a newspaper headline to be read and interpreted by optical devices in a satellite. Such extraordinary resolution is not really required, however, and most operational systems are thought to be able to resolve objects measuring perhaps 6 to 18 feet. Even this is sufficient to spot an individual car and determine its make and model. The buildup of troops during the Czechoslovak crisis in 1968 was accurately monitored by satellite; no major movement of forces on the ground can ever again escape detection from space.

Spy satellites can also build up collections of pictures taken over a period of time. When "riffled through," these provide a kind of time-lapse film showing every change in the area such as new roads built, new buildings put up, and even trees cleared away. Side-looking radar systems carried on Agena satellites are said to be able to "see" through several inches of soil or as much as three layers of foliage. New factories can be spotted easily and their output determined by measurements of the amount of heat exhausted from chimney stacks, vents, or into nearby rivers—the heat showing up on specially developed infrared sensors. "Ferret" satellites carry electronic apparatus which listen in to other countries' electronic babble—anything from coded radio signals to the electronic noises made by new machinery. Some applications extend far beyond normally recognized military objectives. China's wheat and rice crops, for instance, can now be accurately gauged year by year—satellite sensors show not only how much of a crop is being grown but also how much is made useless by disease.

When President Johnson said that the space program would be worth "ten times the money spent on it," he undoubtedly was referring principally to the importance of spy satellites. The cost to the United States of believing, in the late 1950s, that an enormous missile gap was building up ran to tens of billions of dollars. But it was data from reconnaissance satellites that revealed the missile gap to be fictitious. And similar data have often since shown there to be no need to close other equally expensive and equally fictitious gaps. Enormous though the United States defense expenditure may be, it would probably have been much greater were it not for the spies in space.

While this aspect of reconnaissance has not yet been put to positive use in the field of arms control and disarmament, it may soon. Nearly all major talks between the super powers have broken down over the issue of inspection—one side insisting that if both agree to reduce their level of missiles or refrain from nuclear testing, this must not only happen but be seen to happen. And for that to occur without deception, there has always been an insistence, particularly by the United States, that it should send inspectors onto foreign territory to check that what was promised was carried out. But recently the inspection issue has become less important; the reason undoubtedly is that inspectors are made redundant by spy satellites. Each side can monitor the other quite effectively as it is. "The camera," as President Kennedy put it, "is going to be our best inspector."

Unfortunately, there is another side to the story; it arises when more than two countries are brought into the equation. All space photos taken by spy satellites are classified in the United States; so, too, are any photos taken on civilian flights which show any detail in communist countries. There is, however, nothing to prevent such pictures being privately transferred to other countries. If one of the superpowers, for instance, wished to foment a war between two smaller neighbors, it could easily supply space spy data to one of them—claiming that the photographs or other information showed a massing of forces on the other side of the border. The importance of this kind of knowledge was shown by the Israelis' first strike against the Egyptians in 1967. This strike was initiated solely on the strength of espionage information as to what the other side was doing. Who can say that neither Egypt nor Israel is being supplied with satellite data from the United States or Russia?

Arguments such as this perhaps partly explain why both sides have been so secretive about their reconnaissance activities of late. For if spy satellites are really to be used as a force for peace, it would appear to be more efficient to be open about their findings. A Russian secret is still a secret if it is known only by the Russians and a few people in the Pentagon. There is an analogy here with effective deterrence—the Americans soon realized their deterrents would deter only if potential enemies knew what they were. Why the same deduction has not been made about spy satellites is not clear.

In fact, a great deal of excessive secrecy surrounds the whole affair—an enigmatic situation considering the program is designed to break down secrecy. "There no longer seems any point to the special security arrangements apparently surrounding these activities," writes the distinguished Hudson Institute strategist Donald Brennan. "It is quite likely that the special arrangements are continued only because of bureaucratic inertia and not because of genuine needs." Nevertheless, the prolonged nature of this inertia must make us all suspicious that neither the United States nor the Soviet Union intends to exploit the peaceful applications of spy satellites to the exclusion of their undeniable military and commercial advantage.

In 1969 Geoffrey Pardoe, an engineer with Hawker Siddeley, accused NASA of releasing only 13 of the 8,000 photographs taken on the Apollo 7 flight. Another scientist claimed that Americans had been buying land which they thought contained valuable minerals because of pictures they had obtained privately from NASA. NASA retorted that 450 of the Apollo pictures had been released and refused to "dignify with a comment" the land-buying accusation. Whatever the truth, it is clear that space pictures are a mixed blessing in this respect, giving untold economic advantage to the only two nations with major space programs.

Spy satellites also pose one threat to the security of the superpowers themselves. One of the participants in the aborted MOL project was the U.S. Navy. And the reason was clear enough. It seems possible that submarines can be tracked accurately, however deep they may be, from space. They produce slipstreams of water at a different temperature from that of the ocean surface; the nuclear reactor in even a stationary submarine also emits heat which rises to the surface. These temperature differences may be detectable by an infrared device on a satellite, and the Navy planned to use MOL to see how efficient such detection might be. MOL has been canceled, but similar experiments must by now have been carried out in other satellites. If the infrared technique works, the rationale of the Polaris fleet is partially lost. Nuclear missiles are deployed under the sea because they cannot be detected there by an enemy and put out of action. They provide an assured second strike. If that assurance is now in doubt, a new source of instability may follow, and perhaps a new round in the arms race. We will look at some of these possibilities in the next chapter.

ABM: The Great Debate

"One can deter with nuclear weapons," said Sir Solly Zuckerman in 1962 (see page 36). "Can one defend?" At that time the answer was no; today, as anyone who has followed the great debate over the antiballistic missile knows, it is a qualified yes. Nuclear weapons can be used to destroy other nuclear weapons before they strike their targets. How efficiently they can do this, at what cost, and to what advantage have been the subject of the only massive arms debate ever to have been publicly staged.

The issue really dates back as far as 1956, when the first United States contracts were let for studying the problem of the ABM. The weapon envisaged for this role was the Nike-Zeus, and the rocket was used in 1962 and 1963 to intercept trial ICBM missiles over the Pacific. The long-term plan was to stud the United States with thousands of these missiles and their complicated radars; the aim was to prevent all but a fraction of incoming Soviet missiles from exploding on United States soil.

If this was ever feasible, it did not remain so long. As the world began to learn of MIRVs, it learned too of "pen-aids"—decoy warheads such as metal balloons designed to confuse radars as to what was warhead and what was space rubbish. Nike-Zeus was deemed impractical, the ABM program renamed Nike-X, and a second missile and better radars added to the system—which at this time was still only a gleam in the Pentagon's eye.

The second missile was called Sprint—and its job was to knock out those enemy missiles that eluded the longer range Nike-Zeus missile. Sprint, as its name suggested, accelerated quickly even for a missile, and the Army was fond of saying it could reach 50,000 feet "in two heartbeats." But its range was only 25 to 30 miles and it exploded well inside the atmosphere—by which time the incoming missiles' pen-aids would have been burned up by the atmosphere during re-entry.

By 1964 the Secretary of Defense had learned a lot about the ABM problem, much of it from a 23-volume classified report prepared for him by the Hudson Institute. The report, it is said, took 20 analysts a whole year to research and write. Perhaps the report was a little verbose; in any event, McNamara later announced that the benefits to be accrued from protecting the United States with an ABM system were at best "marginal"; and he resisted pressures to deploy an ABM until September 1967, when he announced that a very limited or "thin" system would be erected, mainly to protect some United States missiles against a Soviet attack. He called the system "Sentinel." Its cost was estimated at $5,000 million—not including most of the research or the subsequent maintenance.

From this point on there came a mounting crescendo of public and scientific protest. And the first issue to be raised was that the new "defensive" missiles would carry large nuclear warheads and would be sited very near to large cities. The Sprints, with kiloton warheads, would even be designed to explode in the atmosphere above the cities. The other missile, now known as Spartan, had meanwhile been made larger to carry a warhead of some two megatons capable of destroying pen-aids and warheads over a large area; and from 600 to 700 Spartans were to be deployed. The American people, perhaps with good cause, professed anxiety on every conceivable issue. They were worried, they said, in case the missiles went off by accident "in their own backyards"; they were worried that if all chance of this was prevented by safety devices, the missile might not go off when it was meant to; and, finally, if it did go off as planned, they were worried about the fallout, heat, and blast generated above their own homes.

McNamara was not so concerned about these issues as another one: "The danger in deploying this relatively light and reliable Chinese-oriented ABM system," he said, "is going to be that pressures will develop to expand it into a heavy Soviet-oriented ABM system." These pressures, it emerged, were likely to come from the military-industrial complex, a suspicion which was confirmed when it was revealed that more than 3,000 firms were expected to profit from the decision to build a heavy ABM.

Dr. Jerome Wiesner, former science adviser to both Presidents Kennedy and Johnson and provost of MIT, also worried about this danger. In an article "The Cold War Is Dead, but the Arms Race Rumbles On," he explained how similar pressure groups had lobbied for the B-70 aircraft, the original Nike-Zeus, the nuclear-powered aircraft, and space-based attack weapons. "Today," he wrote, "the same groups that pressed Kennedy to build those weapons are leading the fight for the new ABM system and using most of the same arguments. While the fact that they were completely wrong does not automatically insure that they are wrong today, it does mean that their emotional entreaties should be viewed with some suspicion."

Suspicion increased around election time and increased still more when it was learned that Richard Nixon would move to the White House. A halt was called to the previous ABM plan while the new administration revalued the arguments.

They did so with some vigor. When Sentinel emerged from the revaluation, it had changed its name again, this time to Safeguard. It pointed no longer toward the Chinese but toward the Russians. And it protected not cities but missile bases, the national command center in Washington, and bomber and Polaris bases.

The change was apparently fundamental (though technically very minor), for it took the pressure off the cities issue. Strategically as well as democratically, this seemed to many an improvement. The implication of defending cities had always been to deny the Russians or Chinese an effective deterrent—of exercising the threat which was meant to prevent nuclear war. To the Russians, a United States decision to protect cities must look like a decision that the United States will carry out a first strike because it would now have little to fear from the Soviet second strike aimed at United States cities.

The reasons for these sweeping changes also seemed logical. It was claimed that the Chinese ICBM had been delayed and the threat from that quarter had diminished, temporarily. The Russians, on the other hand, had stepped up their missile production and their production of Polaris-type submarines—the latter meaning that U.S. bombers might not now have time to get off the ground, for submarine missiles could eliminate them with little warning from near the United States coast. And the new Safeguard was also equipped to deal with the Russian FOBS system—which a number of authorities claimed was now being deployed, as distinct from being developed. Nobody gave any authority for this last dubious statement.

Public interest in the ABM had already been whetted; so the controversy did not die down. It was fiercely fought out in the newspapers, in the periodicals, and finally in the Senate. There, on August 6, 1969, the administration won its case for Safeguard deployment on a very gradual scale, by 51 votes to 49. But the victory was a Pyrrhic one likely to influence the whole strategic and military future of the United States. The *Financial Times'* United States editor, John Graham, claimed that the narrowness of the victory

> . . . will have a profound effect on future de-
> fence planning. For half the Senate to stand
> against the U.S. President on the most important
> national security matter ever put to it, when the
> White House mustered every force it could and
> when the full military establishment was in agree-
> ment that Safeguard had to be approved of, is an
> almost unheard-of rebellion. It would be churlish
> to deny the President his victory in the end,
> even though it was a mini-victory. The sobering
> thought is that a defeat, any defeat, even by the
> same one-vote margin as the actual victory, would
> have been a huge defeat.

I do not intend to debate the strategic issues about ABM deployment. Suffice to say that even if one wants to make a purely strategic decision about building antimissiles, the issues are far from clear-cut. The critics, who included three former DoD Directors of Research and Engineering, four former presidential science advisors, 49 senators, including Edward Kennedy, and several Nobel Laureates, claimed that the ABM was not needed strategically. In addition, it would:

1. Not work
2. Increase the risk of nuclear accidents
3. Upset the strategic balance
4. Lead to a new arms race
5. Cost too much ($10,300 million for the complete program)
6. Increase the risk of war
7. Make talks with the Russians less likely
8. Imperil the test-ban treaty

The administration denied every point. Defense Secretary Melvin Laird did not, however, improve the tone of debate by his simplistic assertions. "Safeguard," he told a Congressional Armed Services Committee on March 20, 1969, "is a building block for peace." And with a supreme piece of tautology he claimed that one advantage of the decision was to "offer the Soviet Union added incentive for productive arms control talks."

But the ABM debate does contain some useful lessons. It pointed up many of the essential dilemmas of nuclear deterrence. The first, of course, is that the antimissiles were being used to protect not people but other missiles. Any humane analysis suggests that in a nuclear war it is better to protect a country's population than its weapons. But nuclear strategy leads to the opposite conclusion with undeniable logic. Nuclear deterrence is a game in which a country's population is used as the hostage for its government's good intentions. If deterrence is to work, the population must be left unprotected. With every twist of the arms race, nuclear strategy becomes morally more repellent.

The second lesson is that the debate might have been more meaningful if conducted in less strategic terms. This point was raised in the form of questions about the United States' best long-term interest. As Professor Marvin Kalkstein suggested, "The threat to our country is not from foreign missiles but from a breakdown of our society from within." He was echoing the thoughts of Boston Councilman Tom Aitkens, who had earlier expressed his displeasure at the irrelevance of the ABM debate to people. "You talk of megatons," he said. "We are interested in snow removal. You talk of penetration aids. What we want is housing. You talk of nuclear sufficiency. I say there is massive insufficiency as far as our domestic sanity is concerned."

In an impassioned speech during the August Senate debate, Senator John Sherman Cooper succinctly summarized the nonstrategic dilemma of deterrence:

> The pursuit of security through nuclear power alone will never end. It will waste the fruits of the earth and make the labor of men empty. It will increase the sense of futility, particularly among the young. For we and the Soviets, with all our technology, can be reduced to dust at any moment. The green earth and millions who live on it can be burned to grey ashes. This specter is the essence of the nuclear arms race. This is our present security.

The ABM's last lesson is the most important. How can the effect of a decision of such magnitude on the rest of the world be gauged? In a thoughtful article in the *Bulletin of the Atomic Scien-*

tists, Dr. Jerome Wiesner had earlier charged that the ABM would lead to arms escalation. What does this do, he asked, "to the effectiveness of the United Nations and the conduct of all of the other nations of the world? There are no analytically derived answers to these questions, but they must be weighed very seriously when making a final decision about an ABM system." How seriously they were weighed we do not know. But the fact that such questions cannot be turned into convenient statistics, and are not amenable to cost-effectiveness studies, suggests they may not have formed an important subject of internal debate. When important questions are too difficult to answer, they may be shelved.

The most important of all these questions was never debated in the ABM controversy. It was, however, raised by Professor Ernest Sternglass, who had earlier published some alarming new results about the long-term effects of fallout. These results are still unproven. But, assuming for the moment that they are only one-tenth true, they raise a problem of unparalleled enormity. If nuclear war occurs, the installation of ABMs means that the total of nuclear warheads exploded is greatly increased, as they are now used for defense as well as offense. One result of the fallout produced, Professor Sternglass suggested, is that society might survive a nuclear war only "to come to an end as the infants born to the survivors die in their first year of life." Professor Sternglass then asks:

> Does any nation have the right to destroy the
> lives of innocent children in countries throughout
> the world in a vain effort to ensure the survival
> of its own particular ideology and way of life,
> by weapons that release an indiscriminately-acting,
> long-lasting biological poison into the world's at-
> mosphere?

ASM: The Next Debate?

In retrospect, it is amazing that the savage attacks of the ABM critics came so near to victory. For whatever the advantages of public debate in the strategic arena, they never occur until long after the die has been cast. The United States' long and devoted commitment to antimissile defense is vividly illustrated by one staggering statistic. By 1965 the Pentagon had spent more on ABM research and development than it spent on the whole of the Manhattan Project during World War II.

It was virtually inevitable that that research program would not be allowed to expire into oblivion. The technical arms race of today is carried on by its own momentum. The systems to be deployed in the next decade are virtually determined by the research priorities of the previous decade; and it takes a gargantuan political effort to deflect the science of destruction from its apparently predestined course.

It is against this background that we should judge the future possibilities. For as the Safeguard system lurched into the 1970s by its one-vote majority, it was carried forward by a ground wave of military spending guaranteed to make it redundant in the not-too-distant future. President Johnson, in his last budget, allocated no less than $175 million for research and development in fiscal 1970 into advanced ABM systems that would supersede Sentinel and Safeguard.

What is publicly known about the ABM is in fact only the tip of a vast military iceberg. Some clue as to the nature of the iceberg was given by a DoD press release dated March 14, 1969. As alternatives to Safeguard, the release said, "modified Minuteman missiles and modified Poseidon missiles (SABMIS) were also examined. . . . They may serve to complement the Modified Sentinel system at a later time and are still under consideration for that function." The release might also have mentioned the Advanced Research Projects Agency's Defender program, which is still actively investigating a whole range of ABM concepts.

It is from these areas that the pressure predicted by McNamara to develop the ABM further is likely to come. McNamara thought it would take the form of an anti-Russian city defense, but this seems less likely now. The current pressures are to improve ground-based ABMs and to develop other ABMs that would be operated from the sea or from space. In all cases, the defense may cover not only missiles but enemy satellites. It is significant that Safeguard is really the first "space weapon"—its functions include that of countering the Soviet semiorbiting FOBS threat. Anti-satellite missiles (ASMs) could well become the subject of the next great strategic debate.

The Navy has long had an interest in ABMs, arguing that its Poseidon would make an excellent antimissile. Their proposal, SABMIS, stands for "sea-based antiballistic missile system." The alleged advantage is that interception of Soviet missiles could be made much earlier and the resulting nuclear carnage would take place over sparsely populated ocean areas.

Strange though it may seem, the Navy is likely to play an important part in future space wars. The reason is that it is mobile, enabling it to get close to Soviet launch sites and thus track hostile missiles and satellites soon after launch. It already operates a missile warning system of its own as well as space surveillance radars (Navy programs 474N and Spasur).

And it claims for itself a particular role in antisatellite warfare. If Russia ever launches nuclear weapons into orbit or fractional orbit (FOBS), they will pass over the antipodes of the launch site and the target area—in other words, the points on the opposite side of the globe to the launch and the target. It is from these antipodal points that such weapons are best detected and from where intercepting missiles are best launched. And as might be expected, nearly all of them are in the Pacific or Indian oceans, in Antarctica, or extreme southern America. In none of these places is there much land available for United States military activities. And so, the Navy says, antisatellite warfare is Navy business, best conducted from mobile seagoing platforms.

Most of the Navy's work on such concepts—including even the name of its current program—is highly classified. Some indication of its activity is given by two publicly known programs. The first, Early Spring, studied the idea of using the 10 Polaris submarines not being refitted with Poseidon missiles as launch platforms for antimissile and antisatellite weapons. And under Project Skipper, the Navy developed a nonnuclear means of eliminating hostile satellites. The idea was to fire very fast-moving steel pellets into the satellite's path.

The concept of antisatellite warfare is no longer a military dream. In 1969 Secretary of Defense Melvin Laird increased the Air Force's request for $114 million for an antisatellite early warning system by $43 million. The Army has had an "operational" antisatellite system, based on the Nike-Zeus on Kwajalein Atoll, since 1963. Also operational is the Air Force's modified Thor rocket based on Johnston Island, also in the Pacific.

Although these systems have theoretically knocked down U.S. satellites during testing, they are as yet not really effective. The Air Force still hopes to use a modified Minuteman missile—known as the Minutemaid—to improve ABMs in the future. And it has been alleged that some of today's Minutemen are already targeted onto Soviet satellites. Certainly the Air Force operates its own space detection and tracking system (Spadats), which keeps careful watch on all orbiting craft. One bizarre reason for this is the fear that the Soviet Union could launch over a month or so a great many satellites, all carrying nuclear weapons. Their orbits would all be different but designed so that after a set period they all passed simultaneously over selected targets in the United States. The Soviet Union could then deliver a surprise blow from space. To take the surprise out of this, the Air Force operates a computer that continually charts the future predicted paths of enemy satellites. If its calculations show that a large number of these are programmed to pass simultaneously over the United States in the future, it presumably emits a warning shriek.

But the Air Force is mainly interested in missile and space defense from space itself. One of its first studies into this was known as Saint, standing first for "satellite interceptor" and later for "satellite inspector." By 1962 it had absorbed more than $100 million and was stopped, in order to be merged with the manned space program and the now-canceled MOL. Project Bambi (Basic Antimissile Ballistic Intercept) lasted longer but suffered the same fate after it had come up with a random barrage satellite antimissile system. This envisaged the launching of from 20,000 to 100,000 satellites in random orbit. Each was to be equipped with a means of detecting a missile launch, tracking the missile, and firing a nonnuclear warhead to destroy the missile and its warhead or satellite. It had the advantage of speed but the disadvantage of being the most costly defense system ever devised.

Such ideas still rumble on, mainly for the reason that it is theoretically possible to destroy an enemy missile from space sooner than from anywhere else. Furthermore, if the job is to be done with nuclear warheads, the explosion can take place over enemy territory, where it might be felt to more justly belong.

The Air Force has also claimed that space is the best place in which to deal with enemy satellites. It has developed the concept of "buddy" satellites which fly in formation with those of an enemy. If the enemy's satellite is for reconnaissance, the "buddy" could blind its cameras with laser light, spray paint over its windows, and confuse its electronics with spurious signals. The "lamprey" satellite would go one better by attaching itself to the enemy satellite. Having found out what the enemy was up to, the lamprey would then either blow itself up, together with its mate, or detach itself peacefully.

These concepts are now being born not mainly from fear of nuclear orbiting weapons—although a close eye is being kept on their possibilities. The main worry is that, as nations become more and more dependent on satellite reconnaissance, navigation, and communication, these satellites will become progressively more important targets. Antisatellite defense, already imperceptibly merged with antimissile defense in the Safeguard system, may well become an important military objective of the 1970s and 1980s.

The Future in Space

"History has shown," wrote U.S. Air Force General Bernard A. Schriever in 1965, "that every medium which affords military possibilities has been exploited for military purposes. This has been the case for land, sea and atmosphere; and . . . there is little reason to believe that space will be an exception." There is one reason, of course, which is the insistence that both the United States and the Soviet Union have shown in describing their space activities as "peaceful." But the word is confusing. Consider, for example, the following "peaceful" application of space technology.

In 1962 Dr. Alton Frye suggested that the United States moon program should be subordinated to "another, more proximate goal . . . the development of an efficient interception system." Dr. Frye's system was to include an antimissile defense as well as a means of intercepting hostile satellites. This, he claimed, would give us "a new vista of political opportunities"—by which he meant the opportunity to lay down the conditions under which the Soviet Union would be allowed to play the space game. The paramount condition would be that all the Soviet Union's activities should be nonmilitary. If the condition was not observed, "the United States will be compelled to destroy every vehicle which the Soviets fire into orbit or in a trajectory toward our territory."

Dr. Frye's notion of peace may be far from universal, and his ideas about space colonialism now seem politically very distant. Perhaps we can congratulate ourselves in avoiding the first military space trap. But there are others to be surmounted if General Schriever's prediction is not to come true.

The greatest danger comes from military space technology. The way military space laboratories keep worrying away at the edges of the advancing frontier does suggest they may one day tear off something quite big. "I have thought all the while," Senator John Stennis told the Committee on Aeronautical and Space Sciences on November 8, 1967, "that great military value could result from orbital operations, that out of space technology could come a weapon that transcended anything we already had. For a long time this has not been publicly discussed, but we are now beginning to get news of this kind."

The senator was probably not referring to any specific weapon but to the activities of the Air Force SPAD project (Space Principles, Applications and Doctrine). One part of this program, with the help of industry and some 200 analysts, was aimed at exploring space "scenarios" in the period 1972–85. Dangerously, the group postulated ideas "with maximum freedom"—which meant ignoring any constraints which might come from lack of money, international law, or even technological impossibility. Even by 1966 this group had come up with more than 70 detailed suggestions of how space might be exploited by the military—including such possibilities as how antisatellite missiles might be launched from aircraft, how satellites might be used to control the weather and interfere with normal patterns of night and day on earth, and even how one of the minor planets known as asteroids could be used as a Doomsday weapon.

The late Dandridge M. Cole of General Electric also waxed lyrical on these possibilities. "The Moon," he wrote, "is a 'Panama Canal' to the riches of the deep space 'Pacific Beyond.'" From this he concluded that there are "strategic areas in space—vital to future scientific, military and commercial space programs—which must be occupied by the United States, lest their use be forever denied us through prior occupation by hostile powers."

But in the last analysis it is not space that matters, but what the existence of it makes us do down on the earth below. It is time to take stock, to forge from this confusing story of rockets and missiles, bombs and satellites some pattern of the shape of things to come. The situation is perilous. Today's military research labs are even now laying down the blueprints for a whole series of vicious new twists in the arms race spiral.

The first of these—the move toward the new ABMs and MIRVs —has already been described. It remains only to link them together. Senior American defense officials argue that it was the Soviet decision to deploy 67 Galosh missiles for their Moscow ABM that really started the chain of events. It was then that the Americans first began to take their multiple warhead systems—then still at the research stage—with great seriousness. They argued that a missile with several warheads might easily penetrate an ABM system, whereas a missile with one warhead had a much smaller chance of doing so. In the space of a few years' time a Soviet decision to deploy 67 missiles had resulted in a United States decision to increase its number of warheads by between 5,000 and 7,500. This move in the arms race thus amplified itself some 100 times.

The next move was for the Russians to copy the United States MIRV system. At once the U.S. land-based missiles were threatened and had to be protected. The U.S. Safeguard ABM system, with hundreds of more missiles, resulted. Even as that system is being deployed, its successor is emerging from the drawing boards based on two missiles known as the "Improved Spartan" and the "Remote Sprint." After them, the range of possibilities seems infinite.

I have already mentioned the Navy's SABMIS program, designed to destroy enemy missiles before they have a chance to release their multiple warheads. A more bizarre approach to the same problem would involve mounting ABMs on hovercraft vehicles on the polar ice caps. And of course the Air Force has produced a counter to the Navy's SABMIS, known as ABMIS (Airborne Ballistic Missile Intercept System), in which the antimissiles would be fired from constantly alert cruising aircraft such as the giant C-5A Galaxy.

ABMs of the future may not necessarily make use of nuclear warheads to destroy enemy missiles. Extensive research has been carried out into using thousands of extremely high-velocity steel pellets. In Project RUDI (Regional Urban Defense Intercept) attention is being given to using high explosives to shower gravel in the path of incoming missiles. Nor has the destructive power of laser beams been lost to ABM planners.

But if the missiles cannot be destroyed early enough, improved ways of knocking them out closer to home may have to be used. Projects Hibex and Upstage are studying the possibilities of making short range ABMs even faster, and giving them a chance to maneuver in flight—to counter the possibility that by this time the MIRVs themselves may be maneuvering, weaving their way through space in an attempt to avoid the ABMs. But if the MIRVs are maneuvering and the ABMs have to as well, the distinction between a missile and an antimissile may finally disappear. The ABM may itself be "MIRVed": Project Janus is studying the possibility of using the Minuteman missile or its successor as both a missile and an antimissile.

But ABMs are not the only means by which missile silos can be protected from MIRVs. The most expensive way is to increase the number of missiles so enormously that there can never be enough MIRVs to knock them all out. This possibility, too, is being studied in spite of the implications of the numbers race between missile and MIRV that would inevitably follow. Alternatively, the missiles can be made movable so that the MIRVs never know exactly where to find them. Both sides are studying the possibility of making land-mobile missiles, presumably traveling on railway tracks or hovercraft. A more sophisticated United States idea is Project Ranger, which would provide each missile with five protected firing positions each more than a mile away from the storage position. When there was warning of an attack, the missile could be moved by truck to any one of the five positions within a few minutes. The MIRVs would never know where to find their missile targets.

Other studies are examining the possibilities of making the silos super-hard with vast quantities of concrete. The HRS program (Hard Rock Silo) aims at making the silos impervious to explosive blasts creating pressures of more than 3,000 pounds per square inch. Project Vulcan would achieve the same end by burying the missiles 3,000 feet below the earth's surface.

We are still nowhere near the end of the story. Every move by the ABMers will be countered by the MIRVers. The first technique is to confuse the ABM radars by including in the attacking missile's payload assorted quantities of space junk—metal decoys, space balloons, "chaff," and tiny needles. In the United States alone just the research and development for this have already cost between $1,000 and $2,000 million.

Alternatively, the MIRVs themselves may be made maneuverable. Currently the United States MIRVs are carried on a bus or platform. This bus releases the individual warheads one at a time and changes its direction between releases. In the future each warhead may have its own inertial guidance system and thus become much more accurate. Coupled with this may be the ability for the individual warhead to steer itself through the atmosphere. Two programs—the BGRV (Boost Glide Reentry Vehicle) and the MBRV (Maneuvering Ballistic Reentry Vehicle)—aim at doing just this.

After that, each warhead may be equipped with its own propulsion system, as in the plans for an ARV (Advanced Reentry Vehicle) which would steer its way around the ABM system and onto the target. Even more sophisticated is the SABRE (Self-aligning Boost Reentry) concept: each missile would be equipped with sensors and would scan the ground to identify its target. It would compare this with a satellite reconnaissance map of the terrain below, which would be stored in the warhead's memory. This ultimate idea in weapon automation would have, in theory, an absolute accuracy.

To those professionally outside the strategic nightmare, the idea of increased accuracy is not so frightening as increased bomb power. In fact, a twofold increase in accuracy produces the same increase in destructive power as a tenfold increase in bomb power. And this is why the efforts of the past decade have been to increase accuracy rather than to make warheads larger. It is this philosophy that lies behind the next generation of missiles themselves.

For the Navy, ULMS (Undersea Long-range Missile System) will replace the Poseidon, which is itself still being deployed. This new missile will have increased range and greatly increased accuracy. On land, Project Strat-X is looking at the possibilities of new land-based missiles. In the design stage is the WS-120A or Improved Capability Missile (ICM). It will have longer range, greater accuracy, and a much greater payload than the Minuteman III.

The picture would not be complete without some reference to nuclear bombers. At the beginning of 1970 the United States had 540 strategic bombers (B-52s and a few B-50s). Between them they could deliver some 1,853 nuclear warheads. These took the form of nuclear bombs plus air-to-surface missiles known as "Hound Dogs" (with warheads in the megaton range). In a sense each of these bombers is already MIRVed, for like the single missile it can release a number of warheads at different targets.

The MIRV trend on bombers is likely to continue. In the future the B-52s and the F-111s now coming into service will also be equipped with short-range attack missiles (SRAMS) of greater speed and accuracy but smaller size. The number of warheads per bomber is thus likely to increase. Later SCADs (Subsonic Cruise Armed Decoys) will be added to the bomber armory. Nuclear missiles in their own right, they also appear to enemy radars as a separate bomber, thus greatly increasing the confusion of the defender. By 1977 we may find the SRAMs and SCADs not on B-52s but on its successor—the Advanced Strategic Manned Aircraft or B-1A. By then the number of warheads deliverable by bombers may, according to the Institute for Strategic Studies, have increased from 1,853 to more than 3,500. The total number of warheads, including those delivered by bombers and land- and sea-based missiles, may have risen from 4,235 to more than 11,000. These figures, of course, do not include the nuclear warheads of whatever ABMs are likely to be in existence by then.

This, then, is the future in space to which we can look forward. It bears little relation to the glamorous world of the Apollo program, the dreams of landing men on Mars, the absurd fantasies of those who would pepper the solar system with the human species. The stuff of which space science and technology is really made lies closer home and closer to the German doodlebug from which it was conceived. It is a grim future, spurred on by man's senseless urge to destroy and to seek ever more costly ways of doing it.

When we marvel at the way three men can be brought back from the moon to land on earth within seconds and a few hundred yards of the appointed time and place, we should not forget one thing. Those men could have been three nuclear warheads and on the accuracy of their arrival could have depended the lives of a million men, women, and children. For the nuclear weapons of tomorrow could not have been born without the space program that led to the lunar landing. And the lunar landing could not have been achieved without the military interest from which it stemmed. Such is the genesis of "man's finest achievement."

CHAPTER III

Military Control of the Oceans

Riches of the Deep–The Submarine Deterrent–Antisubmarine Warfare– Vehicles for Inner Space–Submarine Colonialists–The Ocean Dilemma

"We are involved in deep ocean engineering because it contributes to our assigned missions; we are not in the business of exploiting the ocean's abundant mineral or living resources."

Robert H. Baldwin
Under Secretary of the U.S. Navy
January 11, 1966

Dr. Wernher von Braun—the prophet of the space age—has his counterparts in the oceans. Like him, they dream of journeying into a new environment and of walking where man has never trod before. But for the most part their flights of fancy are more prosaic than Dr. von Braun's. Although the ocean is a new environment for man, it is much nearer to hand than outer space. And for that reason discoveries in "inner space" promise more for man's welfare than discoveries in outer space.

Dr. von Braun's ambitions were achieved by milking the German military cow for funds for research. The technique was successful but it provided the world with the military spin-off of the V-2 rocket and the intercontinental ballistic missile. The prophets of inner space are now following in the same footsteps. They are milking the U.S. Navy of research funds to achieve their ambitions and are thus creating their share of military spin-off. The first objective of all this research is naval supremacy; it may come in the form of missile silos on the sea floor, submarines that can dive to the deepest parts of the ocean, or antiballistic missile systems on the mid-Atlantic ridge. It is already providing an energetic new fuel for the arms race and a new environment in which to wage it.

In the long run, other effects may prove yet more insidious. In the oceans only scientific problems of interest to navies produce easily obtainable research funds. Consequently, our knowledge of the ocean environment is being accumulated in a lopsided way. Today it is easier to get funds to work on the noises fish make than it is to work on methods of catching fish. The motivation is not to provide more food but to improve methods of detecting enemy submarines.

In this chapter I shall explore these two dangers of our headlong race into the oceans in more detail. But first let us look at just what promise the oceans hold for man, bearing in mind that those who hold most of the purse strings are "not in the business of exploiting the ocean's abundant mineral or living resources."

Riches of the Deep

About 71 per cent of the earth's surface is covered by salt water. It has an average depth of 12,500 feet and covers a total area of 139,440,000 square miles, eight times larger than the whole of Asia. This vast watery resource, containing some 330,000,000,-000,000,000,000 gallons, is at once the least known and the most important source of human welfare. One reason is that it is a renewable resource; the oceans are a dynamic chemical and biological factory, churning out products faster than we can use them. A second reason is that the products themselves coincide closely with the things we are likely to need most in the coming decades: food, drugs, minerals, oil and petroleum, building materials, and even fresh water itself.

Perhaps the most remarkable thing about the ocean is that so much of it is not water. Every cubic mile of seawater contains an average of 165 million tons of solid material—a total for all the seas of something like 60 quadrillion tons. This material probably includes every chemical constituent known on earth, as well as a few exotic combinations not found naturally on land. The best-known chemicals, of course, are sodium and chlorine—the two main constituents of table salt. But anyone who cares to look for them will find also gold, silver, uranium, tungsten, and tin—not to mention less well-known but almost equally valuable metals such as manganese, vanadium, and cobalt.

John Mero, an American scientist who dreams of exploiting this wealth, has estimated that even the ocean floor is covered with sufficient minerals to support man far into the future. The bed of the Pacific, for instance, is studded with manganese nodules—small accretions of metals which have formed and grown of their own accord. These nodules, according to Dr. Mero, contain sufficient aluminum to last man 20,000 years, enough cobalt for 200,000 years, copper for 6,000 years, manganese for 400,000 years, and zirconium for 100,000 years. In addition they contain thousands of millions of tons of iron, magnesium, and lead. Nodules of this kind are not confined to the Pacific; they occur also in the Atlantic, the Indian Ocean, the Great Lakes of North America, and even the lochs of Scotland.

They are, however, mostly confined to great depths, and this is what has prevented their being exploited to date. To do so would require new types of dredging equipment, consisting perhaps of giant vacuum cleaners sweeping the ocean floor for its mineral fall-out. Even with today's technology, it would be possible to design and build such apparatus. It would be expensive, but expense is always a relative thing; if we had decided to go to the ocean floor and not the moon, if we had run out of a badly needed mineral, or if its price had been forced up too high, we would by now be relying on the ocean's chemical factory to satiate technology's hunger for exotic metals. As it is, the metals are lying on the ocean floor waiting for us and no one is doing much about them.

The nodules are not the only thing of potential value lying on the deep ocean floor. All the material that is not eaten in the oceans either dissolves or falls eventually to the floor, there to form deep sediments of mudlike oozes. Those consisting mainly of the skeletal remains of animals are known as calcareous oozes, and the oceans are estimated to contain about 100,000 million million tons of them. They could be used in the manufacture of cement; and the siliceous oozes, of which there is about one-tenth as much, could provide material for the manufacture of insulating brick, absorbents, and abrasives.

Nearer to land lie the submerged bottoms of the land masses that link coasts with deep ocean. These shelves, in some places reaching nearly a thousand miles out to sea and lying below 1,500 feet of water, occupy an area one-fifth the size of all the earth's land masses. Being relatively close to shore, and in shallow depths, they have been the first areas to be exploited—notably for petroleum and oil. Natural gas reserves off the United States alone were estimated at 50 million cubic feet in 1965. World offshore petroleum reserves are thought to contain 2.5 million million barrels. With more than 200 drilling rigs already at work on the continental shelves, offshore prospecting has become a multibillion-dollar industry stretching right around the globe. But it has only just begun to tap the vast energy potential lying hidden under the waves.

The ocean's most abundant constituent is, of course, water. And thirsty eyes in the Sahara, in Israel's Negev desert, and even in North America have for long looked with hatred at the 139 million tons of salt which every cubic mile of the ocean contains. How to get rid of it? There are several methods, but they all consume large amounts of energy, and so produce water which is usually too expensive for drinking or irrigation. But as the costs of nuclear energy fall, so too will the costs of desalting water. It is no pipe dream to imagine vast areas of desert again turned green, supporting the trees and crops they did thousands of years ago. But, again, water desalination has not ranked high enough in the priorities of the past 20 years; as a result the technical barriers to desalination are yielding only slowly to a feeble scientific assault.

Our thinking here may even be myopic. Dr. Mero has put on his farsighted spectacles to show just what might be achieved with more ambitious plans. If we set up a desalting plant to provide for a coastal population of 100 million people, he calculates, the volume of sea water processed annually would contain 6,400,000 million tons of salt, 240 million tons of magnesium, 160 million tons of sulfur, 800,000 tons of boron, 2,000 tons of aluminum, and several hundred tons of manganese, copper, and uranium, as well as smaller quantities of other elements. Furthermore, if the uranium and thorium could be extracted, they would probably provide enough nuclear fuel to supply the electricity demands of the whole plant.

Revitalized deserts offer more than living space for man; they also offer an important new source of food. If that is to be an urgent requirement—and it already is—the ocean can provide it more directly. Today we dip into the ocean's larder for about 60 million tons of food every year. Fish provides about one-tenth our total intake of protein, and over the past two decades the fish catch has been growing somewhat faster than the human population. In this it is almost unique; the quantity of nearly all other kinds of food that is available per head of population has been growing smaller for many years.

Unhappily, the ocean's larder is not unlimited. Some stocks have already been overfished and their yield is now on the decline rather than the increase. Yet there is much that could be done. The total fish catch, if properly managed, could still increase by three or four times until the fish were in effect "mined" and could no longer support their own populations. And there are other sorts of food in the ocean still hardly investigated. These include krill—the small prawnlike creatures which the blue whale feeds on—as well as the animal and plant plankton which live in the top few feet of the ocean. So far neither has been exploited even though it is technically possible to catch them and to convert them into nutritious and reasonably palatable dishes.

And what is to stop us turning over a new leaf in the ocean, as it were? Why do we persist in hunting fish with "bow and arrow" methods when we abandoned the hunting of animals in favor of agriculture several thousand years ago? In time, we will surely farm saltwater fish as we farm today the cow, the pig, the trout, and the carp. Of course, there are technical problems to be solved before the ocean's 350 million cubic miles become the largest food farm in the world. Yet the attention we give to fish farming does not seem to tally with its promise. On the research scale sea farming is not big science; it is not even little science; it is microscopic science.

There are, of course, also several things in the ocean that have no business there at all. Among these are hundreds of thousands of tons of chemical weapons—mainly mustard gas and nerve gas—sunk by the British and the Americans in the sea off Ireland, in the Baltic, and in the Atlantic. In spite of vigorous protests in the United States, another load of nerve gas found its way into the Atlantic in 1970. Nuclear weapons, too, have left their mark. Fifty gallons of seawater from any ocean in the world contain detectable traces of radioactive fallout from nuclear weapon tests. The concentration of lead in the Pacific has increased ten times since lead was introduced into petrol. DDT has been found in the Bay of Bengal after having drifted with the wind from Africa. General pollution has made more than one-tenth of all the shellfish-producing areas near the United States unusable.

Yet pollution is not the main factor preventing ocean exploitation. "Much remains for us and our children to do," writes Dr. S.

J. Holt, a scientist from the United Nations Food and Agricultural Organization, "to make sure that the ocean is not a contaminated wilderness or a battlefield for ever sharper clashes between nations and between the different users of its resources." It is the prospect of the oceans becoming a three-dimensional battlefield which has dictated the form of most of our oceanographic research. Today the U.S. Navy pays for more than half of all the marine research conducted in the United States. And it does so not for any altruistic reasons. Robert H. Baldwin, Under Secretary of the U.S. Navy, made the point quite clear when addressing a naval conference on January 11, 1966. "Our oceanographic and ocean engineering programs," he said, "are specifically and directly responsive to military requirements. . . . We are involved in deep ocean engineering because it contributes to our assigned missions; we are not in the business of exploiting the ocean's abundant mineral or living resources."

The fact that some 90 per cent of the ocean is still unexplored has even been described as a military plot by the Soviet Union. Dr. B. D. Thomas, president of the Battelle Memorial Institute, has said:

> What a brilliant military exploit it would be to
> send us off to the Moon, while they seize the
> oceans. By some logic I have never been able to
> understand, it has been asserted that the power
> that controls the Moon can conquer the Earth.
> We might add . . . that the power that controls
> the oceans can control the power that governs the
> Moon.

Throughout the last decade this idea has grown in credibility. Today the Navy is the tail that wags the oceanographic dog. It is now wagging it so hard that Tony Loftas, describing the oceans in *The Last Resource,* has warned that the oceans, "instead of providing the means for a satisfactory life for the Earth's family of nations could become the new location for the planet's Armageddon." The basic reason is that our "last resource" has become the perfect hiding place for submarines capable of firing nuclear missiles while still submerged. This one fact has set the world's most powerful nations off in another of their probably illusory searches for greater national security. In doing so it has grossly distorted what should have been our real priorities for ocean research.

The Submarine Deterrent

When Robert Fulton showed William Pitt the blueprints of his "electric torpedo" in 1804, the First Sea Lord, Admiral Sir John Jervis, was mortified. "Don't look at it," he cried. "If we take it up, other nations will, and that will be the strongest blow against our supremacy on the sea that can be imagined." Sir John's predictions turned out to be correct but took much longer to materialize than he could have imagined. The last traces of Britain's naval supremacy did not finally disappear until 1956, the year in which the electric torpedo was theoretically fashioned into a submarine carrying nuclear-tipped missiles.

The occasion was the NOBSKA summer study organized by the U.S. Navy and the National Academy of Science's Committee on Undersea Warfare. The study took the form of a brainstorming session among leading scientists connected with the defense establishment. And it was then that it was first realized that the new solid-fuel missiles could be launched from a nuclear-powered submarine with sufficient accuracy to provide a deterrent force. In an incredibly short time, the main feature of the Polaris missile had emerged and been tested.

On July 20, 1960, the submarine *George Washington* fired its first two missiles while still submerged. Within a few years the United States was able to boast 41 submarines, each armed with 16 nuclear Polaris missiles. The earlier A-1 Polaris had a range of 1,200 nautical miles. The A-2 model could reach 1,500 or more nautical miles, and the later A-3 models could carry their warheads a full 2,500 nautical miles. Theoretically, the last could strike any point on the earth's surface, for no point on land is more than 1,700 nautical miles from the sea.

Currently, however, the U.S. nuclear submarine force is undergoing change. It is planned to leave 10 of the submarines with their A-3 Polaris missiles. By 1975 the other 31 will be equipped with the completely new Poseidon missile. Capable of carrying a warhead of more than two megatons, the Poseidon will have a yet longer range, a completely new design, and much improved accuracy. More importantly, however, the Poseidon may also be equipped with multiple warheads, each of which can be independently targeted. Each Poseidon could carry between 3 and 14 of these warheads, raising the strike force of the submarine fleet very considerably. Thus equipped, a single submarine could launch as many as 224 warheads within five minutes while remaining concealed beneath the ocean surface.

The strength of the submarine deterrent is that, at the moment, it cannot be detected or located. It is thus invulnerable to surprise attack and cannot be eliminated in a first strike. And so, unlike many other nuclear weapons, it may help stabilize a precarious nuclear balance. Whether the Poseidon and its MIRVs will help preserve that stability is very doubtful. Speaking before the Senate Armed Services Committee on March 19, 1969, U.S. Defense Secretary Melvin Laird referred to an improved guidance system for the Poseidon. "This is an important program," he said, "since it promises to improve significantly the accuracy of the Poseidon missile, thus enhancing its effectiveness against hard targets."

What he meant was that the new submarine missiles might be aimed at enemy missile silos, whereas the older Polaris missiles, because they were less accurate, were targeted on cities, and therefore could only be used in retaliation. The Soviet Union is thus likely to interpret the Poseidon as a possible first-strike weapon rather than as a means of keeping the nuclear peace. This is just one example of the glaring gap that exists between the theory of submarine deterrence and the practical advances now being implemented..

Part of the submarine's strength is that it is nuclear powered as well as nuclear armed. This means it can stay submerged for several months. In August 1958 the *Nautilus* made the first submerged journey under the North Pole. The next year the *Triton* traveled round the world without surfacing, making the journey of 41,500 miles in 84 days. This is something no conventionally powered submarine could ever do, for it would have to surface frequently to recharge its batteries.

In 1969 the United States had 81 nuclear-powered submarines. Of the 41 equipped with nuclear ballistic missiles, 32 are usually at sea at any one time. Seven of these patrol the Pacific, and the remainder sail in the Arctic, Atlantic, and Mediterranean. The submarines are serviced at bases in Guam, Rota in Spain, Holy Loch in Scotland, and Charleston in South Carolina.

The Soviet Union had about 60 nuclear-powered submarines in 1969. According to the Institute for Strategic Studies, only about 18 of these can fire ballistic missiles, but a further 35 conventionally powered submarines may also be able to do so. Together they carry about 160 missiles, an average of only three per submarine, each carrying a warhead of around 1 megaton. The missiles that can be launched underwater are the Sark and the Serb, with maximum ranges of 300 and 650 statute miles respectively. Another missile, the Sawfly, claimed to have a range of 1,500–2,000 nautical miles and is being deployed in a new class of submarine, capable of carrying 16 missiles and coming into service at the rate of 4 to 8 a year. China still has no nuclear submarine force, though it does have one or two submarines, each equipped with three ballistic missile tubes.

In July 1969 Britain's nuclear deterrent was formally handed over to the Navy—in fact to four submarines, *Resolution, Repulse, Renown,* and *Revenge.* The third of these came into service in 1969 at a cost of £52 million; an estimated £5.5 million a year will be needed to keep it in service. By the end of 1968 Britain's Polaris program had cost £280 million, her submarine base £30 million, and her Polaris missile depot £11 million. All the submarines carry 16 Polaris A-3 missiles, some already equipped with up to three warheads—though not of the type that can be individually targeted. France also plans to have four ballistic missile submarines in service by 1975; the first was tested in 1969. Progress has been considerably held up, notably because of the difficulty of making nuclear warheads small enough for the missiles. France, unlike Britain, has not benefited from an exchange of technical information on nuclear weapons with the United States.

In a saner world we might expect that in time the submarine deterrent would come to be the only deterrent—that the vulnerable land-based missiles and bombers would disappear and there would be no need to search out new forms of nuclear delivery systems. But the operation of Polaris-type submarines is not so simple as it might appear.

To remain hidden, the submarine must never surface in the open sea. To do so risks identification and the chance that it will be tagged by a hostile submarine when it submerges again. Nor must a submarine send out radio messages when on patrol, for its position may be identified. The only effective Polaris submarine is a silent one, and a submerged one.

Yet the submarine must also know exactly where it is and must be instantaneously ready to respond to orders from its base. Neither condition can be easily met without breaking radio silence or without surfacing. The reason is first that radio waves do not travel through water as they do through the atmosphere. All but the lowest frequencies are rapidly absorbed and so are useless for underwater communication. This communication problem has plagued nuclear submarines since they were first thought of. Currently, submerged submarines can be communicated with by very low-frequency radio waves, vibrating some 10,000–18,000 times a second. Very expensive communication systems have been set up to do this but even these radio waves are strongly absorbed by a few feet of seawater. So the submarine has to travel relatively close to the surface to receive radio signals from the aerial which it floats to the surface.

Furthermore, the submarine must also acknowledge the signals it receives—particularly if they are orders to use its weapons. No one has yet revealed exactly how this can be done by a submerged submarine in a way which does not also reveal its position. One possibility is that peculiar effects in the way that the ocean transmits sounds can be exploited to send an underwater signal over hundreds of miles—or at least over a few miles to the nearest underwater relay station.

Another problem is that the submarine must be able to land its missile on a target two or three thousand miles away with an accuracy of half a mile or less. To do this, of course, the submarine must know its own position to much better than half a mile. While submerged at its patrol depth it cannot take fixes on the sun or stars or on well-known features such as land masses or lighthouses.

Most reliance, therefore, is placed on a device known as the ship's inertial navigation systems (SINS). Each of these consists of three precisely mounted accelerometers and gyroscopes designed to record the submarine's acceleration in three planes. Each submarine is equipped with three SINS and a computer to work out a position from their readings. In theory, this system is completely independent of the outside world and, of course, works at any depth. It has been claimed that it is accurate to several hundred feet. What is less often said is that all errors in the system are cumulative—they mount up as the journey progresses. Any submarine that relied entirely on SINS for a three-month submerged journey would have no chance of delivering its missiles with the required accuracy. If missiles are to be fired, the readings from the SINS may have to be updated every 12 to 24 hours.

But updating is not so easy. One system of sea navigation in widespread use, called "Omega," was developed in the United States for military as well as civilian vessels. The system includes eight transmitting stations, each separated from the next by 5,000 to 6,000 nautical miles and thus spread widely over the globe. These stations transmit very low-frequency waves vibrating between about 10,000 and 14,000 times a second. Any vessel at sea which can receive these signals from two stations at the same time can fix its own position by triangulation.

The manufacturers of the system claim these radio waves can be detected up to 50 feet below the surface. This may be optimistic, and in less than ideal conditions adequate penetration is not likely to be more than a dozen feet or so. But in any case Omega's accuracy is not sufficient for a missile-firing submarine. The best fix that can be obtained is about ½ nautical mile by day, and 1 nautical mile by night, when conditions for radio transmission are less satisfactory.

Polaris submarines also carry a special star-fixing periscope. This can also be used for updating the SINS, but it suffers from two disadvantages. First, it is not sufficiently accurate. And secondly, even a few feet of periscope sticking out of the water can be detected by aircraft radars.

However, there is at least one system that does give the required accuracy. This is the Transit satellite navigation system mentioned in Chapter 2. In the late 1960s this was giving vessels fixes accurate to ¼ nautical mile. Eventually, it is hoped, an accuracy of 0.1 nautical mile may be obtainable. The only problem here is whether or not the submarine must surface to receive the Transit signals. Some technical writers have claimed that they can be received underwater, but how this is done has not been revealed. The Transit satellites emit radio signals vibrating at more than one million times a second and these must be absorbed in the top few inches of seawater. If a submarine is to pick up these signals while submerged, as it reputedly does with its AN/BRN-3 receiving equipment, it must float an aerial to the surface. This need not constitute a significant radar target. There is no doubt that Transit is the principal means used by U.S. Polaris submarines to update their SINS.

However, Commander F. G. Haines, writing of the British Polaris fleet, has this to say: "The problem of underwater fixing is solved at present by three main approaches: inertial navigation systems, the deep sound channel (SOFAR) together with sonar in conjunction with underwater beacons, and thirdly the doppler log." The deep sound channel is a layer of water, about 4,000 feet deep near the equator and almost at the surface near the poles, which transmits sound over very long distances. Listening stations at the same depth can thus pick up submarine signals which never enter the atmosphere. If two stations pick up such signals simultaneously, they can fix the position of the submarine and presumably then radio it to the submarine commander. Alternatively, it may be possible for the submarine itself to pick up signals from sound-emitting beacons placed underwater at known positions. Such navigation aids are known to be already positioned in the ocean.

The doppler log is basically a sonar system which bounces waves off the sea bed. The returning signal gives a measure of the submarine's speed. In addition, such signals may identify known features on the sea floor and hence tell the submarine exactly where it is. This system, however, cannot be operationally very important. For one thing, only about 10 per cent of the sea floor has ever been mapped in detail. Secondly, the system only works in water depths of less than about 1,000 feet. And, thirdly, if the doppler sonar is being used, the system gives only a dead-reckoning system less accurate than SINS itself.

These are the problems which have determined the main directions of ocean research over the past decade. A visit to almost any oceanographic research center in the West will show that work is being done on the following types of problems: mapping the ocean floor; studying the behavior of sound and radio waves underwater; designing powerful emitters of sound and low-frequency radio waves; analyzing the ocean's natural sounds made by fish; inventing new types of submerged "buoy"; and so on.

Much of this work is supported by the relevant navy or defense department. Most of the work paid for from civilian funds is directed by oceanographers who have in the past been involved in defense areas—and hence have had their interests subtly molded by military requirements. Whichever way one turns in the oceans, it seems, one is eventually led back to the requirements of war. This unhealthy situation, now apparently accepted as natural by most oceanographers, has done more than distort our research priorities. It promises, through the insidious nature of technological advance, to set up a novel and expensive arms race under the sea. And like the ABM-MIRV race on land, this race is not being run between two political blocs. Instead the technical experts on both sides are in a race with themselves, alternately trying to find better ways of concealing underwater weapons and then seeking ways of identifying and destroying them. By definition, the only result of such a race can be an expensive and dangerous failure.

Antisubmarine Warfare

The U.S. Office of Naval Research has funded many apparently bizarre experiments. To hard-nosed sea commanders, none can have seemed stranger than a project that took place in the Caribbean in

October 1965. With ONR's help, biologists there collected 30,000 baby green turtles and moved them to a new location in an attempt to find out how the turtle navigates. Scientifically, the problem is a real one. As soon as the baby turtle hatches, it makes a hazardous 100-yard journey straight to the sea, dives through the surf, and sets off on a long swim to distant pastures of sea grass. When mature, it swims back again to its ancestral beach to lay its eggs.

The Office of Naval Research reasoned that the techniques used by turtles in this remarkable navigational feat might hold some lessons for the Navy. And there was some precedent for their interest. Several years earlier extensive research had revealed the system of sound signals the dolphin uses to navigate. This work led directly to a Navy project known as "Artemis." In this the Navy's "dolphin" was the tanker *Mission Capistrano,* and strapped to its belly was a huge sound generator measuring 30 by 50 feet. As the tanker steamed the North Atlantic, it belted out massive underwater blasts of noise.

Sound travels some four times faster in the surface of the ocean than it does through the air. But its path gets bent in complex ways because pressure and temperature change with depth. The top 200 feet of water, however, act as a kind of sound channel, and sound hitting the deeper and colder water below is reflected back toward the surface. The sound from the *Mission Capistrano* traveled in this way over great distances. It was picked up first by a chain of hydrophones which the Navy had installed. From them the signals were relayed to a tower, extending 67 feet above the water and 200 feet below it, which was located on a seamount 30 miles southwest of Bermuda. And from there the signals were transferred to a computer processing laboratory in Bermuda for analysis. What the Navy was listening for was the way underwater objects distorted the sounds made by the *Capistrano.* And by 1961, they claimed, their system could detect anything that moved underwater within a range of 500 miles.

The ocean's extraordinary ability to conduct sound over great distances had been proved much earlier. In 1945 Dr. Maurice Ewing had detected an underwater explosion made near Dakar at a listening post in Bermuda. For this work he was awarded the Navy's highest civilian honor, the Distinguished Public Service Award. His record was broken on March 21, 1960, in an experiment carried out by one of his own research teams at Columbia University, which was financed by the Navy. On that day the research vessel *Vema* detonated an underwater charge of 50 pounds of TNT off Australia.

The noise was picked up 2½ hours later at the Bermuda underwater listening post, after it had traveled 12,000 miles halfway around the world.

This kind of research, triggered off by German submarine successes in World War II, received an enormous boost when nuclear-armed submarines became a reality. Although the Polaris appeared to be a near-perfect deterrent, neither side was anxious to learn to live with it. To do so meant that Americans would have to accept the permanent presence of a Russian fleet of nuclear-armed submarines cruising off their shores and able to obliterate many American cities or bomber bases within minutes. Accordingly, the Navy mounted a massive antisubmarine warfare program in the late 1950s. Apart from Polaris itself, this program has been the Navy's principal obsession for the past decade.

Because every 100 meters a submarine can dive provides it with an extra 2½ million cubic miles of water in which to hide (Polaris submarines are thought to operate down to about 1,000 feet), the first problem to be explored was submarine detection. Initially, thoughts turned to setting up curtains of underwater listening devices strung all the way down the coast of North America.

The first two plans to do this, Projects Caesar and Colossus, were made operational on the floor of the Continental Shelf in 1965. They were followed by SOSUS, standing for "sound system for underwater surveillance," and by Project Trident, in which Western Electric installed a curtain of hydrophones on the continental shelf, listening upward. SOSUS made use of the deep sound channel al ready mentioned and involved listening devices not on the sea floor but anchored at the depth of the sound channel. To what extent these systems were operational or experimental is not clear. But in 1968 the Navy requested a further $39 million for research and development on new sonar "nets."

A year later the American journalist Frank Leary summed the situation up thus:

> The technology of ocean surveillance from bottom-mounted fixed sonars and inverted transducers suspended at depth has been greatly refined over years of experimentation. Thirteen new listening posts were surveyed in along the Kurile-Kamchatka trench only two years ago, to monitor submarine traffic out of Petropavlosk. Another net was installed in the central Pacific. The Navy has also extended the fixed-site surveillance

concept to the inshore coastal regime, and has
several mobile inshore surveillance units operating
in western Pacific harbors.

The Navy's interest in sonar sparked off an investigation of all kinds of noise in the ocean. Marine biologists discovered that one of the easiest ways to attract naval research funds was to study the noises made by marine animals—from the whistling dolphins and clicking crustaceans to the belching and burping of the fish that have gas-filled bladders. While such sounds could be distinguished fairly easily from the noise of a submarine, they could be confused with signals picked up by active sonar devices such as the Artemis. Many forms of marine life emit noises at frequencies which travel through the water most effectively—and these, not surprisingly, often turn out to be the frequencies that are best for sonar work. Accordingly, in 1969 the U.S. Navy was supporting studies of the sounds made by more than 200 different species of fish.

The performance of underwater detection systems is one of the most highly classified of all fields. What slips out about them in the technical literature reveals only the tip of a massive military program. But the kinds of "pure" research the Navy supports does reveal some of its lines of thinking.

In 1960, for instance, NATO announced that it had supported an important piece of civilian oceanography. It had hired Professor Haken Mosby, of Bergen University, to chart the ocean floor in great detail. The areas chosen were the Gibraltar Strait and the passage between the Faeroes and the Shetlands. Both regions are of crucial strategic importance to submarines wishing to slip unnoticed from one sea to another. This survey has now made it possible to deploy curtains of underwater hydrophones in both straits. Oceanography, incidentally, is the only scientific field which NATO has honored with a special subcommittee to collect knowledge and support research.

The U.S. Navy is concerned with the five main oceanic gateways through which Soviet submarines could slip into the Atlantic. The two big ones are between South America and Africa, and between Iceland and the United Kingdom. There are also three small ones—between Greenland and Iceland, Greenland and Canada, and the Strait of Gibraltar. With the possible exception of the large southern gap, all these channels must by now be studded with underwater detection equipment.

Britain is also concerned about submarines traveling east across the Atlantic. Accordingly, she has made plans to string a row of 300 "weather station" buoys from Iceland to Portugal. The kind of "weather" these buoys would report on is classified. But the makers of oceanographic equipment are eagerly awaiting the £1 million worth of orders which the plan would generate.

Submarines can be detected from above as well as below. One possibility, mentioned in Chapter 2, is that reconnaissance satellites may eventually be able to track nuclear submarines because of the heat disturbances they create. And antisubmarine aircraft carry a whole battery of devices for submarine detection. These include radar devices of the kind originally developed in World War II, apparatus for detecting submarine radar or radio messages, an instrument for detecting traces of exhaust emitted by diesel-powered submarines, as well as a device called "MAD." This stands for "magnetic anomaly detector" and has been the cause of prolific research into the nature of the earth's magnetic field. It works on the principle that the presence of a submarine affects the reading of the earth's magnetic field received on an aircraft flying overhead. The submarine appears as a "magnetic anomaly." But to complicate matters further, there are regions of the ocean floor that have the same effect, and the existence of a certain type of rock can easily register on an aircraft MAD as a submarine. For this reason many navies have been supporting research into the nature and distribution of natural magnetic anomalies over the ocean floor.

Some underwater listening devices are capable of relaying their information to aircraft. In one form of submarine detection the aircraft lays its own listening devices called sonobuoys over an area of sea. Having planted these in a pattern, it can then overfly an area of some 30,000 square miles listening for submarine noises. Antisubmarine helicopters also dip listening apparatus called sonoballs into the ocean in the hope of detecting submarines lying in the deeper "shadow area" where they tend to hide.

Finally, there is a whole range of submarine detection equipment carried on ships—both on surface vessels and on submarines themselves. Some of the devices emit no signals but simply listen for all submarine noises in the neighborhood. The longer-range devices can detect echoes from objects as far away as 100 miles. This is made possible by so-called convergence zones in the ocean. These cause sound waves to be bent downward and then upward, rising to the surface at regular intervals. The first convergence zone surfaces about 30 miles away, the second 60 miles away, and the third about 100 miles away. No operational sonar can routinely detect objects more distant than the third convergence zone. Yet again there are exceptions—sonars operating in the deep sound channel may have an even greater range if conditions are good. But there is usually a penalty for long range. This is that the device has to emit so much sound that enemy submarines can detect the sonars, and hence avoid them, at much greater range than they themselves can be detected.

These detection systems are often coupled to antisubmarine weapons such as torpedoes, depth charges, and even missiles. Some of these are tactical nuclear weapons. SUBROC, for instance, is a missile which is launched underwater, breaks surface to travel through the air, and then homes in on its submarine target. It carries a nuclear depth charge as its warhead. The Mark 45 Astor antisubmarine torpedo carries the biggest nuclear charge and has a range of 10–20 miles. But the conventional Mark 48 torpedo is perhaps the cleverest. This first listens for submarine noises to aim at. If nothing is detected, it sends out sonar signals and listens for the echoes. And if that fails, it is programmed to carry out its own "random" search for enemy objects.

Each of these items of equipment requires its own research and development program. In addition, of course, they all depend on oceanographic research in general. To this end, the official *Marine Science Affairs* report of 1968 was able to boast that in the previous year the U.S. Navy had collected "over 100,000 miles of seismic sub-bottom profiles and ship-towed magnetic data; 860 Nansen casts for submerged water analysis; hundreds of bottom photographs, geological cores, biological and radiological samples, and current measurements; and many thousands of measurements of propagation of acoustic energy over a wide spectrum of frequency."

It might be thought that this kind of information could at least be profitably used by industry and civilian science. But the report went on: "While the above oceanographic surveys are intended for military use, others which are closely allied to them are available for civilian use." In other words, the results of this basic research were classified.

The process works the other way as well—open research can quickly be exploited in classified programs. Robert A. Frosch, Assistant Secretary of the Navy for research and development, told a meeting of civilian scientists on December 27, 1967, of the importance of their work on underwater destruction. "Developments in oceanography and ocean engineering," he said, "are important to over-all objectives in mine warfare. Since the field which sets off the destructive force of the mine explosion is transmitted through the water, a knowledge of various water properties as well as of bottom conditions is necessary for intelligent employment of both mines and mine countermeasures."

Measures and countermeasures are the essence of the underwater battle. But in spite of intensive research, it seems that the submarine still has the edge on the detector. The limits of effective sonar range are still thought to be 25 miles or less, and longer-range systems are still unreliable. How long that will remain true at the current level of research is another matter. Consider another passage from the 1968 *Marine Science Affairs* report:

> Marine science and technology in support of
> specific weapons systems is budgeted at $37.7
> million for FY 1969. Most of this money will
> support studies of the characteristics and behavior
> of sound energy in the ocean. The primary
> objective is to advance the Navy capability to
> detect, identify, seek and destroy hostile submarine
> forces, but the knowledge gained serves the con-
> verse purpose of helping to conceal Polaris sub-
> marines and, thus, preserving the invulnerability
> of the Fleet Ballistic Missile System.

This paragraph could serve as a casebook illustration of the dilemma of military technology. First, it assumes that a breakthrough in submarine detection would benefit only one side—that Soviet submarines could be detected but that United States ones could not, since they would be equipped with some device to overcome the new advance. Second, it assumes that such an advance would be to United States advantage and that therefore this goal should be pursued. Underwater, it would seem, the Navy is not prepared to accept the position of parity which the advocates of nuclear deterrence claim to be the only stable one. Instead, the aim is a spiraling arms race under the sea—a kind of inner-space race with many more real strategic issues at stake than ever existed in the outer-space race.

"The race may already have started," writes Arvid Pardo, Malta's permanent representative at the United Nations.

> An informed guess is that the United States Navy
> is currently spending about $400 million for
> submarine tracking and detection devices installed
> on the ocean floor. An intense nuclear and con-
> ventional arms race already exists in the at-
> mosphere, on land, on the surface, and
> immediately under the surface, of the sea; the

addition of an arms race in a new environment, as now appears to be in prospect, would further strain the financial resources of the major powers, causing postponement of those comprehensive measures for the improvement of standards of living which are widely considered to be imperative. The disappointment of impatient expectations could increase both internal and international tensions.

Mr. Pardo has become an eloquent spokesman for those who claim that the deep ocean floor should be owned by an international organization. In honor of this, Malta has issued a postage stamp with the inscription "*Qiegh il-bahar ghall-gid tad-dinja*"—meaning "sea's bed for the world's good." But there are other slogans about. The U.S. Naval Academy crest bears the words "*Ex scientia tridens*" —"from knowledge, sea power." In the United States the words have apparently been taken so literally that Rear Admiral "Muddy" Waters has been forced to issue a warning to the industrialists who read the Pentagon's *Defense Industry Bulletin*. "Oceanography," he writes, "is not to be confused with anti-submarine warfare, nor the Polaris system, nor amphibious or mine warfare operations. Oceanography is a necessary support element in all of the warfare areas."

Vehicles for Inner Space

In the early 1960s it seemed that the race to inner space was really on. From the United States, in particular, there came a mountain of popular literature describing in glowing terms the bounty that lay hidden under the ocean. The key to its exploitation, it was argued, was to build a mammoth fleet of ocean "spacecraft"—submersible vehicles that would glide silently beneath the waves guiding prospectors and food gatherers to the sites of the richest hauls. This was an exciting technological dream, freely coupled to heady visions of man's first steps into the second unknown environment to have been conquered in a decade. "Current underwater research," wrote the American biologist Dr. Andreas Rechnitzer in 1965, "is centred on extending the range of 'free' dives and the development of a new fleet of highly mobile submersible craft. The ultimate aim is to exploit the ocean's vast resources of proteins and minerals."

In point of fact, the ultimate aim was quite different. Dr. Rechnitzer earned his oceanographic fame in the bathyscaphe *Trieste,* which he, together with Jacques Piccard, took down to 18,150 feet in the Mariana Trench in the western Pacific. His trip was paid for by the U.S. Navy, which a year previously had bought the *Trieste* from the French Navy.

Elsewhere, Dr. Rechnitzer has written about the more specific military roles of deep ocean exploration. "We expect that the ocean floor will be used as a maneuvering ground for super-submarines," he says. "We must learn infinitely more about it." To that end the *Trieste* has been used to study underwater sound and visibility and the effect of very deep water pressure on a range of mechanical devices.

Nor is this an isolated instance. At least 60 per cent of the best-known submersibles are used wholly or partly for military research. And if one considers only the 30-odd craft capable of descending below 2,000 feet, all but four have been, are being, or will be used for military research. Such is the stranglehold of military research on oceanography.

A cursory study of submersibles suggests that many of the craft are industrial adventures aimed at some form of mineral prospecting. Unhappily, this is not the case. Take, for example, the *Aluminaut*—a much-publicized vehicle used to symbolize man's move into the oceans. This vessel was built for Reynolds Metals Company and was then leased to the U.S. Navy and the Scripps Institute of Oceanography in California. At Scripps it is operated on a grant from the U.S. Office of Naval Research. Ultimately, then, it was the Navy that called the tune as to what research was done. Furthermore, the main reason why Reynolds had the craft made in the first place was to prove that the next generation of military submarines could be built, like the *Aluminaut,* from aluminum.

The point is even better made with *Alvin,* a craft which the Office of Naval Research had built specially for the Woods Hole Oceanographic Institution. While there it was supported by a contract with the U.S. Dept. of Defense—Navy. Its studies "were divided among geology, biology, geophysics, and engineering. The results will contribute to the ability to use the deep ocean floor and the sea floor in support of the National Purpose. . . . The biologic studies will encompass life forms and benthic animals that will affect sea floor structures." No one, of course, doubts that information of this type, if released by the Navy, is of benefit to civilian research. But it is as well to be clear that the first purpose of the study is to provide information of importance to the Navy in erecting sea floor structures. What those structures might house we shall see in the next section.

Most of the other submersibles are in a similar situation. Westinghouse's *Deepstar-4000,* for instance, has been leased in turn to the Navy's Underwater Sound Laboratory, Oceanographic Office, and Electronics Laboratory. In 1968 it was selected by the Naval Undersea Warfare Center for "a variety of undersea programs." Similarly, Lockheed's *Deep Quest* is used primarily in antisubmarine warfare research. General Dynamics has built two submersibles for exclusive use on the Navy's underwater test range off Bermuda. *DOWB* was built by General Motors Defense Research Laboratories. When it went into service in 1968, Dr. David S. Potter, director of GM's defense and space laboratories in Santa Barbara, said: "The deep ocean work boat (*DOWB*) will provide a new dimension to us in our acoustic work and in our physical research. It also will enhance our capabilities for surveillance, placement and recovery activities on the ocean floor and in searching or mapping operations." Dr. Potter had earlier directed an acoustic bottom survey for the Navy's underwater range BARSTUR near Hawaii. GM's specialty in oceanography is deep-ocean acoustic tracking, particularly under Arctic ice, and it helped the Navy set up its AUTEC range in the Bahamas (see p. 131). It operates its own submarine detection range near Santa Cruz, where the *DOWB* has been working.

Some of the other submersibles are operated exclusively by the Navy for classical research. These include the *Dolphin, Moray, Deep Jeep, NR-I, Hikino,* and *Deep View.* Many of these are never publicly mentioned, even in the technical oceanographic literature. The *NR-I,* the first nuclear-powered submersible, cost $100 million, but nothing is known of its tasks since launch. Even the depth at which it can operate is classified. "Briefly, then," writes Nick Valery of *Science Journal,* "this is how the U.S. government is using defence dollars to encourage a wider and more profitable industrial participation in ocean research and development: the Department of Defense puts up the money, the Navy proposes an R and D program with military objectives, industry tenders for various sub-systems and, finally, any non-strategic information resulting from the Navy's operating experience is released for commercial exploitation." The order of priorities is important here; and because the priorities are somewhat different in England, there are hardly any British submersibles in operation.

Britain's first submersible was called SURV. Built by a small company in the south of England, it was scheduled to reach 1,000 feet and was greeted with much delight from those interested in oceanography. But after scarcely a year of life, its makers announced there was no demand for the submersible and it would have to be scrapped. At that time Nigel Hawkes from *Science Journal* reported the views of its makers in some detail. When his article appeared, the Natural Environment Research Council—the British government body responsible for oceanography—was apparently surprised to find the blame for the craft's failure laid at its doorstep. And in a letter to *Science Journal,* NERC's secretary, Dr. R. J. H. Beverton, explained what the trouble really was.

"The story of small manned submersibles has not been a happy one," he wrote. "Enthusiasm for what appeared at first sight to be an exciting technological breakthrough obscured the fact that the original incentive behind their explosive development in the United States was a military one, with no relation to their cost/benefit for oceanographic research."

To trace the origin of this "explosive military development," one must go back to April 10, 1963. That was the day on which the U.S. submarine *Thresher* submerged off the New England coast. The craft, carrying 129 men and worth $50 million, never resurfaced. At that time the bathyscaphe *Trieste* was the only U.S. craft capable of finding her in the 8,400 feet of water in which she lay. After a prolonged search, parts of the submarine were located and brought to the surface. The cause of the disaster was only vaguely identified, and nothing of importance was recovered.

This event hit the U.S. Navy where it hurt most. Just as it was beginning to deploy its powerful arguments for improving sea-based deterrents, and scrapping land-based ones, the loss of one of its vessels exposed to public view the force's complete incompetence to achieve anything in water deeper than a few hundred feet. A committee was formed to recommend action and to ponder the technological absurdity that man was shortly to reach the moon while two-thirds of the earth's surface remained unexplored and almost impenetrable alien territory.

The result was the Navy's Deep Submergence Systems Project (DSSP), initially budgeted at a total of $332 million. The project was to include programs for (1) submarine location, escape, and rescue; (2) object location and small-object recovery; (3) large-object salvage; and (4) a man-in-the-sea program.

At first it seemed as though this program would itself beget no less than 16 new submersibles. The largest part of the program called for 12 deep submergence rescue vehicles capable of reaching 6,000 feet. They were to be able to mate with a distressed submarine and bring her crew back to a surface vessel in seven round trips taking 17 hours. They were to be airlifted and deployed around the world in such a way that any submarine crew could be recovered within 50 hours of a disaster. But only one of the craft had been launched by 1970, and its operating depth had slipped substantially. The full force will not be operational before 1975. The 12 vehicles originally planned have now been cut by a half.

The program to recover large objects, which means intact submarines, has slipped even further. Using specially designed lifting ships, it was originally hoped to bring up 1,000-ton weights by 1970 from a depth of 1,850 feet. It was thought that objects could be recovered from 600 feet by 1966, and that eventually weights of even 2,000 to 10,000 tons could be lifted from 20,000 feet of water. By 1970 the situation looked very different. It was hoped to be able to lift 1,000-ton weights from 850 feet of water by 1974. Advanced development had still not been begun.

A similar story surrounds the program to locate objects in deep water and recover light aircraft debris. Four vessels were originally planned, each able to descend to 20,000 feet and bring up bombs or other equipment weighing 250 pounds. Again, they were to be operational by 1970. But by that year the vehicles were still in the design stage and not expected to be operational before 1975.

On January 17, 1966, the Navy's problems were further compounded. On that day a nuclear armed B-52 collided with an aircraft tanker over Spain. Three of the bombs were scattered over land, two releasing radioactivity. But the fourth parachuted down and was blown out to sea, there to sink 6 miles off the coast in 2,850 feet of water. For 82 days the search went on. It took three weeks to get the *Alvin* and the *Aluminaut* to the scene, where they were assisted by one of the Perry Cubmarines and by a remote-controlled device for recovering torpedoes called "CURV." Four other research ships were used, together with 25 Navy vessels and some 3,000 men. Existing sonar systems for locating the bomb proved inadequate, and it was only when an experimental system was hurriedly put together that the recovery operation could begin in earnest.

While this drama was going on, a panel of presidential science advisors was debating ocean strategy. Its report, "Effective Use of the Sea," was published in June 1966. It took the Navy to task over a good many issues, not the least being the slow progress made in the DSSP project. But its criticism went deeper still. "Academic oceanography," it said, "would hardly exist if the Navy, chiefly through the Office of Naval Research, had not provided leadership and imaginative support during the past 20 years." It continued: "Both direct evidence from budgets and indirect evidence from excellent research proposals for basic studies which have been refused suggest the need for increased Navy support of the basic oceanographic sciences and technologies."

This was advice the Navy took quickly to heart. One result was the launching of the highly classified Deep Ocean Technology (DOT) program in 1967. Its broad purpose was to provide technical knowledge for the development of underwater weapon systems of advanced design. There are few clues as to what directions the program is now taking, but consider the following statement about DOT by Rear Admiral O. D. Waters in a talk given in June 1967.

> I suggest that industrialists with an interest in future developments in oceanography keep an eye on it. As a line item in next year's requested budget it accounts for only $4 million but this is largely for basic studies that will soon lead to bigger things. . . . Immediately it includes experimental work on such things as deep mooring devices, super-strength plastic material, power packages and the whole complex of problems involved in facilities implanted on the deep ocean floor. For the bureaucratic locution "facilities implanted," let's just substitute the more interesting statement that the Jules Verne idea of cities under the sea is no longer just a science fiction idea. This calls now for research and development for life support in a new and most hostile environment, new problems in underwater communication, in deep underwater navigation and a host of other problems that arise in connection with the whole new enterprise of sea floor engineering.

There is now evidence that one reason why the DSSP project has gone so slowly is that the Navy has found more interesting things than recovery and rescue to do in the deep ocean. With some foresight, Nick Valery wrote in *Science Journal* in 1967:

> The military aspects of DSSP include the possibility of placing missile silos on the sea bed and,

> with this, the ability to seek out and counter
> similar establishments built by a potential enemy.
> But a more immediate military objective covered
> by DSSP funds is the development of new pres-
> sure hull designs and materials which ultimately
> should permit the collapse depth of combatant
> submarines to be pushed even lower—perhaps
> down to 2500 metres—and underwater speeds
> raised to 50 knots.

Official confirmation of this was slow in coming. But there was a significant addition to the President's report to Congress on Marine Science Affairs in 1969. Every year this report summarizes progress and follows a standard pattern. But the 1969 report included the following paragraph after the introduction to DSSP, which was not included in 1968.

> Application of deep submergence and ocean
> engineering technologies also now appears feas-
> ible in the areas of mine warfare, amphibious
> operations, undersea command and control sys-
> tems, advanced undersea strategic weaponry, and
> underwater surveillance and reconnaissance.

Clearly a game of double-bluff is being played out beneath the sea. What poses as civilian scientific research often turns out to be naval research, with naval applications in mind. And what appear to be specific military programs for the rescue of submarine crews and objects turn out to be at least partly geared to quite other purposes—purposes which if openly acknowledged might not receive financial support quite so readily.

All this makes it difficult to assess where we are going in oceanography and just how far we have gone. The magazine *Scientific American* made a valiant effort to do this in a special issue dated September 1969. The editorial material made hardly any mention of military involvement, although the advertisements carried the message loud and clear. Willard Bascom, president of Ocean Science and Engineering, Inc., was given the unenviable job of telling his audience about technology and the ocean. "The entire area of military technology, which is the most sophisticated of all, must be outside the scope of this article," he wrote, virtually admitting defeat. "The best of modern seaborne military technology is done in secrecy, with budgets far in excess of those spent for any of the other areas."

Submarine Colonialists

The first Polaris submarine was deployed in 1960. As we have by now come to expect, work on the next generation of sea-based deterrents began in the same year. For the U.S. Navy, Project Hydra began to sketch in the many ugly heads which nuclear weapons could sprout when placed on or in the ocean and on or under the ocean floor. And in the summer of 1964 the Navy's more scholarly advisers were called to another summer study, known as Seabed, to thrash out the ways the last ounce of deterrent value could be squeezed from the ocean's vast bulk.

The prime area of interest, according to Erwin J. Bulban, was "the basing of medium-to-long-range ballistic missile systems in the ocean in specially designed, submersible vessels capable of operating in depths of from approximately 1,000 ft. to 11,000 ft." By a happy accident the Navy's DSSP program, with its 16 submarine rescue vehicles able to operate down to 6,000 feet, got off the ground in the same year. Thus was the Navy able to get a good deal of the research needed for its next generation of weapons done under a more peaceful guise.

But the Seabed study produced other ideas. From it stemmed research on a submarine able to launch 32 missiles stowed horizontally and fired like torpedoes (Polaris and Poseidon are stowed vertically). Another study investigated a 40-missile submarine, with the missiles stored outside the pressure hull. The Dolphin and the NR-I were launched to investigate the depth capabilities of submarines. Late in 1968 approval was given for $150 million to be spent on a specially designed, quiet turboelectric submarine to be launched in 1970. And in that year work began on three new submarines, priced at $536 million, which would be able to reach 40 knots and 2,000 feet. The Navy's submarine construction bill soared from $149 million in fiscal 1969 to $505 million in 1970.

The missile systems ULMS and SABMIS, mentioned in the last chapter, also turned into multimillion-dollar programs. They were all part of the Navy's plan to prove that the only safe place to keep nuclear weapons was where the Navy could control them— and in so doing show that there was yet another arena into which the American military presence could be extended. Like the Air Force a decade before, the Navy argued that two things needed to be done to the oceans. The first was to fill them with naval weapons. And the second was to colonize them with naval aquanauts to look after the weapons. Both ideas were heavily concealed within a dense fabric of pretense about the importance of ocean exploration for the future of mankind.

When forced to admit its plans should have some relevance to strategy as well as human welfare, the Navy argued along the same lines as the Air Force had. Nuclear wars, it said, would be safer if they were fought over, on, or under the sea rather than on land. For the benefit of the Pentagon and Congress, one naval jingle writer managed to put all this in three lines and stress its fiscal wisdom at the same time:

> Move deterrence out to sea,
> Where real estate is free,
> And where it's far away from me.

The Navy's case was given a helpful boost in 1968 by the "effective use of the sea" report already mentioned. One such effective use, the report suggested, might take the form of "missiles of Polaris' size or even considerably larger placed on relatively shallow underwater barge systems on the Continental Shelf in a way which conceals their location and requires the system to move infrequently so that the potential of its being tracked by motion-generated noise is minimized. In addition one might consider a slightly mobile ocean-bottom system which creeps along." In fact, this had already been considered. According to the American journalist Seymour Hersh, the Westinghouse research facilities in Baltimore, Maryland, received an $82,000 contract in 1964 for studies of a "bottom-mobile weapon system."

The report went on to suggest that such systems might require "underwater maintenance by personnel also located underwater." Earlier it had been argued that if space was to become a battlefield, the moon was "high ground" that should be occupied. If the ocean floor is also to become a battleground, the Navy now suggested, there was oceanic high ground, in the form of seamounts, which should be occupied. Technically, these are features on the sea floor standing at least 1,000 meters above their surroundings. About 1,400 seamounts have been found in the Pacific, and these represent perhaps only 10 per cent of the total.

Dr. John Craven, who led the Seabed study and later the DSSP program, has this to say about seamounts:

> In the Pacific, the extensive chains of sea mounts
> divide the Pacific Ocean into a specific number of
> basins which are now identifiable by the sea
> mounts which constitute Wake, Guam, the New

Hebrides, the Fijis, the Gilberts, the Marshalls, the Ryukyus, the Kuriles, etc. Even now, these islands are important elements in the strategic outer periphery of the Asian land mass. The occupation and utilization of the undersea portion of these strategic barriers will make even more effective the utilization of the outer islands as a commercial, political, and military balance to the mainland.

The first seamount to be occupied by the U.S. Navy, in 1964, was an extinct volcano 192 feet below the sea surface to the south of Bermuda. There, in a metal tank called "Sealab I," four Navy divers spent 10 uncomfortable days getting used to the high-pressure atmosphere of helium, oxygen, and nitrogen which filled the tank. Afterward Captain George Bond, projects officer for DSSP, wrote:

This means that the riches of the continental shelves of the world, so long protected by the ocean environment, are now within the reach of man for purposes of sensible exploitation and wide exploration. Thus, submerged continents equal in total to the land mass of Africa are available for the use of mankind. Now the petroleum, mineral and food resources of the sea will be accessible to our civilization.

For the next Navy experiment, Sealab II, a crew of 18 military and 10 civilian divers was assembled. Scott Carpenter was appointed chief aquanaut for the project. This move invited comparisons of the exploration of inner and outer space, and the Navy was able to point with satisfaction to the benefits for mankind to which their studies, but not those of outer space, might lead. There was less talk about the actual jobs of the military divers, which included the salvage of a jet aircraft, patching a submarine hull, testing new recovery tools, and construction of an underwater weather station.

These experiments were run entirely by the Navy, and it is not surprising that they should have been for Navy use—perhaps it is more surprising that they have also helped civilian ocean technology along. But there are other ocean projects which appear to be mainly civilian but where in fact the Navy calls the tune. One such project is Tektite, an experiment run by General Electric with financial help from the Department of the Interior, NASA, and the U.S. Navy. It enabled four civilian scientists to spend 60 days at a depth of 50 feet in the sea off St. John in the Virgin Islands. The Navy's role in this project was larger than it superficially appeared to be. It assumed, for instance, "operational direction for implementation of the scientific mission's plans and objectives." A press release from the Navy continued:

> Tektite I provides the Navy an opportunity for exploration in related areas of underwater technology. These areas include underwater medicine and safety, and engineering and construction, to name but a few. The experience gained by the Naval Command Submarine Medical Center and the Naval Facilities Engineering Command in the Tektite program will have impact on future long duration scientific studies, and will provide new tools for Naval Operation readiness.

What the Navy should have operation readiness for was outlined earlier by Rear Admiral John K. Leydon. "The hypothesized missions used for structuring the deep sea program in ocean technology are: occupation, for the purpose of exploiting critical ocean floor sites on the continental shelf off the U.S., seamounts located near the U.S., continental slopes off the U.S., and similar areas located elsewhere; . . . installation and operation of surveillance systems both on the ocean floor and at mid-depth." Another writer, H. D. Palmer, is more specific. "Applications of manned stations," he claims, "include submerged repair facilities, supply depots, re-arming and communications relay stations."

The complex way in which the affairs of the Navy and the university are intermeshed is well-illustrated by Project Tektite. One of the participants was the University of Pennsylvania. A scientist from that university proved in 1947 that midget submarines could take off from and return to larger submarines moving underwater. In the experiments the university scientist piloted the midget submarine; the same scientist was partly responsible for the idea of Tektite.

The Navy's interest in Tektite was through its DSSP man-in-the-sea program, which, as I have pointed out, became relevant to "amphibious warfare," among other things, in 1969. And in that year it was announced that the Navy submarine *Grayback* had been refitted to enable it to land troops underwater. *Grayback* had been converted to carry two electrically driven "pods" housing aqualung troops. The pods make their journey to land underwater and the troops disembark, still underwater, near the coast. After their surprise attack they can return via their pods to their mother submarine. Howard M. Wittner, general manager of GE's Missile and Space Division, chose not to stress this kind of application when discussing Tektite at a conference in Brighton. "The Tektite marine science mission now underway," he said, "is a very 'real' mission as it is responsive to mankind's needs for intensifying the use of food from the sea in the War on Hunger."

General Electric has more ambitious plans for ocean exploration. Its project Bottom-Fix is designed to provide manned stations at depths down to 12,000 feet, and eventually 20,000 feet, suitable for "a wide variety of deep-ocean missions, both military and scientific." These stations are to consist of spherical modules linked together and made from a glass-ceramic manufactured by Corning (the Navy's military submersibles *Deep View* and *Hikino* are to have pressure hulls of a similar material, also provided by Corning). The spheres can be linked together in the ocean depths, where they would be tethered to the ocean floor. It is hoped that such stations could be operational by 1980; they will have their first trial on the mid-Atlantic ridge at a depth of 6,800 feet.

There are several other plans for deep ocean stations. General Dynamics, the manufacturer of many submersibles, including the military NR-I, and the Autec I and Alvin II, both of which operate at 6,500 feet, is working on a station to operate at 6,000 feet for 30 days. Called DOMAINS (Deep Ocean Manned Instrumented Stations), they will be anchored about 50 feet above the seabed in such a way that by releasing anchor and ballast the station can be quickly floated to the surface if danger threatens. The station itself consists of two vertical cylinders, each 48 feet high, in which five men can live on four floors. The station is being developed for the U.S. Navy Civil Engineering Laboratory. As such, it is just one of the concepts developed for that laboratory's Manned Underwater Station (MUS) project. This has been underway since 1966 and calls for one of the two cylinders to house a 30-ton, 100-kilowatt nuclear power plant. The station, models of which have been test-towed at San Diego, would be buoyant and anchored to the sea floor. It would then be winched down to the desired depth. First tests of the station are due for the early 1970s.

On January 5, 1968, the *Philadelphia Inquirer* told its readers of another Navy-supported industrial project. "Working under Navy contract, researchers here are studying ways to house up to 1,000 men on the deep ocean floor to establish advanced undersea warfare systems, claim U.S. territory or assist industrial ventures." The contract was with North American Rockwell's Ocean Systems Operations for a study known as "SOAMUS," the study of one-atmosphere manned underwater structures. Operating depth of this enormous military colony is to be 6,000 feet. North American is also designing the Beaver submersible, "intended primarily for oil well servicing." Later in 1968 North American president John R. Moore put the shoe on the other foot when addressing the American Society of Oceanography. "Only rapidly diminishing technical barriers," he said, "are preventing a foreign power from establishing a deep ocean base a few miles off the Los Angeles shoreline."

One of the largest underwater contracts, worth from $70 million to $100 million, has gone to the University of Miami and the Chrysler Research Department for Project Atlantis. The first Atlantis station, a cylinder 12 feet in diameter and 75 feet long, will be moored in 1,000 feet of water off the east coast of Florida in 1972 or 1973. A year or so later it is hoped to deploy five of these stations at 6,000 feet. This Atlantis network will serve as a command and control center for antisubmarine warfare. Each station will have a nuclear power supply and will house 10 to 12 men for up to 30 days. Crews will be delivered to the stations by a submersible which can mate with the underwater structure. Eventually it is hoped that the stations can be deployed at 12,000 feet.

Although not openly acknowledged as such, these programs are probably part of the Navy's Deep Ocean Technology program. And there are almost certainly others which have not been publicly mentioned. Lockheed, for instance, is said to be working on a Project Turtle, a station which could support a submerged and manned missile base capable of crawling along the ocean floor and setting up thermal gradients in the water to confuse enemy sonars.

But the most intriguing Navy project is Rock Site, about which there appears to be only one piece of published information. This was an article written by Dr. Carl F. Austin of the U.S. Naval Weapons Center which appeared in the November–December issue of *Sea Frontiers*. In it Dr. Austin described how bases under the sea floor could be constructed by drilling out from the land, as is already done for some undersea coal and mineral mines. Dr. Austin described in detail how the undersea shaft could be linked to the ocean floor and made accessible from above. "The tools and technology," he said, "exist today." To prove the point, the article was accompanied by several photographs, all credited to the U.S. Navy. Their captions read:

> Eel Point on San Clemente is under consideration
> as the location for the Rock Site installation. A
> 1200 foot deep shaft at the shoreline would extend

to nearly 2½ miles offshore where access and
vehicle locks would be constructed (U.S. Navy).

Hole in one. This 108-inch diameter drill bit, used
to drill a mine shaft through difficult water-bearing
sediments with one pass of the bit, is examined by
the author (U.S. Navy).

Keeping the sea out, this bulkhead and lock door,
designed by a mining company, can withstand 520
pounds per square inch of water when closed
(U.S. Navy).

Beneath the Atlantic, 3 miles offshore and 2700
feet below sea level, this undersea rail haulage
line is located off the east coast of North America
(U.S. Navy).

Undersea machine shop, 500 feet long and 30 feet
high, is located 1500 feet below sea level and 2½
miles offshore. It is beneath 400 feet of water
(U.S. Navy).

Dr. Austin's article talked about the applications of this program
as offshore production of minerals and petroleum and tapping geothermal energy beneath the sea bed. *Ocean Science News,* however,
made the following comment:

The Navy's interest is not primarily ocean mining
or geothermal energy. The Navy is thinking specifically in terms of sub-seafloor military bases
operating surveillance gear, manning missile
stations, and providing logistic support and staging
areas for the undersea military forces of the future.

It might, for instance, be possible to service a submarine fleet from
such installations, meaning that the subs need never surface at all.
Eventually, if missiles on the sea floor are thought to be less detectable than submarines, how much more secure might be a silo
actually under the ocean floor? The only clue to its existence would
be a series of small underwater hatches constructed on the ocean bed.
   Undersea mines are today all connected with land by a tunnel.
"A major goal of the Rock Site program," writes Dr. Austin, "is
cutting this air umbilical and achieving completely submerged and
isolated undersea operations wherever valuable and geologically possible." He goes on to describe how such stations might support 50
men obtaining their oxygen from the electrolysis of seawater and
their power from a nuclear generator. Cost might be $40 million to

$80 million for stations beneath 500 or 1,000 feet of water. Of the possible uses of such a station, "military bases" is quoted first.

Thus the race to colonize the oceans is well under way. It has some similarities with the space race, and the arguments used to goad it along have often been identical. Thus Dr. Athelstan F. Spilhaus, Dean of Minnesota's Institute of Technology, wrote in 1964: "Man *is* going to colonize the oceans, and it might just as well be *our* men." If Commander Jacques Cousteau's dream of breeding a new race of man, *Homo aquaticus,* able to survive and breathe underwater is to be fulfilled, there seems little doubt that the race will have American nationality and military intentions. "It seems clear," writes Seymour Hersh, "that the Navy has the technology and the desire to expand the miseries of the present arms race to the 70 per cent of the world's surface under the sea. It may be too late to stop the Navy's ambition."

The Ocean Dilemma

In August 1967 Malta asked the United Nations to debate a proposal that the seabed and the ocean floor be reserved exclusively for peaceful purposes. These regions, the Maltese memorandum suggested, "are the only areas of our planet which have not yet been appropriated for national use, because they have been relatively inaccessible and their use for defence purposes or the economic exploitation of their resources was not technologically feasible."

In subsequent hearings before the House of Representatives, Robert A. Frosch, Assistant Secretary of the U.S. Navy, challenged this view. "That is an incorrect statement," he said. "I would prefer to deal with some of the details of it in closed session." Dr. Frosch was referring to the installation of sound-emitting, direction-finding beacons and sonar detection networks already sited on the deep ocean bottom. And these are not the only instruments deployed there. The Advanced Research Projects Agency has put down 30 seismic recording units on the ocean floor, 10 of them in water deeper than 15,000 feet. It has designed units for operating at 30,-000 feet. And it has an unmanned station working at 12,600 feet some 80 miles off the coast of California and linked to the mainland by cable.

The Maltese resolution also proposed that financial benefits from ocean-bottom exploitation be used primarily to promote the development of poor countries. Dr. Frosch had other comments to make.

The Maltese resolution, he said, and certain phrases therein, were what he would propose if the aim was to "slow down the exploitation of the seabed for the longest possible time."

The point is not an obscure one. The U.S. Navy currently spends about $2,100 million a year on applied research and development. Some of this, of course, is spent on such developments as new naval aircraft of no relevance to ocean science or technology. But the rest —by far the larger part—goes to projects of real oceanographic interest. It is used to support more than 30 research laboratories, each spending more than $1 million a year, some a great deal more. These include the Naval Electronics Laboratory, the Radiological Defense Laboratory, the Underwater Weapons Systems Engineering Center, the Mine Defense Laboratory, the Ordnance Laboratory, the Oceanographic Instrumentation Center, the Ordnance Test Station, the Underwater Sound Laboratory, the David Taylor Model Basin, the Underwater Ordnance Station, the Naval Research Laboratory, the Training Device Center, the Naval Missile Center, and the new Ocean Engineering Facility on San Clemente. The latter, a small island some 60 miles off the California coast, seems destined to become the Navy's equivalent of the Air Force Vandenberg Base— the military space center. San Clemente was to have been the site of the Sealab III experiment, of the launch and repair facilities for the Deep Sea Rescue Vehicles, and was under consideration as the base for Project Rock Site. The island is owned and administered by the U.S. Navy. It forms part of the San Clemente Island Range, which is operated by the nearby Naval Underwater Warfare Center in Pasadena. Polaris, Subroc, and Poseidon have all been tested on this range.

In addition, the Navy runs several other ranges. The latest of these is AUTEC, the Atlantic Undersea Test and Evaluation Center situated in the Tongue of the Ocean area off the Bahamas (near Andros Island). The site was leased from Britain in an agreement made in 1963 and occupies an area about 100 miles long and 15 miles wide. In places the range is more than a mile deep, and some 1,000 hydrophones have been installed there. The range was surveyed by the Alvin research submersible while working for the Woods Hole Oceanographic Institution. Cost of the whole project has been estimated at more than $150 million.

A good deal of the Navy's applied research money goes to industry. An assessment for 1964, and a forecast for 1970, shows just how much of the U.S. government ocean funds spent by industry lies in the defense field:

	1964	1970
Defense	$454 million	$1,000 million
Civil	$127 million	$300 million
Waste treatment	$335 million	$305 million
Total	$916 million	$1,605 million

Even this table is misleading, for it does not include funds for anti-submarine warfare. In 1970 the Navy spent almost exactly $2,000 million in this area, of which some $600 million went to research, development, testing, and evaluation. Even in 1967 more than 160 private industrial concerns had some practical interest in antisubmarine warfare work.

In addition, the Navy claims considerably more than half of its government's spending on basic ocean science. United States funds for marine science totaled $528 million in 1970, and of that the Navy spent $298 million. This money is used to support Navy oceanographic research. In 1970 the Navy was operating 31 of its own research and survey vessels, five aircraft, and at least three submarines. In addition, it was providing more than 50 per cent of the funds required to operate a further 28 privately owned research ships. Occasionally, the Navy abuses its privileged position in this field. Although it had only one oceanographer on board, the U.S. spy ship *Pueblo,* which was captured by North Korea in 1968, sailed under the guise of oceanographic research—to the fury of many oceanographers who saw it as a precedent which would eventually curtail the international nature of their work.

Most Navy support of civil laboratories is done through the Office of Naval Research. The ONR, according to one of its spokesmen, Rear Admiral John K. Leydon, has helped build up the Scripps Institute of Oceanography, the Woods Hole Oceanographic Institution, and oceanographic study at New York University and the University of Washington. In addition, it has provided these institutes with nine research ships and was largely responsible for establishing oceanographic research at Johns Hopkins University, Texas A & M University, Oregon State University, MIT, and the Universities of Miami and Rhode Island. "The marine geophysics area, in particular," the admiral notes, "has received increased emphasis over the years because of its growing importance to undersea warfare." He was also careful to make clear that support of civil research has no altruistic aims. "The Navy must continue to play a dominant role in the support of basic oceanography," he writes, "in order that: (1) major parts of the national effort go into those phases of the science which have the greatest Naval Application; and (2) no broad area is neglected because of changing fads in the research community."

The ONR also takes care to learn about those bits of oceanography that it does not support directly. To this end the ONR branch in London visits about 300 European laboratories every year. The information gathered during these visits is transmitted back to Washington in the form of an average of 200 reports every year. In addition, the branch publishes a journal, *European Scientific Notes,* which is distributed to some 7,000 selected people in U.S. government agencies and laboratories. Most of the content concerns so far unpublished work and the journal is marked "not part of the scientific literature." It is not available to members of the press. ONR London also transmits back to Washington copies of about 2,500 published articles every year, 75 per cent of them from Britain. ONR's activity from London is called "foreign scientific liaison." European scientists who have found their work "developed" by American naval laboratories even before they have had time to publish it in Europe have coined some less-complimentary terms for this type of information collecting.

Perhaps significantly, ONR London has recently become more concerned with applied research of immediate interest to naval development programs. It has been given an important role in the Mutual Weapons Development Program, in which it acts as a link between the U.S. Navy and British and other European military establishments.

Another device by which the Navy attracts the interest of non-naval scientists is its series of summer studies. These began in 1948 and were instrumental in leading to the Polaris concept and many of the new sea-based weapons. They often last for several months, involve very eminent scientists, and are always classified. J. R. Marvin, Deputy Director of the Naval Analysis Group, and F. J. Weyl, once ONR's chief scientist but since appointed as the National Academy of Science's Special Assistant to the President, have this to say about summer studies: "From the mid-fifties onward, summer studies became regular activities, conducted in considerable number and engaging summer after summer most of the prominent members of the scientific community. A wide variety of subjects of graduated difficulty is thus being studied by teams that operate essentially according to the rules we have outlined."

I have written at length about the American naval position because the information is publicly available. But probably a similar position exists in other advanced countries. For instance, Nick Valery had this to say of the British situation in 1967: "The biggest spender in the oceanography business in Britain is still the Ministry of Defence. Not counting the Royal Navy's military research programme, something like £4.25 million is being spent this year on surveying operations. This work is being carried out by Royal Naval personnel who have at their disposal five ocean survey ships, four coastal and inshore ships and two Antarctic survey vessels."

From all this it is clear that the pace of oceanographic research is largely controlled by the military. Because of this, as Dr. Frosch points out, if the seabed were to be preserved only for peaceful uses, the pace would slacken. But what about the direction of oceanographic research? Senator Claiborne Pell of Rhode Island has spelled out the implications. "Our national dependence on the Navy for the major sponsorship of ocean development has left gaps in the national program. . . . We trail the Soviet Union in fisheries, we are far behind the Japanese in aquaculture, and we have left to the French most of the development of systems to obtain sea power."

Looked at globally, of course, the situation is much worse than that. In a saner age it would be unthinkable that most of our knowledge of 70 per cent of the earth's surface could be locked up in the confidential drawers of the world's military establishments. It would be unthinkable that so much money could ever be wasted on activities that have done so little to provide the fruits of an unowned resource to those who so badly need it. And it would be unthinkable for anyone to believe that the search for nuclear security under the oceans could ever be any more successful than the search for it proved to be on land, in the air, or in space.

Our priorities in the past, it would seem, were more wisely assessed. "Give a man a fish," an old motto runs, "and he will eat a meal; teach a man to fish and he will eat forever."

CHAPTER IV

The Environment Wreckers

Tests and Fallout–Swords into Plow-shares–Ecological War–Human In-secticides–MilitaryDinosaurs–Earth-quake Hazards

---

"We are running an arms race with
ourselves, and very frequently the threats
that we can see five years ahead,
for example, are the threats that we
ourselves pose."

> Dr. Jerome Wiesner
> *Industrial Research* (July 1969)

No two points on the earth's surface are farther than 45 minutes away from one another by missile. No city could survive attack from one large thermonuclear weapon. No continent could last out the full blast of a nuclear holocaust. What is there left for military technology to do? And, having thoroughly explored the strategic potential of space and the oceans, where is there left for it to go?

The answers to these questions are probably "nothing" and "no-where." There are few, if any, ways left of making life cheaper than it is. There are no longer any technical avenues to increased na-tional security. But to assume that military technology will therefore grind slowly to a halt is unfortunately too optimistic. The research shows few signs of coming to an end. And its continuance is likely to pose a threat to survival in more ways than one.

One quite distinct danger, common to nearly all the military tech-nologies of the future, is the danger of accident—a danger inherent in an arms race that requires our military technologists to run a race with themselves toward the new destructive powers that lurk in every test tube. On this score, I believe, our main worry is not that they will be successful. It is rather that in the process of failure they will be led to experiment with forces they do not understand and thus expose the civilians they are trying to protect to the chance of massive accident, massive pollution, or both.

As much, as we shall see, has already happened in Vietnam. The chemical poisons that have been spewed over that country in the name of peacemaking have now produced the "unpredictable" side effects which many scientists, of course, predicted. Equally "unpredictable" is the chance that continued nuclear testing will eventually trigger off an earthquake in a populated area or that military experiments in weather control may meet with more results than now seem likely.

A related problem, which we will explore in passing, results from the way military technology forces the pace in a research area and then hands over the results to industry. Thus have our civil engineers been given nuclear explosives on a plate and told to find peaceful uses for them. By and large, nuclear excavation, for example, is an unwanted technology and one whose hidden risks may well exceed its dubious value. In the decades to come, our civil meteorologists may likewise find themselves saddled with the techniques of weather control which they neither sought nor wanted and are certain not to know how to use.

Finally, it would be a mistake to think that this problem of military catastrophe is anything new. The seeds of destruction, sown many years ago, may even now be sprouting their shoots of death. They first promised to do so in 1945, the year in which military technologists turned themselves into environment wreckers *par excellence.*

The day before the first atomic bomb was exploded the physicists who had gathered to watch the test fell to discussing one of the more alarming possibilities of success. It was conceivable, they argued, that the heat from the bomb would be sufficiently intense to start a fusion reaction in the air. If that happened, the atmosphere itself would ignite in a blazing fireball that would encircle the earth. "I invite bets," said the famous Italian-born physicist Enrico Fermi, "against first the destruction of all human life and second just that of human life in New Mexico."

Taken literally, his fears proved groundless. Yet that explosion, and those that followed it, did release into the atmosphere an accidental form of pollution whose effects are still being felt and evaluated.

Tests and Fallout

On October 2, 1956, President Eisenhower addressed himself to the question of fallout from nuclear tests. "The continuance of the present rate of H-bomb testing by the most sober and responsible scientific judgment," he said, "does not imperil the health of humanity." President Johnson's complete about-face on this question, in a television address almost exactly eight years later, contains many lessons. "Atomic explosions," he told the nation, "were poisoning our soil and our food and the milk our children drank and the air we all breathe. . . . Radioactive poisons were beginning to threaten the safety of people throughout the world. They were a growing menace to the health of every unborn child."

Johnson could say this because a year earlier the partial test-ban treaty had been signed. Eisenhower could say what he did because at that time there was a body of scientific opinion that held that tests were almost harmless. New evidence, some as recent as 1969, shows that no respectable scientist can ever again hold that opinion. At the same time pressures are building up for atmospheric nuclear tests to be restarted.

In fact, even as early as 1956, Eisenhower was on shaky ground. After 1945 the United States defense authorities showed a marked reluctance to come clean on the question of radioactive fallout. Their reluctance was understandable, because in fact they knew very little about it. There were bitter quarrels in those early years between the authorities and the scientists who had helped develop the bomb —many of the latter arguing that the public should be told more about the hazards of fallout and testing.

But in 1954 the changing wind blew heavy fallout from the Bravo test over four Marshallese islands and over the Japanese fishing vessel, *Lucky Dragon*. This was a disaster that could not be hushed up. For two years the affected islanders required intensive medical care, and one of the fishermen eventually died. In the light of this Eisenhower's remark appears particularly unfortunate.

It has now been made doubly unfortunate, for radiation effects on the Marshallese islanders have come to light which were quite unexpected. The radiation has proved to have a 10-year delayed effect.

By 1969 it was found that 17 out of the 19 children on the island of Rongelap who were under ten at the time of the 1954 explosion had contracted thyroid growths. The first case was not

discovered until 1963, although some of the children had been observed to be growing only slowly. As the thyroid gland is impli-
cated in the control of growth, it now seems clear why the children
grew so slowly. (Two of the children when aged twelve were only
as tall as a normal seven-year-old, and their bones had matured
only to the extent expected of a five- and a three-year-old.) Tests
have shown that the growths—some of which have now proved to
be malignant—were caused by radiation, probably through drinking
water contaminated by radioiodine. Many of the thyroid growths
have had to be surgically removed.

Such is the legacy of radioactive fallout. And while these particular effects were not appreciated in the 1950s, there was even then
a body of scientific opinion that realized full well the dangers inherent in testing. By 1958 concern had become so strong that the
American Nobel Laureate Dr. Linus Pauling organized a petition
to the United Nations. It urged the case for a test ban and pointed
out that continued testing might cause "an increase in the number
of seriously defective children that will be born in the future generations."

Pauling's petition collected the signatures of more than 9,000
scientists from 43 countries. There can be no doubt it helped in
negotiating the test ban five years later. The United Nations itself
reported twice on the question of fallout, in 1958 and again in
1962. The second time round it resolved all ambiguity about how
much of what kind of fallout or radiation caused detectable damage. "All research has confirmed the fact," the report read, "that
ionizing radiation produces genetic damage at all doses and dose
rates so far tested."

The next year the test-ban treaty, prohibiting nuclear tests in
space, in the atmosphere, and under the sea, was signed in Geneva.
But by that time at least 423 nuclear weapons had been tested—
5 by France, 23 by Great Britain, 124 by the Soviet Union, and
271 by the United States. Together they had a total yield of 511
megatons. We can be sure that these tests have added significantly
to the deaths and casualties of the atom bomb's first victims at
Hiroshima and at Nagasaki. The extent of the damage already inflicted—and still occurring—is only now becoming clear.

In 1969 Professor Ernest J. Sternglass of the University of Pittsburgh published some alarming results from a long computer study
of the effects of radiation on the fetus and the infant. His first
research had led him to the towns of Albany and Troy in New

York. Relatively heavy fallout had occurred there after a 43-kiloton explosion in Nevada in April 1953. Five years later a dramatic increase in leukemia had been found in both towns.

Professor Sternglass found that there were also more fetal deaths or stillbirths than would normally have been expected, and these even as long as 13 years after the test. He then looked at the data for the United States as a whole and found much the same was occurring. The rate of decline of fetal deaths—expected from improved medical practice—had begun to decrease sharply soon after atmospheric tests began in Nevada in 1951. Actual rises in fetal death rates were first found in 1954—the year the first large H-bombs were tested—and the same happened again in 1961, when the Soviet Union began its tests of large-megaton weapons.

Other figures showed that many more children died under the age of one than would have been expected. By 1964 the infant death rate in Sweden was nearly half what it was in the United States. The percentage of live births in the United States had dropped from second highest in the world in 1946 to eighteenth place by 1964.

Most alarming of all, Professor Sternglass calculated that between 1951 and 1966 there had been in the United States 375,000 more infant deaths than would normally have been expected—and this, he added, "has continued at a rate close to 34,000 a year" ever since. "Public health organizations," he added, "have made a world-wide effort to understand the origin of this disturbing trend that has by now started to affect the whole world."

Professor Sternglass was convinced that the cause was strontium-90—a long-lived radio isotope that is produced by atomic explosions. His evidence was that the number of excess fetal or infant deaths rose in step with the total amount of strontium-90 produced, the amount deposited as fallout, the amount found in children's teeth and bones, and the amount found in American milk. He analyzed figures not only for the United States as a whole but for each individual state and for a number of individual towns. "It now appears," he wrote, "that what we may have witnessed was a totally unanticipated genetic action of strontium-90 on the human reproductive cells of such a magnitude that it may well have turned the world's existing stockpiles of nuclear weapons into a biological doomsday machine for all mankind."

These facts are grim enough. What would they mean translated into the terms of nuclear war? Professor Sternglass explains:

> In the 20 years of atmospheric testing, 200 mega-
> tons of fission energy was released. If this was
> responsible for the increase in the death rate of
> one in every hundred live births, then a release
> of 20,000 megatons anywhere in the world—the
> amount which would be needed for an effective
> first strike along with the defensive warheads
> that would be used against it—would mean that
> virtually no infant would survive to produce
> another generation.

I do not want to include in this book information which is of dubious scientific value. And it is only fair to record that Professor Sternglass's argument has been heavily criticized—by doves and hawks alike. There is, however, no doubt that a real problem exists. Even some of Professor Sternglass's severest critics now regard the fallout situation as one requiring immediate and drastic action.

Thus Drs. John Goffman and Arthur Tamplin, of the AEC's Lawrence Radiation Laboratory in California, had this to say to a congressional committee in November 1969. "The most crucial pressing problem," they warned, "is to secure the earliest possible revision downward by at least a factor of ten fold of the allowable radiation dosage to the population from peaceful nuclear energy activities."

They went on to claim that there would be "disastrous consequences to the health of the public if this recommendation receives less than immediate serious attention." These consequences included an increase of 16,000 additional deaths from cancer in the United States for every year of inaction.

The situation is now doubly unfortunate. Just as this kind of alarming new assessment of the dangers of fallout is beginning to appear, pressures are mounting for nuclear weapon tests to be resumed in the atmosphere. The reason is that it may be difficult to develop the next generation of ABMs without these tests.

There is also renewed pressure for increasing still further the rate of underground nuclear testing. This pressure comes not so much from the makers of nuclear weapons as from those who would like to see nuclear explosives used for peaceful purposes. The idea of turning the nuclear sword into a plowshare may be praiseworthy enough in principle. In practice, the whole affair provides an unhappy illustration of what can happen when a powerful military technology is thrust forcibly into the hands of industrialists who, by and large, neither wanted it nor believed that it could be used safely.

Swords into Plowshares

Project Plowshare was the name given by the Atomic Energy Commission in 1957 to their plan for making nuclear explosives available to civil engineers. It was argued that nuclear excavation could make possible enormous engineering schemes, such as the digging of a new Panama canal, which would simply be too expensive if conventional explosives were used. It was also hoped that nuclear explosives could be used in the recovery of oil and natural gas at greatly reduced cost.

The program was politically suspect from the start. It provided an excellent excuse for continued underground testing for military purposes—yet the testing could be publicly declared to be for civil applications. Furthermore, the program's existence was later to become a powerful argument against a comprehensive test-ban treaty —who in their right mind would ban all nuclear tests when they might give rise to such exciting things as Plowshare promised?

The oil industry, however, was, for the most part, skeptical about Plowshare. Thus Dr. Tom Gaskell of British Petroleum wrote in 1963: "There will have to be a revulsion against the Plowshare type of scientist, who wishes to keep the bomb in business whatever the political danger." Describing the Plowshare reports as "ostensibly humane effusions which have been the bane of oil production departments for some years," he went on to suggest that we should "bury our proud aspirations" and that "before we embark on grandiose schemes which may change things irreversibly we should be grinding out the facts of how nature works."

In spite of this, the danger also spread to Europe, with the setting up in Paris of an industrial consortium ready to reap the rewards of nuclear engineering should they materialize. This firm, Geonuclear Nobel Paso, was formed in July 1968 with a capital of $1 million provided by the American El Paso Natural Gas Company, the French Nobel Bozel, the German Dynamit Nobel, and Poudreries Reunies de Belgique. The firm thought that the underdeveloped countries were the most likely venue for the first nuclear projects and by June 1969 they "had not yet ruled out" the possibility of obtaining nuclear explosives from either France or the United Kingdom.

Plowshare raised in acute form the question of radioactive contamination. The first important point concerned the wording of the 1963 test-ban treaty. The most liberal interpretation of that treaty allows nuclear tests which vent radioactivity into the atmosphere providing the radioactivity is contained within the national boundaries of the state conducting the test.

To provide the required information, some of Plowshare's experimental tests had to be of the kind which formed a crater. It was hoped that the explosive could be buried in such a way that the overlying earth would fall back into the crater, trapping the radiation beneath it. But in April 1965 the 4-kiloton Palanquin test burst through its covering and released most of its radioactivity into the air. The Cabriolet test of January 1968 threw radioactive rocks and dust up as high as 1,900 feet. And a 35-kiloton explosion, Project Schooner, at the Nevada test site on December 8, 1968, released into the atmosphere the highest levels of radioactivity recorded in many cities of western and northwestern United States since the test-ban treaty came into effect.

Between three and seven days later a rise in radioactivity was detected at four sampling stations in Canada. The amounts were small, but according to a Canadian parliamentary reply, "The coincidence with correspondingly higher levels in the United States some days earlier was brought to the attention of the United States authorities." Mexican authorities also reported higher-than-normal levels after a test in January 1968 and concluded, "Any activities higher than normal would be ascribed to atmospheric nuclear tests or to leakage of activity from underground tests near the Mexican border." From this it appears that Plowshare tests have contravened the test-ban treaty, in a minor way, on at least two occasions. In fact between 1963 and 1970, 19 tests vented radioactivity into the atmosphere; and on at least two occasions that radioactivity crossed national boundaries.

It is not surprising, then, that no practical Plowshare venture has so far got off the ground. One of the earliest plans, Project Chariot, was dropped because of strenuous protests about radiation hazards; this project was to excavate with nuclear explosives a harbor in Alaska. A similar plan to blast out a harbor in northwestern Australia was dropped in 1969.

But the Plowshare enthusiasts continued to spread their gospel, claiming they could provide a 2-megaton explosion for as little as $600,000 and in this way move a cubic yard of earth for only 3 cents. Their eyes were firmly fixed on the most massive undertaking they could conjure up—that of digging a new Panama canal.

Scientists argued against the project from many different standpoints. One was that any new canal, however excavated, would upset the ecology drastically by providing another link between two separate oceans. Others claimed that nuclear techniques were too unpredictable, would produce so much fallout that large populations in the neighborhood would have to be moved out, and that this would make the project prohibitively expensive. Professor A. E. Martell, at one time a staff member of the Armed Forces Special Weapons Project and an expert on the effects of nuclear weapons, summarized the objections thus: "The use of nuclear explosives, unlike other proposals, would involve still unpredictable risks of earthquake and of local and world-wide radioactive contamination as well as greater dislocation of local populations." He went on to suggest that digging the canal through one of the proposed routes might require "three 25-megaton and one 50-megaton explosives set off together—an explosion of 125 megatons. If such massive yields are required, the difficulties of nuclear canal construction, perhaps already insurmountable, would be magnified greatly."

They might also have disastrous side effects, for 125 megatons is a blast of considerably more energy than the 1908 earthquake which brought San Francisco to the ground.

It seems very doubtful whether a nuclear Panama will ever be dug. Nevertheless a series of tests is planned in the event that the project goes ahead. In a letter to the chairman of the Canal Study Commission in August 1968, the chairman of the AEC, Dr. Glenn T. Seaborg, summarized the experimental testing that would be needed for the project during 1970 and 1971:

> Project Yawl: several 100-kiloton cratering
> experiments
> Project Galley: seven explosives each in the
> range of a few kilotons to a few hundred kilotons
> Project Gondola: a cratering experiment, design
> dependent on site selection
> Project Phaeton: a 1-megaton cratering experi-
> ment in hard rock

Professor Martell concluded: "There is little doubt that conduct of the proposed cratering tests would be contrary to our obligations under the Nuclear Test Ban Treaty. If these high yield cratering tests were carried out at a continental site, they would also constitute a threat to the public health and safety."

The danger from such tests lies not only in the radiation they may release into the atmosphere but also in the radioactive elements released in the immediate environment of the crater. Professor Barry Commoner, writing in *Environment,* has summarized the issues thus:

> A study of the Sedan shot at the Nevada Test Site provides direct evidence that considerable fallout radioactivity at the site is in the form of readily airborne dust. . . . Pendleton finds that radioactivity is carried by wind from the Nevada Test Site even though no tests are underway. It has been observed that the radioactivity of airborne dust increases sharply in Salt Lake City when there is a strong wind from the southwest. This means that winds travelling from Nevada to Salt Lake City carry dust-borne radioactivity.
>
> The largest concentration of population close to the Nevada Test Site is in Las Vegas, a distance of about 65 miles. It would be of interest to know how much of the huge amount of radioactivity deposited on the soil of the site over the years has been carried by wind into Las Vegas. To what extent have radioactive dust particles lodged in the lungs of residents of Las Vegas? To my knowledge there have been no reported studies of this problem.

The difficulties and dangers inherent in Project Plowshare are such that no single useful civilian project may ever be accomplished. In the meantime, however, the scheme will have acted as a powerful and dangerous political tool. The experimental tests have worsened the test-ban environment, and American and Russian officials have already discussed ways by which the existing treaty might be "relaxed." The optimistic claims of Plowshare exponents also made the nonproliferation treaty considerably more difficult to negotiate, for nonnuclear countries did not want to sign away their rights to what they had been told was a cheap means of earth excavation.

There is, however, another important aspect to the Plowshare affair. During the 1960s there developed a widespread concern for the earth's environment. Past experience had indicated that grandiose engineering schemes invariably harbored hidden catastrophe. No one believed Plowshare was likely to be an exception. And opposition to it was heightened by vigorous battles with the Department of Defense over just what was being carried on in the name of United States policy in Vietnam. The argument did not concern the politics of the situation as much as its ecology.

Ecological War

The first reports that American forces were using chemical weapons in Vietnam made the headlines in 1964. As alarm mounted, press conferences were held in Washington and Secretary of State Dean Rusk tried to reassure the nation and the world that nothing exceptional was afoot. "We do not expect," he told Congress on March 24, 1965, "that gas will be used in ordinary military operations. . . . The anticipation is, of course, that these weapons will be used only in those situations involving riot control or situations analogous to riot control."

Five years later, it was clear either that the anticipation had gone badly wrong or that the whole Vietnam war was regarded as an extensive operation in riot control. For by the end of 1969 the U.S. Army had procured no less than 13,736,000 pounds (about 7,000 tons) of the most widely used gas—CS, an irritant chemical powder which is the modern form of tear gas. And it was not reassuring to recall that chemical warfare in the First World War had begun with tear gas and had quickly escalated to include the use of chlorine, mustard gas, and other agents which together caused more than a million casualties and nearly 100,000 deaths. Furthermore, in that war the total amount of tear gas used by both sides was only about 12,000 tons. The U.S. Army was proposing to use more than half as much in a limited war in one country for "riot control."

But unless B-52 bombers are accepted as a legitimate means of riot control, it soon became clear that CS was being used for something quite different. The *New York Times* reported on February 22, 1966, that CS had been dropped from the air in preparation for a B-52 raid. The Department of Defense was quoted as saying that the purpose of the gas attack was to force enemy troops to the surface where they would be vulnerable to the fragmentation effects of the bomb bursts. And several reports since then have made it clear that CS has been used in loads of several tons to flush enemies out of hiding before bombing and artillery attacks began.

The escalation that followed, however, did not parallel that of

World War I. The mustard gases and the nerve agents, extensively stockpiled in several United States centers, were never brought into action. But in their place appeared an equally insidious and far more novel weapon—the herbicide. It brought to Vietnam a new concept in warfare, one wholly characteristic of the troubled and polluted decade of the 1960s: ecological war.

"Only we can prevent forests" is the motto hung up on the headquarters of the pilots charged with the conduct of ecological war. The motto is not a jest nor even a vain boast. By March 1969 these pilots had dropped from their C-123 Provider planes enough herbicide to treat more than 4,500,000 acres of jungle and cropland.

"Treat" is a euphemism in this context. The word actually means "kill" when the herbicide is sprayed onto crops and it means "remove the leaves from trees" (and probably kill) where it is sprayed onto jungle. The intention is to deprive the Vietcong of both food and camouflage. The results have been something quite different and will be recorded in history as one of the greatest military obscenities of the twentieth century. The total effect has to be considered in relation to the concentration of high explosive also dropped on a limited land space—by 1969 more than the total tonnage of bombs dropped by the United States in Europe and Asia in World War II.

"Whole forests have been smashed into kindling by B-52 strikes," wrote Douglas Robinson for the *New York Times* on September 13, 1968. He continued:

> Both American and South Vietnamese experts are concerned that the war may be changing the entire ecology of the region. . . . Machines, explosives, and chemicals have devastated wide areas where the Viet Cong were thought to be hiding. In many of these areas there is no sign of life except, of course, the Viet Cong who still manage to appear when all else is gone. There are other places where major battles have reduced the land to desert. At Khe San millions of tons of bombs have turned the once green hills into a moonscape of craters and scorched dirt.

The final cost to Vietnam's ecology cannot be counted yet. It is already clear, however, that large numbers of deer, tiger, elephant, monkey, and wild boar are leaving that ravaged land for the relatively more peaceful countryside of Cambodia and Laos. The rhinoceros is no longer seen in South Vietnam; and the elephant has been one of the biggest losers as a result of its useful role as a pack animal. It has been shot down by patrols and by gunfire from helicopters and even jet aircraft.

The effect on the soil may be much more serious. The heavy concentration of chemicals dropped on many areas suggests three dangers: that the more persistent chemicals will prevent regrowth; that the soil will be converted to a hard red rock, a natural process which occurs only slowly under normal conditions; and that the rate of soil erosion will be much increased. No one could make any serious assessment of the long-term future of the soil by 1970. But it takes 20 years for a forest to reestablish itself under normal conditions. Under these particular conditions it seems unlikely the forest will ever return naturally; in its place is arising a dense tangle of shrubs and the ubiquitous bamboo. Once established, of course, these fast-growing weeds leave larger trees little chance of reseeding themselves.

Thus the ecological war becomes a generation war; whatever political settlement is finally agreed may matter less to the next generation of Vietnamese than that their paddy fields and jungles have been destroyed.

Unhappily, the chemical war in Vietnam has become a generation war in more ways than this. Nine years after the defoliation program had got under way, a research study revealed that some of the herbicides might have a "dangerous effect" on the unborn child. Small amounts of some herbicides, it was found, caused rats and mice to produce malformed offspring. Slightly larger amounts of the most widely used herbicide, 2,4,5-T, produced deformed offspring with 100 per cent regularity if administered between the tenth and fifteenth day of pregnancy in these animals.

There is no doubt that these "thalidomide" effects will already be widespread on animal life in Vietnam. Whether they have also affected human life is more difficult to say. But in the summer of 1968 several Vietnamese newspapers printed pictures of badly deformed babies; some of them even then attributed the defects to the herbicide program.

The grim saga that then followed has been meticulously detailed by Thomas Whiteside in the magazine New Yorker. The original report that the defoliants, particularly 2,4,5-T, caused fetal abnormalities was apparently deliberately hushed up. Eventually the details found their way into the hands of the press, and the presidential science adviser, Dr. Lee DuBridge, was forced to make an announcement. He played the matter down but did say that use of the material within the United States would be restricted to areas from which the material could not reach man.

In his announcement, Dr. DuBridge said that studies had shown that "relatively large oral doses" produced a "higher than expected number of deformities." He suggested that it was "improbable" that any person could receive harmful doses of the agent as a result of the way the material was currently being used, and then cast doubt on the validity of extrapolating from animal tests to possible results on humans.

But as Whiteside so convincingly showed, the facts are these. The "higher than expected number of deformities" revealed by the study was actually 90–100 per cent. In some of the experiments all the treated rats that produced live offspring produced deformed ones. And the same experiments showed that 80 per cent of the fetuses were killed before birth—a matter not mentioned by the President's science adviser.

Secondly, the rat is an animal apparently rather resistant to drugs that produce fetal deformation. In the late 1950s scientists who tried to show that thalidomide was teratogenic (induced fetal changes) could find no effects even if rats were given very high dosages. Yet 1 in 10 of the women who took the drug in the crucial stage of pregnancy produced malformed offspring.

Finally, how likely were human beings to ingest potentially dangerous amounts of 2,4,5-T? About 20,000 tons of this material have been sprayed or dumped on South Vietnam in military operations. After reviewing all the evidence, Whiteside reached these conclusions. A pregnant Vietnamese woman could absorb from drinking water "a percentage of 2,4,5-T only slightly less than the percentage that deformed one out of every three fetuses of the pregnant experimental rats. . . ." Furthermore, "A pregnant Vietnamese woman who ingested 120 milligrams of 2,4,5-T in two liters of water a day would be exposed to 2,4,5-T at 600 times the concentration officially considered safe for Americans."

Matters were not improved when the manufacturers of the herbicide claimed that the effect was due not to the herbicide but to a trace contaminant in it. If this were true, it was pointed out, the contaminant must be an incredibly dangerous material. One estimate suggested that it must be some 10,000 times more teratogenically active in rats than thalidomide had proved to be in rabbits (and thalidomide was found to be between 50 and 200 times more teratogenic in humans than in rabbits).

The inevitable soon happened. When the citizens of the small town of Globe in Arizona learned of the newly discovered effects of defoliants, they were finally able to explain—to their satisfaction at least—the curious disease from which Globe had been suffering for five years. Throughout that time neighboring areas had been heavily sprayed with defoliants identical to those used in Vietnam. For five years the inhabitants of Globe had noticed their animal life dying before their eyes. One dog gave birth to a litter of 13 pups, one of which was deformed. Guinea pigs, hamsters, and mice died after having produced deformed offspring. Some 60 per cent of the kids born to a goat herd were either deformed or dead. Birds were found in the gardens unable to stand or move, and a tame peacock was found paralyzed. One woman who was actually directly sprayed while out walking subsequently complained of vaginal bleeding, numbness of the limbs, and painful discharge of milk from her breasts—even though she had had her uterus removed 12 years previously.

As I write, a barrage of American officials is denying that any of these effects have any connection with the spraying that has gone on near Globe. Another barrage is denying that the deformed offspring born to Vietnamese women have any connection with the military defoliation program. And a third barrage is denying that the defoliants produce any harmful effects at all.

All this is bad enough. Yet it is now clear that the ecological war in Vietnam could have had—and may yet have—more profound effects. In any ecological disaster it is not the immediate effects that constitute the greatest danger. The prospect that far greater changes will be brought about by little-understood mechanisms is much more alarming. Let us look at one possibility.

Plague is a disease that is always present in Vietnam. It is carried by wild rats which for the most part remain in the more inaccessible regions of mountainous jungle. Normally, the Vietnamese are reluctant to journey into these areas, citing fear of disease as the principal reason.

The war has brought two changes. Guerillas and antiguerilla patrols have journeyed deep into the jungle in order to execute the war. They have thus been brought into close contact with the animal reservoirs of infection. And the widespread destruction of jungle has driven the wild rat into more populated areas and even the cities. There they have passed plague on to human populations and to the domestic rats that were not previously carriers of the disease.

The figures speak for themselves. In 1961 plague was reported in only one of Vietnam's 29 provinces. By 1966 it had infected 22 of them. And the number of plague cases increased as follows: 1954–1962, less than 40 cases a year; 1963, 119 cases; 1964, 290 cases; and 1965, 4,454 cases. American soldiers as well as the Vietnamese have caught the disease.

The figures do not look potentially disastrous until one realizes the implications. American public health officials are desperately worried about the chances of a plague outbreak in the United States. So far the sources of infection have been confined to the Vietnamese countryside. But it would need only one infected soldier to return to the United States and be bitten by a city rat for the chance of an epidemic to become high indeed. Had this happened when the New York garbage strike was in progress, and when rats ran amok throughout the city, a major disaster could well have occurred. Such are the dangers of tampering with ecology in an age in which disease can be transferred from one side of the globe to another in a matter of hours.

The ecological rape of Vietnam makes unedifying reading. At a time when the world was first realizing that its peacetime activities in agriculture and industry might pollute the planet sufficiently to threaten human survival, massive and deliberate pollution of an entire countryside was being carried out as an act of policy. Even worse, research teams and production plants were hard at it perfecting and manufacturing pollutants that would attack man directly. The object of this research, as one scientist has aptly put it, is to find a "cure for metabolism."

Human Insecticides

Along the west coast of Scotland there is a series of antilitter notices. They remind sightseers to respect the countryside, and to:

> Resemble not the slimy snails
> That with their filth record their trails
> Let it be said where you have been
> You leave the face of nature clean.

Immediately opposite one of these notices, just a few miles offshore, lies the island of Gruinard, the polluted property of the Ministry of Defense. In the 1940s it was sprayed with a disease called anthrax to determine whether biological warfare posed a serious threat. It did. The island is still dangerously contaminated, and, according to the director of Britain's biological warfare defense establishment, is likely to remain so for at least another hundred years.

Gruinard stands as a now more or less permanent reminder that nuclear weapons are not the only ones that threaten our future. Research on chemical and biological weapons has produced agents that could well rival the killing power of nuclear weapons and at the same time wreak changes on the environment of perhaps uncontrollable proportions.

The technical details need not concern us very much. Suffice it to say that a 1-megaton nuclear weapon could destroy a city with a population of 1 million people. Fifteen tons of the most powerful chemical weapons—which are closely related to some agricultural sprays and insecticides—could cause the death of every other human being over an area of 60 square kilometers. Just 10 tons of the organisms that produce crippling diseases such as anthrax and plague might kill one in four people over an area of 100,000 square kilometers. As these are weapons that might be afforded even by less-developed nations, the threat is real enough. It has several dimensions.

The first is that no one quite knows what would happen if the weapons were used. In 1969 a special committee reported to the Secretary General of the United Nations, "The fact that certain chemical and biological agents are potentially unconfined in their effects both in time and space, and that their large scale use could conceivably have irreversible effects on the balance of nature, adds to the sense of insecurity and tension which the existence of this class of weapon engenders." In other words, they increase the chance of war.

But the report continued: "If these weapons were ever used on a large scale in war, no one could predict how enduring the effects would be and how they would affect the structure of the society and the environment in which we live." So if there were a war of this kind, it is not clear how many would survive and what problems the survivors would have to cope with.

A year later a report from the World Health Organization made a brave attempt to probe some of the unknowns. Even a limited use of some of these agents, it suggested, "could cause illness to a degree that would overwhelm existing health resources and facilities." The report's authors were particularly concerned that there would be long-term dangers to human health coming from chronic illness, delayed effects of the agents, the creation of new reservoirs of human disease, and unpredictable changes in ecological conditions.

But in fact neither of these reports dealt in any detail with another related problem. How does the very existence of these weapons affect our chance of survival? Vietnam apart, chemical weapons have not been used on a massive scale since 1918. Biological weapons have never been used. And we may be able to avoid an all-out chemical or biological war in the future. But if the stockpiles remain, if the research continues, if the production plants are not shut down, for how long can we avoid a major accident—one that might produce quite unpredictable effects? The record is not encouraging.

In the United States chemical and biological weapons are tested at the Dugway Proving Ground in Utah—which occupies an area somewhat larger than the state of Rhode Island. But in spite of its size, tests do not always end up on target. In 1969 Congressman Richard McCarthy produced an Air Force map of the area showing a region some 10 miles in diameter labeled "Permanent Bio Contaminated Area." The area lay outside the proving ground on the Wendover Air Force Range situated to the east. Faced with this evidence, the Army admitted that it had put a "teacupful" of anthrax bacteria on the site 15 years previously.

The congressman later charged that dangerous tests had been carried out with a disease called Venezuelan equine encephalitis—a rare and lethal form of sleeping sickness. Hardly had he done so when a United States stockpile of nerve gas on the island of Okinawa sprang a leak and 24 people had to be taken to the hospital. They suffered a happier fate than the 6,400 sheep that got in the way of a cloud of nerve gas a year earlier in Utah, for they all survived. The sheep died.

It was this event, more than any other, that brought home the dangers of the situation. Nerve gas has frequently been tested at Dugway, but the experiment conducted on March 13, 1968, proved an extraordinarily ill-fated one. The jet aircraft that was spraying 320 gallons of nerve gas opened its tanks over the target area, but one of them failed to respond to the subsequent "jettison" command—and was still spraying when the pilot pulled out of his dive. A cloud of nerve gas was swept over 30 miles of country into Skull Valley, where it settled on sheep pastures and fodder. Had the wind been blowing in another direction, the cloud would have passed over a road.

Nine months later the Army was still denying that its test had affected the sheep in any way. But congressional hearings eventually wrung a confession from the Army. There was the additional confession that in the first six months of 1969 there had been five tests with nerve gas contained in 8-inch howitzer shells and four more in which 17 pounds of nerve gas were released 18 feet above ground.

The hearings were held by a subcommittee under Chairman Henry S. Reuss and started late in May 1969. Unusually, the Army witnesses were sworn in to tell "the truth, the whole truth, and nothing but the truth." What came out revealed that many previous statements had been a good deal less than the whole truth—a discovery which led Representative Guy Vander Jagt to detect a "pattern of deception" which had clouded the whole issue. The chairman was equally forthright. When Army witnesses failed to provide relevant information, he ordered them to "call the man at the Pentagon who has it and get him up here as fast as he can come." The chief scientist at Dugway also invoked the chairman's indignation. Asked why he thought the gas could be sprayed without danger, the scientist replied, "Well, it never had in the past escaped from the proving ground." Chairman Reuss replied: "Doctor, you frighten me. You really do. Who gave you your authority to spew these poisons all over the environment? Who told you to do that?"

Testing extremely toxic weapons is not the only hazard. These materials also have to be manufactured, stored, and when their "useful" lifetime has expired, disposed of. The story of the Rocky Mountain Arsenal at Denver is the story of all three hazards.

The arsenal became one of the main centers of chemical warfare during World War II. It learned the tricks of making nerve gases first from the Germans and then from the British—whose initiative had discovered a chemical so toxic that two or three drops placed on human skin would cause death within minutes. A decision was made to manufacture vast quantities of both types of nerve gas, and the arsenal soon realized it had a disposal problem on its hands. What to do with the toxic sideproducts of the manufacture of nerve gas and related commercial compounds?

The arsenal's answer was to dig a 12,000-foot-deep well and sluice the chemicals down it. The well was connected to a 20-mile-long reservoir of porous rock deep below the earth's surface. Between March 1962 and February 1968, no less than 163 million gallons of toxic waste were poured down the well.

But a month after the well was first used, Denver had its first earthquake in 80 years. This was no coincidence. For four years earth tremors followed every large disposal of waste down the well. Some were strong enough to break windows in houses 20 miles away. An investigation showed a near-perfect correlation between the rate of waste disposal and the occurrence of tremors. The chance that one did not cause the other, said Dr. Maurice Major of the Colorado School of Mines, was only "two or three chances in 1000."

The trouble was that when the disposal was stopped after four years, the earth tremors went on. Geologists suggested that the liquid waste had acted as a lubricant between layers of rock deep below which were under stress. As long as the liquid remained there, tremors seemed likely to continue. So plans were made to pump the liquid out again. But a study showed that no more than 300 gallons a day could be pumped up and at that rate it would take 1,488 years to clear the lot. The liquid was there to stay. Meanwhile geologists predicted an increasing chance of a relatively severe earthquake in the area.

This itself made worse a not entirely novel problem. For many years both mustard gas and nerve gas had been stored in the arsenal. The arsenal's boundaries join those of Denver's main international airport, and one of its chemical storage areas lay in direct line with the airport's north-south runway. An aircraft making a crash landing might well have produced an accident affecting much of Colorado. And the chance that the arsenal's own waste disposal techniques would trigger an earthquake in an area where so much toxic material was stored appeared as a very vicious circle indeed. The upshot was that the Army decided to relocate many of its toxic agents and to dispose of its oldest stocks.

It was then discovered that this plan involved the dumping in the Atlantic of 27,000 tons of obsolete chemical weapons. Material from four arsenals was to be moved halfway across the United States in four trains consisting in all of 809 cars. The material was found to include 3.4 tons of the tear gas CS, 4,786 tons of mustard gas, and 2,152 tons of nerve gas. This was not all. The nerve gas was contained in weapons ready for use. The weapons consisted mainly of bomb clusters—each cluster containing 76 individual bombs, each of which contained 2.6 pounds of the nerve gas. There were also 13,000 rockets filled with nerve gas ready for firing.

Although the Army had dumped chemical weapons into the

Atlantic on at least three previous occasions, it now emerged that no detailed studies of what might happen had been carried out. Nor had adequate precautions been taken to eliminate the chance of an accident as the toxic material was shipped across the country. The trains were not required to follow a rail route avoiding big cities, they were not given a speed limit, and they were not to be paced by a pilot train to lessen the chance of accident. In the congressional hearings that followed, Senator Harrison A. Williams called the plan a "poisonous parade across America" which represented the "ultimate in railroading risk." A high-level scientific committee was called in to advise on how else the weapons could be disposed of. Even they, however, were forced to admit that some of the material would probably have to end up in the Atlantic—as indeed it did in 1970.

In the final analysis, the point about the Rocky Mountain Arsenal affair is not whether the plans for the testing, stockpiling, and transporting of toxic weapons had adequate safeguards. Whatever safety precautions are taken, it is simply not possible to handle such large quantities of lethal materials for any length of time without incurring the risk of accident. At Fort Detrick, for instance, where most of the research into biological warfare is carried out, the safety precautions are reportedly superb. Nevertheless, there have been 420 accidents there in 26 years. And in 1969 it was reported that 270 cows grazing downstream from the laboratory's sewage disposal plant had suffered from an inexplicable illness.

In the long run the chance of an accident is virtually inevitable. In the last third of the twentieth century it is rising particularly fast because of external threats. Airports and railways are busier and accidents there more likely. Sparsely populated areas where weapons might be tested are becoming rarer. And, of course, as population densities go up, the effects of an accident become more serious.

In the civil field, the prospect of technological catastrophe has already been recognized. Speaking before a Senate subcommittee in 1969 Dr. Jerome Wiesner, past science adviser to two American Presidents, claimed that "we are engaged in a race between catastrophe and the intelligent use of technology, that it's not at all clear we are going to win." To what extent the pace of that race is governed by military technology has not yet been established. Few people have pointed out that if we are worried about aircraft pollution, for instance, the accusing finger should be pointed at air forces before civil airlines. Over Britain, at any rate, there are twice as many military aircraft movements a year as there are civil ones.

One of the greatest dangers of future military research is accidental or deliberate pollution. And military pollution may be harder to combat than its civil counterpart. For one thing, it is conducted in the name of national security and thus is often held to be above criticism. For a second, it is often done in secrecy and therefore is not subject to the checks and restraints which protect us from other technological follies. It is in this context that we should examine the big military technologies of tomorrow.

Military Dinosaurs

In July 1960 William J. Kotsch of the U.S. Navy published an article called "Weather Control and National Strategy." It is worth quoting from in some detail.

> Recent advances in the weather science demand the immediate establishment of a vigorous, comprehensive, and imaginative atmospheric research program under governmental sponsorship. The lowest price for procrastination in this regard will be political, economic, social and military paralysis. The highest price will be absolute obedience to the leaders in the Kremlin.
>
> The ability to control the weather and climate will become America's and the Free World's key to survival. . . . With all that is at stake, it is inconceivable that the Soviets would not employ large-scale weather control techniques as soon as it is within their powers to do so, *regardless of the effects upon the Free World.*

This kind of pleading is not unusual in the technical press that serves the U.S. armed forces. Indeed, the phraseology is almost standard and can be used to whip up concern about any and every new scientific field which may have military relevance. Space weapons, laser death rays, antisubmarine warfare, and ocean technology have all had the same treatment. What is surprising is that anyone takes them seriously. But they apparently do, and weather control has been no exception.

For instance, the Office of Naval Research has supported Project ACE, standing for "Atmospheric Control Experimentation."

The Naval Ordnance Test Station first developed a method of producing large quantities of silver iodide from silver iodate. The chemical is used in large amounts in the Navy's Project Stormfury, for instance, in which experiments have been done in dispersing fog and clouds, suppressing hailstorms, and seeding hurricanes to dissipate their energy or to steer them away from United States coastal towns. The U.S. Army has been involved in experiments in which small pieces of metal chaff are scattered into thunderclouds. The chaff is the same material as that packed in nuclear warheads to confuse enemy radar. In the thundercloud it serves a different purpose—it appears to trigger lightning discharges in the cloud, thus making ground strikes less likely.

These programs have civil equivalents in several other countries. And clearly their primary purpose is not to develop a new and aggressive military technique but to improve the weather close to home—and particularly close to important military establishments where fog and storms can delay important strategic flights. But the fact that they are financed by defense agencies is worrying. It means that important results can be easily classified and that defense scientists are always at hand to exploit any new and unforeseen military potential. Nor should we overlook the fact that if lightning strikes can be suppressed, they can probably be triggered; and that if hurricanes can be steered away from U.S. coasts, they can be steered toward other, less friendly regions.

The destructive potential of weather control should not be lightly dismissed. A single lightning strike can release the energy equivalent to 1 ton of TNT—and more than a hundred lightning strikes occur every second over the globe. In the western United States, they cause more than 10,000 fires annually. The energy contained in a thunderstorm cloud is about the same as that released by a 1-megaton bomb. A moderate Atlantic hurricane is equivalent to perhaps 1,000 megatons. And a large Atlantic depression rates 10,000 megatons—roughly the explosive force that would be used in an all-out nuclear war.

But if such large forces are involved, man's puny efforts to exploit them might well be thought ineffective. Not at all. The art of weather control lies in exploiting the instabilities of the weather system—in finding the triggers that will delay or set off the massive energy displays that we call weather. There is every chance of success. Dr. Gordon J. F. MacDonald, executive vice-president of the Institute for Defense Analyses and chairman of a special panel appointed to study weather control, claims that "No matter how deeply disturbing the thought of using the environment to manipulate behaviour for national advantage is to some, the technology permitting such use will very probably develop within the next few decades."

The phraseology is a little misleading, for the technology will not develop of its own accord—it will be developed as a result of a deliberate decision to vote money to this end and to try to get results. But Dr. MacDonald is quite clear about the implications:

> The political, legal, economic and sociological consequences of deliberate weather modification can be so complex and far-reaching that our present involvement with nuclear affairs will seem simple. . . . Past experience demonstrates that much smaller technological changes than environmental control can transform political and social relationships. Experience also shows that such transformations are not entirely predictable and that guesses based on precedent . . . are likely to be quite wrong. . . .

This, in a nutshell, is the classic case of what we might call the military dinosaur. A technical possibility emerges for the large-scale manipulation of behavior for national advantage. The advantages of such manipulation have not been specified, nor has it been outlined how any weapon of this kind could be used to achieve ends not already possible by other, more direct military means. The defense agencies back a research and development program. And then it is pointed out that the implications of success are unpredictable and far-reaching. The parallels with Enrico Fermi's atmospheric fireball are obvious—except that we have no evidence that our fears will prove to be as groundless as were his.

The problem of weather control illustrates these points clearly—but the emphasis I have put on it is accidental. Instead I could have mentioned again the plan dreamed up by the U.S. civil space agency to put into orbit a large mirror to reflect sunlight onto Vietnamese forests during the night and thus make guerilla infiltration more difficult. I could have dwelt on the Navy's Project Sanguine—a plan to crisscross 22,500 square miles of Wisconsin with buried cables carrying as much as 800 megawatts of power (enough to supply a large city). The object of this piece of technological mania is to provide a communication system for submarines that would remain functioning after most of the United States was obliterated in a nuclear war.

Or I could have raised the alarm, as Sir Bernard Lovell has done, about the prospect of seriously depleting the ozone layer in the atmosphere by continually thrusting through it rockets burning up to 15 tons of fuel every second of their journey. And I would have stressed that substantially more than half of these rockets were financed by defense agencies and that many of the civil ones also had military implications.

But to have dwelt on these prospects, and other similar ones, would still have left one question unanswered. Can even defense agencies get away with experiments likely to have profound and instantaneous effects on the environment? The historical record is not encouraging.

In 1958 the United States exploded three hydrogen bombs 310 miles above the earth. Each of these "Argus" explosions produced an artificial aurora as bright as a full moon and each severely interrupted long-distance radio communication. The experiments were not announced by the Pentagon, either before or after the event. Only some smart detective work by the *New York Times* science editor, Walter Sullivan, made public to the world that an experiment affecting the environment of the entire earth had been carried out in secret.

The depressing thing about this experiment was that the ensuing public outcry did not stop its repetition. In 1962 it was learned that a 1.4-megaton bomb was now to be exploded at a height of 250 miles. Strong protests were made to the United States both by astronomers and by politicians. The Americans replied that the explosion could have no lasting consequences on the environment.

The device—known as "Starfish"—was set off as planned above Johnston Island on July 9, 1962. "The American predictions," Sir Bernard Lovell wrote, "turned out to be entirely wrong." The explosion released into the earth's magnetic field some 10^{27} fission particles. Instead of dropping quickly into the atmosphere, they became trapped in space in a band stretching right round the globe. Magnetic disturbances, interruptions of radio communication, and auroral displays followed. The presence of this space pollution thwarted, perhaps forever, scientific experiments designed to find out what space was like in the important region in which the particles were trapped. And for many years the particles acted as a source of confusion and irritation to radio astronomers trying to study the heavens. The Russians did not improve matters by carrying out similar experiments a few months later.

It is now clear that neither the Argus nor the Starfish explosions increased the national security of the United States. Nor did they lead to radical new weapons that could be used in space. We can expect similar negative results from the military technology of the future. But because it is likely to be carried out nearer home—and not in the distant regions of space—there are few reasons for thinking that its effects will be harmless. There are some for thinking they may be disastrous.

Earthquake Hazards

It is a geographical accident that the Nevada Test Site lies only 240 miles from the San Andreas fault—a fracture in the earth's crust that slices through California in a grim reminder of the 1908 earthquake that reduced San Francisco to a pile of disease-ridden rubble. The small earthquake that took place in this region in 1971 bears witness to its seismic activity. Seismologists point with alarm to two underground 1-megaton nuclear weapon tests carried out in 1968. Both caused fracturing and faulting of surface rock 5 miles from the test site. A third test, unhappily called Faultless, produced a 5,000-yard fissure in the earth's crust. More tests of this kind, they claim, could easily trigger off an earthquake disaster in the western United States. They are probably right.

The Atomic Energy Commission, while publicly dismissing the danger, has clearly found the problem worrying. For one thing, it was threatened by court action from Howard Hughes, multimillionaire and owner of a large tract of the Nevada desert. No doubt partly because Hughes' resources could well afford a massive court case, the AEC deemed its Nevada Test Site unsuitable for very large underground tests and developed a new one farther from Hughes' hometown of Las Vegas. Less happily, it decided to conduct the very large tests that were needed for the development of antiballistic missiles on the island of Amchitka off western Alaska.

And in spite of widespread public protest, it carried out a megaton test there in October 1969. Two more tests, each of several megatons, were planned for the future. Amchitka's remoteness from population centers, however, did not still the critics. They pointed out that the island lay in an earthquake-prone area and that geological knowledge of the surrounding sea floor was minimal. About all that was known was that the Aleutian Islands, of which Amchitka is one, are part of the Pacific seismic belt which is the most active earthquake area in the world. The largest earthquake of 1965, the Rat Island earthquake, originated just 20 miles from Amchitka. And the October test was detonated underground between 20 and 60 miles from the Aleutian Island fault system. Several scientists pointed out that no one would dare to set off a large explosion that close to the San Andreas fault in California.

What, then, is the evidence that underground tests could trigger off earthquakes? First, there is the undeniable evidence that they already have. When pressed on the matter, the AEC eventually admitted that one of its 1968 tests had produced around 10,000 measurable aftershocks which continued for a period of four weeks after the test. The announcement gave rise to some frenzied activity among seismologists.

At the Massachusetts Institute of Technology, the Japanese seismologist Dr. Keiiti Aki reported that one of the 1968 tests produced an earthquake of magnitude 5.9 almost immediately after the test. By earthquake standards this is small; a very large earthquake often reaches magnitude 8 or more.

However, three seismologists at the University of Nevada then went back to examine their records of 21 tests carried out in the Nevada Desert. They found that all of them increased seismic activity, sometimes dramatically, for at least several days after the explosion. The effects extended up to 12½ miles from the explosion and in one instance for twice that distance. They found, for example, that in the 83 hours before one test their instruments had recorded only one natural earthquake. In the eight hours following it, they recorded no less than 32 earthquakes, all detectable but small enough not to produce damage.

Such findings were made more alarming by new knowledge about earthquakes themselves. Addressing a meeting of geophysicists in 1969, Dr. James N. Brune of the California Institute of Technology claimed that "in many cases large earthquakes may be considered successions of triggered events rather than smoothly propagating ruptures." He pointed out that the great Alaskan earthquake of 1964 was started by an event of magnitude 6.5 and was soon followed by one of magnitude 7.8 which did all the damage. It was no comfort at all to learn that the largest underground nuclear test ever carried out by the AEC recorded itself as an earthquake of magnitude 6.5.

Three scientists from the University of Miami, C. Emiliani, C. G. A. Harrison and M. Swanson, then went on to examine the effects of 171 underground explosions at the Nevada Test Site between 1961 and 1966. They concluded:

> It is clear that underground explosions trigger
> earthquakes up to about 32 hours afterwards. The
> data available to us show that in the 32-hour
> interval after the explosions there were 228 earth-
> quakes, or an increase of about 62 per cent over
> the expected number of 141. . . . We have verified
> that the seismic effect of the explosions extends to
> the 860-km limit of our search. It may still be
> noticeable at greater distances.

There are other ways by which tests could make themselves felt at great distances. One of the greatest hazards of earthquakes is that those originating under the sea floor give rise to tsunamis or tidal waves. Their effects are disastrous and widely spread, frequently spanning the entire width of the Pacific Ocean. And the Aleutian area, where the AEC's Amchitka test site is situated, is infamous for the tsunamis that have originated there. Writing in *Science Journal,* John Phillips began an article on tsunamis with these words:

> Early in the morning of April 1, 1956, a heavy
> earthquake occurred in the Aleutian Trench. It
> generated a tsunami which covered the 3600 km
> to Honolulu in 4 hours and 34 minutes, an average
> speed of 784 kilometres an hour. The waves were
> over 15 meters high on some parts of the coast:
> they smashed hundreds of buildings, tore up roads
> and railways tracks and swept the debris out to
> sea. Twenty-five million dollars worth of damage
> was done; 173 people were killed and many more
> injured.

It would be scientific to conclude this section with an estimate of the probability that future nuclear tests will trigger earthquakes and tidal waves. No such figures are available. We know only that a test could cause an earthquake and a tidal wave. But we also know that the results of such a catastrophe become potentially more serious every year.

In Denver nerve gas manufacture led to an earthquake hazard to the nerve gas storage tanks. The same vicious circle is apparent in the nuclear field. The plutonium that comprised the Nagasaki atomic bomb was made by reactors in Hanford in Washington State. After the war nine more reactors were built there and their radioactive wastes stored in 140 underground tanks. The tanks are still there, containing 55 million gallons of waste which has to be artificially cooled to keep it from bursting through the walls of its containers.

Twenty-four years after the site was selected, it was given a geological survey. The results showed the area to be one of "moderate earthquake activity" and to be covered with an unusual pattern of fissures reminiscent of those found at the site of the 1964 Alaskan earthquake.

Each of these tanks probably contains more radioactivity than the fallout produced by all weapons tests since 1945. The tanks are not designed to withstand earthquake shock. If the cooling system or pipes leading to the tanks were ruptured, hot radioactive gases would be released into the wind and might travel large distances. If the tanks themselves were ruptured, the wastes might find their way through groundwater into the Columbia River.

Such cumulative effects of military technology cannot be ignored for very much longer. It remains quite impossible to estimate the chance of a disaster from any single cause such as ecological change, weather control experiments, nuclear tests, or accidents with biological weapons. But the risk goes up with every new hazard that is added to the list. The further ahead we care to look, the higher the chance of accident becomes. And the more possibilities we add to the already large range, the higher is the chance of a cumulative catastrophe. To list all the possible combinations in a world of increasing complexity would merely turn this book into a catalogue of potential disasters. If any insight into the problem is to be gained, it is more instructive to examine the nature of the scientific effort which is so unwisely turning the possibility of disaster into probability.

CHAPTER V

Science in the Warfare State

The *Military-Industrial Complex–*
The Military-Scientific Complex–
Colonizing Civilian Science–Tech-
nological War

"The needs of defence, or the presumed
needs of defence, to a considerable
extent condition the kind of technology,
and to a lesser extent the kind of
science, that is encouraged in countries
which by political circumstances have
been forced into the arms race."

Sir Solly Zuckerman
Scientists and War (1966)

The deep malaise that confronts today's science and
technology can be illustrated by two statistics: (1) In one year, 60
per cent of all those people studying for doctor's degrees in mathematics in the United States applied for jobs at RAND—the Air
Force's military think tank. (2) In ten years United States industry
increased its scientific manpower by 160,000 people. Of these,
130,000 went to work on government-supported military projects.

These figures are evidence of the massive demand for scientific
manpower that exists in the "warfare state." But it should not be
thought that this is a special problem of the United States (or of
the Soviet Union, for that matter). It exists in all countries that are
involved in the technical arms race. And its effects are felt even in
those nations which long ago decided to play no part in the nuclear
nightmare.

164

If one country decides to spend 32 million technical man-hours to develop just one missile—the Atlas D, for example—so much gets sucked down into the military whirlpool that the effects of the decision are felt the world over. First, the civilian centers go short. Second, the flow of scientists and technologists through the educational machine is stepped up. A time lag is inevitably involved, and so the conditions are laid for a future situation in which jobs have to be found for the new graduates; the forces then provide a public service by taking them on to study more military possibilities.

Meanwhile, the civilian centers have been hard at it recruiting from elsewhere. Today about 10,000 scientists, technologists, and doctors emigrate to the United States every year. According to Professor Richard Titmuss of the London School of Economics, this influx of manpower has since 1949 saved the United States taxpayer more money than the total amount spent by the United States in foreign aid over the same period. The net result, we all know, is a brain drain from the poor to the rich countries.

What is more rarely pointed out is that it is ultimately a brain drain from the civil laboratories of the developing nations to the military complexes of the rich nations. Thus do the hungry and over-populated regions of the world help nurture the nuclear fixations of the rich. Viewed as a threat to survival, this phenomenon is doubly alarming. Not only does it help perpetuate the nuclear instability of East-West relationships, but it is a source of great tension between the Northern and Southern nations. Not only does it hasten the onset of World War III, but it makes more real the prospect of World War IV.

This is the background against which we should judge the role of science in the warfare state. My aim in this chapter is to show how close science and war have become. Their marriage, if not harmonious, is intimate: neither can now exist without the other and neither can see where the other is leading it. Nor has the marriage been a fertile one: science has not improved any country's "national security"; and the clarion call of national security has not provided those particular scientific fruits which might otherwise have scattered their seed over a hungry and overpopulated earth.

But, like other marriages, this one has produced things that no one quite foresaw and which certainly no one wanted. The first and most fearsome of these—judged alone by its power and ultimate uselessness—is the arms industry. The military-industrial complex owns more scientists than any other sector of the economy. In relation to its output, it uses them far more intensively than any other industry. And its influence has been felt throughout the world.

The Military-
Industrial Complex

President Eisenhower made his famous and much-quoted warning against the military-industrial complex in 1961. "We have been compelled to create a permanent armaments industry of vast proportions," he said. "We must not fail to comprehend its grave implications. . . . In the councils of government we must guard against the acquisition of unwarranted influence, whether sought or unsought, by the military-industrial complex. The potential for this disastrous rise of misplaced power exists and will persist."

How seriously was Eisenhower's warning taken? For a simple indicator of progress, one can turn to the level of spending of the U.S. Department of Defense. In 1961 the DoD was spending $47,-808 million a year. Today its budget has almost doubled, to $80,600 million in 1970. With that rise has come full justification for Eisenhower's concern. In 1968 an unsuccessful presidential candidate, Senator Eugene McCarthy, was led to conclude, "With military missions in many parts of the world . . . with its own business of selling billions of dollars worth of arms—for cash or credit—all around the world, with its involvement now in 'civil action' or 'nation-building' in many of the underdeveloped countries, the Defense Department has become perhaps the strongest independent power in world affairs."

This was more than a politician's clever turn of phrase: it was a statement of fact. In 1970 the DoD received more money than the national income of any country in the world except the Soviet Union, the United Kingdom, France, West Germany, or Japan; it was larger than the Gross National Product of the whole of Latin America. To put it another way, one American government department had an income roughly the size of the income of Canada and India put together.

Approximately half this income goes to industry in the form of $40,000 million worth of contracts and orders every year. In 1967 this complex of military and industrial forces employed 103 out of every 1,000 working Americans. Thus military activities involved one-tenth of the labor force and consumed about one-tenth of the country's Gross National Product. Something in the region of 120,-

000 individual suppliers helped DoD to dispose of its largesse. The aircraft industry was the biggest beneficiary in 1969 with $7,000 million of defense sales. Close behind came ammunition ($2,900 million) and ships ($898 million), with furniture ($20.2 million) and even musical instruments ($1.6 million) bringing up the rear.

But though there are many defense suppliers, there are only a few important ones. Two-thirds of military spending goes to the top 100 firms, and half the total goes to only 25 companies. In 1968 the top five companies were General Dynamics ($2,200 million), Lockheed ($1,900 million), General Electric ($1,500 million), United Aircraft ($1,300 million), and McDonnell Douglas ($1,100 million). GE, for instance, was involved in work on sophisticated radars for the ABM system, reentry systems for new Minuteman missiles, and swiveling gunners' stations for the Army's combat helicopter, Cheyenne. In addition, its annual report for 1968 claimed, "As a socio-economic contribution, the Missile and Space Division played a major role in establishing the first Negro owned and operated aerospace company, Progress Aerospace Enterprises, Inc. The division assisted in training technicians, awarded the firm its first contract and evaluated its first piece of delivered hardware, a component for a GE space project."

Another characteristic of the defense market is its stability. Of the top 25 defense firms in 1966, 21 had been in the top 25 a decade earlier. Here, clearly, is one of the causes of the "mad momentum" of the nuclear arms race which Robert McNamara referred to in his famous speech of 1967.

However, a more careful analysis suggests that the momentum is not so much mad as carefully controlled. The first level of control is within the Defense Department itself. In 1969 the DoD had on its own payroll no less than 6,140 public relations officials. In addition there was a special band of "legislative liaison" lobbyists whose job it was to promote defense interests on Capitol Hill—in 1969, for example, 339 of these had a special budget of $4.1 million.

Industry itself cements its relationship with the defense establishment by hiring senior officers of the armed forces as they reach retiring age. A congressional subcommittee revealed in 1960 that the firms that supplied 80 per cent of U.S. armaments employed no less than 261 retired admirals and generals, and 485 officers of the rank of colonel or Navy captain and above. General Dynamics, at that time still the top defense firm, had 186 retired officers on its payroll, and its board chairman was a former Secretary of the Army.

Here we have another indication of what has happened since

Eisenhower's warning. In 1969—less than a decade later—Senator William Proxmire charged that the top 100 defense firms now employed 2,062 retired officers of the rank of colonel and above.

As well as competing with one another for military contracts, the defense firms also unite for their common good. Through their membership in the National Security Industrial Association, they provide the Defense Department with about 7,000 advisers. The Aerospace Industries Association provides another powerful voice for the space and defense lobby.

Geography also acts as a lever on the system—in the form of the senators and congressmen anxious to divert defense money into their own districts. *Newsweek* cites the Charleston, South Carolina, district of the former House Armed Services Committee chairman, the late L. Mendel Rivers, as an extreme example:

> Rivers's South Carolina district has an Air Force base, an Army depot, a Naval shipyard, a Marine air station, the Parris Island boot camp, two Naval hospitals, a Naval station, a Naval supply center, a Naval weapons station, a fleet ballistic-missile-submarine training center, a Polaris missile facility, an Avco Corp. plant, a Lockheed plant, a General Electric plant under construction and an 800-acre plot of ground that has just been purchased by the Sikorsky Aircraft Division of United Aircraft. The military payroll alone is $2 billion a year. The main gate at the Air Force base is "Rivers Gate," Route 52 through Charleston is "Rivers Avenue," a housing project on the Navy base is "Men-Riv Park." Rivers has claimed credit for landing 90 per cent of this. And he runs on a perennial campaign platform of "Rivers delivers."

But only a very few states benefit to this extent. In 1967 three states—California, Texas, and New York—received one-third of all defense contracts. Two-thirds of the contracts went to only 10 states. In his book *How to Control the Military,* the economist John Kenneth Galbraith has pointed to the absurdities to which this leads. "In all but a handful of cases," he writes, "the congressman or senator who votes for military spending is voting for the enrichment of people he does not represent at the expense of those who elect him."

To many the most alarming feature of all this is not that the Pentagon dominates such a vast empire: it is that the industry which is meant to serve it actually *leads it toward* those contracts and weapons systems which its corporations would like to work on. During the summer of 1969 a group of 11 students organized by the Institute for Policy Studies conducted an investigation into what they called the "National Security State." Their report was a remarkable one, particularly for the information it produced on where ideas for new weapon systems come from. Peter Schenck, an official of the Raytheon Corporation and former president of the Air Force Association, is quoted as saying:

> The day has passed when the military requirement
> for a major weapon system is set by the military
> and passed on to industry to build the hardware.
> Today it is more likely that the military require-
> ment is the result of joint participation of military
> and industrial personnel, and it is not unusual for
> industry's participation to be a key contribution.
> Indeed, there are highly placed military men who
> sincerely feel that industry is currently setting the
> pace in the research and development of new
> weapons systems.

A representative of Pratt and Whitney was blunter still:

> We have the technical superiority and are on the
> offensive. We spoon-feed them. We ultimately try
> to load them with our own ideas and designs, but
> in such a way that, when they walk away from the
> conference table, they are convinced it was their
> idea all along.

Nor was this student report impressed by the defense industry's much publicized moves to "diversify" into the civilian market.

> A recent sampling of the views of industry leaders
> indicated that they . . . have no intention of gam-
> bling in the civilian market. While much industry
> advertising refers to their potential contribution to
> solving the nation's ills, in fact there have been
> little industry funds invested in this area, and
> defense firms have shown little capacity for par-
> ticipating successfully in the civilian market.

The situation may be even worse than this suggests. A look at the way government spending has been divided up over the past few decades shows that the growth of the defense business has actually slowed down the process of healing the nation's ills. In 1939 44 cents of every budget dollar was used in welfare spending, but in

1963 the figure was only 7 cents. In 1939 the government spent $30 a head on welfare programs; in 1963 the figure was $16. And according to Senator George McGovern, the United States military budget in 1963 was higher than the cost of all social welfare programs from 1933 to 1940 combined.

From all this, many people have been led to conclude that conspiracy is afoot; that the military-industrial complex deliberately conspires to impede progress; and that the whole affair simply illustrates the abundant evil of the military mind. Such a view, in my opinion, is actually damaging to the cause of those who hold these views. The military complex is no more, or less, than one admittedly very large part of the economic system. Viewed in this light, it is natural that it should assiduously seek to expand its business and be slow to take up industrial opportunities in civil areas. Furthermore, the ethic of free enterprise on which United States industry is based dictates that the defense industry will grow in times of increasing defense budgets.

Professor Galbraith has a more profound charge to make about the power of the military-industrial-bureaucratic organization. "How," he asks, "did these three forces come to assert authority over a tenth of the economy and something closer to ten-tenths of our future?" This, he claims, really is a reversal of the principles on which American society was founded. At no point in the system can the electorate exert any control on the decisions made. It is not elected leaders but government and industrial officials who in fact determine policy and procedure. This is the real point at issue; and it is the point we should bear in mind when looking at the situation in other countries.

In the United Kingdom the defense budget is much smaller— £2,266 million for 1969–70, representing 6.4 per cent of GNP or about 14 per cent of total central government expenditure. Nevertheless, the industry to which this gives rise is large enough. During the 1960s the Ministry of Defense spent £5,704 million on procurement. To this, of course, must be added figures for arms exports, which over the same period and for major weapons alone came to around £500 million.

At this point information about the British military-industrial complex appears to end. There are no figures available of how many retired officers the firms employ, of how the revenue is divided geographically, or even of how many firms get what share of the market. In this sense, the situation is more alarming than in the United States. How the system operates long ago disappeared from public view and from public control. The nature and number of contracts are not publicly available, nor are there Parliamentary committees constantly probing the workings of the defense establishment.

During 1968, however, the Select Committee on Science and Technology did investigate defense research. The inquiry unearthed a good deal of previously unavailable information but came to some surprising conclusions. Among these were:

> All those involved in initiating and carrying out
> the defence research and development programme
> [i.e., the Defence Departments, Industry, the
> Treasury and the Foreign Office] must be able to
> participate in its formulation.

> We welcome the setting up of a joint research
> committee between the Ministry of Technology
> and the aerospace industry . . . this collaboration
> should be extended to other branches of industry
> that can contribute to the defence programme
> . . . there should be defined channels of com-
> munication between the Defence Departments
> and industry. . . .

> . . . we recommend that consideration should
> be given to a system of joint direction of some
> establishments by Government and industry.

Such quotes, and frequent references to the virtues of the American system, might lead to the conclusion that the committee members were deliberately advocating the setting up of a military-industrial complex of American type. In fact their motivation was Britain's balance of payments. If industry could play a larger part, the argument ran, exports of both civil and military equipment would improve. It seems questionable whether increased exports would be sufficient compensation for a more powerful military-industrial complex. And there was no indication in the report of the fact that balance of payment battles are, in reality, another form of warfare themselves. Any improvement in one country's position must be reflected in corresponding declines in the positions of other countries. On all this, the report was mute.

The situation in many other advanced countries is much the same, and it would serve little purpose to document each individually. But it is important to record the way the arms industries of the advanced nations manage to ensnare the governments of smaller powers into huge military spending. For the rich countries not only cajole the developing world's scientists to emigrate, but they then sell back to the developing countries, at enormous cost, the military products which their more advanced industries are able to manufacture as a result of their greater accumulation of scientific talent.

Considered globally, and not nationally, the implications are terrifying. In 1957, for instance, none of the Third World countries had long-range air-to-surface missiles. But by 1968 these weapons had spread to 19 of the world's poorer countries. Supersonic aircraft—which in 1969 had only military uses—spread to 32 countries of the Third World in 14 years.

The result is a world arms bill of $180,000 million a year. According to the U.S. Arms Control and Disarmament Agency, "Global military expenditures . . . are equivalent to the total annual income produced by the one billion people living in Latin America, South Asia and the Near East. They are greater by 40 per cent than world-wide expenditures on education by all levels of government and more than three times world-wide expenditure on health."

The Stockholm International Peace Research Institute has looked at the long-term implications of these expenditures. If things go on as they are, it concluded,

> . . . then military spending will continue to double
> every fifteen years. By the early years of the next
> century the world will be devoting to military
> uses a quantum of resources which is equal to
> the whole world's present [1968] output. This
> is not so preposterous as it sounds. The world
> is now devoting to military purposes an amount
> of resources which exceeds the world's total
> output in the year 1900.

Here, I think, one can approach an ultimate truth about the military-industrial complex. It is a complex fueled not by conspiracy but by science and technology. Conspiracy alone could never threaten to double military spending every 15 years. New knowledge can. For as soon as one weapon system is out of the factory and on to the battlefield, advances in the military and civilian laboratories have made it obsolete. The result is technical innovation at a rate unknown in any other field of human endeavor.

The Military-Scientific Complex

Senator Barry Goldwater is one of the few people to have pointed up the real nature of the military-industrial complex. On April 15, 1969, he told the U.S. Senate:

> Rather than deploring the existence of the military-industrial complex, I say we should thank heavens for it. That complex gives us our protective shield. It is the bubble under which our nation thrives and prospers. . . . What is more, I believe it is fair to inquire whether the name presently applied is inclusive enough. Consider the large numbers of scientists who contributed all of the fundamental research necessary to develop and build nuclear weapons and other products of today's defense industries. Viewing this, should we not call it the scientific-military-industrial complex?

Indeed we should. The Pentagon operates the largest research and development business in the world. With a current budget of around $8,000 million a year, it is surpassed in size by none. And within the United States it dwarfs all other research and development efforts. In 1970 the Defense Department was spending very nearly one-half of all the money spent by government on research and development. It was spending nearly one-third of all the money used in the United States for research and development, including the money industry itself puts up.

One-quarter of this budget goes to Defense Department laboratories. There are currently about 130 of these, and they employed in 1968 131,641 people, 37,284 of them scientists and engineers. The other three-quarters of the budget goes in the form of contracts to industry, universities, and nonprofit organizations. By far the largest portion—about two-thirds—ends up in industry.

But this is not the end of the story. There are two other agencies, NASA and the Atomic Energy Commission, which also have significant military functions. At least half of the AEC's budget is for weapons research, and nearly all of it is used in projects which have some defense significance. How much NASA money should properly be described as defense-oriented depends on one's view of NASA. But as we saw in Chapter 2, that agency's impact on military affairs is not inconsiderable.

Pulling all this together produces some extraordinary figures. Defense proper, space, and atomic energy command nearly all the money the U.S. government spends on research and development. In 1968, for instance, these three agencies spent $13,243 million out of a total government R&D budget of just less than $15,000 million; their share of the market was 88 per cent. The other 29 agencies provided 12 per cent among them.

"In all," writes Steven R. Rivkin, referring to the situation in 1964, "350,000 scientists and engineers, one out of every four in the country, were employed in industry, universities, nonprofit institutions and government on a full-time basis (or its equivalent) on work connected with defense." This is still true. And it means that a scientist or engineer who does not want to work on defense has to search hard for his money.

There are currently about 2 million scientists and engineers in the United States. Those who have wished to sound the alarm about defense research have claimed that one in five or six of these work on defense projects. In reality the situation is more alarming than even this implies.

About one-third of all scientists and engineers in the United States do research and development—say two-thirds of a million of them. As one-third of a million work for defense-related agencies, one could conclude that every scientist and engineer doing R&D is doing it for the military. This is confirmed by a rough check on budgets. The three defense agencies spend $13,250 million out of a total of $27,000 million—almost exactly one-half. And even this does not include people industries employ at their own expense to do defense research.

This extraordinary situation merits closer examination. The Department of Defense itself pays for about one-third of the United States scientists and engineers doing research and development. But as we have seen, the DoD controls "only" one-tenth of the economy. So if its budget is considered out of all proportion to civil requirements, the use it makes of scientists is much more so. It operates, in fact, the most research-intensive industry of all.

Professor Galbraith, probably rightly, ascribes this situation to the Soviet bomb and Sputnik.

> The natural reaction was to delegate power and concentrate resources. The military services and their industrial allies were given unprecedented authority . . . to match the Soviet technological initiative. And the effort of the nation's scientists

(and other scholars) was concentrated in equally impressive fashion. None or almost none remained outside. Robert Oppenheimer was excluded, not because he opposed weapons development in general or the hydrogen bomb in particular, but because he thought the latter unnecessary and undeliverable. That anyone, on the grounds of principle, should refuse his services to the Pentagon or Dow Chemical was nearly unthinkable. Social scientists also responded eagerly to invitations to spend the summer at RAND. They devoted their winters to seminars on the strategy of defense and deterrence.

While President Kennedy was clearly concerned about the situation, his conclusion was a lame one. "We have paid a price," he said, "by sharply limiting the scarce scientific and engineering resources available to the civilian sectors of the economy." It was left to Professor Galbraith to spell out what that price was:

> The effect of this concentration of talent was to add to the autonomy and power of the organizations responsible for the effort. Criticism or dissent requires knowledge; the knowledgeable men were nearly all inside.

This price, of course, is one that has to be paid only in the context of national security and development. In terms of global security the price is higher. There are currently some five million scientists and engineers in the world. The most optimistic assumption is that perhaps one-third of them are doing research and development. If this is true, it means that one out of every five people working at the world's scientific and technical frontiers is doing so with American military funds; and one in eight of them is working for the U.S. Department of Defense directly. In reality the proportion must be higher still.

The situation in the United Kingdom is on a similar but smaller scale. The UK spends about £1,000 million a year on research and development; and the defense budget for research and development is one-quarter of that, falling from £260 million in 1968 to £236 million in 1970.

In the UK it costs about £10,000 a year to keep one person working on research and development. So of the 100,000 British scientists and engineers doing research and development, 25,000 work with defense money. Again, then, defense is an extremely research-intensive industry. While defense accounts for about 7 per cent of the British Gross National Product, 25 per cent of the country's R&D scientists and engineers are on the defense payroll.

Defense research is not, of course, limited to only the United States and Britain. The situation in France, the other Western nuclear power, is roughly comparable. Figures for China and the Soviet Union are not available but clearly are very large. In the nonnuclear countries, such as Germany, Italy, Sweden, and Canada, defense also requires the services of large numbers of scientists, but the process is not so research-intensive as it is in nuclear countries. Even so, proportionately many more scientists are used in defense than in civilian industry.

As I have said, world military expenditure is about $180,000 million a year—some 7 per cent of total world output. By comparison about 20 per cent of the world's scientists and engineers are employed in military research. This 3-to-1 superconcentration of scientific talent in defense is the essence of the modern arms race; it is the fuel which powers it and the force which drives the world ever closer to extinction. All of it is expended in the name of national security. And all of it, by denying to civil and social programs so much of the driving scientific force of the twentieth century, helps to slow down the rate of human progress.

This point is worth stressing. It is fashionable to complain today about the material resources consumed by defense. But few have pointed out the size of the much more valuable scientific resource being consumed by defense needs. And not only is it more valuable but it is used for defense in proportionally much greater amounts than money itself.

Dr. Eugene Rabinowitch puts it like this:

> The fundamental difference between natural
> wealth and wealth derived from scientific and
> technological effort is that the first one is strictly
> limited . . . while the other has no such limitation.
> Dividing limited natural wealth between individ-
> uals and nations is a "zero-sum" game; one wins
> what others lose. Production of wealth by science
> and technology is, on the other hand, a game
> in which all can win at the same time.

One might add that diversion of scientific talent into defense fields is quite another kind of game: one in which nobody wins any of the time and everybody loses all of the time.

Colonizing Civilian Science

With this in mind, we should look briefly at what has happened to civilian science. Military funds are not restricted to industry and government establishments, but have found their way in increasing amounts into educational institutions. The universities, the power houses of learning, have become outstations for defense departments. In the process they have flourished from their newfound source of wealth, and their research has borne military fruit. Society has yet to work out the cost of this remarkable twentieth-century phenomenon.

During World War II, scientists in universities throughout the world turned their hand to military research without a qualm. Most of them did so in the belief that their efforts would bring the war to a close more quickly and they would then return to their civilian way of life. But in the process defense departments discovered the powerful ally they had fostered in science and technology. And in a cold war environment, they were not prepared to let go that easily. After a period of deliberation, the U.S. Department of Defense laid down its "policy of basic research" on June 19, 1952. It states:

> To provide the essential foundation for the techniques of war, the DoD must assure that basic research is adequately supported in all areas where the presence of knowledge is important to the military effort. . . . Research in universities, non-profits . . . may be of a kind which does not have specific aims but holds promise of some ultimate military application.

At the time few university scientists saw this document. Most of them still do not know of its existence. And if they had seen it, they would doubtless have scoffed at the idea that the DoD could lay down what kind of research universities might or might not do. It is now clear that in the United States the DoD pursued its policy with care and deliberation. And over the past two decades it has effectively controlled many of the directions of university research. The proof lies in the figures.

In 1968 American universities and colleges received $1,548.5 million for research and development. More than one-fifth of this —$319.1 million—came from the Department of Defense. If the other defense-related agencies—AEC and NASA—are added in, these three agencies together contributed one-third of the R&D funds for universities and colleges, a total of $513.5 million. The Department of Defense alone supplied grants of more than $1 billion to 65 universities and colleges, the largest being $22.1 million to the Massachusetts Institute of Technology.

But this is not the end of the story. One of the results of the wartime alliance between science and defense was the setting up by universities of research centers either on or off their campuses. These centers are not involved in education as such but undertake sponsored research for agencies and act as healthy financial centers in their own right. The University of California, for instance, runs the Los Alamos Scientific Laboratory—the nuclear weapons center—for the Atomic Energy Commission; MIT operates the Lincoln Laboratory for the Department of Defense.

In all there are some 25 of these university research centers, and in 1968 they received $657 million for research and development. Of this, no less than $641 million came from the three defense-related agencies. And if these totals are added on to the university and college figures, it turns out that DoD, NASA, and the AEC provided $1,154.5 million for research and development out of a total of $2,195.5 million—more than half. And although the Department of Defense's original plan stated that the research it sponsored need have no specific military applications, more than one-third of the money it provided in 1968 to universities, colleges, and their research centers was for classified work.

In September 1965 the President added fuel to this already swiftly burning fire. He asked all federal agencies to administer their grants in such a way as to improve university research and science education. This gave rise to the DoD's Project Themis, which was designed to bring universities not already heavily committed to defense into the fold. In 1967 the DoD contacted 400 universities, identifying research areas of defense interest. As a result the department received applications for grants from 173 universities, of which 42 were selected. The following year 43 additional institutions were brought into the scheme. In every case priority was given to universities not already receiving large amounts of defense money.

In Britain the situation is different and much less easy to document. In 1967–68 universities and colleges had about 775 defense grants, worth in all about £1.5 million (these included defense grants from the Ministry of Technology). Though this seems small enough, it is quite large compared with other sources of university revenue. For instance, the figure was about the same as the total money supplied to university and college staffs by three of the research councils which support university research. In other words, in terms of direct government funding, a similar importance was attached to defense as to environmental research, agriculture, and social science put together. In overall effect, this situation is corrected by two factors. First, the research councils spend a lot of money supporting their own staff in universities; and, second, the government gives universities a lot of money to do with as they please.

The fact remains, however, that defense money has penetrated deep within the educational structure of Western nations. It turns up in surprising places and in ways which give an indication of the situation much more vivid than mere statistics. Britain's most famous monument to civil science, the huge Jodrell Bank radio telescope, was at one time part of the defense network. On September 22, 1961, the Ministry of Aviation issued this press release:

> The Air Ministry is installing some equipment
> which will be of assistance to Professor Lovell
> in his work on satellite behaviour, and which will
> in addition offer some capacity for the detection
> of ballistic missiles.

Jodrell Bank, it turned out, was to act as a standby for the Fylingdale Early Warning Station and, it was claimed, was to be electronically linked to Bomber Command.

In the United States the situation was more blatant. The equivalent of Jodrell Bank was the even-bigger but less-versatile radar telescope at Arecibo in Puerto Rico. This 1,000-foot-diameter dish, built into a natural mountain bowl, was constructed at a cost of $8.3 million for Cornell University by DoD's Advanced Research Projects Agency. It was widely hailed as a major milestone in the progress of radio astronomy. But this was not its primary purpose. It was financed by ARPA as part of the Defender program to explore methods of defense against ballistic missiles. Its contribution would be to map the ionosphere in great detail and thus provide important information about the detection of missiles and their decoys.

There were other motives, too. It was thought the new telescope would be able to detect nuclear explosions in space, and this application was accordingly classified. It was also planned to use the instrument to eavesdrop on Soviet military communications that were bounced off the moon. But by the time the telescope became operational, both these jobs could be better done by satellite. For several years the telescope provided useful information to defense agencies as well as to radio astronomy. Then during an economy drive in the late 1960s the Defense Department announced that it would now have to close down the facility. Only intervention from the National Science Foundation saved an important radar telescope from becoming just another piece of obsolete military equipment.

Of course, this use of defense money has benefited civilian science enormously. This has never been in doubt, and from the statistics quoted it is clear that if defense funds were denied science, the scientific community would more or less have to pack up and make a fresh start. At the same time, no money coming from defense is given altruistically. The money is given primarily for military reasons, and any civilian uses that emerge are secondary. Many scientists find this hard to believe, for the research they perform with defense money seems far removed from military applications.

Late in 1969 a bill was presented to Congress which tried to prevent the Department of Defense from supporting studies not directly related to military functions. According to a report in *Science* by Andrew Hamilton, the DoD thought the bill would be without effect. "As a matter of policy," the DoD said, "and surely as a matter of rhetoric, all the work we support is relevant to military needs."

Nor are the connections really so remote. Work on infrared radiation leads to new missile homing devices; work on star photometry improves submarine navigation; work on flame spectroscopy leads to better methods of missile detection; a study of meteors suggests that military communications might be made secure by bouncing signals off meteor trails; research on large molecules leads to a better fuel for Polaris missiles; and a geophysical study of thermal properties of land masses tells defense departments where Early Warning sites are best constructed. This list, which could be extended indefinitely, is a real one taken from congressional committee hearings in the United States.

More direct proof comes from the agencies themselves. Dr. William J. Price, Executive Director of the Air Force Office of Scientific Research, has elucidated several times exactly why AFOSR supports so much science. "This research support," he writes, "is of such a magnitude and nature as to help significantly in colonizing the scientific fields of potential interest to the Air Force." In another article he refers to the international nature of this colonial effort. "Colonizing," he says, "may be described as increasing the chance of important discovery in an area deemed to hold promise for the Air Force by 'raising the temperature' of the world's scientific activity in that field."

The colonial parallel is a good one. Early in colonial history most countries found they had much to benefit from colonial rule. Only later, when they sought independence, did they discover their hands had been tied and their resources exploited in such a way as to make escape very difficult.

Now that universities are beginning to examine their escape routes, they are also beginning to count the costs. "We cannot afford much more bounty upon the terms on which we have been receiving it," Yale's graduate dean John Perry Miller told an educational conference in October 1968. In a new book Harold Orlans asks a blunter question: "Has the dispassionate pursuit of truth been redirected to the pursuit of truths useful to government and to that subgovernment to which the power of sparing life or inflicting death has so often been delegated: the Department of Defense?"

The answer to this blunt question can only be a blunt yes. Today, no research interest is secure from the inquisitive stare of the military. It is no longer of much importance to distinguish between pure and applied science, between science and technology, or between science paid for from civil funds and that paid for by defense funds. Most of what gets done has some military interest, and nearly all the rest serves some national interest.

And thus, to the extent that modern society relies on science to point up the pathways of future progress, defense and the national interest are putting the stamp on all our futures. The ways in which such things happen are not all obvious.

The reasons are complicated and depend partly on the fact that foreign policy is made through the interaction of many government agencies and that all research agencies are essentially furthering a national cause of some kind. For this reason funds and high-level positions in civilian jobs are often denied those with unconventional views.

Back in 1954 the U.S. Department of Health, Education and Welfare issued a press release that read: "In those instances where it is established to the satisfaction of this Department that the individual has engaged in or is engaging in subversive activities or that there is serious question of his loyalty to the United States, it is the practice of the Department to deny support." In his book *American Universities and Federal Research* Charles V. Kidd charges that research funds have been denied university scientists for "political unorthodoxy, improper associations, past contributions to currently unpopular causes and leftist tendencies."

Much more recently, the Office of Naval Research and the Army Research Office wrote letters to their contractees raising questions about the renewal of their contracts. The letters were sent only to the signatories of an anti-Vietnam war advertisement, which urged mathematicians to regard themselves as responsible for the uses to which their talents were put. The advertisement ended: "We believe that this responsibility forbids putting mathematics in the service of this cruel war."

Then in 1969 a major storm blew up in Washington as to who should be the new director of the National Science Foundation. A distinguished scientist, Dr. Franklin A. Long, who had served on Pugwash's continuing committee, had been offered the job. Press releases had been prepared announcing his appointment and a meeting with President Nixon arranged. Then, at the last minute, Dr. Long's appointment was stopped by the administration. The reason was apparently Dr. Long's views on arms control, and more particularly an article he had written the previous year about anti-ballistic missiles—stating, among other things, that their deployment would be a "strong pressure toward acceleration of the arms race." Dr. Long never got the job, and the affair aroused great fury among liberal scientists. It also provided conclusive evidence that "correct" attitudes toward the military-industrial complex and its scientific counterparts were a prerequisite to high-level jobs even in the most civilian of all science agencies.

The ultimate absurdity in this interwoven relationship between civil and military science can be seen in the Atomic Energy Commission. After World War II a number of influential physicists expressed concern that the atom should not become the exclusive concern of the military. In the prolonged battle with the administration that followed, the physicists lost many rounds; but one they did win was to create a new civilian agency, the AEC, which had all government responsibility for atomic energy and which was not run by the Department of Defense. One result is that peaceful uses of nuclear energy have resulted faster than might have been the case. But other results show that the AEC has served as a stout shield behind which the Defense Department has been able to shelter.

With zealous enthusiasm the AEC first pushed for nuclear-powered submarines, aircraft, and aircraft carriers much harder than the Defense Department would have done. It pushed "atoms for peace" so hard that the underdeveloped countries are now studded with nuclear reactors—with all the potential for disaster that that implies.

And from the military viewpoint the AEC had one important advantage in being a civilian agency. It supplied nuclear warheads free of charge to the Department of Defense. Thus, writes Don K. Price, "For more than a decade every military staff planner, as he computed the alternative advantages and costs of using different types of weapons to accomplish any particular objective, was given a powerful incentive to choose nuclear weapons because they were free."

This issue came to a head in the debate over the antiballistic missile. Critics of the program argued that the Department of Defense had been stringing the public and Congress along with its estimates of costs. And it emerged that the much-quoted official figures contained no allowance for the nuclear warheads the ABM missiles would carry. Quite correct, replied the Defense Department; the warheads will be provided free of charge by the Atomic Energy Commission. AEC's charge to the taxpayer, it later turned out, would be $1,200 million.

Technological War

Science and war have not always been so intimately connected. But within the narrow confines of the twentieth century it is difficult to see the situation in perspective. Even 300 years ago it was possible for scientists to exert some control on the uses to which their inventions were put. At that time a handful of men manned the technical frontiers, secure in the knowledge that what they did not discover might remain unmolested for hundreds of years. Leonardo da Vinci, for instance, invented the submarine but deliberately suppressed it "on account of the evil nature of men, who would practice assassination at the bottom of the sea."

Any scientist who today suppressed his findings would be quickly ridiculed; and of course, with 5 million scientists and engineers at work, his discovery would emerge in short order somewhere else. And there would be pompous talk of how far human progress had been set back by the suppression of new knowledge. Yet no one seriously stops to count the cost of the world's being without the submarine during the three centuries after da Vinci's death. In fact, his contribution was a positive one: he delayed "assassination at the bottom of the sea"—now practiced on a larger scale than he could ever have foreseen—for 300 years.

For an objective assessment of where we stand today, it seems we have to go outside science and outside contemporary studies. In 1936, the professor of classics at the University College of Swansea, Benjamin Farrington, published an important book on Greek science. When he came to revise the second edition in 1969, he was moved to write a new conclusion—one which contrasts strongly with the Greek inspiration on which science was founded.

> "In the space of 300 years or a little more," he wrote, "the face of the world has been transformed. But so has the image of the scientist. Research, now multiplied a millionfold, is mainly for war and therefore mainly secret. To publish results from inside is treason; to try to get at them from outside is spying. Much industrial research suffers from the same restrictions. Poverty has not been overcome. The gap between the fed and the hungry peoples of the world increases. The sea is threaded by submarines and the air winnowed by aircraft capable of causing within minutes the death of more people than existed on earth when the Royal Society was founded. We are back again at square one."

How, then, did we get back there? One cause, undoubtedly, was the arrogant scientific assumption that technical advance could put an end to war. This myth seems to have haunted the minds of nearly all the great weapons inventors of the past. In 1844 *Punch* printed a cartoon showing a Captain Warner testing a new shell. The commentary opposite read: "Hurrah then, for the WARNER shell, from which—all terrible as it is—peace may be hatched, to the true happiness of man, and the best glory of nations!"

Alfred Nobel, with equally misguided sincerity, saw in his dynamite factories great hope for peace. The disasters of the two world wars which soon followed—based mainly on Nobel technology—

did little to shake scientists' blinding faith in the peaceful nature of their inventions. In 1946 two nuclear physicists, P. B. Moon and Eric Burhop, were echoing Nobel's thoughts. "The advent of the atomic bomb," they wrote, "has given us a rare opportunity to make future warfare less likely on account of the horrors of mass destruction it will entail."

And in 1964, when the debate on chemical and biological weapons was beginning to heat up, the argument was given a novel twist by a former commanding general of the U.S. Army Chemical Corps Research and Development Command, Brigadier General J. H. Rothschild. He foresaw a world in which war could be made not less likely but less bloody, in which buildings could be left unharmed at the expense of people. "Such is the versatility of these weapons," he claimed, "that they can either bring death and defeat to a military aggressor, or provide a more humane means of insuring peace in a disarmed world."

Hollow though these arguments appear, there remains a nagging doubt: has the nuclear weapon prevented a third world war? It seems possible. But that is not to say that it will continue to do so. Nor is this any longer a question in which any element of doubt can be tolerated. Another world war will have to be avoided if the result is not to be global suicide. And even with nuclear weapons extensively stockpiled, it has proved possible for major ideologies to wage war against one another in countries such as Korea, Malaya, and Vietnam. Even more important, the existence of the bomb has itself given rise to quite a new kind of war.

This is the technological war. It was declared in 1945 and has been fought out ever since on the battlefields of the scientific laboratory. While it may once have had the object of producing the ultimate weapon to preserve the peace, it has long since become an end in itself. General Curtis E. LeMay made the point quite clear in a book published in 1968. "I sincerely believe," he wrote, "any arms race with the Soviet Union would act to our benefit. I believe that we can out-invent, out-research, out-develop, out-engineer and out-produce the U.S.S.R. in any area from sling shots to space weapons, and in doing so become more and more prosperous while the Soviets become progressively poorer."

This concept of technological war is rather a startling one. It is one in which the medium has become the message. What has become significant is not what new weapons military research has produced but the very act of producing them; the aim of technological war has been to force the nose of the other side's most prized scientific talent to the military grindstone. The result, writes Don K. Price, has been that

> another boundary was blurred: the boundary
> between war and peace. So we had to turn not
> merely to a state of constant armament and psy-
> chological warfare, but to a process of looking a
> decade ahead with respect to the production of
> the scientists who were to carry on the basic re-
> search that would serve as the technological basis
> for future weapons systems. Industry was no
> longer to be mobilized by government only in
> time of a hot war and then demobilized as
> quickly as possible. The mobilization had to be
> a permanent arrangement. . . . It required the
> continuous managerial supervision by government
> of a large segment of private industry and the
> continuous subsidy by government of the higher
> education of scientists and others.

A closer look at the nature of military research reveals another characteristic of the technological war. No major new weapon has been invented since the missile and the H-bomb more than 15 years ago. The 10 million man-years of military research that have elapsed since then have been concerned with "improving" the weapons systems which depend on them. The goal has been to make warheads smaller and more powerful, more accurate and more controllable, to improve the electronics on which they depend, and to make the delivery systems less vulnerable to attack. The goal has not been the discovery of a new ultimate weapon for peace keeping but a rate of product improvement in which each side just manages to keep up with the other. In other words, military science has to run as fast as its grossly inflated budgets will allow just to maintain a previous position of security.

The goal of product improvement is not restricted to the research side of defense departments; it characterizes the whole world defense budget. The world military expenditure of some $2,000 million over the past decade and a half has not been spent mainly on increasing the total number of weapons; it has been spent on improving them. Indeed some weapons are in shorter supply now than they were 15 years ago. The number of aircraft carriers has dropped from 130 to 75, and the number of submarines has fallen from 900 to 700.

But those submarines and aircraft carriers are today a great deal more effective. Intrigued by this trend, in 1969 economists at the Stockholm International Peace Research Institute tried to measure what the rate of military product improvement really was. As there was no obvious measure—such as destructiveness—that could be used, they looked at the real cost over the years of a number of weapons: four specific types of aircraft, the attack submarine, the aircraft carrier, and the destroyer. Having allowed for world price increases, they found that the real cost of each of these weapons increased over two decades by between 6.6 per cent per year for the aircraft carrier to 18 per cent per year for the fighter plane. These increases give some indication of the product's increased performance. In comparable prices, for instance, the Air Force fighter cost $110,000 in 1945 but $6.8 million in 1968. From this the SIPRI team was able to make a startling conclusion:

> The figures for the seven weapons . . . suggest
> an average increase in performance of something
> over 10 per cent a year. This implies a doubling
> every seven years, and a twenty-fold increase
> over thirty years. Civil goods do not increase in
> performance or capability in this way. The per-
> formance or capability of a present-day car
> is not twice that of a 1962 model, or twenty
> times that of a 1939 model. If calculations were
> made on the same basis . . . for a typical collec-
> tion of consumer goods, they would show very
> little rise at all.

The SIPRI study went on to single out the major cause of this vast rate of weapons improvement. We have already seen that military industry employs far more scientists and engineers in rela-tion to its budget than do other sectors of the economy. SIPRI showed that the research input in the military field was at least twelve times greater than in the civilian field. For instance, in the United Kingdom, which in 1964–65 operated the most research-intensive military industry in the world, $62.20 was spent for every $100 worth of military equipment bought. The comparable figure for civilian industry was $4.90 for every $100 of manufacturing output. Similar figures were found for the United States and for France: $54 compared to $7.50 for the United States, and $51 compared to $1.90 for France. This work also shows the research cost of being a nuclear power. The next highest country in the league was nonnuclear Canada; she spent "only" $20.40 on military

R&D for every $100 of military procurement, compared with $1.30 for manufacturing industry as a whole.

These figures go a long way toward explaining the momentum of the arms race. If large R&D departments exist for weapons, improvements will be made. It must then be assumed that potential enemies have found the same improvements. The weapon is then developed and deployed and the same process repeats itself with the development of new countermeasures. The result is the vast and expensive security deadlock which is the ultimate aim of technological war.

But there are yet broader implications. One is that it does not really matter who pays for the research or who does it. The results are equally accessible to the military if they are produced in laboratories with no formal connections with defense of any kind. The important thing in the technological war is to keep scientific momentum forging ahead at maximum speed with minimum thought for the consequences.

Dr. Edward Teller, the scientific superhawk known as the father of the H-bomb, actually goes so far as to advocate the research being done outside defense laboratories where it will not be curtailed by limitations of the military imagination. "Generally," he wrote in 1963, "it is much better not to ask for military requirements but to push scientific advancements to the limit; the military requirements will soon follow. The military often lacks the vision to see the potential for new scientific developments."

This statement by Teller must rank as one of the most remarkable of the nuclear age. For he continues:

> I have heard scientists say quite frequently, "our main problem is no longer one of technological advance but rather is to make the best human use of the advances already achieved." This is an extremely grave symptom. The whole dynamic civilization of the West, for which America is the spearhead, is based upon scientific and technological advancements. We must trust our social processes to use these advancements in the right manner. We must not be deterred by arguments involving consequences or costs.

This argument appears more extraordinary when one realizes that the chief "consequence or cost" involved is the survival of mankind. But even viewed from the narrow confines of national security this whole philosophy has turned out to be the most expensive, disastrous, and futile experiment ever conducted. Nor is this a view confined simply to those who wish to play no part in the defense establishment. For confirmation it seems more reasonable to turn to a man who for many years controlled the largest collection of scientific defense talent in the world—Dr. Herbert York, former director of defense research and engineering for the Pentagon.

In 1969 Dr. York was moved to write a condemnation of the decision to deploy antiballistic missiles in the United States. His conclusion was that:

> ... the ABM issue constitutes a particularly clear example of the futility of searching for technical solutions to what is essentially a political problem, namely the problem of national security.
> ... The arms race is not so much a series of political provocations followed by hot emotional reactions as it is a series of technical challenges followed by cool, calculated responses in the form of ever more costly, more complex and more fully developed automatic devices. ... Thus the steady advance of arms technology may not be leading us to the ultimate weapon but rather to the ultimate absurdity: a completely automatic system for deciding whether or not doomsday has arrived.

As far as I know, this is the most authoritative and most devastating critique of the aims of technological war yet to appear in print. It is a fitting point at which to change gear, to close this grim narrative of how abortive, dangerous, and unsuccessful has been our search for the hardware of peace. During the rest of this book we shall examine the "software" approach—the efforts made by the biologists, the social scientists, and the peace researchers to find some way out of the deadly course on which we appear set. But I should warn that though their efforts are a great deal more enlightening, and their approach infinitely more sympathetic, even these scientists are fast on the way to proving Dr. York's point: there are no technical solutions to political problems.

CHAPTER VI

The Psychology of Aggression

---

*Aggression in Animals–Man as an
Animal–The Nature of Aggression–
Substitutes for War–The Population
Drive–Man as Man*

"Since wars are made in the minds
of men, it is in the minds of
men that the defences of peace must
be constructed."

UNESCO Charter

Psychologists, sociologists, and anthropologists all play their part in the war machine. Their advice is sought—and paid for—by governments interested in the future of the power struggle. But only a handful of them ever turn to consider the other side of the coin. If wars are made in the minds of men, social scientists of one kind or another should be able to tell us something about why men fight.

Yet the psychology of peace features in almost no university course. As a discipline, it is young and essentially amateur, for few governments invest funds in basic studies with only a small chance of any payoff.

In this chapter I shall examine some of the findings that may have relevance to the psychology of war and peace. But a warning note should be sounded. Because the field is young and poorly funded, the evidence that can be drawn on is limited. Most of it has been produced by scientists whose first interest is in other fields. Most of it has relevance to war and peace by implication only. In quality, it compares unfavorably with the mass of painfully acquired literature available on, say, the theoretical accuracy of low-level bombing. In short, we know far more about how to kill than about *why* we kill.

The grass roots of war, some biologists tell us, lie in the teeth and claws of the other animals to which man is related. I should make it clear that I do not believe a more extensive study of Macaque monkeys, for instance, has much to tell us about nuclear warfare. But it might provide new information about the nature of aggression, and it would almost certainly help us see our own history and future in a more realistic perspective. So I make no apology for starting this chapter with an account of animal aggression nor for harking back to that subject in the pages that follow.

Aggression in Animals

There are two popular views of animal aggression. One is that animals in the wild spend all their time fighting. The other is that if wild animals are not interfered with they will never fight. Both ideas have been perpetuated by Walt Disney's films, and they are as wrong as they are different. They do grave injustice to the richness of animal behavior patterns and serve only to confuse those who turn to animals to seek knowledge of human aggression. So before starting we must dispose of some hoary old myths.

The first is that animal species habitually fight other species. On the contrary, snakes do not fight lions and kangaroos do not attack cows. And when we are shown gory pictures of one animal tearing another limb from limb, we would do well to forget about aggression. Almost certainly the animal is stocking its larder. If this process has any message for humanity, it is not one for generals or politicians but one for the managers of abattoirs. Nature is no redder in tooth and claw than is a slaughterhouse. And that is not the place to start any inquiry about the origin of war.

The second myth is that because some species seem to spend most of their time fighting other members of the same species, they are engaged in killing one another. Catfights and dogfights have now entered the human language as a means of describing any vicious and bloody duel. The analogy is precisely wrong. Such fights rarely end in death and only occasionally do they draw blood. Here a better understanding of the significance of these displays of animal aggression is more rewarding.

Conventional wisdom has it that the brilliant colors of many tropical and subtropical fish are the means by which different sexes attract their mates. In fact, they are the signals used to warn other members of the species that they are on foreign ground. Fish that live singly or in pairs mark out their own territory by parading their colors around the edges of it. Birds do the same thing with their characteristic songs, which warn not only that a territory is occupied but tell a potential intruder something of the age and ferocity of the defender. Cats and many other animals stake out their hunting grounds with their characteristic smells.

All these signs signify that "trespassers will be prosecuted." But it is what happens during the process of prosecution that may have relevance for man. To an inexperienced eye, the sight of deer with their antlers interlocked, swaying to and fro in apparently mortal combat, looks like the prelude to a bloody death. What is actually happening is more nearly the culmination of the conflict. Sometime before, the two deer will have paced one another, side by side. Then, instead of swinging their antlers viciously into the haunches of their opponent, they stop, lower their heads, engage antlers, and wrestle. The winner is the one who stays the course the longer. And if one should start the fight before the other, rarely if ever will it drive its antlers into its opponent's body. Instead it stops short, as if brought up by some unseen command.

Much the same process marks the combats of other species. Fish will bite ineffectively at one another's mouths, but, as the famous ethologist Konrad Lorenz has written, "never, never does a fish bite into an opponent's unprotected flank." In fact, most animal combatants never touch one another. Instead they engage in an elaborate but entirely psychological trial of strength. Fish will turn sideways on to one another, extending their fins to show their opponent just how large they are. Cats arch their backs and apes stand their hair on end for the same reason. These are the symbols of aggression, the deterrent threats of the animal world. They are designed to bring the opponent's escape mechanism into play, and they are markedly successful.

They are also functional. In territorial animals, these encounters occur mainly when one animal is venturing onto the territory of another. And it seems that the amount of aggression an animal will display is related to its distance from home. Near its lair, it has no alternative but to show that its deterrent is real and will be used if necessary. Further from home the animal becomes less aggressive and quickly yields to the threat display of an animal on its own territory. All this is also regulated by the size of the animal. Larger animals need larger territories on which to forage for food, and, appropriately, larger animals are able to make more convincing threats.

Animals that live in flocks use similar techniques to establish a hierarchy of rank or "pecking order"—so named because the phenomenon was first observed in chickens. The pecking order, too, has social functions. Once established by trial fights or psychological showmanship, it eliminates unnecessary competition. Only those close to one another will jockey for position, and senior and junior animals rarely fight. In jackdaws the order is so well-established that senior members will interfere in fights breaking out among junior members, thus controlling their squabbling. And it is usually the more experienced members that become the leaders, taking on themselves the task of warning their fellows against dangers which their greater experience enables them to judge more effectively. From them the junior members of the group learn the tricks of survival.

With so many vital aspects of wild life depending on aggressive encounters, it is surprising that all forms of higher life have not long ago fought themselves off the face of the earth. But the fact that so few fights end in death means that some very powerful rules of animal warfare have evolved to protect the species.

These rules are the basis of the ritual that underlies each animal combat. Weapons evolved by animal life have two functions: to protect the species from attack by predators and to catch prey, and to provoke fright in other members of the same species for the territorial or other reasons which I have mentioned. Significantly, an animal species does not always use the same weapon for the same job. Many of what appear to us as the most ferocious bits of animal armory are for threat only—but like all realistic threats can be put to effective use if need be. Thus the deer's antlers have been evolved for the exclusive function of ritualized fighting within the species. If a deer is attacked by another animal for prey, it defends itself not with its antlers but with its forelimbs (the reindeer also uses its antlers as a snow scoop, but that is another matter). So the first rule of animal warfare is that the ritual weapons, and not the real ones, are used in interspecies combat.

The second rule is that even the ritualized weapons are used as rarely as possible. The first "control system" is for the losing animal to turn off its threatening signals. The cock turns its bright red comb away and the cat's arched back resumes its normal shape. These are signs of impending defeat, but they are often insufficiently strong to deter the victor quickly. And here a second mechanism comes into play.

The defeated animal then offers up to the victor the most vulnerable parts of its body. This may be part of the same movement in which the aggressive signals are turned off, or it may occur as an almost separate signal. The wolf, in this situation, turns his head away from his opponent, offering his jugular vein to the teeth of the winner. The jackdaw holds the unprotected base of its skull under the beak of its rival. And the dog, as everyone has seen, rolls onto his back, offering his throat and belly to the victor.

All these actions evoke a reaction as positive as did the original signs of aggression. They are aggression inhibitors and they have saved countless millions of animals from death by their own species. The attacking animal, perhaps with a final gesture of triumph such as a quick worry at a dog's throat or a slap on a monkey's behind, calls the contest off. The defeated then has the chance to flee back to his own territory or knows that he has fallen by one in the pecking order of his species. Either result is beneficial for both the species and the individuals.

To zoologists I must now apologize for the inadequacy of this description of animal behavior. What I have said does grave injustice to the richness and variability of the rituals that compose animal aggression. But it should be sufficient to provide the background against which we might view human aggression. Our need is not to examine the intricate social life of the tropical fish but to see if the principles on which it rests carry any message for humanity.

Man as an Animal

Biologically, man is the type of animal best described as an unarmed vertebrate. His bare hands are no substitute for the aggressive weapons of claws and hoof, antlers and fangs, poisons and tusks. But perversely this physical weakling is the most murderous species ever to have dominated the earth.

One might wonder how much worse his fate would have been had he been equipped with the natural weapons of his animal ancestors. The answer, again perversely, is that it might have been a good deal less bloody. "If men had tusks or horns," Dr. Anthony Storr has written, "they would be less, rather than more, likely to kill one another." The reason for this is that the natural killer must be an evolutionary failure. Nature's solution, as we have seen, is to provide heavily armed animals with powerful inhibitory instincts. The more powerful the weapons, this rule runs, the more powerful the inhibitions.

Whatever the nature of this inhibition, according to the mammal expert Dr. L. Harrison Matthews, "only one species of mammal habitually disregards it—and he is at present in a very insecure state, in spite of the fact that he is the world's dominant species." It is precisely because man finds it so difficult to kill his own kind with his bare hands that he is so poorly endowed with killing inhibitions. All this would run strictly in accord with the natural plan if man had not also evolved culturally—if he had not discovered that he could fashion with his hands substitutes for the natural weapons he lacked.

Anthropologists would have us believe that it is man's ability to make and use tools that distinguishes him fundamentally from other animals. When they discover in the fossil record bone or stone tools that have been fashioned, the bones of the animal that did the fashioning are automatically dubbed "human." The first function of these tools, it is argued, was for food preparation—the killing and dismembering of animal prey and the gathering and preparation of plant foods (man has been an omnivore, eating both plants and animals, since the records begin). From this gastronomic start, there developed a culture based on the hand-held tool, and the capacity for speech, which led to man's dominance over the world.

But there is lively argument as to what the first tool was actually used for. There is some evidence that about the first thing man did with his newfound ability was to murder his brother by striking him on the head with a stone. Slightly later, when he invented fire, he may have roasted and eaten other members of his group. As yet the matter cannot be decided either way from the fossil record. But it is not an unreasonable assumption that an animal, without a powerful killing inhibition and with a murderous tool in his hand (plowshares and swords are easily confused), might well strike the first blow for death. Robert Ardrey seems totally convinced. "In the first hour of the human emergence," he writes, "we became sufficiently skilled in the use of weapons to render redundant our natural primate daggers. I know of no scientific explanation for the remarkable reduction in our canine teeth other than substitution of the weapon in the hand."

This idea leads naturally to a reassessment of man the tool-maker. What man really made was not a tool but a weapon. "Our history reveals the development and contest of superior weapons as *Homo sapiens'* single, universal cultural preoccupation," writes Ardrey. "Peoples may perish, nations dwindle, empires fall; one civilization may surrender its memories to another civilization's sands. But mankind as a whole, with an instinct as true as a meadow lark's song, has never in a single instance allowed local failure to impede the

progress of the weapon, its most significant cultural endowment."
According to this view, man did not father the tool. Nor did he
father the weapon. It was the weapon that fathered man.

Whatever its origins, there can be no doubt as to the weapon's
biological significance. It introduces distance between attacker and
victim. And with that distance comes the virtual elimination of any
residual inhibitions man may have about killing his brothers. Desmond Morris suggests that if "the appeasement signals of the losers
cannot be read by the winners, then violent aggression is going to
go raging on. It can only be consummated by a direct confrontation
with abject submission, or the enemy's headlong flight. Neither of
these can be witnessed in the remoteness of modern aggression, and
the result is wholesale slaughter on a scale unheard of in any other
species."

This can be expressed in more direct terms. It is today not very
difficult for any nation to persuade its airmen to fly a bombing raid
with napalm bombs—indeed, the flying crew of any air force would
accept this as part of their everyday requirement. But it would be
remarkably difficult to persuade the same men to round up 300
men, women, and children, cover them with petroleum jelly, and
ignite them. Why this should be is still not clear. It may be simply
that humans do still possess a residual measure of killing inhibition
which prevents them from carrying out such wholesale and painful
slaughter at close range where they must witness the result. Our
"weak stomachs" may be an evolutionary relic of ancestral inhibition. Alternatively, it might be that our capacity for rational thought
has developed a concept of mercy which is—in that form—unknown
in the rest of the animal kingdom. If this is so, one cannot help
wondering why our rationale cannot easily recognize that napalm
bombing at a distance is the direct equivalent of igniting human
flesh at close quarters.

Further research is required to throw light on the concepts of
mercy and inhibition and their biological relationship. It is easy to
see, however, that human reason has tried to force on society the
social equivalent of animal inhibition. "All the culturally evolved
forms of fair fighting," writes Dr. Lorenz, "from primitive chivalry
to the Geneva Convention, are functionally analogous to ritualized
combat in animals." It is a sad fact that because these social con-
ventions are not biologically based, they have rarely been so effective
as those of other animals.

All this tells us something about why man finds it difficult to resist
the temptation to fight. But it does not give any indication of how

to help solve the problem nor does it explain why man has an urge to fight in the first place. These are points we shall come to later, but the study of man's place in evolution has, I think, already pointed up an important message.

That message is that there is no biological reason to suppose that *Homo sapiens* is not bound for extinction. During the past two million years, roughly the time over which some kind of man has existed, many animal species have died off. Some owe their demise to man's aggression, but most have simply found the evolutionary race too fast. The expectation of life for a bird species has dropped from an average length of 1½ million years to 40,000 years. A mammal species is no longer expected to live half a million years but only 20,000 years. On this basis man's extinction, were he not such an exceptional animal, is long overdue.

In working out this equation we have to balance man's intelligence against the fact that biologically he is an instinctive killer with no or few inhibitions. Our only parallel in the animal world is the rat, virtually the only other animal known to wage systematic, prolonged, and bloody war on its own species in the wild.

Human arrogance prevents us from comparing ourselves with any objectivity with the rat. For this purpose, Dr. Lorenz has invented a mythical Martian with a sound knowledge of the principles of animal behavior. Such a Martian, Dr. Lorenz warns,

> . . . would unavoidably draw the conclusion that man's social organization is very similar to that of rats which, like humans, are social and peaceful beings within their clans, but veritable devils towards all fellow-members of their species not belonging to their own community. If, furthermore, our Martian naturalist knew of the explosive rise in human populations, the ever-increasing destructiveness of weapons and the division of mankind into a few political camps, he would not expect the future of humanity to be any rosier than than that of several hostile clans of rats on a ship almost devoid of food. And this prognosis would even be optimistic, for in the case of rats reproduction stops automatically when a certain state of overcrowding is reached, while man as yet has no workable system for preventing the so-called population explosion. Furthermore, in the case of rats it is likely that after the wholesale slaughter enough individuals would be left over to propagate

the species. In the case of man, this would not be
so certain after the use of the hydrogen bomb.

The Nature of Aggression

"A powerful measure of desire for aggression," wrote Freud shortly
after the First World War, "has to be reckoned as part of man's
instinctual endowment . . . *Homo homini lupus;* who has the courage
to dispute it in the face of all the evidence in his own life and in
history?" In claiming that man treats man like a wolf, Freud certainly did the wolf an injustice; the wolf, as ethologists have stressed,
turns out to be a rather peaceful animal in the wild. But was Freud
also doing an injustice to man? Is there really evidence that man is
instinctively aggressive?

With 60 million human beings dead from 11 years of world war
in this century, the fact that man is aggressive for whatever reason
seems to need little proving. But the relationship between war, as
an organized social activity, and aggression in the individual is not
clear. However, the story of social violence unrelated to war in this
century is unequivocal. Aggression is present and getting worse.
Among its more inexplicable facets is that in one year alone in England the National Society for the Prevention of Cruelty to Children
saw 114,641 children and summoned their parents to appear in
court in no less than 39,223 cases. During every hour of 1964 one
person was murdered in the United States and two to three people
were wounded in Britain. Violent crimes have risen by 57 per cent
in the United States in seven years. Robbery in London has become
ten times more frequent in the past decade. Three prominent American politicians—one a President—have been assassinated in five
years in a country which claims freedom and democracy as its essential doctrines.

"The inborn bases of our behavior," writes the German ethologist
Dr. Paul Leyhausen, "are given to the individual just as are the
number of his cranial bones or the maximum and minimum limits of
his heart frequency; he cannot choose them but must live with them
as best he can." In saying this, Dr. Leyhausen does not mean that
there is nothing we can do about the 114,641 maltreated children
every year. He means simply that there are certain drives basic to
man which are inherited and must be expressed. There is now a
great deal of experimental evidence that some forms of behavior are
inherited and not learned—though they are modified by learning.

Dr. Daniel Freedman of the University of Chicago has studied the problem in puppies, in human identical twins—which are genetically identical—and in genetically differing (fraternal) twins. "Like puppies," he writes, "human babies show genetically based differences in behaviour from the earliest weeks of life. The human is not a *tabula rasa.*" If we accept that some of our inherited behavior may be connected with aggression, our extraordinary treatment of our own species becomes more understandable.

It is also clear that there are regions of the brain that in many animals are connected with aggression and defense. Experiments have shown that if these brain centers are stimulated chemically or with an electrode, characteristic and uncontrollable actions result. Monkeys may behave like emotional idiots, eating nuts and bolts as happily as raisins. More significantly, they become confused as to when to respond with appreciation and when with fear. In this way, too, animals can be made to eat or drink when they are already satiated. They can be made to show sexual reactions and will even learn to tread a pedal that produces the electric current that causes the reaction. This activity they will repeat hundreds of times in succession without pause.

If part of the brain of the cat or dog is surgically removed, these animals can be made to exhibit "sham rage." The hair stands on end, the eyes dilate, the tail lashes, and the animal snarls—but may at the same time start to lap milk as if nothing of importance were actually going on. One area of the brain of the cock has been found which when stimulated causes the animal to search for an object on which to discharge its aggression. Another area appears to control courtship behavior in much the same way. "In other words," Dr. Anthony Storr concludes, "it looks as though aggression is as much an innate drive as sexuality."

In humans, as might be expected, such experiments are rare and the evidence less clear-cut. But there is a connection between certain kinds of brain damage and some aggressive forms of mental illness. Many of the children who suffered from the 1920 pandemic of encephalitis lethargica—a disease which damages certain brain areas—were later found to be extremely aggressive. They inflicted violent attacks and even murder on others and resorted to self-mutilation. They set fire to property and committed many sexual offenses.

Brain surgery is also used in the treatment of some forms of aggressive mental illness. The severing of certain brain connections causes patients to become less anxious and less self-centered. "Self-directed violence in the form of suicide, mutilation or starvation," writes Sir Denis Hill of the Maudsley Hospital, "yields better to the operation than externally directed violence, such as irritability, belligerence and defiance."

Such forms of aggression are today described as pathological. But there is plenty of evidence that aggression is also part of everyday human activity. Indeed, in the form of assertiveness it is an essential requirement for success in almost every activity in Western civilization.

The connection between aggression and sex is particularly close. Love and hate, philosophers and poets have told us for centuries, are never very far apart. The more intense our sexual arousal, the more violent is likely to be its expression. While sadism and masochism are now usually regarded as abnormal, the borderline between them and "normal" sex activity is hard to define.

The roots of all this behavior can be observed in other animals. In cichlid fish, for example, a newly found mate arouses aggression almost as quickly as does a territorial intruder. But as the pair get used to one another, a startling and perhaps vitally important form of behavior begins to emerge. When approaching the female, the male undergoes all the characteristic changes that indicate he is preparing to attack. But just as he seems about to engage in combat, he swims straight past his mate and vents his worked-up feelings on the first territorial intruder he can find. In this way, his aggression is redirected toward another fish and away from his mate. Dr. Lorenz has described how his daughter-in-law kept two pairs of cichlids separated from each other by a glass panel. The pairs never fought but each male continually threatened the other through the glass. Only when this glass became partially obscured by algal growth did marital squabbling break out. Whenever mates began to attack each other, it was always found that the glass panel had become covered by algae.

This redirection of aggression away from the mate and toward territorial invaders is found in many animals. During evolution this behavior mechanism must have arisen independently many times, and it is not difficult to see why it has been of such value. Not only does it allow a pair to mate instead of frightening one another off, but it stimulates the male to defend his territory frequently and with vigor just at the right time. The female and the young both benefit greatly. "I consider this behavior supremely ingenious," writes Dr. Lorenz, "and much more chivalrous than the reverse analogous behavior of a man who, angry with his employer during the day, discharges his pent-up irritation on his unfortunate wife in the evening."

Biologically, it seems that aggression and the bonds that form between individual higher animals are inseparable. Some animals, notably fish, live in large, impersonal shoals where no individual recognizes another and there is no pecking order. Such shoals never behave aggressively or territorially and there is never any bond formation between individuals. They live communally, it seems, solely for strength in numbers against predators—who rarely attack the shoal but try to isolate one member of it from the others. When animals behave aggressively in some seasons and not others, bonds between individuals form only during the aggressive periods.

The connection between threat and greeting, attack and appeasement can be seen in higher animals, but it is often much more ritualized. The redirection of aggression almost always seems to be present. The goose redirects towards another nearby male or interrupts his courting to threaten a nearby rock or tree. As in man, only occasionally—when passions seem to be deeply aroused—do the courting ceremonies take on much of the form of the aggression displays from which they evolved. Dr. Lorenz, who has worked a great deal with geese, claims actually to observe a rebound effect in which the release of aggression seems to increase affection between the pair. "Aggression having been discharged at the hostile neighbor," he writes, "tenderness towards the mate and children wells up unchecked." (The Duchess of Marlborough noted a similar effect in her diary: "My lord returned from the war today," she wrote, "and pleasured me twice in his top-boots.")

In man, there are still some vestigial remains of the connection between friendship and aggression. The excitement of greeting an old and loved friend may well produce goose pimples—a sign that man is trying to stand his hair on end as do other animals during aggressive displays. Even more convincing is the laugh—a gesture which we use to dissipate tension but which is closely related to the baring of an attacking row of teeth in a threat display.

But it is the principle of redirection itself which may be important —a form of behavior we all use when banging a fist on the table instead of into the face of the man sitting opposite. Ethologists argue that we have too few opportunities for redirection of aggression in modern life. If this is so, it might well be profitable to consider what we might substitute for destructive violence and even what we might substitute for war.

Substitutes for War

"It may seem stupidly naïve to think that we can substitute ritual struggles for war," Dr. Storr told a London conference in 1963, "but in my view this has already happened." He gave as an example the fact that the English no longer battle with the Scots but engage them in the less-bloody and more ritualistic combat known as rugby football. The analogy is provocative and becoming more so as football spectators wreak progressively more damage both before and after the game itself.

Other forms of human ritualized aggression have existed much longer than football. They are also woven more closely into the fabric of society. Known as avoidance and joking relationships, they have been found by anthropologists in societies as far apart as the Australian aborigines and the North American Indians. Once recognized, of course, they soon became evident in modern Western society as well.

The avoidance relationship exists typically between a man and his mother-in-law. In some tribes, all contact between these relations was and still is rigorously avoided by social convention. They rarely meet and when they do there is a strict taboo on conversation. The function of the custom is to eliminate the possibility of conflict between two people who, until a marriage occurred, had no relationship with each other. After the marriage a new form of kinship structure is set up which must survive if the marriage is to last. As there is no natural bond between a man and his mother-in-law, all chance of conflict must be eliminated by avoidance. Nevertheless, the two regard each other as close friends. The late Professor A. R. Radcliffe-Brown once asked an Australian aborigine why he avoided his mother-in-law. "Because she is my best friend in the world," the answer came back. "She has given me my wife."

Fascinating though this relationship is, an ethologist might observe that it provides no outlet for aggression, but merely stifles it. This is not true of the joking relationship in which teasing, taunting, and even obscenities are allowed. But custom dictates that neither side must take offense, providing the rules of the verbal combat are closely followed. Such relationships are widespread in human society and often exist between a man and his wife's brothers and sisters. Sometimes they also exist between grandparents and grandchildren. Here the grandchild may joke that he plans to marry his grandmother when his grandfather dies. In turn, the grandfather may pretend that he is already married to his grandson's wife. The point of this ritual is to deemphasize the age difference between the two "combatants"; it is, in fact, a neat way of sidestepping the conflict of interests that occurs across not one but two generation gaps.

The joking relationship is not limited to individuals. It extends, particularly in some parts of Africa, to a relationship between one clan and another. These clans are usually those which must live near one another, competing perhaps for the same commodities but relying on each other for a certain amount of cooperation. Again, open conflict must be avoided for the sake of both tribes and it is channeled into harmlessness through humor. Behind all joking relationships lies the laugh and the smile, symbolizing simultaneously aggression and friendship.

There are many parallels in Western society. There is, for instance, a classic joking relationship between the universities of Oxford and Cambridge. More recently, something similar has been evolving between the newer "red-brick" universities and the older Oxbridge establishments. And at the personal level, nearly all of us subconsciously make use of the same device—typically when forced, through work or marriage, to spend a lot of time in the company of a quarrelsome individual. The latent aggression is then channeled into controlled forms of teasing. Joking relationships also exist between countries, especially those adjacent to each other. They can be seen in the verbal sparring matches that take place between groups of Welshmen and Englishmen meeting for the first time. The Scots, incidentally, rarely seem to take advantage of this convenient convention, so perhaps there is some substance to their proverbial lack of humor.

No one believes that a better knowledge of tribal society is going to solve the problem of global conflict. But it does, I think, enlarge our view of the capabilities of human society and explode the myth that war is inevitable. And so I make no apology for describing the rituals of a tribe which show that, even if war is inevitable, it can be made practically harmless. For the Dani people of western New Guinea have ritualized war itself.

There are about 50,000 Dani and they are split into a dozen or so alliances, each a potential enemy of the others. They were studied extensively by a team of anthropologists from Harvard University in 1961, although the society and its customs had been generally known for years. To the Dani, war is an almost constant preoccupation. Its functions, as described by Drs. Robert Gardner and Karl Reider, would delight Dr. Lorenz:

> The Dani engage in "war" to promote the success and well-being of their social order. In large measure, their health, welfare and happiness depend on the pursuit of aggression against their traditional enemies. Since their enemies share a common culture, the same considerations motivate them. For both, the various forms that aggression takes are their means to secure, even if only temporarily, a sort of harmony between their desires for personal safety and certain inescapable pressures that militate against such desires.

The Dani fight in two ways. The first are formal battles which last for a whole day—providing the weather is neither too hot nor too wet, in which case the conflict is postponed. The decision to fight is taken early in the morning by the war leaders and shouted across the no-man's-land that separates one alliance from the next. Most of the morning is taken up with elaborate preparation, and by noon the two "armies" are lined up facing one another some 500 yards apart. The combat is started by a small group advancing to within some 50 yards of the enemy and firing their arrows. They retreat, and this ritual attack is repeated again and again. The rest of the war consists of bursts of activity in which groups of 200 or more discharge their arrows for a 10- to 15-minute period. Most energy is spent in dodging the arrows and in trying to ambush the enemy—which is almost impossible, as few of the battlegrounds provide any cover. After 10 or 20 clashes the warriors that live farthest away begin to leave the battlefield to be home by nightfall. Verbal taunts begin to replace the arrows, often directed against individual enemies, because most of the men are known by name to those of the other side. As twilight approaches, both armies break up and run for home. The cost will have been several flesh wounds caused by the arrows and spears. Occasionally, there is the "unmentionable shock of death to someone who acts stupidly or clumsily." But death is more common during the raids that occur when the specific purpose is to avenge a death—invariably only one—incurred in a previous conflict.

Drs. Gardner and Reider conclude:

> In a year, the toll on each side of deaths resulting from wounds received in formal battle, am-

bush or raids will number between ten and
twenty. An equal or even greater number of Dani
perish prematurely from complications arising
from the common cold; hence, since Dani war is
an institution involving virtually all male members of the society, the death rate is not excessive.

Western society has made its own efforts to ritualize war, mainly
in the form of laws designed to minimize the involvement of prisoners, civilians, and the wounded. That these laws are not built-in
is seen only too clearly by the fact that the global war for which
we are now preparing will inevitably kill a far higher percentage
of civilians than ever before. In fact, the only survivors may be
the military and the senior politicians.

There is, however, another form of ritualized combat which is
more comparable to the Dani system. This is the battle being fought
out in space using modern technology as weapons. The space race
can be seen as a harmless redirection of the aggression that has
built up between the Americans and the Russians. If it has indeed
prevented conflict between these countries, it would be churlish to
complain about the billions of dollars the space race has cost.
Furthermore, it would now be an urgent priority to make sure that
both countries raced hard and fast to get a man on Mars first—
perhaps financing it by a cut back in defense spending.

Former Vice-president Hubert Humphrey was one who saw the
value of this redirection. "Space activities, even space competition,"
he said in September 1966, "can be a substitute for aggression, a
bridge for mutual understanding and the identification of common
interests with other nations, and a major tool of arms control and
disarmament." Unhappily, there is a flaw to this argument which
we examined in detail in Chapter 2. Space activity is mainly in-
dulged in because it might bring strategic advantage in the earthly
wars fought out below. It is thus a form of redirection which could
quite suddenly reveal itself in its true colors of open, nonritualized
conflict.

But the space race does substitute an inanimate object for a
human enemy. It is space and not man that has to be conquered.
All the world knows the value of an enemy and is fond of rem-
iniscing about the comradeship that exists in war. Human societies
are united by an external threat and sometimes by an external
goal. At such times of stress we work better together and achieve
more. If there were hostile beings on Mars, we could quickly

mount a global effort against them. Yet the threats within our midst —such as famine and the population explosion—seem incapable of fully rousing our cooperative efforts.

One kind of inanimate enemy that makes us forget our differences is a natural disaster. Major earthquakes, floods, hurricanes, or landslides usually evoke a global response. The number of people killed or threatened by these events is usually much smaller than the numbers involved in a war or in a famine. They stimulate a greater universal response because they are caused by natural forces beyond our control—forces which cannot be allied to any political ideology. A natural disaster of unprecedented scale, some psychologists have suggested, might galvanize us into such activity that war would have to be forgotten for a long time to come.

A disaster of just this kind may be in the offing. We may be on the verge of another ice age. Some scientists believe that ice ages are caused by the building up of enormous ice caps near the North and South Poles. When these caps become thick enough, the pressure at the bottom becomes so great that the ice and snow liquefy. The whole cap slips, spreading out into the surrounding area. The result is a tidal wave of enormous size which would engulf many coastal areas. If the Antarctic cap slipped, ice floes with an average thickness of 200 yards would spread out as far as latitude 55° south.

The volume of melted ice would also raise the general level of water in the oceans by 20 or 30 yards. This would make most of the densely populated regions of the globe uninhabitable. It would also lead to a new ice age. Existing, unmelted ice would be spread over a much larger area, and its whiteness would reflect back much more of the sun's heat. The earth would cool down.

The present thickness of ice and snow in the Antarctic may already be unstable. It is now more than 4,000 yards thick, and there is enough ice in the Antarctic and in Greenland to cover the whole earth to a depth of 100 yards. A new ice age might come at any time.

Dr. Ernst Hass, medical superintendent of the Doren district hospital in West Germany, suggests that this new ice age may be "an ideal enemy for mankind." As our own destruction is in question, the threat might be real enough to cause us to attempt to halt the buildup of further ice. This might be done, he says, by melting some of the existing ice by blasting or by spreading black powder on it to heat it up. If the results could be controlled, this might even provide a use for some of our excessive stockpiles of nuclear weapons. The melting ice would, of course, raise the level of the oceans unless some action were taken. Dr. Hass suggests the extra water be used to irrigate the drier regions of the world, desalting it first where necessary.

Such a global hydraulic scheme would absorb funds on an unprecedented scale. Its complexity would make a lunar landing look trivial. And its cost would leave few funds with which to continue the arms race. Even if the threat of the next ice age is not imminent, Dr. Hass suggests, we will lose little and gain much by fighting this common enemy. "Why should we not replace the present arms race among nations with a common fight against a global opponent?" he asks. "If we actually have to expect the next ice age, we will have won first prize with this change in attitude. Even if the Antarctic ice cap does not show any tendency toward sliding into the ocean, it still will have caused us to utilize huge invested means, presently completely unproductive, for the expansion or the improvement of our common living space."

Melting the snows of the Antarctic is a global game played for very high stakes. In my view the chances are that it could end in a human disaster quite as catastrophic as global war. But it is useful as a model, for it highlights those aspects of games which might help in a quest for peace. One of these aspects has already been mentioned: competitive games provide an outlet for aggressive actions. But if games in general—taking the word to embrace activities ranging from the space race to the Olympics to international debates—have any major importance, it may be for other reasons as well. We shall see later that an almost essential prerequisite for war is an ability to make an enemy of the enemy—to see him in terms other than those we would use to describe ourselves.

From this emerges a fact which at first appears trite. The better we know our enemies the less hostile they appear. International competitions of any kind are in this sense educative; in them we can see potential enemies participating in the same activities as ourselves and thus proving a common identity. This may provide some reason—though in my view not a good enough one—for "keeping politics out of sport." It is certainly a good reason for keeping politics out of science which, like the Olympics, is a game that has to be played across international frontiers.

Few people claim that by turning fights into games we will eliminate war. The idea is just one among a thousand slender straws at which we might grasp to lessen the chances of annihilation. We turn now to a single idea which some biologists claim could eliminate not only war but civil violence as well.

The Population Drive

A young chaffinch brought up in solitary confinement will never warble like a chaffinch. For this, it needs to hear and imitate the songs of its seniors. A human baby, as every mother knows, needs a good deal of encouragement and assistance if it is to learn to breast-feed. A human adult, some biologists tell us, would never copulate unless he or she were told how to do it. From observations such as these arises the idea that no form of behavior is entirely innate—it must either be learned or stimulated by a reaction with the environment.

Violence may be a form of behavior which falls into this class. Certainly, it is not indispensable either to animal or to human societies. Among those tribes which do not engage in war, and seem to find little pleasure in violence of any kind, are the Himalayan Lepchas, the pygmies that live in the Ituri rain forest of the Congo, and the Arapesh of New Guinea. "These small societies," writes Geoffrey Gorer, "living in the most inaccessible deserts and forests and mountains of four continents, have a number of traits in common, besides the fact that they do not dominate over, hurt or kill one another or their neighbours, though they possess the weapons to do so." Among these traits is the fact that none of these tribes makes much distinction between the ideal characters of men and women. There is, for instance, no warrior class. They also derive enormous pleasure from physical acts—eating, drinking, sex, and laughter. Our Puritanical forefathers, as Dr. Storr has remarked, may have a lot to answer for.

In the wild, animal societies function along similar lines. Aggression is always present, but physical violence is rare, particularly among higher mammals such as gorillas and chimpanzees. George Schaller, who observed mountain gorillas for 466 hours in the Congo, wrote afterwards: "I have not witnessed serious aggressive contacts between gorillas." Jane Goodall, who has watched chimpanzees at close quarters for more than 3,000 hours, reports 73 brief episodes of tension but only one fight. Even that produced "no visible signs of injury."

Yet all our experience of monkeys and apes in zoos shows that they fight frequently and to the death. Sir Solly Zuckerman, whose expertise embraces both defense technology and animal behavior, studied a large colony of baboons in the London Zoo during 1929–30. Initially the colony consisted of some 140 individuals, but this number was rapidly reduced by wholesale massacres. Thirty of thirty-three female deaths were caused by fighting, and 8 of the 61 males died by violence. Fifteen of the females died in one month of particularly savage attacks.

At that time, little was known of the natural behavior of primates and it was thought these massacres—also found in other zoos— were a natural part of monkey behavior. Work in the field, most of it quite recent, now indicates that this is far from true. "The reports from the plains and forests," write the biologists Claire and William Russell,

> bring a message of hope for mankind. The violence of zoo monkeys is not a product of inherent aggressiveness; monkey societies in ideal conditions live in peace and harmony. Violence is not some ultimate and irreducible feature of the universe; it is simply a problem to be solved, and mankind has solved many problems.

Why, then, do animals in captivity fight so fiercely? To the Russells, and many other biologists, the answer is connected with population density. Experiments with almost every kind of animal, notably rats, deer, and monkeys, have shown that violence erupts when living space is compressed. Why this should be is not clear, but there are some clues. There is a "critical distance" for every animal —a separation smaller than which will not be tolerated by any two animals if there is any aggressive tension between them. Cats, for instance, can often be seen "stuck" too close to one another in a position in which neither dares move. Both know that any movement from the other will spark off a violent attack. Generally, this critical distance is such that neither animal has room to turn around and flee before being struck; unless the distance can be increased, violence is inevitable, although it may be short-lived. As the fight starts, rapid movements break the critical distance deadlock so that the defeated can flee in safety. Animals in cages or enclosures violate the personal space of their fellows more frequently than in the wild.

But there are probably more subtle causes of this violence. The pecking order of communal animals can be described as an absolute hierarchy, because it is valid at all times and in all places. Noncommunal animals establish a relative hierarchy in which one animal is boss but only on his own territory and sometimes only at certain times on that territory. On other territories he becomes a second-class citizen. Frequently, of course, the distinction between communal and noncommunal is not clear-cut. Cats, for instance, are partly territorial and so have a relative hierarchy. But they also have an absolute one which appears on neutral territory. There they will fight out their own equivalent of a pecking order which determines, among other things, the sexual seniority of the males. But the bottom cat in this pecking order becomes the top cat when he returns to his own ground. Even wholly communal animals maintain a critical distance from one another, over which relative hierarchy obtains hidden within the absolute hierarchy of the flock as a whole.

In zoos, where there is not much room for territorial behavior, one can now begin to see how this natural balance between absolute and relative hierarchy gets upset. As living space is compressed, the relative hierarchy associated with territory becomes eliminated. There is room only for an absolute system, maintained by brute force. Captive monkey societies have their own despots, their own dictators, and their own tyrants. And they suffer as viciously and as frequently from coups d'état as do their human analogues. Perpetual and lethal squabbling is the order of the day. It is caused by social stress in the form of too many animals per square foot of cage.

This social theory is now to some extent backed up by physiological evidence of the effects of crowding. "At critical levels," writes Dr. Hudson Hoagland,

> the social organization of groups is disrupted and this is accompanied by fighting, reproduction failure, cannibalism and increased death rates. Postmortem examination of the animals shows evidence of overactivity of the pituitary adrenal complex with signs of adrenocortical exhaustion. Crowding of people in concentration camps is highly stressful and has resulted in pathology and deaths with evidence of exhaustion of the adrenal cortex. Increased artherosclerosis, psychoses, neuroses, crime, delinquency, and reduced fertility may accompany the stress of crowding in slums and ghettos.

In plain language, crowding causes hormonal upsets which lead to fighting and to physical disease—in animals and in man.

That crowding has as profound an effect on man as on other animals is difficult to prove. We do know, however, that man also has the equivalent of a critical distance. We all need "personal space," and the American psychiatrist, Dr. Augustus F. Kinzel, has investigated the shape of the circle of protection which we subconsciously form around ourselves. If anyone invades this circle, Dr. Kinzel believes, it can induce panic and violent assault, particularly from men accustomed to violence. He has measured the size of this circle in both violent and nonviolent individuals. In the latter it is a perfect circle, some 18 inches in radius and 7 square feet in area. In violent individuals it is much larger, nearly 30 square feet, and extends farther behind the individual than in front of him. Its size can be roughly judged by anyone prepared to undergo the slightly dangerous experiment of approaching and standing close to someone waiting in a hotel lobby. An angry reaction usually occurs when the separation is around 2 feet.

This only provides confirmatory evidence that we do not like being crowded. The Russells have sought hard to show that crowding—at least in the form of competition for natural resources—has motivated every major and well-documented massive outbreak of violence throughout history. Used in this way, history is a malleable tool, and examples can be picked at random to support almost any conceivable viewpoint of sufficient generality. It is intriguing, however, that the seventeenth and twentieth centuries have been much more warlike for Europe than the eighteenth and nineteenth centuries. The Russells explain this from the observation that there was massive migration from Europe in the eighteenth and nineteenth centuries which relieved population pressure. The colonies, in other words, acted as a kind of safety valve. And when the valve was clamped shut in the twentieth century, Europe saw conflict on a scale it had never envisaged.

The Russells conclude:

> Alike at the level of the individual and that of
> the whole society, the case seems clear that man-
> kind has indeed retained the whole system of
> violence as a means for drastic population reduc-
> tion in face of population crisis, and that this,
> and this alone, is the ultimate significance of
> human violence.

Dr. Paul Leyhausen is among the biologists who have taken the population threat seriously. He sees, as we all do with varying degrees of urgency, that a continuously increasing population must eventually lead to massive famine or massive bloodshed. But he goes on to ascribe to population pressure nearly all the ills of modern man. The relative hierarchy which we call democracy, he argues, cannot thrive in overcrowded societies. Individual freedom is lost and bureaucracy replaces government. The frustrated electorate then tries to introduce concepts of relative hierarchy into fields such as education where more authoritarian systems may be more appropriate. "I have never yet heard or read a reasonable argument as to why ever more and more people should live on the limited space of our Earth," he writes. "The sickness of mankind is too many people. Like any other natural product, they too lose their value when present in excess."

I am unsure to what extent past population pressures can be held responsible for war and violence. But we can all see that many of today's troubles stem from gross overcrowding. In a world in which every other child exists at starvation level, we have no cause for complacency. We have few reasons for not heeding the message of the biologists who warn us that man, like the other animals, cannot live peacefully in the pressure cooker surroundings of modern life. And anyone who can count can work out that in only 30 years' time the situation will be twice as bad as it is now.

Of the 130 or so ministries of defense that are scattered around the globe, all but a handful describe their function as peace keeping. I am therefore quite serious in suggesting that these ministries will soon have to make contraception their first priority. Halting the population explosion is an essential requirement for peace. The pill and the loop, rather than the tank and rifle, may soon become the best form of military aid. "Soon" really means *now,* for as Dr. Paul Ehrlich has remarked, "Most of the people who are going to die in the greatest cataclysm in the history of man have already been born." Dr. Ehrlich's articles on the immediate dangers of the population explosion should become the field manuals of tomorrow's generals.

Man as Man

"Arguments based on fish, birds and other animals are strictly for them," wrote Professor Ashley Montagu in 1968. "They have no relevance for man." And in a book-length work he and 13 other colleagues tried to undermine the tentative conclusions which ethologists such as Dr. Lorenz had been making. Among the more penetrating critics was Dr. Edmund Leach, the anthropologist who delivered the BBC Reith lectures in 1967. Dr. Leach compared the study of animal society by those who seek enlightenment about human society with the man who analyzes a wheelbarrow to try to discover how a jet aircraft works.

He also made a telling semantic point. We can never know, he claimed, what animals think or feel. So when we study their social organization, the best we can do is to see them in the image of man —using terms such as aggression, love, and fear to describe their actions. Having verbally turned animal societies into human ones, is it then logical to reverse the process—to think that animals falsely given human attributes can tell us anything about human behavior? The argument, said Dr. Leach, is circular.

It may also be dangerous. According to Dr. J. P. Scott:

> The erroneous notion that fighting over the
> possession of land is a powerful, inevitable, and
> uncontrollable instinct might well lead to the con-
> clusion that war is inevitable and therefore a
> nation must attack first and fight best in order to
> survive and prosper. It is to be hoped that the
> persons in power in our society are too sophisti-
> cated to fall for any such adolescent interpreta-
> tion of world affairs, but history will, as usual,
> have the last word.

It will not serve any great purpose for us to get deeply enmeshed in this argument. Fortunately, the recommendations that emerge from a study of animal societies are far from revolutionary and in themselves quite inadequate to ensure lasting peace. They may, however, propel us marginally in the right directions and should therefore not be dismissed too hastily. More important, as I have stressed, is the fact that they broaden our view of aggression and violence. In particular, they give no cause for complacency that man will inevitably survive the cataclysmic course on which he seems set.

But one vital question has still not been posed. Even if animal aggression is related to human aggression, does either have any connection with war? It seems doubtful if any aggressive urge makes us push the nuclear button. And it is difficult to connect the verbal sparring matches of politicians with the pecking order of chickens.

On the contrary, there is a great deal of evidence that men as individuals do not fight wars through choice. For instance, a survey by the American Institute of International Order asked, "Do you have any doubts about the desirability of peace?" Eighty-one per cent of the poll had no doubts. Ninety-four per cent thought there was some use in working for peace. There are few absolute standards here, but it is a fact that people's attitudes become much more warlike after a war has been declared than before it.

Even then a good deal of coercion is needed; as Trotsky said, a soldier must be faced with the choice of a probable death if he advances and a certain death if he retreats. Most armies impose the death penalty for desertion. And until recently most armies were conscripted, at least partially, by force. Until 1914, it has been estimated, less than 1 per cent of the British population was ever actually involved in a war; even those that were spent more time in the barracks than on the battlefield. Dr. Stanislav Andreski puts it this way:

> If human beings were in fact endowed with an
> innate proclivity for war, it would not be necessary
> to indoctrinate them with warlike virtues; and
> the mere fact that in so many societies past and
> present so much time has been devoted to such
> an indoctrination proves that there is no instinct
> for war.

The evidence that man must be taught to be warlike is copious. And what we are taught in Western society is that killing within the tribe is murder, and killing outside it is a proof of manhood and bravery. Fleeing from the enemy, a perfectly respectable defense mechanism in animals, is dubbed cowardly in human society. That things could be otherwise is suggested by what will be the final animal example in this chapter. A kitten reared apart from its own species will learn to accept a rat as a companion in its own cage. And never afterward can it be induced to kill or even to pursue rats. Unhappily, it is not difficult to teach humans violent behavior or to instill in them warlike attitudes. This might be expected from our knowledge of animal behavior, but the evidence for it comes from experiments on man. I will summarize the results of one such experiment.

Stanley Milgram, professor of psychology at New York's City University, has investigated how easy it is to make people carry out orders which are harmful to other humans. His subjects were told to test the learning ability of students trying to learn a list of words. When the learners made a mistake, the "teachers" were told to administer an electric shock to the student. For this purpose they were supplied with an electric shock machine calibrated from 15 to 450 volts, with "Danger: Severe Shock" marked on the top range. The subjects could see the students through a partly silvered glass, and they nearly all increased the intensity of shock to the maximum when told to do so.

In later experiments, the subjects were allowed to hear the reactions of the students—which ranged typically from grunts at about 75 volts to agonized screams followed by silence at the maximum intensity. When these cries could be heard, but the victim could not be seen, 62.5 per cent of the subjects administered the full shock when told to. When the victim was in the same room, the number dropped to 40 per cent. When the subjects were told to force the hands of the victims down onto the shock terminals, in spite of their shrieks, as many as 30 per cent still obeyed the orders of those in charge of the experiment. Professor Milgram concludes: "A substantial proportion of people do what they are told to do, irrespective of the content of the act and without limitations of conscience, so long as they perceive that the command comes from a legitimate authority." In other words, we may all be potential Eichmanns willing to excuse ourselves that we were only following orders. (To put readers' minds at rest, I should add that the shocks were fake ones, and the students' screams were simulated—although this was not known to the subjects taking part in the experiment.)

The process of indoctrination is made even easier by the fact that a small success rate is sufficient. During World War II Dr. H. V. Dicks made an extensive study of the psychological and political characteristics of German prisoners. Only 11 per cent were Nazi "fanatics," all others having some or many reservations about Nazi doctrine. This percentage did not change with the fortunes of war, nor did it change much after the war ended. In 1943, 15 per cent of Germans expressed an admiration for Goebbels; and even by 1955, 10 or 11 per cent of Germans under 25 still admired Hitler.

Today, we are constantly told that only 5 per cent of students are militant and that only 5 per cent of the Irish want anything other than to live peacefully with their Protestant or Catholic neighbors. Five per cent is enough. Ten per cent, coupled with powerful leaders, can bring about world war. War, it seems, is an activity fomented by the few to the detriment of the many.

Social scientists have made countless studies of the psychology of the militant 5 or 10 per cent. And the most militant appear in societies with pronounced patriarchal values where masculinity is viewed as an end in itself. Women play an inferior secondary role and there is often a "tenderness taboo." The male must be strong, athletic, brave, and authoritarian—all the characteristics, incidentally, which are lacking from the peaceful tribes mentioned earlier.

A notable feature of the militant is a form of asceticism which eschews pleasure. For this reason, some anthropologists see hope in the hedonistic drives of today's youth. "Mankind is safer when men seek pleasure than when they seek the power and the glory," writes Geoffrey Gorer.

> If the members of the youth international—the beats and the swingers, the *provos* and the *stilyagi* —maintain the same scale of values and the same sex ideals 20 years hence when they themselves are middle-aged and parents, then they may, just possibly, have produced a permanent change in the value systems and sex roles of their societies, which will turn the joy of killing into an unhappy episode of man's historic past, analogous to human sacrifice, which ascribed joy in killing to the gods also.

Unisex, in other words, may be more than just a fashion in clothes.

From this optimistic forecast, we should turn to inquire what contribution biologists might make in the future to the art of peace. The most useful, according to Dr. John Burton, would be for the biologist to admit that he had

> no contribution, that the cause of war is not directly related to aggressiveness, and that in fact he had no reason to believe that aggressiveness is an attribute of a sovereign state. . . . Political leaders of states who accuse other states of being aggressive would then know where the responsibility for aggression finally lies.

But the biologists have already made other contributions. They have exposed our ignorance. While we have studied the cichlid fish and the mountain gorilla with care, we have omitted to study group behavior patterns in man in all except the most primitive societies—what Desmond Morris has called "remote cultural backwaters so atypical and unsuccessful that they are nearly extinct." Biologists have tried to fill the gap, but what is needed is a human ethology with an interdisciplinary mix of animal behaviorists, social scientists, and anthropologists. Natural history has been for the birds and the bees for too long. We need a natural history of man as well.

Those who have tried to study the behavior of men in groups have found it difficult. The underlying patterns are less apparent than they appear to be in animal society. Hegel warned as much when he said that peoples and governments have never acted on principles deduced from history. Dr. Lorenz put it more simply: "The ever-recurrent phenomena of history do not have reasonable causes." Because man is a thinking being, the basic drives that may underlie his behavior are heavily disguised. His collective behavior in groups depends on so many variables that the outcome of specific situations is almost impossible to predict. It may be a vain hope to try to discover a biological or even a psychological basis for man's history of warmaking.

But much of our knowledge of man comes not from the study of his biology and psychology but from the study of his institutions, his cultures, and his social and political organizations. War is a social phenomenon. It can be studied as objectively as economics or town planning. And the natural history of war does tell us a good deal about why and when wars happen. For this new knowledge we owe a debt to a small band of scientists who for more than a decade have been struggling to start a new discipline —peace research.

CHAPTER VII

The Natural History of War

---

*The War Disease–"Natural" Causes
of War–The Arms Race–Paranoids
and Reality–The International Game
–Architects of the Future*

"The idea of turning the cold and
brilliant light of mathematics on
a subject where passions obscure reason
is in itself the embodiment of the best
in scientific ethics."

Anatol Rapaport
Journal of Conflict Resolution
September 1957

Lewis Richardson was a Quaker, a meteorologist, a mathematician, and a psychologist. In 1916 he was also an ambulance driver for the Friends' Ambulance Unit in France. Between runs he could be seen hunched over a notebook working out an apparently endless series of mathematical equations.

Thus it was that the first real attempt at numerical weather forecasting was made. During breaks in the carnage of World War I, Richardson tried to forecast the weather over a six-hour period for a region south of Hamburg. And instead of using the mixture of hunch and folklore which characterized forecasting at that time, he chose mathematics as his weapon of attack. He wrote down all the equations he could deduce which described the way the sun heated the earth and the ways in which winds developed from pressure differences. His forecast, made by laborious hand calculations, took more than a year of his spare time. And in April 1917, during the chaos of the Battle of Champagne, his manuscript was lost under a heap of coal.

Miraculously, it was recovered a few months later. It was found to be so hopelessly wrong that meteorologists were discouraged from repeating the experiment. But their complacency was to be shattered shortly after World War II by the arrival of the computer. Calculations which took Richardson a year could then be done in less than five minutes. A group of scientists at Yale University used Richardson's equations and a computer to produce a remarkably accurate numerical weather forecast. And today numerical weather forecasting is a common technique. At the National Center for Atmospheric Research in Colorado there is now a computer that will plot maps of temperature and pressure over the whole world up to 28 days in advance.

The weather was not the only thing that fascinated Richardson. During the war in France, he also dreamed of a numerical theory of war and wrote a paper called *Mathematical Psychology of War*. "There was no learned society to which I dared to offer so unconventional a work," he said later. "Therefore I had 300 copies made by multigraph, at a cost of about £35, and gave them nearly all away. It was little noticed. Some of my friends thought it funny."

The mathematics of war, at first a hobby for Richardson, soon became a passion. And in 1940 he retired to study the subject full time. It was an uphill struggle. "It is still difficult to publish work on that subject," he wrote shortly before his death in 1953. "There are many anti-war societies, but they are concerned with propaganda, not research. There is a wide public interest in the subject provided it is expressed in bold rhetoric, but not if it is a quantitative scientific study involving statistics and mathematics."

Had Richardson lived just a few more years, he might have been more optimistic. Four years after his death, the *Journal of Conflict Resolution,* which encompassed aims similar to his own, was started. And in 1960 the results of his 13 years of full-time research were published posthumously as his two already classic books, *The Statistics of Deadly Quarrels* and *Arms and Insecurity.*

Lewis Richardson was thus the father of two new sciences. One, numerical weather forecasting, is already highly developed. The other, the mathematics of war, has developed more slowly. Its progress has been hindered by a society accustomed to centuries of diplomacy and political "hunchmanship." There was, and still is, deep-felt resistance to the idea that anything as complex as international relations could be examined in the cold light of mathematics. Were it not for this, Richardson's second science might have borne fruit two or three decades ago. We might by now have had a science which would predict when and where wars would break out, how they might be prevented, and what could be done to lessen the impact of arms races. Even more important, we would have had a science which, simply by its existence, might have changed our whole attitude to war.

The War Disease

Of all the ills that have plagued the human race since history began, war has been the least researched. Why this should be is not clear, but the fact remains that until at most 40 years ago it seems to have occurred to no one to study war as a social phenomenon —as an affliction of the human condition which has remorselessly brought death to millions and an end to most of the great civilizations. Individual wars, to be sure, have been diligently investigated, but few historians have looked up from their case studies to seek the global picture. Had they done so, who knows what advances they might have produced?

An analogy with medicine is instructive. Until 1848 no one knew what caused cholera. But in that year a Dr. John Snow looked up from his individual patients and sought a social pattern for the disease. On a map he plotted the addresses of 500 people who had died from cholera in Soho in a period of 10 days. All the deaths clustered around a central spot which, investigation proved, was the site of a water pump. When its handle was removed, the epidemic died and Dr. Snow had proved that cholera was caused by contaminated water. Why the world had to wait another hundred years before anyone applied the same principle to the study of war is inexplicable.

Professor Quincey Wright, at the University of Chicago, was perhaps the first man to mount a monumental and objective study of the "war disease." He led a team of scientists and politicians who for 15 years amassed and analyzed every war statistic they could gather. His project involved more than 75 separate studies, generated 66 manuscripts, and produced theses for 45 students studying for higher degrees. Ten specialist books were published, but the job of assimilating the whole study fell to Professor Wright himself. And in 1942 he published his enormous *Study of War*. The latest edition, published in 1965, runs to 1,637 pages, 40 chapters, 52 appendixes, 51 illustrations, and 77 tables. As just one example, the study included an analysis of the "warlikeness" of 652 primitive peoples, together with details of their race, culture, environment, and social and political organizations. We shall see later what uses can be made of facts such as these.

Professor Wright also contributed entirely new data about war itself. In modern civilization—since about 1500—he found there had been at least 284 wars and some 3,000 battles. He defined a battle as involving more than 1,000 casualties on land or more than 500 at sea; a war was a hostile encounter which involved more than 50,000 troops or which was legally declared as war. But, he warned, these were inadequate measures of human violence. The United States, for instance, had been involved in only 165 of the "official" battles. But she had fought in more than 9,000 hostile encounters. "There have probably been over a quarter of a million such hostile encounters in the civilized world since 1500, an average of over 500 a year," Professor Wright estimated.

The accompanying table shows some of the main statistics of war over the past four centuries. Battles, as well as becoming more frequent, are becoming much larger—as their names reveal. They were once called after the bridges or towns where they took place. By World War I they were named after rivers—the Battle of the Somme—or even regions—the Battle of Champagne. By World War II they were called after countries or oceans, the Battle of Britain, the Battle of France, and the Battle of the Atlantic. The trend appears to lead inevitably to the nuclear holocaust that would be the Battle of the Globe.

Another American scientist, Dr. Frank L. Klingberg, was asked during World War II to find some means of predicting how heavy Japanese losses would have to be before the Japanese surrendered. The question became academic when the atomic bomb was dropped, but in the course of his work Dr. Klingberg discovered how quickly violence was escalating:

War	Date	Average deaths per day
Napoleonic	1790–1815	233
Crimean	1854–1856	1075
Balkan	1912–1913	1941
World War I	1914–1918	5449
World War II	1939–1945	7738
(Hiroshima)	August 6, 1945	80,000

TABLE 2					
Century	16th	17th	18th	19th	20th
No. of wars	63	64	38	89	30 (to 1964)
No. of battles	87	239	781	651	more than 1,000
No. of battles/war	1-2	4	20	7	more than 30
Average length of war (years)	2.9	2.7	2.7	1.4	4.0
% of time at war	65	65	38	28	18
Average no. of nations/war	2.4	2.6	3.7	3.2	4.8
Average size of forces on each side in each battle	18,000	22,000	22,000	35,000	100,000 (to 1940)
% of battles outside Europe	0	0	2	13	25 (to 1964)
% forces killed in battle	–	25	15	10	6
% of warring nations killed as direct result of war	1.5	3.7	3.3	1.5	8.8
Intensity of wars (violence index)	180	500	370	120	3,080

Wars: those legally declared or involving more than 50,000 troops

Battles: those involving more than 1,000 casualties on land or 500 at sea

Data: from Wright, Quincey. *A Study of War*. Chicago and London: University of Chicago Press, 2nd edition, 1965

Sorokin, Pitirim. *Social and Cultural Dynamics*. London: Allen & Unwin, 1937

Institut Français de Polémologie. "Périodicité et Intensité des Actions de Guerre (1200 à 1945)" in *Guerres et Paix* (1960/2)

The sociologist Pitirim Sorokin found another measure of the same thing in 1933. He calculated an index of violence based on factors such as the size of population, size of fighting force, and the numbers of wars and casualties involved in combat since the twelfth century. His violence index is the last line of Table 3. It shows that even before World War II violence was more than 25 times greater in this century than the last; it was more than 150 times greater than in the twelfth century.

There are other indications that the twentieth century is the time of violent upheaval which we all intuitively believe it to be. So far nearly 90 people out of every 1,000 have been killed as a direct result of war in this century compared with only 15 in the last. The number of people involved in the increasing number of battles is also getting much larger. The battles themselves last much longer than they used to. Since the last world war about 20 million men have been under arms, roughly 7 out of every 1,000 (and this excludes the huge numbers of people employed in war industries of various kinds). In seventeenth-century Europe only 3 in every 1,000 were under arms.

Finally, there are signs that war has recently become more common. Lt. Col. Fielding L. Greaves has counted no less than 14,542 wars in the period 3600 B.C. to A.D. 1962. He found that there was an average of 2.61 new wars every year up to the beginning of World War II. Since that war ended, however, the average has risen to 2.94. In view of all this, it is not surprising that we think things are getting worse. "There is a more widespread opinion than in any other period of history that war has not functioned well in the twentieth century," Professor Wright concludes with scholarly understatement. "From being a generally accepted instrument of statesmanship, deplored by only a few, war has, during the modern period, come to be generally recognized as a problem."

If there is a brighter side to the coin, one has to look hard for it. Table 3 does show that the percentage of forces killed in battle has gone down over the centuries. At the same time the percentage of civilians killed has gone up. In World War I about 13 per cent of the dead were civilians; in World War II, about 70 per cent; in the Korean War, 84 per cent; and in Vietnam the percentage may be over 90. In the Battle of the Globe, if it occurs, mankind's fate may be sealed with the final statistical absurdity: civilians killed, 100 per cent; military forces killed, 0 per cent.

The other figures which seem to give reassurance are equally illusory. Thus we have spent progressively less time fighting wars over the centuries. But that is only because we have learned to fight them faster and more efficiently. World War III may be measured in minutes rather than years, but its brevity will hardly compensate for its effects.

More and more nations seem to be joining each war, and more and more of the battles are being fought outside Europe. Wars, of course, are no less undesirable because they are fought by Africans, Asians, and South Americans. Indeed, there is some evidence to the contrary. The Lopez war of 1865–70, in which Paraguay fought Brazil, Argentina, and Uruguay, did not end until 83.5 per cent of Paraguay's population had been killed. One estimate claims that at the end only 3 per cent of the men and less than 14 per cent of the women survived. A country that started with a population of 1,337,000 ended up with only 221,000 inhabitants.

Lewis Richardson, consulting more than 70 history books, compiled the vital statistics of all the wars he could trace since 1820. His interest was actually in what he called "deadly quarrels," and he classified them according to the logarithm of the number of people killed in each "quarrel." As the logarithm of 10,000,000 is 7, he called a war in which that number of people were killed a quarrel of magnitude 7; similarly, a quarrel in which 10,000 people were killed was magnitude 4. He then added up how many quarrels there had been in the following size ranges:

Magnitude	People killed	No of quarrels since 1820
7.5 to 6.5	6.5 to 5.5	5.5 to 4.5
31,622,777 to 3,162,278	3,162,277 to 316,228	316,227 to 31,623
2	5	24
4.5 to 3.5	3.5 to 2.5	smaller than 0.5
31,622 to 3163	3162 to 317	3 or less
63	more than 188	6 million

Thus the figure 2 in the table above refers to the two world wars, in both of which millions of people were killed. At the other end of the scale, quarrels of magnitudes less than 0.5 involved three, two, or one deaths—they were either murders or multiple murders. Richardson arrived at his figure of 6 million murders after consulting the criminal records of a score of countries and allowing for some of the possible errors. He admitted his figure might be wrong by several times, but such a relatively "small" error was insignificant on the log scale.

There is, however, a gap in the table for quarrels between magnitude 2.5 and 0.5—those involving between 4 and 316 deaths. Such "quarrels" were too large to be of interest to criminal departments and too small to be of interest to the military. But with all his other data at hand Richardson could now propose a theory. He plotted on a graph the number of quarrels against their magnitude. He found they fell on an almost perfectly smooth curve. He was then able to read off the graph how many quarrels there had been in the missing size range. He concluded that there had been 397,000 quarrels of magnitude 0.5 to 1.5 (those involving between 4 and 31 deaths); and that there had been 5,630 quarrels of magnitude 1.5 to 2.5 (involving between 32 and 316 deaths).

This information could have been obtained in no other way. We can never prove that Richardson was right, for the records do not exist. But the technique is a classic example of the power of the scientific approach applied to a novel problem. It gives good reason to believe that if science is used to study warfare, spectacular results may emerge.

One further example should suffice to make the point. Richardson was intrigued by the idea that arms are an insurance against war. He presented his argument in the form of a Socratic dialogue between himself and a "Colonial Official," speaking in the year 1910. "It is absurd," the official told Richardson, "for people to make a fuss about the cost of the British Navy. That cost should be regarded as an insurance premium on the value of British overseas trade. And, indeed, the rate of premium is remarkably low, only about 3 per cent on the imports and exports of the United Kingdom."

Richardson decided to test this theory. He generalized it to the form that expenditure on arms should minimize suffering if war breaks out. And after painstaking research he found out the military expenditure of some score of European nations during 1913, 1914, and 1915. He also estimated the deaths the same countries incurred as a result of the war. This time there was no smooth curve. The countries that spent most did not suffer the least damage. Richardson concluded there was no relationship between how much a country spent on arms and what its losses were in a subsequent war. His Socratic critic sprang to the attack.

"CRITIC: You have misunderstood the point. To
be well-armed may not keep a nation out of war,

> but it does enable it to emerge victorious, with larger territory or other advantages, and to forget its casualties, which, though they seemed severe at the time, are easily outlived in the long subsequent peace.
>
> "AUTHOR: That is quite a different theory. Do all well-armed nations emerge victorious? Please look at the point marked Germany in the diagram of empires."

The diagram, of course, showed that the defeated Germany had spent more on arms than any of the other 20 empires and countries. And Richardson went on to suggest that expenditure on arms was an important cause of war, rather than a means of preventing it.

"Natural" Causes of War

The massing of war statistics is not in itself a particularly useful activity. It is only when the data are used to test theories that we can expect helpful insights. Just as Richardson used his data to test some theories of how spending on armaments might reduce the risk of defeat, so other scientists—of what one might call the "cataclysmic school"—have looked for natural events which might explain why wars occur. And, like the results of any social science poll, the findings they have come up with range from the absurd to the obvious. Occasionally, they have also been revealing.

In 1923 a Russian astronomer and archaeologist, Professor A. L. Tchijevsky, published what he called an Index of Mass Human Excitability. His information was collected from 72 countries and covered the period 500 B.C. to A.D. 1922. His principal conclusion was that humans behave excitedly—and violently—in waves which break upon society nine times every century. Each wave, the professor claimed, lasts for 11.1 years and reaches its peak one year before the time of maximum sunspot activity.

An American psychologist, Professor Raymond H. Wheeler, followed up with a similar study in 1943. His conclusions were no less startling. Civil wars, according to Professor Wheeler, occurred in waves with a 170-year period between them. Every third wave was more severe than the other two, giving a cycle of drastic civil violence every 510 years. The cause, he claimed, was not sunspots but droughts—which also occurred every 170 years.

Are those the findings of the crank fringe of science? Not entirely.

Lewis Richardson and Quincey Wright—both sane and level-headed scholars—have also found natural cycles to human hostilities. "Tabulations of the dates at which battle honours have been given to British regiments," says Professor Wright, "show a remarkable fifty-year fluctuation in the frequency of such battles." He found similar evidence from other battles and in the war casualty rate in England, France, and the United States.

This 50-year cycle Professor Wright attributes to the passage of two generations—the first is thought to regard war as undesirable, and the second believes it to be romantic. (Interestingly, economists have also found a 50-year cycle in their subject, and in England and the United States 50 years is about the time for which one political party dominates.)

All this might be dismissed as fantasy did Richardson not find something similar. His cycle seemed to be 15 to 30 years long but Richardson writes: "We may suppose that the generation who had not fought in the earlier war, but who were brought up on tales about its romance, heroism, and about the wickedness of the enemy, became influential from 30 to 60 years after the war ended and so delayed the process of forgiving and forgetting."

Two American scientists, Frank Denton and Warren Phillips, were sufficiently struck by this to study the cycle in more detail—examining fluctuations in the number of wars, the number of people involved in them, and the number of casualties. They found that a 25- to 30-year cycle did indeed exist, within which was a 5-year cycle of war. Thus they found the following warlike periods: 1840–44, 1865–69, 1890–94, 1915–19, 1940–44.

Like Richardson and Wright, they also sought an explanation in terms of the generations. Those too young to fight in a war, they reasoned, would have to wait 25 years or so before becoming influential decision makers. The latters' age of power, too, spans roughly 25 years—from the age of 40 or 45 to 65 or 70. In other words, the power elite undergoes a complete turnover every generation or every 25 years.

Cycles of war are neither very important nor inevitable. What is important, however, are the explanations given for them. What started as a sunspot explanation in the 1920s has now become a human explanation, which is far more understandable. In the last analysis all wars are declared by humans and so caused by them. But there do seem to be certain physical and geographical conditions which make a country more likely to go to war.

I have already mentioned that one of Professor Wright's monumental contributions to the study of war was to compile a list of 652 primitive societies and their characteristics. Two Norwegian scientists, Drs. Tom Broch and Johan Galtung, decided to use this data to see whether more primitive tribes were more warlike than less primitive ones. Their conclusions are unusual for conflict research for they are unequivocal: there are virtually no "ifs or buts" and few qualifications or exceptions. One-third of the tribes were found to "engage in aggressive warfare for economic or political purpose." And the most primitive were the *least* belligerent. The least primitive—societies we would today call "traditional"—were the most belligerent. If the tribes also had much contact with their neighbors, they were found to be even more belligerent. Drs. Galtung and Broch are pessimistic about the implications of this finding. As society becomes progressively more civilized, they suggest, and "instant communications" become available to everyone, the world may become more warlike than ever.

This finding ties in with many others in the field of conflict research—and most notably with one made by the father of the subject, Richardson himself. He worked out the average number of frontiers each of 33 states had with other states during the period 1820 to 1945. A seacoast counted as only one frontier, and if two countries had a common frontier at several points—as when their colonies were adjacent to each other—this also counted as one. Richardson then compared the number of frontiers a nation had with the number of wars fought:

Country	Frontiers	Wars
Japan	1.6	8
Nepal	2	3
Sweden	2.3	0
Greece	2.7	6
Denmark	3	2
. . . .		
China	10	9
Prussia	10.6	7
Brazil	11.5	3
France	15	19
British Empire	22.5	26

This list of ten countries includes three exceptions—Japan, Greece, and Brazil—to the rule that the more frontiers a state has the more wars it fights. When the figures for all 33 states are put on a graph, this rule can be seen to apply rather accurately. Even the exceptions are interesting; Japan and Greece appear more belligerent than the rule suggests they "should" be, and Brazil appears less belligerent. But Brazil's north and west frontiers are sparsely populated and in regions where transport is difficult except by river; wars across those frontiers would be very unlikely.

Frontiers, of course, are a measure of "contact" between one nation and another. So the frontier law ties in well with the Norwegian scientists' finding. The implication for peace keeping is obvious. "But," as Richardson wryly remarked, "frontiers are not easily altered."

These findings shed a much more sinister light on what has been going on in the world since 1945. About 59 of the world's underdeveloped countries have achieved independence since then—most of them since 1961. As a result the total number of national frontiers has shot up, and so has the average number of frontiers per country. It cannot be an accident that the number of conflicts in the world seems to have been increasing just as fast. Alan Wood of the Institute for Strategic Studies in London has calculated that since 1938 the total number of conflicts has almost doubled every decade. Most of the increase comes from Africa, the Middle East, and Asia.

This brings us to the poverty gap. Today 90 per cent of the world's wealth is concentrated in about 30 rich countries. The other 10 per cent is spread thinly over about 100 developing countries. Even California's Gross "National" Product is bigger than the whole of Latin America's; in 1969 it was also larger than any one of the 137 states except the United States, the U.S.S.R., the UK, and West Germany.

This may seem extraordinary enough. But the situation is getting much worse. Two-thirds of the world's population already lives in the developing countries—and 85 per cent of all the births that take place occur there. As a result the developing countries are doubling their populations three times faster than the developed countries. The race for equality is being run backward, and every year the gap widens.

It should surprise no one to learn that this trend is being matched in terms of human violence. "Of the 73 armed conflicts occurring in the period 1958–65," writes the American scientist Dalimil Kybal, "63 (86 per cent) occurred in poor or very poor countries." The former U.S. Defense Secretary, Robert McNamara, was quick to point up the implications. "There is a direct and constant relationship," he said on May 18, 1966, "between the incidence of violence and the economic status of the countries afflicted. . . . The conclusion is blunt and inescapable: the years that lie ahead for the nations in the southern half of the globe are pregnant with violence."

Of all the cataclysmic theories of war, only this seems to have held up to repeated investigation. The poverty gap, whether between nations or between classes within a nation, is an important source of conflict. As such, it frequently gives rise to violence—in the form of revolution, a war of liberation, or even international strife. As the world's resources and wealth are currently so unevenly spread, this should give us great cause for concern. There is every indication that the situation is getting worse rather than better, and I shall consider the implications of all this in more detail in Chapter 9.

But the "violence of imbalance" is not a sufficient explanation of all war. All the most recent examples of large-scale international conflict have occurred between sides that were roughly balanced. To understand these any better, we have to examine them for what they are—a violent relationship between nations. And the relationship that currently concerns us most of all is the arms race between East and West.

The Arms Race

"There have been only three great arms races," wrote Richardson in 1951. "The first two of them ended in wars in 1914 and 1939; the third is still going on." Like all of us, Richardson wanted to know how the third arms race would end. Earlier he had become the first man to devise a mathematical theory of how arms races work. He was sufficiently impressed with his theory to write an article shortly before World War II comparing the situation with the arms race before World War I. He urged the editor of the journal to which he sent his paper to publish quickly—because, he said, this might prevent another world war. The editor rejected the paper; the world war occurred: and no one seriously thinks that Richardson's article could have stopped it.

But his work, and that of his followers, has undoubtedly shed light on the hidden dynamics of the arms race. Consider the following sequence of events.

On July 3, 1961, President Khrushchev announced that he was suspending the Soviet Union's unilateral reduction of armed forces. Instead, he had decided to increase the military budget by $3,000 million because of "the growing military budgets in NATO countries."

Later the same day President Kennedy ordered a review of United

States military capability. Six months after that he announced that defense expenditure had increased by 15 per cent in the past year. And, he said, we have "more than doubled our acquisition rate of Polaris submarines—doubled the production capacity of Minuteman missiles—and increased by 50 per cent the number of manned bombers ready on 15-minute alert."

This is how arms races are kept going. The process looks chaotic but is not. It is a steady escalation in which one side increases weapons or expenditure according to its assessment of what the other side is doing. In his equations Richardson made allowances for the fact that countries get tired of the race—there comes a time when the cost looks excessive and the race slows down. He also realized that other events may increase the goodwill between the sides—and this also slows down the race. But provocations—such as the Cuban missile crisis—speed it up again.

Richardson's equations are mathematically simple and they can be put, somewhat clumsily and inaccurately, into words. The rate at which one nation arms, Richardson said, depends on the grievances or goodwill it feels towards the other side, plus some measure of their difference in military power. Even from this, some intriguing ideas follow:

1. If neither side has grievances nor arms, neither side starts an arms race. There is "permanent peace by disarmament and satisfaction"—as has existed between the United States and Canada since 1817 and between Norway and Sweden since 1905.

2. If there are grievances but no arms, an arms race will start.

3. If there are grievances and one side disarms, it will not stay disarmed for long.

By putting all this into equations, Richardson was able to deduce many important characteristics of an arms race. When he began to put numbers into his equations, he used the value of trade between nations as a measure of their goodwill toward one another. His equations were so simple that the condition for an arms race not to start turns out to be this: the value of trade between two alliances must be larger than the sum they spend on armaments.

"As love covereth a multitude of sins," wrote Richardson of the arms race leading to World War I,

> so the goodwill between the opposing alliances
> would just have covered £194 million of defense
> expenditure on the part of the four nations
> concerned. Their actual expenditure in 1909 was
> £199 million; and so began an arms race which

> led to World War I. . . . In the years 1907
> and 1908 a small mutual obligement between the
> opposing groups of nations, such as a reduction of
> their warlike annual budgets by an amount equal
> to the cost of two days of the subsequent war,
> would have prevented the arms race from
> developing and so, presumably, would have
> avoided the war altogether.

The "theory" behind an arms race—its political justification—is that it is necessary to preserve a "balance of power." Richardson's equations showed that nations could reach a stable balance of power in this way. But the cost of doing this was that what they spent on arms was not necessarily stable—the cost might run away with them until one side declared war or began disarmament.

An arms race, Richardson said, is like a ball placed on top of a horse's saddle. If it rolls in the head-to-tail direction, it is not likely to fall off; a balance of power situation prevails. But if it rolls from side to side, it will fall off straight away; a runaway arms race has started.

Can human affairs such as these be properly expressed in the language of mathematics? Richardson thought so.

> The equations are merely a description of what
> people would do if they did not stop to think. Why
> are so many nations reluctantly but steadily in-
> creasing their armaments as if they were mechan-
> ically compelled to do so? Because, I say, they
> follow their traditions, which are fixtures, and their
> instincts, which are mechanical, and because they
> have not yet made a strenuous intellectual and
> moral effort to control the situation. . . . In this
> respect the equations have some analogy to a
> dream. For a dream often warns an individual of
> the antisocial acts that his instincts would lead him
> to commit, if he were not wakeful.

In saying this, Richardson suggests that politicians do not stop to think. Today, perhaps, we are less cynical. I recommend anyone who thinks he can act more rationally than a politician to try the following arms race game, invented by the Danish scientists Mats Friberg and Dan Jonsson. Their "guns and butter" exercise illustrates beautifully just how deep is the arms race trap and how difficult it is to get out of it.

"Guns and butter" needs three players; one for each side and one controller. Each player has two dishes, one for guns and one for butter, and the controller has a large supply of coins or chips. At each deal the controller gives each player one coin. The players, who must be out of sight of one another, then decide into which dish to place their coin. The deals continue until one of the players declares "war." He then compares the number of coins in his gun dish with that of his opponent. The winner is the one with the most guns; he takes his opponent's butter coins and pockets them; both dishes of gun coins are returned to the controller. And at some point unknown to the players the controller declares the game ended; each player can then pocket what he has in his butter dish. This is the payoff for playing the game peacefully.

The Danish scientists ran a long series of controlled experiments using 30 pairs of players. Their most surprising result was that almost everyone opted for a warlike approach. Only 18 per cent of all the coins used were put into the butter dish; 82 per cent were spent, and inevitably wasted (returned to controller), on guns. And this in spite of the fact that had each player put every coin into the butter dish, each would have come away with a profit amounting to half the kitty. Although this form of cooperation was the best bet for both of them, very few players even attempted to play this way.

The scientists made the game more interesting by allowing the controller to tell the players after certain deals what their opponent had done with his last coin. This is analogous to one nation announcing to the other what it intends to spend on armaments in the coming year. They found that this increased still further the number of coins spent on guns.

They also found that the players, like nations, nearly always tended to overestimate how much their opponents had spent on guns. Furthermore, the higher the level of the armaments, the higher the overestimates—a situation somewhat similar to the "runaway" arms race predicted by Richardson. In fact, most of the games ran a course which corresponded very closely to Richardson's mathematical model of the arms race.

Richardson's model was made before nuclear weapons were invented. Paul Smoker, a British peace researcher, believes that the model now needs modifying. One reason is that there was no fear before the two world wars that the coming war would bring the world to an end. Today, a nuclear war might do this and so another brake has been applied to the arms race. Furthermore, today's arms race is not simply between two sides. Richardson himself tried to use his model to explain an arms race among up to 10 nations, but he was not very successful. Today, any model must obviously include China, France, and Britain; probably it should include West Germany and Poland as well.

Paul Smoker has therefore tried several variations on the Richardson scheme. He found that the race between the United States and the U.S.S.R. was growing in size during 1948–52 but dampened down during 1952–60. Another round of escalation—perhaps related to the "missile gap" mentioned earlier—then started. From his new models, Smoker predicted in 1962 that a new dampening would occur in 1964. Sure enough, on December 15, 1963, it was announced that Khrushchev planned to curb military spending and to reduce his country's armed forces. And two weeks later Robert McNamara announced a planned cut in the defense budget of $1,000 million—the first cut since 1958.

After this remarkable prediction, Smoker went on to develop a wave model of the arms race. He compared the race to ripples on the surface of a pond. The size of the ripple is equivalent to expenditure on armaments. As the race heats up, the ripples get larger, and as it cools down they get smaller. Outside disturbances can then be compared to stones—or sometimes rocks—being thrown into the pond.

One such stone was identified by Smoker—the entry into NATO of West Germany at the end of 1954 and the formation of the Warsaw Pact in May 1955. The significance of Germany's move may have been underestimated in the West. In the Napoleonic War and in World War I Russia suffered heavily from invading forces. In World War II she was again invaded by a much smaller nation which advanced nearly to her capital city. New estimates suggest that in that war the Russians lost nearly 20 million people (the Americans have lost less than 1 million people in war during the whole of the past century).

Thus one result of Germany's entry into NATO was much ripple making on the arms race pond. According to Smoker's model, these ripples took a long time to die away. By 1961 his measure of hostility between the two sides showed it to be twice as intense as it would have been were it not for the German ripple. Smoker concluded: "Alliances are intended to prevent war but in fact such shocks could disrupt the system and cause the war they are trying to prevent. Decision makers should consider the effect on the whole system before forming, strengthening or expanding alliances."

Smoker's models provided some other important pointers. He found, for instance, that as long as the theory of deterrence exists, the arms race will oscillate between large and small values but never die away. "Coupled with the accidental war risks," he said, "this presents a very black picture if survival is our aim . . . the fact that there is a finite probability of accidental war makes deterrence as a long-term policy insanity."

His ripple theory also threw up some practical recommendations. One of the items that affect ripples is the information released about what one side intends to spend on armaments. Smoker found that when the system was being dampened, frequent announcements—of decreasing military budgets—helped to increase the dampening effect. He suggested that at such times military spending should be publicly announced every six or nine months, instead of every year. But when things were getting worse, information about defense spending made the ripples even larger. At such times, he said, military budgets should be announced only every two years. An analogous situation was found in the guns-and-butter game—when players were told what the other had done, they spent more on armaments.

Today an arms race cannot be distinguished from a war as sharply as in 1914 or 1939. Nuclear weapons have forced us to adopt the concept of limited war. Hostility starts gradually and war may never be declared in its formal sense—as it never has been in Vietnam. This prompted Drs. Norman Alcock and Keith Lowe to see if the Vietnam war followed Richardson's equations. Their work, at the Canadian Peace Research Institute, showed that it did. It showed also that there were two parts to this war—one ending in about 1964 and the other following the next year.

Intriguingly, Dr. John Voevodsky, while at Stanford University, published a general article on the structure of war at about the same time. He, too, found two parts to the Vietnam war, with the changeover dating from the same time as the Canadians suggested. And, like the Canadians, he also suggested in 1969 that "we are approaching a crisis point in the Vietnam war where either a settlement is possible or another major escalation is indicated." As we now know, settlement and not escalation was the order of the day.

Dr. Voevodsky's work is among the most fascinating of all theories to emerge on the structure of war. He found, for instance, that the ratio of casualties to deaths follows the same course whatever the war—and he included the American Civil War, both World Wars, and Korea and Vietnam. He showed that the number of casualties was also related to the size of the forces in the battle zone. He found that if forces were doubled, casualties went up about six times in all wars except the Korean one—where they went up nearly four times. He found too that the war "variables" were closely related on each side—if deaths, casualties, or forces were changed on one side, they invariably changed by a related amount on the other. And, finally, he found that as time went on, the rate of increase of forces at the front leveled off. The way in which it did so could be used to predict when the war would end. By June 30, 1968, Dr. Voevodsky forecast, both sides in the Vietnam war had committed to the front 86 per cent of all the troops they would use in that war.

Common sense, one might argue, would lead to similar conclusions. But what is surprising is that these rules should apply so accurately for all wars. "Each war forms a pattern over time," Dr. Voevodsky writes, "and then history repeats each pattern. . . . Instead of complete chaos, which is the expected characteristic of human affairs, the exact opposite condition seems to exist when the human affair is warfare. . . . Wars appear to be remarkably orderly events."

I suspect the importance of this work does not lie in predicting the number of deaths in a war or when it will end. Much more important is the fact that it changes our attitude to war. It changes the role of the soldier to that of an inevitable statistic engaged in a repetitive historical pattern.

"We will hope that it is not true," said the wife of a canon of Worcester Cathedral when she heard of Darwin's theory of evolution; "but if it is true let us pray that it not become generally known." Those who seek to govern by military force may be praying the same thing about the new scientific analysis of war—an analysis which is increasingly turning its attention on the decision makers themselves.

Paranoids and Reality

On June 28, 1914, a Serbian nationalist in Sarajevo assassinated the heir apparent to the throne of Austria-Hungary. Within weeks Austria-Hungary had declared war on Serbia; Germany on Russia and then France; and England on Germany. Four years later 10 million men had been killed, twice as many wounded, the German empire lay in ruins, and the map of Europe had been completely redrawn. The seeds had been sown for a worldwide economic depression and a second, even bloodier, world war.

The genesis of this onslaught, as we have seen, can be found in the European arms race of the first few years of this century. But it is more difficult to see how a murder in Serbia could have provided the trigger for such a chain of events. The six weeks that followed therefore provide a unique case history for the analysis of how nations and their leaders behave in times of stress.

Not content with the standard historical description, scientists at Stanford University in California have made a detailed analysis of the attitudes of the six principal powers during this period. They accumulated the most authentic documents written by the half dozen or so most influential leaders in each country over the six weeks. Their interest lay in perceptions—perceptions of how each leader saw the moves of other nations and of how he perceived the significance of his own moves. Content analysis of these documents revealed about 5,000 perceptions, which were then characterized into type—such as hostility, friendship, frustration, and satisfaction —and graded on a 1-to-9 intensity scale. This information was then used to analyze the events of Europe's most crucial six weeks.

"The results," write Drs. Ole Holsti and Robert North, "reveal that the decision makers of each major power in the crisis felt their own nation to be the undeserved victim of a hostile environment. Together the nations apparently perceived more than twice as much hostility directed at them as they directed at other nations. And each nation perceived itself as the main agent of a friendship which was not reciprocated by the other nations.

From their data, the scientists were able to construct an index of injury which reflected the feelings of paranoia that the leaders felt at various times during the crisis. It was found that at the times of the most crucial decisions, the leaders were at their most paranoiac —seeing themselves as being the object of hostility and the non-recipient of friendship, while they themselves were not being hostile and were dispensing friendship to others.

A critic of this analysis might point out that the documents could not be reflecting the truth very accurately; it is logically impossible for all five nations to act in a friendly way and yet regard their neighbors as hostile. This is precisely the point. Leaders can act only on their perceptions of the truth, and during a crisis, these are particularly likely to depart from reality.

The documents used also reveal something about the personality of the various leaders involved. At Northwestern University a "model" of the start of World War I has been used to investigate the role of personality further. First a team of subjects was selected whose members, according to psychological tests, matched the personalities of the real leaders rather closely. The scientists Charles and Margaret Hermann then used the team to play out the principal events of the start of World War I. They effectively made it into a war game, but all the clues that the game was really World War I were removed. Another team, with different psychological characteristics, was also made to play the game. Its members' records were then analyzed in the same way as were the actual records of the leaders in the Stanford study. The analysis showed that the psychologically matched team behaved much as did the real leaders. But the other team found a way out of the dilemma and ended up in negotiation.

These studies are highly suggestive. Specifically, they suggest that the personalities of national leaders must be taken into account when war is studied. They also indicate that nations—or at least their leaders—tend to behave paranoically during a crisis. In 1959, before either of these studies had been completed, Professor Kenneth Boulding leapt intuitively to the same conclusion. "Most nations," he wrote, "seem to feel that their enemies are more hostile toward them than they are toward their enemies. This is a typical paranoid reaction."

It can be no accident that the leaders of totalitarian states have often shown paranoid tendencies—Hitler, Stalin, and even Mussolini are all examples. To explore the idea much further, however, means treading on dangerous ground. Scientists may be allowed to poke their icy fingers into many novel situations, but one area is definitely out of bounds: detailed and public assessments of the mental derangements of living politicians. The fact that psychologists have found that Nebuchadnezzar suffered from icyanthropy (believing he was a wolf), that Saul was a manic depressive, that Cromwell had paranoid delusions, and that Napoleon was a hypomanic is intriguing but scarcely helpful in dealing with today's problems.

Our thanks are therefore due to Dr. Brent M. Rutherford, also of Northwestern, for devising an elliptical means of saying what needed to be said. Dr. Rutherford was struck by the fact that mental illness sufficiently severe to need treatment is remarkably common in most of Western society. Symptoms that indicate this have been found in 81.5 per cent of a sample of 1,666 people living in Manhattan; in 84.5 per cent of the population of a nonurban community in Nova Scotia; in 86 per cent of Copenhagen schoolchildren; and in 79 per cent of Stockholm schoolchildren.

Presumably, therefore, democracy acts as a kind of filter which allows the more mentally stable personalities to be elected to positions of great responsibility. Without being able to psychoanalyze large numbers of politicians there is no way of knowing. But Dr. Rutherford knew that mental hospitals have recently allowed their patients active roles in running the hospital. The various wards elect their own leaders and councils. The psychological background of all the patients is well-known; furthermore, studies have shown that mental patients participate in and show roughly as much enthusiasm for political activity as does the population at large. Dr. Rutherford therefore compared the personalities of the hospital leaders with the personalities of all the patients in the hospital. Which types, he asked, tend to get elected to high offices?

Nearly all the leaders were found to be either manic depressives or schizophrenic paranoids. There were nearly four times as many paranoids—those suffering from grandiose or persecution delusions —in the leaders as would be expected from a study of the hospital population as a whole. In a sense this is not surprising, for paranoids show few signs of mental instability; outwardly they behave almost normally for most of the time. Care is needed in interpreting this study, and I will let Dr. Rutherford speak for himself:

> I do not intend to suggest here that high political participants are psychotic paranoids: rather I suggest that substantial elements of paranoid behavior and belief may be present among higher level participants. . . . If decision makers tend to possess paranoid personality systems, with attendant belief rigidity and suspicion, their ability to adopt creative and innovative perspectives may be curtailed. The ability of their organizations may likewise be curtailed. The peculiar rhetoric of disarmament is a possible case in point.

It is rather remarkable that two quite separate studies should show that both nations and their leaders tend to behave paranoically. The findings can be made less emotive if we simply say that states and their governments perceive realities in characteristic ways; when they make decisions, they do so rationally, having assessed what they regard as the true situation. What is crucial here is the business of assessment—whether it be by a leader, a high-level committee, or even a political party.

Appropriately, scientists who have tried to shed light on this process have borrowed analogies from the science of optics. A leader's beliefs, for instance, act as a kind of lens between himself and the events on which he must act. Sometimes the lens produces gross distortion, as Dr. Holsti has elegantly shown in analyzing the speeches of John Foster Dulles.

From a study of 434 documents of Dulles' written and spoken thoughts, Dr. Holsti concluded that Dulles' beliefs were strictly in line with what has been called "the inherent bad faith of the communists" model. Every move by the Russians of any significance was interpreted by Dulles as though he viewed them through a lens which eliminated any chance of "good faith." Cuts in Soviet military spending were interpreted as a sign that the Russian economy was failing—as Dulles believed it inevitably would. And when the Russians announced a cut in armed forces, Dulles suggested the men saved would be used to manufacture yet more lethal weapons. "Clearly as long as decision-makers on either side of the Cold War adhere to rigid images of the other party," says Dr. Holsti, "there is little likelihood that even genuine 'bids' to decrease tension will have the desired effect."

The "belief lens" is a rather curious piece of optical equipment, because it appears also to act as a mirror. In 1960 Dr. Urie Bronfenbrenner, speaker of fluent Russian, visited the Soviet Union and spoke with some 100 people about their perceptions of the United States. "Slowly and painfully," he writes, "it forced itself upon me that the Russians' distorted picture of us was curiously similar to our view of them—a mirror image. But of course our image was real. Or could it be that our views too were distorted and irrational—a mirror image in a twisted glass?"

Since then an enormous amount of work has been done on the mirror image in international relations. A classic example is that an American will regard a Russian defecting to the United States as a hero and an American defecting to the Soviet Union as a traitor. He rarely sees a logical inconsistency in this—even though for a Russian the exact opposite is true. The American psychologist Ralph K. White has produced the most striking example of the mirror image, after extensive interviews with Americans and Russians. He tabulates the images as follows:

AMERICAN IMAGE OF THE U.S.S.R.	SOVIET IMAGE OF THE U.S.
1. *They (the rulers) are bad.* The men in the Kremlin are aggressive, power-seeking, brutal in suppressing Hungary, ruthless in dealing with their people.	1. *They (the rulers) are bad.* The Wall Street bankers, politicians and militarists want a war because they fear loss of wealth and power in a communist revolution.

2. *They are imperialistic.*
The Communists want to
dominate the world.

3. *They exploit their own
people.*
They hold down consumer
goods, keep standard of
living low except for
Communist bureaucrats.

4. *They are against democracy.*
Democratic forms are mere
pretense; people can vote
only for Communist
candidates.

2. *They are imperialistic.*
The capitalist nations dominate colonial areas, keeping
them in submission.

3. *They exploit their own people.*
All capitalists live in luxury
by exploiting workers, who
suffer insecurity, unemploy-
ment, etc.

4. *They are against democracy.*
Democratic forms are mere
pretense; people can vote
only for capitalist candidates.

The mirror image idea is connected with what anthropologists call "ethnocentrism"—the tendency for a group of people to see themselves as the center of the universe and as the sole purveyors of justice and goodness; it is always the enemy that is bad, evil, and aggressive in spite of sometimes quite obvious indications of the opposite. In this the mirror is not only reflecting but also projecting; it acts as a kind of psychological epidiascope for one nation to project its faults onto the other side.

By making value analyses of President Kennedy's and Premier Khrushchev's most important speeches, Drs. White and William Eckhardt were able to study a situation where lens, mirror, and projector were all acting together. They wrote:

> Both presented their respective nations as cham-
> pions of peace and freedom, and as wanting dis-
> armament but as requiring military strength to
> defend themselves against the aggression of the
> other. In each case the speaker's own nation, and
> his bloc, was described as unified in spite of di-
> versity. Its foreign aid was referred to as an act
> of friendship, and never as an attempt to inter-
> fere with the internal affairs of other nations.
> . . . On the other hand, both Kennedy and
> Khrushchev depicted the other side as the enemy
> of peace and freedom and as not wanting dis-
> armament. . . . The other nation's foreign aid was
> seen as an act of imperialism, their workers as
> slaves, their press had no real freedom and
> their government was undemocratic.

The mirror image in international relations is a curiously new concept—considering that it must have been operating for centuries if not millennia. That it has been recognized and analyzed is almost entirely due to the work of conflict researchers in the past decade. It has already explained a good deal of the origin of conflict and the processes by which conflicts are escalated. But in the last analysis it is only part of a much larger system of relationships between nations. The international system itself, the backdrop against which individual leaders play out their fantasies and psychoses, is also coming under close scrutiny.

The International Game

"Big two agree on all nation meet with big two summit conference first," flashed a headline from the American newspaper, *The Intelligencer,* of about a decade ago. "Four nations have agreed to attend a world Peace Meeting proposed by Utro," the report continued. "First acceptance came from Omne which has also agreed to a Big Two summit meeting conference to take place prior to the world meeting."

When the summit conference took place, several students got up from their desks and moved next door to exchange written messages over a table. They were playing one of the most elaborate and realistic of the games invented to simulate the international system. Known as INS (Inter-Nation Simulation), it was developed in the late 1950s at Northwestern University. Academically, it was significant as a meeting point between experts in group behavior and those interested in international politics. The object was partly to discover how realistic such a simulation could be made and partly to see how different personality types behaved as national leaders.

Besides Omne and Utro, several other nations—each represented by two or three decision makers—took part in the game. They communicated by written message and a central information room kept stock of each country's "resources," the political standing of the leaders (who could be thrown out of office by simulated lack of support), and the strategic balance of the various sides. The written messages also found their way to the professionally produced newspaper which acted as an information source to all the nations. Described thus, it is difficult to visualize the intense involvement of the participants. Yet in one game when the controller asked the newspaper editor to make certain changes in the way he was presenting the news, the editor stormed up to the controller and threatened his resignation. Game or no game, he said, he was not prepared to work on a censored publication.

INS is one of a score or so of games which attempt to simulate the problems connected with war and peace. To outsiders, and especially diplomats and politicians, they are highly intriguing but usually dismissed as academic frivolities. What, then, can be learned from simulations of this kind?

"In a simulation held a number of years ago," writes Professor Harold Guetzkow of Northwestern, "one of the participants suggested that the Russians build a wall to divide East and West Berlin. The umpire ruled out the idea on the basis that it was preposterous. A few months later construction started on the now famous Berlin Wall."

This is by no means the only example of smart prediction from an internation game. Richard Brody, also of Northwestern, ran 16 carefully controlled simulations of the effect of nuclear weapons spreading to more and more countries. His study showed that the various alliances of nations tended to fragment as individual countries got their hands on the weapons. This work was done in the summer of 1960, before France and China were nuclear powers and before they subsequently parted company with their respective alliances.

Thus there is no doubt that simulations can predict the future accurately. The trouble is that they don't *always* do so and there is no means of telling in advance whether or not the simulation is realistic. Rumor has it that one simulation has shown that in a few years' time Poland will be the United States' most important ally. We can only wait and see.

Meanwhile there are many who would prefer to put their faith in the predictions—equally scientific, some argue—of the Provençal writer, Nostradamus. His book *The Centuries* was published in 1555 and, purely for the record, I acknowledge that he also predicted the Berlin Wall, as well as trouble over a land in the middle East, and the installation of a "cold thing" (Polaris missiles?) on the island of Scotland. "One day," he wrote, "the two great leaders shall be friends. Those of the Arctic Pole shall be united together. There shall be in the East great fear and dread." Nostradamus clearly predicted a Soviet-American alliance, and he also predicted a war between it and China three years and seven months after the alliance was formed. This from a man who in the sixteenth century foresaw the rise to power of *"un Empereur naistra près d'Italie"* called "Napoloron" and a German captain called "Hister"!

In spite of this, Nostradamus's predictions are scientifically much less useful than the results of simulations. Anyone now involved in these exercises is sharply aware of the dangers: no model of a war or an international situation can ever be made truly realistic, and so none of the results can be assumed to apply in real life. But these models do force on their designers a need to ask precise questions—questions which perhaps would never had been thought of if the model had not suggested them.

For instance, those who tried to make a realistic model of the events that led to World War I soon found themselves faced with a novel question. Suppose the model could be made realistic. Should it then be programmed in such a way that the final outcome was always war? Or should war break out only with a certain probability? In other words, if history were to repeat itself, if the same leaders were faced again with the same situations, would war be inevitable? There is no reason to think so. It is certain that the precise wording of the notes exchanged between the powers would have differed in detail, if not intent. And if the words were slightly different, their interpretations would also have been different. An obvious implication is that there may be a "science" of diplomatic note writing which we have not yet begun to develop.

Alternatively, internation simulation can be used to warn of the possible results of future policy decisions. In the early 1960s Drs. Weyman Crow and John Raser ran a simulation of what would happen if one nation developed a "capacity to delay response"—in other words, if it managed to protect its missiles from attack by, for example, an antiballistic missile system. The results of this simulation deserve to be better known. Dr. Raser summarizes them thus:

> . . . upon acquiring invulnerability, the nation was perceived as being stronger, more threatening, more able to deter, and less interested in arms control agreements. . . . The probability of accidental war decreased, but the magnitude of wars which did occur was greater and the frequency of strategic wars increased.

Perhaps more important than this, however, is the information about how the international system works that can be revealed by games and models. The world's 137 nation-states constitute one of the most complicated social systems known to man. Each nation communicates with almost every other at a variety of levels—through national leaders, business organizations, professional associations, trade unions, and so on. Superimposed on all this is a separate communications system composed of what the modelers call "INGOs"—international government organizations such as the United Nations and now many others. When you add to this the diplomatic system and the BINGOs—international systems set up by businesses—as well as the network of trade agreements and defense pacts, one can begin to see that the "wiring diagram" of the international system would make even the most complicated telephone exchange appear simple.

Nor can anyone interested in finding out how nations behave—and hence why they fight—afford to ignore any of the components of the system. But the virtue of the "systems approach" to the international system is that it promises to bring its complexity under control—or at least within grasp of human understanding. This is no idle exercise of the human intellect, for there is a goal at the end of all this analysis that might make any other human achievement seem petty.

It is already possible to make a computer model of a nation's economic system—a model that will show realistically what happens if wages or prices are increased or if income tax is reduced. There is no reason to believe that a model of the international system could not be constructed along the same lines—though it would be more complicated and considerably more difficult to produce.

One crucial factor—the dominating theme of most of this chapter—is that the international political system be understood in terms of numbers rather than hunches. The movement to do this is now in full swing; it is essential because computers can handle numbers but they cannot operate from the indefinable tenets of a hunch. "The test of this process," wrote Professor Kenneth Boulding in 1965, "will be in the increase of human power over social systems, such as those towards (economic) depressions or towards war. It will be surprising, indeed, if we ever have another great depression. The abolition of war is probably not much more difficult than the abolition of depressions."

Another essential requirement is that the business of data collection be greatly expanded. One would need to set up "international stations," analogous to weather stations, into which the indicators of conflict—information about the size of armed forces, the volume of hostile propaganda, the views of the many populations on important issues, and so on—would be continually fed. Like the computer at the beginning of this chapter that mapped temperature and pressure a month in advance, one might then be able to predict where and when future wars were likely to occur. And, even more important, it might be possible to make some small adjustment to the system to reduce the chance of hostility.

Before contemplating a mammoth operation of this kind, one must ask a number of vital questions. First, what kind of return on investment might the project bring? Kenneth Boulding has estimated the cost of this data collection service at about $1,000 million.

> There is a great deal of evidence that investment in fundamental knowledge bears large rates of return on occasion. In this particular case, if the development of a system of scientific reality testing could indeed be a substitute for the war system, the returns are in the order of $120,000 million a year, this being the present cost of the war system. An investment with a potential cost of $1,000 million and a return of $120,000 million surely deserves the epithet of spectacular, if indeed it could be done.

If indeed it could be done—which raises the second question. Currently, there is no evidence of any law which suggests that it could not be done. Is it any more visionary to dream of building a computer model of the international system than it is to dream of putting men on the moon? Obviously not. But is it visionary to suppose that such a system would help reduce the frequency of war?

To answer that question we must turn to peace research, which may already be pointing to an optimistic conclusion. A recurrent theme in this chapter has been that the difference in the conditions that lead to war or peace may be marginal—that the international system can be flipped from one condition to the other by small and apparently insignificant triggers such as the choice of words in a diplomatic note. If this is the case, one does not need to expend enormous amounts of energy in trying to stuff the bullet back down the gun barrel—it is more a question of finding the trigger point and applying some gentle dampening.

Analogies like this are provocative, for the difference between the state of war and the state of peace is enormous. So is the difference in structure between water and ice. Yet only a small temperature change is needed to convert one into the other. And there is a critical temperature near which these changes can take place very suddenly. "In the world social system," writes Professor Boulding, "we may be very close to a critical temperature of this kind. Man has been locked up in the icy trap of his fears and threats and impotences for a long time, and all thaws have been local and in a sense temporary. We may be closer than we think to the great thaw."

Architects of the Future

Professor Boulding's ideas about modeling the world international system are novel and exciting. But his analogies with the world economic system should make us pause. It may be true that economists will be able to prevent another worldwide depression, but their new-found ability to manipulate the economic system has its drawbacks. No one can claim that their machinations have brought economic stability; on the contrary, we seem to live from one economic crisis to the next—and economic growth, trade surpluses, and foreign exchange rates have become the principal preoccupation of our politicians. Is this as it should be? And what would a world in which we had learned to manipulate the warlike behavior of nations in a similar way be like?

For one thing, it seems that it would be as unstable as it is now. The manpower resources and intellectual activity that would have to go into stabilizing the recurrent crises that would occur would be enormous. And because of this, nations might well be slow indeed to learn that their arms and their armies could be dispensed with. In other words, the world might end up with fewer wars but with a greater preoccupation with them than before.

Boulding's critics put up a convincing case—a case that rests mainly on the fact that negative peace, the elimination of international violence, is not enough. Instead, they argue, we should be working for positive peace. The aim should be not only to eliminate violence but also to reduce and eventually eliminate the tensions and conflicts which cause it. Peace researchers, in other words, should aim at a world utopia and nothing less. To do this they need not make a model of the international system as it is but of the international system as it should be. What are the choices?

For many years the stock answer to those who sought world utopias was world government. Nation-states should be eliminated, it was argued, and one world government formed to rule one world-state. Undeniably, there could then be no world wars. Today, perhaps, we are wiser. Aside from the difficulty of ever attaining world government, the prospect of domestic violence—of uprisings, revolutions, and insurrections—is uppermost in everyone's mind. Many of today's conflicts are internal and not international.

Furthermore, one of the principal causes of unrest now appears to be a failure in democracy—a basic fault in the system that prevents the vast majority from playing any constructive part in political decision making. And while the way out of this impasse is not clear, some of the ways in which the situation can be aggravated are well recognized. Large political units with vast bureaucratic organizations tend to increase political deprivation. Viewed in this light, world government of one world-state looks more like a recipe for disaster than utopia.

As much is clear from the present tendency of the world system to fragment, rather than integrate. Few regions are seeking to join together in larger political units, but many are trying to split off —Wales, Scotland, Northern Ireland, French Canada, and until recently, Biafra, to mention only a few. One reason for this is that the new, smaller units will allow more people a direct say in determining their own future. Another is that the example set the rest of the world by the two superpowers has not been universally welcomed. If world government were to be created, the process would presumably have to be a gradual one. And one of the first moves would be the gradual creation of more superpowers—of a united Europe, a united Africa, and a united Southeast Asia, for example. But, as Dr. Johan Galtung warns, "if superpowers make superwars, then this looks like a dangerous road to peace."

A safer road, many peace researchers argue, is to ride the bandwagon of pluralism. To do this means fostering any ideas which increase the complexity of communications within the international system and which tend to decrease the importance in it of the nation-state. This apparently inexorable process has been going on for many years, but few people have changed their attitudes to the nation-state. In spite of all the evidence to the contrary, of all the evidence that the world actually works through a series of systems in which the concept of national territory has only limited relevance, we still think of the nation-state as the most important unit in the system. Even if this were true now, it is not likely to

remain so for long in the face of the mounting problems that wait
to be solved. Overpopulation, pollution, famine, and disease are
no respecters of national frontiers. To fight them will require
further decreases in the significance we attach to national boundaries. Indeed, our current concern with preserving what is left of
the natural environment is a direct expression of the idea that
national frontiers are not, after all, all-important. The war against
pollution, in other words, may turn out to be a particularly good
way of fighting the war against war.

There are, perhaps, a score of scholars throughout the world
concerned with building up a concrete picture of how a utopian
international system might look a long time in the future. Theirs is
an immense undertaking; we have not got, nor should we ask for,
quick and spectacular results. But at the same time we cannot
afford to ignore the alternative futures being prepared, analyzed,
and modeled by those concerned with the more immediate future
for more immediate reasons.

And, living as we do in a warfare state, it is not surprising to
find the main thrust of these efforts centering on war. "I estimate
that between 15,000 and 30,000 officers and scientists are concerned with war gaming of one kind or another at the present time,
in America alone," writes Andrew Wilson in his recent book *The
Bomb and the Computer*. "About a quarter of these are directly
employed by the Department of Defense. The rest are on the pay-
rolls of aerospace and electronics corporations, or staff members
of civilian 'think tanks' which conduct military research on contract."

Many of these games are futuristic in tone and involve such
bizarre concepts as military bases on the moon, new religions
based on the evil of the white man, the building of Russian-Ger-
man missiles in Mexico, and an advanced Chinese space program.
There is, of course, much to be said for thinking about "surprise-
free" futures so that they do not creep up and take us unawares.
But there are also dangers. Military war-gamers appear prone to
apply their findings too easily to the real world. "Because of the
variety of the futures they generate," writes Wilson, "they can give
us little help in planning the future—and could well saddle us
with neuroses more dangerous than the threats they appear to expose. Above all, if taken seriously, they could lead us to even
heavier investment than at present in deterrent systems, at the cost
of human needs less easily dramatized."

All this is a grim reminder of the direction in which the arrow of most of our future research is pointing. It is a reminder, too, of the fact that peace researchers and military technologists are not so distantly separated as might appear. On occasion, the military have provided the funds for peace research to continue, and sometimes peace researchers, often unwittingly, have provided intellectual ammunition for the guns of power politics. Nowhere is this intermingling of research interest more apparent than in the scholars' concern to grasp the real, everyday issues of how to avoid war and conflict—the issues of peacekeeping by deterrence, by disarmament, and by all the techniques of arbitration, conciliation and mediation. In short, the science of conflict—which we will now examine—was the bastard child of an unhappy union: that of nuclear strategy and peace research.

CHAPTER VIII

The Science of Conflict

The Neostrategists–Does Deterrence Deter?–The Great Evasion–The Disarmament Game–Conflict Resolution

---

"Some of the most formidable obstacles to conflict resolution on the international scale are the encrusted ideas of the past."

Professor Anatol Rapaport
Peace Research Reviews
August 1967

From the promise of thermonuclear war, and the operations research that made that war more "efficient," there had emerged in the 1950s a new role for the physical or social scientist: that of strategist. These paper warriors sought, as Herman Kahn was to put it, to "think the unthinkable." They claimed to bring a cold and dispassionate logic to bear on such problems as "how many megadeaths can we afford to achieve this or that political end." They took on the job of contemplating in detail what would happen in a nuclear war. To them the views of the extreme right and of the peace camp were equally facile; emotion, and such intangible things as right and wrong, morals, and conscience, were to be deplored in the new strategic analysis. Such factors merely muddied the issues at stake, which should be viewed only through the crystal-clear waters of reasoned appraisal.

The rise of the strategist, almost exclusively located in the United States, was rapid. A huge network of "independent" institutions— the famous think tanks—arose to cater to the government's demand for analysis of the country's new strategic options. At a time when anything "scientific" commanded almost instantaneous grants, the promise of "scientific" strategy appeared on the governmental horizon as manna from heaven. By the early 1960s the strategist was firmly established. "His influence," wrote Professor Anatol Rapaport in 1964, "is evidenced by the flourishing state of the profession and by the lavish financing of gigantic research organizations devoted to the working out of diplo-military strategies."

It was also evidenced by the writings of Herman Kahn. In 1961 he published *On Thermonuclear War*—a book which purported to show to the general public just what the new strategic issues were and the kind of thinking that had led to them. As an exercise in public relations, it must be judged a failure—if only because of the way it was reviewed in the magazine *Scientific American*. The reviewer was James R. Newman, a numerate lawyer who had earlier played an important role in helping to wrest the atom from the hands of the military.

"Is there really a Herman Kahn?" Newman asked in the first sentence of his review. "It is really hard to believe. Doubts cross one's mind almost from the first page of this deplorable book; no one could write like this; no one could think like this. Perhaps the whole thing is a staff hoax in bad taste."

Newman continued:

> An ecstatic foreword by Klaus Knorr of Princeton University's Center of International Studies states that this is "not a book about the moral aspects of military problems." The disclaimer is much to the point; it is exactly wrong. This is a moral tract on mass murder: how to plan it, how to commit it, how to get away with it, how to justify it. . . .
>
> Herman Kahn, we are told, is "one of the very few who have managed to avoid the 'mental block' so characteristic of writers on nuclear warfare." The mental block consists, if I am not mistaken, of a scruple for life. This evil and tenebrous book, with its loose-lipped pieties and its hayfoot-strawfoot logic, is permeated by a bloodthirsty irrationality such as I have not seen in my years of reading.

The strategists had to wait only three years before they received a book-length broadside in the same vein. It came, in 1964, from Professor Rapaport and was triggered off in part by a university lecture by one of the strategists entitled "Defense and Strategy in the Nuclear Age." At the end of the lecture Rapaport asked whether the strategist would agree to the definition of genocide as the deliberate slaughter of helpless populations for political ends. The strategist agreed. "And how," asked Professor Rapaport, "do you intend to defend yourself?"

Nor did Professor Rapaport mince words in his book *Strategy and Conscience*. He accused many strategists of "unscientific" science based on assumptions conveniently forgotten when the conclusions were presented in order to "rationalize" policies which had already been formulated. But scientific mistakes are common enough, and Professor Rapaport's main argument was at a different level. The strategists had likened their detachment from what nuclear war really meant to the detachment of the surgeon cutting human flesh. Rapaport claimed that this detachment resembled not so much that of the surgeon as "that of a butcher or still more that of all the other organizers of mass exterminations."

He continued: "It is the professional involvement of the strategists that blinds them to the enormity of the evil associated with being positively and 'creatively' involved in a 'game' in which the suffering and death of untold millions of innocent human beings are the payoffs." And he had an even more serious point to make. "Thermonuclear war," he said, "is not a natural disaster. It is being carefully planned and prepared by the strategists themselves."

There was a good deal of justice to this charge. And, if nothing else, it pointed up the strange reversal of aim which the strategists had somehow perpetrated on society. Although nuclear weapons were not invented as deterrents, their continued production in the 1940s and early 1950s was carried out under that guise. A strong nuclear force, it was argued, could inflict so much damage that other nations—nuclear or not—would be frightened into submissive behavior. The new weapons were to be peacekeepers—but those charged with developing the plans for their use were somehow driving us more quickly toward the holocaust they were meant to be avoiding.

It was this situation, more than any other, that spurred scholars to inspect the unpleasant details of nuclear strategy more carefully. Their first reaction was to examine the whole concept of deterrence in a broader framework. They went on to argue, with logic but with scant hope of being listened to, that the concept itself was split with internal inconsistencies and based on faulty premises. From there their interest in peacekeeping turned back to disarmament and to technical insights that might break the dead-lock at Geneva. And, finally, they sought to elaborate a general theory of conflict in an attempt to nurture a technology of conflict prevention that might succeed where deterrence or disarmament failed. These are the subjects which I have clumped together un-der the general head of "the science of conflict."

The Neostrategists

The kind of strategic thinking that was developed in the 1950s was based largely on the theory of games—the word being used in its mathematical, not its recreational, sense. Chess, for example, is a game in which strategy is used to the full; an analysis of several series of moves is used to suggest which move is more likely to lead to victory. The answer, of course, varies with the responses of the opponent—but good guesses can also be made at these, for the opponent's strategy is also to win or, if on the defensive, at least to avoid defeat.

Chess is what is known as a "zero-sum" game. The gains of one side are precisely balanced by the losses of the other. Both sides therefore have identical "value systems" with the possible ex-ception that some players find knights more valuable than bishops and some do not. The looseness of an analogy between chess and two countries involved in war is thus immediately apparent, for the latter is not a zero-sum game. What one side gains in a maneuver may not be equal in value to the loss of the other, because the value systems of the two opponents are not identical; furthermore they both change with time.

It was not until the advent of nuclear weapons that this kind of strategic analysis came to be much admired. This is strange, be-cause a nuclear situation probably has the least to benefit from crude analogies with zero-sum games. As soon as large stockpiles of nuclear weapons became available, it was realized that "victory" had changed its meaning. In all-out nuclear war the sole surviving pawn that would mean victory in chess would denote the most Pyrrhic of all victories in real life. Nuclear weapons, it was inevi-tably argued, could not be used to win wars but could only be *not* used to preserve the peace. The contrast with chess is almost perfect.

Of course, this does not exhaust the possibilities of using game theory to illuminate international relations. There are many other types of games, some of which help at least in framing the right questions. But because the idea of nuclear deterrence was so far removed from any standard game theory, deterrence itself grew up in the 1950s as an idea in a vacuum. "What is impressive," Professor Thomas C. Schelling was to write in 1960, "is not how complicated the idea of deterrence has become, and how carefully it has been refined and developed, but how slow the process has been, how vague the concepts still are, and how inelegant the theory of deterrence is. . . . There is no scientific literature on deterrence that begins to compare with, say, the literature on inflation, Asiatic flu, elementary-school reading, or smog."

At least there was not until Professor Schelling wrote the 1960 book that this quotation comes from. But the intellectual leap then taken was a large one. In *The Strategy of Conflict* Professor Schelling tried and succeeded in showing that there are "enlightening similarities between, say, maneuvering in limited war and jockeying in a traffic jam, between deterring the Russians and deterring one's own children, or between the modern balance of terror and the ancient institution of hostages."

The essence of the book was that all these situations are part of the process of "bargaining." The feature they all have in common is that they involve two parties which have common interests as well as conflicting ones—and by definition nuclear powers, however hostile, do have a common interest in avoiding mutual annihilation. To preserve these interests, players have to follow strategies —but not the strategies of military terminology. " 'Winning' in a conflict," wrote Schelling, "does not have a strictly competitive meaning; it is not winning in relation to one's adversary. It means gaining relative to one's own value system; and this may be done by bargaining, mutual accommodation, and by the avoidance of mutually damaging behavior."

The analysis that Schelling made was thus of how two sides manage to strike bargains which both desire. It is a fact that what often characterizes international relations, parent/child relationships, industrial disputes, or driving a car is the use of force, or, more often, the threat of its use. Schelling took great care to stress the difference. "Strategy—in the sense in which I am using it here," he said, "is not concerned with the efficient application of force but with the exploitation of potential force."

Viewed in this light, many apparently irrational acts can be seen as the valuable moves in the strategy of conflict that they really are. An army advancing on an enemy, for instance, may burn down all the bridges that it has crossed. This "insane" act of denying the army any chance of retreat is not so insane as it might appear. It is a signal to the enemy that no bargaining behind the line of the bridges is possible—for the very reason that the army physically cannot retreat further than that. This puts it in a strong bargaining position—the enemy realizes that business is meant. Similarly, a traffic officer may write down the number of an offending car on a prenumbered form before talking with the driver. Once this is done, the driver realizes the officer has no option but to report the matter: threats and verbal abuse will be of no avail. Negotiators with inflexible briefs from their governments operate from a similar position of bargaining strength.

It may seem generous to call any situation of this kind "bargaining"—but of course the bargaining has gone on before the confrontation. If the army, the traffic officer, or the negotiator has made his actions known beforehand, the opposite party will have had to weigh this when considering his actions. He will realize that the other party not only has a deterrent, not only intends to use it, but actually has no choice but to use it.

There are other ways of making deterrence credible. When driving in big cities it is considered prudent to give taxi drivers a wide berth. The reason is that the taxi driver, unlike the private owner, does not care particularly if his vehicle gets a few knocks. He has less to lose in any physical contest about the right-of-way. Conversely, if the deterrent is made large enough, it may not even matter if its use will wreak more damage to the threatening party than to the threatened. One can threaten costly legal proceedings over small issues, or threaten to drive a new car into an old one, or threaten to drive away at great expense cars that are badly parked. In every case, the threat will work providing it is believed. By analogy so may a threat to use nuclear weapons, however trivial the event which it is specified will trigger off the nuclear response, and however great the cost to the user.

Here one can bring more subtle concepts into play, ones which rarely appear in conventional game theory. One method of deterrence is to hoist the responsibility for use of the threat onto the other party's shoulders. This means specifying in advance precisely what the threat will be used against. The other party must then decide whether it can bear the responsibility of starting an action when it knows precisely what the reaction of the other side will be. Demonstrators use exactly this strategy when they lie down in a road or on a railway track. Schelling retells the (mythical) story of a U.S. Air Force pilot accompanying a ship about to be seized by Communist vessels. The pilot has no authority to fire the first shot. Instead he jettisons burning oil on the sea in front of the Communist ships. Responsibility for first bloodshed is then shifted to the other side, who have to decide whether to sail through the oil or turn back.

Much of Schelling's book is concerned with what happens to the bargaining process when two sides can communicate and when they cannot. In the latter situation there can only be "tacit bargaining"; but Schelling, with the help of intuitive reasoning and a few simple games, was able to show that even bargaining without communication can go further than might appear.

Consider two people told to meet in a big city on a certain day but not told the time or the place. How would they do it? People actually presented with this problem are usually able to solve it even if they cannot communicate. In New York they mostly decide to go to Grand Central Station at noon and in London they probably go to Piccadilly Circus, also at noon. Two players are both told to write down on a piece of paper either "heads" or "tails"; if both write down the same word, both will be rewarded, but if they write different words, both will be penalized. Again, both players manage to win by agreeing intuitively, without communicating, to write heads.

Agreements like this are much easier to make if there is some kind of communication, however limited or imperfect. And in case Schelling's ideas seem remote from real situations, it may be helpful to relate them to a real conflict—the Vietnam war. The story that follows may owe much to Schelling's theory, for one of the principal actors, White House adviser Professor H. A. Kissinger, was at Harvard at the same time as Schelling.

By this I do not mean to imply that there was any deliberate attempt to turn theory into practice. But by the mid-1960s Schelling's "neostrategic" analysis of bargaining situations had made a substantial impact. Indeed, it had given rise to a small but scholarly industry devoted to the task of extending Schelling's insights to new fields. It provided, in effect, a new intellectual lever with which to pry open for analysis all situations in which two parties had both conflicting and common interests. The technique could be used to study disarmament as well as deterrence, arms control as well as strategy. And it is against this background that we should view what may have been the most crucial move in the history of the Vietnam peace talks.

In early 1967 the attempt to begin Vietnam peace negotiations had broken down, and communication between Hanoi and Washington was nonexistent. When the six-day war between Israel and the United Arab Republic broke out on June 5, 1967, the secretary-general of Pugwash, Professor J. Rotblat, summoned a meeting of the Pugwash continuing committee. It took ten days to arrange, and by then the war was over. Talk turned to Vietnam and to Raymond Aubrac, a Pugwash scientist working in Rome. Aubrac had been a personal friend of Ho Chi Minh's in the 1940s. Kissinger, who had attended earlier Pugwash conferences and was present at the June meeting, agreed to investigate the possibility of using Aubrac and another French scientist—Dr. H. Marcovich —as messengers between Washington and Hanoi.

This they did—first from Paris and later through a visit to Hanoi under the guise of a scientific trip to Cambodia. The messages they carried related to what "could, should, or would" happen if the United States were to halt the bombing of North Vietnam. At this time Aubrac and Marcovich were the sole means of communication between Hanoi and Washington. Their role was essentially to reinforce a bargaining suggestion that might well have been reached by tacit agreement: that if the bombing of North Vietnam were halted, Hanoi would talk peace. Note that this is just the kind of "prominent" solution that might suggest itself to two sides seeking peace but unable to communicate.

Aubrac and Marcovich were able to help resolve any ambiguity that might still be present. One way in which this was done was for the United States to agree to a signal that would act as a gesture of goodwill and at the same time acknowledge that they understood the agreement and would keep it—in other words, that Aubrac and Marcovich's messages had got back correctly to President Johnson. The signal that was agreed on was an unannounced halt to the bombing for a period of 11 days. This halt was actually carried out, unknown to the outside world, late in August 1967.

Next month United States officials began to talk openly about halting the bombing, but communication again broke down. Thus it was not until March 31, 1968, that President Johnson actually announced a partial halt to the bombing. But this was the signal for peace talks to start: three days later Hanoi announced it would talk peace.

Anyone who has read Schelling's book cannot fail to see in this story a link between theory and action. But the story also highlights what are considered by many to be the shortcomings of neo-strategic theory. The whole sequence of events was made possible only because Ho Chi Minh agreed to see Aubrac. He did so not for any reasons that can be revealed by bargaining analysis but because the two were old friends. Aubrac had done much for Vietnamese laborers in France at the end of World War II. And when Ho visited Paris in 1946 he sought out Aubrac to thank him. Aubrac offered him hospitality in his country house and Ho later visited Aubrac's wife when she gave birth to a daughter. Aubrac and Ho became good friends.

Schelling's book is about problems that arise where trust and friendship do not exist. He spells this out in some detail:

> We tend to identify peace, stability, and the quiescence of conflict with notions like trust, good faith and mutual respect. To the extent that this point of view actually encourages trust and respect it is good. But where trust and good faith do not exist and cannot be made to by our acting as though they did, we may wish to solicit advice from the underworld, or from ancient despotisms, on how to make agreements work when trust and good faith are lacking and there is no legal recourse for breach of contract. The ancients exchanged hostages, drank wine from the same glass to demonstrate the absence of poison, met in public places to inhibit the massacre of one by the other, and even deliberately exchanged spies to facilitate the transmittal of authentic information. It seems likely that a well-developed theory of strategy could throw some light on the efficacy of these old devices, suggest the circumstances to which they apply, and discover modern equivalents that, though offensive to our taste, may be desperately needed in the regulation of conflict.

And there is no doubt that much of what comes out of the strategy of conflict is offensive to our taste. It is by no means apparent that we want to model international relations on lessons learned from the underworld. To judge from the shocked outrage with which the world reacted in 1970 to the kidnapping of diplomats for political blackmail, the devices of the "underworld" are not to our taste. Yet our double standards are fully in evidence here. When Latin-American rebels held American diplomats hostage for the release of political prisoners, they were in fact only borrowing a neat trick from the repertoire of behavior of the super-powers. For more than a decade deterrent theory has meant that both the United States and the Soviet Union have held each other's civilian populations—consisting of not one but hundreds of millions of people—in similar hostage for the good behavior of their governments. Yet if we are not prepared for the underworld to model its behavior on ours, it seems scarcely reasonable to model ours on its.

The implications of the theory for limited war are no more reassuring. Schelling wrote: "To characterize . . . the maneuvers and actions of limited war as a bargaining process is to emphasize that . . . there is a powerful common interest in reaching an outcome that is not enormously destructive of values on both sides." One Vietnam later, after immense destruction of values on both sides, and countless massacres, one can have serious doubts that the outcome of limited war can ever be anything but destructive.

Equally offensive are the implications of some of the theory: that the most effective deterrent might be a "super-dirty" bomb, designed so that long-lived fallout kills a maximum of the civilian population as slowly as possible; or that the final deterrent might be (ought to be?) a Doomsday machine which can never be turned off and which will blow up the world if any country transgresses certain rules which other countries lay down. Ideas such as these can hardly compensate for the lack of trust which is the reason given for the need for the theory; in that sense they can only worsen the situation.

Indeed the criticism that strategists were actually preparing the way for nuclear war can be extended: the neostrategists have prepared the way for limited war. Said Robert Neild in 1968:

> The calculus of violence and threats of pain, of the kind you find in Schelling's *Arms and Influence,* appears to have helped to provide a rationale for the doctrines of escalation which have been applied in Vietnam. It is not hard, with the benefit of hindsight, to see that it was probably misleading, quite apart from its questionable morality. The obvious defect is that this type of calculus seems mainly to be based on reasoning about individual violence, roughly of the kind portrayed in films about gangsters or in novelettes about Foreign Legionnaires and torture.

Does Deterrence Deter?

Although Schelling's book was not published until 1960, many of his ideas were current long before that. They burst upon the intellectual vacuum that had previously surrounded deterrence with considerable vigor. They helped to turn what had previously been only nagging and poorly expressed doubts into a new and coherent school of thought. Americans had not been happy about their major policy in foreign relations—that if the Soviet Union launched any form of attack, it would simply be wiped off the face of the earth through the then-current doctrine of massive retaliation.

Such doubts were not the exclusive concern of the peace camp; they appeared in universities, in Congress, and even in military establishments. Indeed it was the latter that made the first concrete move of reappraisal. In June 1958 a key study was begun by the Naval Ordnance Test Station at China Lake, in California. Its main purpose was to apply psychological and sociological analysis to questions of deterrence on the premise that "there must be a cheaper, more credible, more moral, and more effective way to deter an opponent than by threatening to obliterate his country if he attacks."

Not long after this, massive retaliation was officially renounced— and replaced by the doctrine of flexible response. This, of course, was only a minivictory, for it did not acknowledge some of the basic premises of the attack on deterrence that was now being mounted. From the Naval Ordnance Test Station, Thomas W. Milburn wrote:

> Both the United States and the Soviet Union seek
> to influence each other's behavior through threat
> of retaliatory punishment. To the extent that they
> concentrate on threat of punishment as the method
> of influencing such behavior, they ignore the
> empirical findings of psychologists about
> individuals and groups, whether human or
> infra-human: outside threat tends to increase the
> cohesiveness of a group . . . punishments (or
> threat of them), while they may tend to suppress
> behavior, serve little to change underlying motives.

The point was a good one. Much had been made by Schelling and others of the idea that deterrence was a weapon that permeated all levels of society, from nations to families. Further, that analysis of the simpler examples might contain lessons on nuclear deterrence. The one lesson that had not been learned was that the threat of punishment had been relentlessly exposed by psychiatrists as the worst and most dangerous ways of making children behave as their elders wished.

But even this seemed only a trivial criticism compared to the fundamental examination deterrence doctrine received in a meeting of social and behavioral scientists and strategists held in Inyokern, California, in June 1959. At that meeting it appeared, perhaps for the first time, that the doctrine was shot through with logical inconsistencies. In exposing them the meeting came to realize that they were based on a fundamental lack of knowledge of what the international power game was all about. As a result the meeting called for a massive research program to investigate:

1. How can a nation understand and hence predict another's goals and values?
2. What is rationality and how does it relate to deterrence?
3. What is the difference between effective deterrence in times of crisis and low tension?
4. How do nations perceive each other's goals?
5. What can be learned from communication and bargaining studies—including the promise of rewards?
6. Is deterrence effective in nuclear war also effective in the control of limited war?
7. What is the relationship between weapons characteristics and deterrence, conflict and the international system?
8. How is the organization of the international system changing?

I have reproduced this list in full because it provides a rough recipe for the fields of peace and conflict research that were soon to get off the ground. Much of the research described in the last chapter is aimed at answering some of these questions—and the substance of this chapter is concerned almost exclusively with them. What is particularly interesting is that this ambitious research program was proposed by a naval laboratory. It soon got off the ground as Project Michelson—its name deriving from the physicist who had earlier tried to "measure the immeasurable," the effect of the earth's velocity on the velocity of light. Michelson succeeded in making his measurements but found no effect. This negative result gave rise to Einstein's theory of relativity.

But we should return to the attack on deterrence. The first approach was to extend the type of logical analysis so brilliantly expounded by Schelling. Much of this debate concerned the assumption of rational behavior by nations, the delicate thread by which the whole nuclear tightrope seemed to be suspended. It was pointed out that deterrence could only prevent wars which would otherwise have been started by rational decision. Yet, as George R. Pitman wrote in 1966, "Major wars have resulted either as a consequence of escalation from lesser conflicts or from accidents and miscalculations." What made this assessment particularly worrying was that the two world wars, Korea, and Vietnam all seemed to fit into this category. The superpowers were spending by far the biggest chunk of their resources on a war-prevention technique which appeared to have no relevance to the massive slaughter that had thus far characterized the twentieth century.

A second question about the assumption of rationality concerned what happened when deterrence failed. If one side attacked there was then no strategic reason for the other to retaliate, even though it had previously declared passionately that it would. To retaliate would, in fact, be an example of irrational behavior because retaliation could achieve nothing except vengeance. Therefore, if one side made its threat credible, the other must conclude that the first side would behave irrationally. Such an attitude would be bound to lead to a worsening of relations. "For if the actual use of force is self-defeating—indeed, is suicidal," John R. Raser wrote, "then *ipso facto,* the threat to use such force is hollow when made by rational men."

In this way the logic of deterrence was shown to break down if deterrence failed. The logic was found equally faulty if it worked. This required both sides to make a rational analysis of their options. This they might do during times of low tension—but at such times no deterrent threat was needed, for attack was not being considered. During crises, however, there was increasing evidence that rational behavior could not be relied upon by nations. So at the very time that deterrence was needed, the behavioral assumptions on which it was based were not likely to exist.

Dr. Raser concluded:

> The major error of the past has been to
> concentrate on how to make nuclear deterrence
> more effective while neglecting the more basic
> questions of whether it even works or whether
> there is any need to deter. . . . Can the process of
> deterrence we observe among individuals (pre-

venting unacceptable behaviour by punishment
threats) be generalized to relations between states?
. . . And, has the whole deterrence effort in fact
been necessary—has any nation really *intended* to
commit the kind of aggression that nuclear
retaliatory forces are designed to deter?

Suggestive answers to the first of these questions came from a
variety of sources. The first was a simple analogy with the game of
chicken—the game in which two cars speed toward each other with
their inside tires running along the center line of the road. The
winner is the one that continues his course, the loser the one that
steers away to avoid the inevitable collision. To win this game,
Schelling had argued convincingly, one should make one's threat absolutely credible by leaving no choice except to continue along the
line—for instance, by throwing away the steering wheel and making
sure your opponent saw you do it.

This maneuver makes victory extremely likely. It does not, however, make it certain because the other side may adopt the same
tactic with inevitable results for both. But let us assume that the
chance of victory is 90 per cent—a good enough chance, perhaps,
to adopt this strategy as policy. It then turns out that the policy
becomes disastrous if the game has to be played repeatedly.

For instance, if the game is played twice, the chance it will be
won on both occasions is only 90 per cent of 90 per cent—in fact,
81 per cent. If the game is played more than seven times, defeat
(elimination) becomes more likely than victory. If it is played 49
times, there is only one chance in a hundred of surviving. Such is
the effect of cumulative risks. Those with a morbid curiosity may
like to calculate how many times this game has already been played
by the superpowers in such forms as the Cuban missile crisis, and
how many more times it is likely to be played before the end of the
century.

The implications of game theory were soon followed up more
rigorously. Until the 1960s no games which included a psychological
threat of deterrence had been examined in detail. A great variety of
them soon appeared, and I shall describe a typical one to illustrate
the problems and implications that they furnished.

"When two dynamite trucks meet on a single track road," Professor Schelling had asked earlier, "who backs up?" Two psychologists, Morton Deutsch and R. M. Krauss, posed a more complex
question: if either or both of the drivers have a deterrent, how

quickly can they deliver their loads? And can they do so more quickly without deterrents?

They sought their answers from a game in which two players were asked to behave as road haulage companies. Each player had one truck and had to get his load from point A to point B, and vice versa. Two single-lane roads joined these points—a long one and a short one. Each player was required to make a maximum profit which was measured by the time taken to make the journey. Both trucks moved at the same constant speed, and the game was so arranged that every journey via the longer road caused the player a loss. He could make a profit by using the shorter road, providing he did not have to stop and argue the right-of-way with the other player. Arguments on the road were time lost and dollars down the drain.

The cooperative way of playing the game is for each player to take turns in using the shorter road. The deterrent threat was to provide first one and then both of the players with a gate which he could lock at his end of the short road. Thus if both players met on the short road, one would have to decide to back up—but the player who did this might lock his gate after him. This move—like using a retaliatory nuclear weapon—availed the player nothing except the gratification of punishing his opponent. The threat to close the gate could, however, be used as a deterrent to prevent the other player from using the short road.

The game was first played without gates, then with one player having a gate, and finally with both players having gates. After 16 pairs of people had each played the game 20 times, their joint average scores were:

no gates	one gate	two gates
+203	−406	−875

The results show that the players fared progressively worse as first one and then both of them acquired the deterrent. Interestingly, the player who had the only gate in the second game did not do nearly so well as when neither side had a deterrent—although, as might be expected, he still beat his opponent quite handsomely.

Let us now make a naïve interpretation of these results. When both sides have the gate (the deterrent), both lose heavily—so heavily in fact that something like a nuclear holocaust appears to have happened. The fact that one of the two sides lost slightly less heavily than the other becomes virtually irrelevant—if the players really had been haulage companies both would have been declared bankrupt. When one side had the gate there was also a net loss but a smaller one; again, both sides lost overall but one can imagine only the loser being declared bankrupt and the winner going on to recover his losses in the next round. And when neither side had the gate, both made a profit—as might happen to two powers who did not have to spend a major portion of their resources on nuclear weapons. Game theory, one might conclude, proves that nuclear deterrence will end in disaster.

Of course, it does no such thing. The game I have described perhaps suggests a conclusion of this kind, if one is happy to ignore all the ways in which gates differ from nuclear deterrents and in which road haulage differs from international relations. But I could equally well have quoted results from similar games which show that players do better when they possess deterrents. What, then, is the relevance of game theory? Has the whole chain of events that started with looking more scientifically at the problem of nuclear war simply led to what one prominent critic, Lord Chalfont (former Minister for Disarmament in the British Foreign Office), has called "an intellectual wilderness"?

Certainly, game theory has not yet led us out of the deterrent maze. That, in itself, is not sufficient reason to reject its findings altogether. Even now, one can begin to discern—if darkly—some light at the end of a tunnel which may lead to alternatives to deterrence. The game of chicken, for instance, brings home quite vividly how important is the concept of cumulative risk when making nuclear policy. If, as a result, policy makers make more effort to assess risk cumulatively over a long period, rather than just one jump ahead, game theory could have fulfilled no more useful purpose. But we cannot draw up any kind of a balance sheet until we have first examined the implications of game theory for disarmament —which must wait until later in the chapter.

There are, of course, other ways of getting a handle on the deterrent situation. Perhaps the most obvious is to turn back the pages of history. Although nuclear deterrence is still novel enough, deterrence itself is unpleasantly old. "If you want peace, prepare for war" has been the unproven and often disastrous policy of nearly every great civilization of the past.

A typical example, which may have awful relevance to our current problems, was the long coexistence of the Roman and Persian empires for 139 years (A.D. 363 to 502). Throughout this period, the two empires peered at one another, eyeball to eyeball, across a vast complex of military apparatus. There were border skirmishes, cold wars, freezes, thaws, and angry words throughout. Eventually, although neither side intended it, full-scale war broke out. It lasted 100 years and neither empire ever recovered.

This suggestive parallel proves nothing. If any lessons are to be drawn from history, the approach must be much more systematic. Raoul Naroll, an anthropologist working at the State University of New York at Buffalo, is about the only man to have attempted a thorough study of historical conditions to test hypotheses of war in a scientific way. He selected, with immense care, 20 historical situations in which two civilizations coexisted at the same time. He drew his examples from 2,000 years of history and assembled huge amounts of information about each situation. He then carried out what the anthropologist would call a cross-cultural survey. He was looking for similar patterns of behavior across time and space.

And he found them. Of the 30 hypotheses of war that he tested, four are of direct concern to deterrence. He asked the question, "Did civilizations which had larger armed forces, more mobile ones, or better quality ones fight in wars less often than when they did not enjoy these military advantages?" He asked the same question about civilizations which had extensive fortifications.

"In all four of these tests," he writes, "it was predicted in accordance with the deterrence hypothesis, that wars would be less frequent during periods when the conspicuous state, while on a defensive stance, enjoyed the specified military advantage than during other periods. None of these predictions was confirmed by the correlation with 'Months of Wars.'. . . If anything, armament tends to make war more likely."

Like all good scientists, he went on to check the obvious loophole. It could be argued that there is a chicken-and-egg problem here—that nations prepare for war when they suspect one is coming, and so it is the wars that produce military preparations and not the other way about. One of the strengths of this study was that the statistical methods used showed this not to be the case. Military preparations were the chickens, and the eggs it laid were wars.

Thus the historical evidence, game theory, and logical analysis all call into question the doctrine of deterrence on which the future of civilization rests. Yet there is still room for doubt. Those who believe in deterrence argue that only one fact is necessary in assessing its usefulness: that in the past 25 years we have not had a nuclear war. This, of course, tells us absolutely nothing about whether or not we will have one in the future. But whether even the nuclear peace of the recent past has been due to the deterrent we can never know. The only sure piece of knowledge is that if there had been no nuclear deterrents, there *could* have been no nuclear war.

In all this there is something reminiscent of the elephant man, who was found scattering newspapers along the corridors of a railway train. This activity, he claimed, was the best way he knew of keeping elephants at bay. When it was pointed out that the nearest elephant must be several thousand miles away, he was far from taken aback. "You see," he said, "it must be working already."

The Great Evasion

The dubious notion of deterrence, fortunately, is not the only route to peace known by civilized man. Regularly, for 25 years, disarmament experts have met at Geneva, New York, London, Paris, and even Helsinki. Their talks have ranged from missiles to germ warfare, from conventional arms to nuclear weapons, and from surprise attack to international inspection. And in a million man-hours of debate, they have produced a mountain of problems and a molehill of results. Their failure, as more than one commentator has put it, has been total.

It has been accompanied by an outpouring of books and articles on disarmament and arms control. Most have been written in the hushed and reverent tones of those who ascribe to disarmament a sacred quality which should not be lightly criticized. Although sympathetic to the idea behind this approach, I do not intend to copy it. If the bizarre rhetoric that has gone on at Geneva has been a mockery and an evasion, it may be in our best interest to say so. It is certainly in our best interest to inquire why so much effort has produced so little result in a field which matters so much.

The idea of general and complete disarmament, born from the appalling memory of World War I, had an exciting adolescence. Through the 1920s and 1930s it was enthusiastically espoused by country after country. Those who played a part in promoting the cause claimed that the world was then nearer a final peace than it has ever been. But high hopes were never so rudely dashed as they were by Hitler, 50 million deaths in six years, and the explosion of the first two nuclear weapons. As the smoke from World War II cleared, those who came back to the disarmament tables did so in grimmer mood. Not only had they been fortunate enough to survive a war so total that it had seemed theoretically impossible, but they had emerged carrying a weapon that made global elimination look not only possible but technically easy.

So naturally their first concern was the bomb. The Americans proposed, in their Baruch Plan, that all atomic materials should be owned and managed by an international body. When that mechanism had been set up, they suggested, nuclear weapons should be prohibited and destroyed. Although this effectively removed the United States monopoly on the atom, the Russians were not enthusiastic. First things first, they said. And Andrei Gromyko proposed that atomic bombs should first be prohibited. Then, and only then, he said, would he debate the secondary issue of control systems for seeing that the agreement was enforced.

In the event, it took ten years for these two powers to agree to differ. By that time so many bombs had been made that no inspection scheme seemed remotely feasible. The world's chance of controlling and eliminating nuclear weapons had disappeared. And the only point on which the Americans and Russians now appeared unanimous was that it would be a good thing if other countries did not also go nuclear.

By 1955 events had taken a novel turn. The Soviet Union now urged that the danger from nuclear weapons lay in surprise attack. An inspection scheme to eliminate this possibility, it was argued, would establish an "atmosphere of trust" in which each side could then dismantle its nuclear weaponry. The Americans appeared to accept the first part of this plan and on July 21, 1955, President Eisenhower outlined his "open-skies" plan: the two powers would exchange military blueprints and allow each other the right of aerial inspection. A month later the Americans in effect withdrew all previous disarmament offers, leaving "open skies" the only talking point. And the presidential disarmament assistant, Harold E. Stassen, soon admitted frankly that he no longer wanted to eliminate nuclear stockpiles.

The American position at this time is fascinating. For what they were actually proposing no longer involved any form of disarmament—they were simply asking for an agreement on an inspection scheme. In short order, the new idea of arms control was born. It involved a fundamental examination of just what was involved at the Geneva talks: were nations trying to eliminate their arms or were they trying to establish a lasting peace?

The arms controllers argued that the two things were not identical. And as they developed the idea of deterrence to explain after the event why they had so many nuclear weapons, they were able to point out that peace might be obtained through stable and mutual deterrence more easily than by arms elimination. It was not long before it was being argued that the aim of arms control was to improve deterrence—either by increasing or decreasing nuclear weapons as appropriate. By 1960 Professor Schelling was writing: "Recently, in connection with the so-called 'measures to safeguard against surprise attack,' we have begun to consider the possibility of improving mutual deterrence through arms control."

This change in philosophy was a gradual one. With hindsight one cannot but wonder how any situation of such importance could be so radically turned on its head with so little fuss. Talks designed to eliminate nuclear weapons had turned into talks designed to preserve them to keep the peace. The Russians, it must be recorded, were not impressed. Nor did they show any enthusiasm for "open skies." This one might have expected, for the fundamental stumbling block in all disarmament talks has always been that the United States operates with relative openness—much more so than even France or Britain —while the Soviet Union apparently regards secrecy as an important part of its defense.

For this reason one can question how much of a bargain Eisenhower was really offering in his open-skies approach. History, unhappily, speaks for itself. The year after his offer, as we now know, the United States accepted its own "disarmament" plan unilaterally by overflying the Soviet Union with its U-2 flights. Both sides were later to turn this into an important strategic operation through their reconnaissance satellites.

There is one thing that must be said in favor of arms control: within a few years it did enable international agreements to be concluded at Geneva. Although the first decade of disarmament talks was unproductive, the second decade produced results. By 1970 the following treaties had been adopted:

Treaty	Signed	In force
Antarctic	December 1, 1959	June 23, 1961
Partial Test-ban	August 5, 1963	October 10, 1963
Outer Space	January 27, 1967	October 10, 1967
Latin American Nuclear Free Zone	February 14, 1967	Partially
Nonproliferation	July 1, 1969	March 5, 1970

This list, compared to the previous situation of impasse, looks quite substantial. The impression may, however, be illusory. So we should ask just what these treaties have achieved and, more specifically, what they have done to check the nuclear arms race and lessen the chance of nuclear war.

The first point is that three of these treaties concern geographical areas remote from those of strategic concern. The preservation of Antarctica for peaceful uses has turned that continent into a useful scientific laboratory—one, it should be noted, operated to some extent by navies rather than purely civilian scientists. However, the effect has been beneficial for science. But the Antarctic Treaty has had no effect on the strategic arms race. Nor has the Latin American Treaty, for no country in that area is anywhere near achieving nuclear status, and only one or two have ever expressed any interest in doing so.

The Space Treaty is more interesting. In effect, it prohibits the setting up of military stations on the moon and the placing into orbit of weapons of mass destruction. We have already seen in Chapter 2 that, despite the claims of some Air Force fanatics, neither of these objectives ever had any strategic merit. The treaty did not prevent, however, an enormous waste of money by both the Soviet Union and the United States, who felt compelled to investigate space as a military insurance policy. Nor does the treaty mention any of the uses of space that have turned out to be strategically important—there is no prohibition of military communication, weather, navigation, or reconnaissance satellites. This is no accident. In the terms of arms control, all these innovations are to be applauded, for they promise to improve the efficiency of deterrent weapons. The point that technical advances of this kind can also be, and often are, destabilizing is ignored.

To be disparaging about the nonproliferation treaty is less justified. A world in which a score or more of nations practiced nuclear deterrence on one another would be a dangerous one indeed. And the treaty does make that world appear less likely and certainly more distant. Yet, as Robert Neild, the Director of SIPRI, said in a lecture in 1968:

> The non-proliferation treaty is not a disarmament measure. It will not reverse or check the main arms race. China and France are again outside the treaty. It is possible that other potential nuclear states, notably India, may yet stay out.

> . . . The main point, however, is that the non-
> proliferation treaty, if it goes through, seems
> unlikely to be effective for long if the great pow-
> ers do not do something to stop their arms race.
> Otherwise it will simply be a measure that con-
> firms the nuclear dominance of the existing nu-
> clear powers.

Finally, one must look at what is almost universally regarded as the most significant of all the treaties: the partial test-ban treaty, which went into operation in 1963. The need for it, as we saw in Chapter 4, was the increasing danger of atmospheric pollution from fallout; and it was public concern about this that eventually forced the hand of government. The original idea, however, was that all nuclear weapon tests should be banned. After incredibly complicated negotiations, it was concluded that no one could be sure that the other side would be able to detect small underground explosions unless they were allowed to inspect foreign territory. On the number and nature of the inspections to be allowed, the Americans and Russians were never able to agree. As a result they signed a treaty prohibiting all tests except those underground. It was designed as a first step to a complete ban, and several studies have since shown that inspection on foreign territory might no longer be required. Nevertheless, a complete ban now looks more distant than it did in 1963.

The partial test-ban treaty is preceded by the following para-graph:

> Seeking to achieve the discontinuance of all test
> explosions of nuclear weapons for all time, deter-
> mined to continue negotiations to this end, and
> desiring to put an end to the contamination of
> man's environment by radioactive substances.

What has happened since these words were solemnly signed has been nothing short of mockery. According to officially announced figures, the United States exploded 170 nuclear devices under-ground between 1963 and 1968; the Soviet Union exploded 49. And in fact the rate of testing after the treaty came into effect went up, not down. According to a SIPRI study, the world as a whole carried out an average of 39.6 nuclear tests a year during the period from 1951 to 1963; the average went up to 46.2 a year during 1963 to 1968.

Astute observers of the scene in 1963 might have predicted something of the kind. In that year the U.S. Secretary of Defense announced what he called his "simple" position on disarmament and arms control. "I think we should engage in such agreements," he told a congressional committee, "if and when, and only if and when, we can do so without reducing our power advantage."

To set everyone's mind at rest, President Kennedy then announced four safeguards that would be undertaken when the treaty was signed. The first of these was "the conduct of comprehensive, aggressive, and continuing underground nuclear test programs designed to add to our knowledge and improve our weapons in all areas of significance to our military posture for the future." Can this really be called disarmament? It seems clear in retrospect that the treaty was no more than a "clean air" bill and that no nation had any intention of letting the treaty interfere with its nuclear weapons program.

And on November 30, 1967, Senator Henry M. Jackson was able to reassure the Senate that no such disaster had befallen the United States.

> The accelerated underground test program for the next 18 to 24 months consists of a relatively large number of tests on new re-entry vehicles, guidance systems, and our antiballistic missile systems now under development. . . . A large number of underground tests were conducted and very significant advances made in the area of weapons technology development, and in new and radically different weapon design concepts. . . . The basic aims of upcoming underground tests are for the furthering of our knowledge of weapon effects, for improving weapon reliability, increasing penetration capability, and advancing technology.

By early 1970 the largest underground test had risen from a few kilotons to 1.2 megatons. There were indications that future tests might be in the 3- to 10-megaton range. There is no strategic need for anything larger, and the partial test ban had proved no serious handicap to those intent on improving strategic weaponry.

And in two ways it has actually acted against our best interest. By limiting the environment in which tests could be made, it catalyzed into being new and large military research and development programs for underground testing and the computer simulation of nuclear explosions. This has probably cost more, in terms of money and manpower, than continued atmospheric testing would have done. But this, even the most hardened cynic must admit, is perhaps a small price to pay for clean air.

The other charge is more serious. It is that the partial treaty has prevented our getting a complete one. If partial measures had been resisted, this argument runs, mounting concern over pollution of the atmosphere, and its apparently ever-graver implications, would have forced nations to agree to a complete test ban. But with the fallout threat removed, the public lost their lever on the situation and a complete test ban now seems unlikely.

I do not intend to make any justification for the deplorable record at Geneva. Even its successes indicate, I think quite unequivocally, that any real disarmament is simply not possible without some powerful new insights. But there is one bright side to the coin. The more or less total failure, particularly of the first decade of disarmament, led intellectuals to ponder the basic problems of disarmament. They found themselves, like Schelling and his followers, faced with the problem of two parties that had both common and conflicting interests. But they sought their answers not from a more "sophisticated" system of military threats but from behavioral studies which suggested how the other party might be persuaded to cooperate.

The Disarmament Game

"A model of stalemate" was the title a Harvard researcher gave to his analysis of what I have called the "Great Evasion": he sought to show just why all that talk at Geneva had produced so little advance. The researcher, Robert A. Levine, refused to acknowledge that any guilt should be attached to either side. It was a fact, he said, that progress had been almost nonexistent and we should seek not to blame either side but to discover the reasons.

Levine's model was simple but illuminating. He argued that every disarmament move produces a certain amount of cooperative gain to both sides. It may also provide a strategic advantage to either side, because their military power situations are never symmetrical —if they were, banning the bomb or destroying aircraft would present no problem. The stalemate model looks like this:

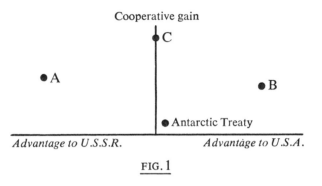

FIG. 1

All the agreements so far made, such as the Antarctic Treaty, have provided only a minute cooperative gain. But they have been concluded because they did not provide either side with much advantage over the other. All treaties which would fall well to the right or the left of the center line have been eschewed. And, the implication is, will be eschewed in the future.

This model suggests one possible way out. I have marked on the figure two disarmament moves, A and B, that give a substantial advantage to one or the other side. Either move is unlikely to be agreed to on its own. But taken together they would constitute disarmament move C—a move which is very cooperative but which gives neither side an advantage over the other. In other words, a package deal of two moves could succeed where either individual move would be bound to fail. Specifically, Levine suggests, it might be possible to conclude a deal whereby the Soviet Union agreed to relinquish a certain amount of secrecy for United States withdrawal from specified overseas bases.

But even if this were done, the problems have not been overcome. There is a class of games, the "Prisoner's Dilemma" games, which can be used to examine any situation where there are both trust and suspicion between two players. I shall use them exclusively to illustrate disarmament problems, but we should remember that this is not their primary function: basically, they are tools for the psychologist who wishes to study the behavior of two people. Their implications for international relations are not yet clear.

The basic game can be set out as follows, and to understand what the game is all about, it is worth playing it mentally for one or two minutes before reading on:

Soviet Union

		Disarm	Arm
United States	Disarm	Soviet Union: +1 United States: +1	Soviet Union: +10 United States: −10
	Arm	Soviet Union: −10 United States: +10	Soviet Union: −1 United States: −1

Consider, now, the problem of playing this game strategically. Together the players do best if they both disarm (+1 each); individually, one will do best if he can arm (+10) but persuade the other to disarm (−10). But the danger here is that if one arms, the other almost certainly will and both players will then together do worse (−1 each). So on any individual starting move, it is strategic suicide to disarm. Strategy dictates that both sides arm and both sides lose. This assumes, of course, that the players cannot communicate and cannot establish an agreement to disarm which they believe the other will honor.

The situation becomes more interesting if the game is played, say, 100 times. If the first player disarms, he may lose the first round; but if he persists, he may convince his opponent that he is trying to reach an agreement that both players always disarm and so make their maximum joint gain. This again makes strategic sense. But when it comes to the one-hundredth game, there is no longer any strategic reason for honoring the agreement, so the second player arms and finishes the game with a move which gives him a 20-point advantage. But if strategic reasoning dictates this as the last move, it inevitably follows that the same applies also to the ninety-ninth game; and to the ninety-eighth game; and to the ninety-seventh game; and so on. Strategically, every move must therefore be to arm, and each side is bound to lose 100 points.

"This conclusion," Drs. Rapaport and Marc Pilisuk told a conference in 1963, "while formally correct, is counter-intuitive. At any rate, there must be something wrong with a definition of rationality, if 'rationality' prescribes a course of action as a result of which two players will lose 100 units each in a situation which enables them to win 100 units each."

This analysis is also relevant to the question of deterrence. In Prisoner's Dilemma the deterrent is the negative score each receives if both sides arm. This should induce the players to disarm. The fact that strategic reasoning does no such thing "leads to the total collapse of the pragmatic argument for continued co-operation based on 'avoidance of reprisals,' i.e., 'deterrence.'"

The insights that can be gained from Prisoner's Dilemma come from recording how subjects play a long series of games. The situation can be made more interesting by varying the scores in each box and thus examining how different punishments and rewards affect the play. Over the years hundreds of thousands of these games have been played under the supervision of psychologists, and some well-established results have emerged. The first two are not surprising. If the reward for unilateral arming is increased, players tend to behave less cooperatively (they both disarm less often). And if the punishment for arming increases (when both arm), they tend to play more cooperatively.

But there is a qualification. If the punishment for both arming is severely increased, sometimes both players arm more often. And it has been found that if the punishment is progressively increased, there is a range over which the players are not deterred but again tend to arm more often. These results suggest that the incentive to cooperate provided by punishment threats is not so simple as it appears; greater punishments can apparently make the players more antagonistic toward each other. Furthermore, the game can be used to compare the effect of increasing the reward for disarming and increasing the punishment for disarming by the same numerical amount. It is found that the reward is more effective in making players cooperate than the punishment.

Hundreds of studies with pairs of subjects actually playing for money have now established some general patterns of how the game is played. Over the first 25 or so games, the amount of cooperation (joint disarmament moves) tends to decrease. It then begins to increase, and by between the two-hundredth and two-hundred-fiftieth game, about 65 per cent of the pairs are disarming on every move; 15 per cent are arming on every move; and the remainder are oscillating between various moves. Psychologists call the first group "Doves," the second, "Hawks," and the third "Mugwumps." They find that once a pattern has been established, it is rarely broken; indeed, the longer the play lasts, the less chance there is of altering a set pattern of responses. In this respect, the game is like Richardson's model of the arms race: it has a self-perpetuating characteristic built into it.

The Doves, or unilateral disarmers, are particularly interesting. By consistently disarming, even though the other player consistently arms and wins that round, they are trying to teach the opponent to play cooperatively. Such "martyr's runs" have been found to occur over many games; one subject playing for real money even played "martyr's choice" on 77 consecutive games. But the prognosis is fairly dismal. For every martyr's run that ends in success (an "agreement" to play cooperatively), 2½ runs end in failure (martyrdom for the martyr and victory for the opponent).

This conclusion receives confirmation from an unexpected source. When Raoul Naroll carried out his historical survey, he compared the frequency of war in civilizations behaving defensively with those behaving aggressively. He found there was no difference in war frequency. "It follows," he writes, "that peace-loving nations are no less likely to be involved in war than warlike nations. Hence, one must conclude that it takes only one nation to make a war, not two nations, a conclusion offering no comfort whatever to advocates of unilateral disarmament."

There are two other intriguing results from Prisoner's Dilemma. One is that players are influenced greatly by the other's play. They tend to play like each other, and they tend to play more and more like each other the longer the game continues. Second, the game can be played without revealing to the players the matrix on page 276. The game then continues very differently. Instead of the amount of cooperative play decreasing for only the first 25 games, it does so for 150 games. And when the game finally settles down, only 35 per cent of the pairs are playing cooperatively instead of the 65 per cent who do so when they can see the whole matrix. I will discuss the significance of these results later.

Prisoner's Dilemma is a very simple game, and one of its great advantages is that it is a "pure" tool for studying behavior. Normally the games are not given the disarmament connotation which I have used. But Marc Pilisuk has invented a whole series of games of this kind which can be used to simulate disarmament more and more closely. The game on which the series is based consists of giving each player 20 cards, white on one side, blue on the other. In these "Michigan Disarmament games," as they are called, one side of the card also has a picture of a factory on it, the other side a picture of a missile. The players start with all their missiles face up. They take turns making secret moves, turning either one, two, or no cards the other way up. Turning the missile side up is, of course, arming; turning the factory side up is disarming. After 20 moves, the results are compared. Both players are punished if they have not disarmed at all, and both are rewarded if they have completely disarmed. At in-between stages the scores can be adjusted in many ways, depending on what values the experimenter puts on a factory or a missile. A player can, for instance, be allowed to win even though he has slightly fewer missiles than the other—on the grounds of the economic gain of converting more missiles to factories.

The game, which is essentially a form of Prisoner's Dilemma, can then be progressively complicated. Inspections of each other's position can be called for at random intervals, or when one player requests it. Players may or may not be allowed to refuse inspections. The game can be stopped after any inspection if the difference in number of missiles is bigger than a certain value—or it may be allowed to proceed. One player may be allowed to launch a surprise attack at any time, which he will win if he has a specified military advantage in number of missiles. The 20 cards can be grouped in sets, representing zones, and the inspections applied to only certain zones; surprise attacks may be made using only certain zones, representing overseas bases. Missiles may be given different values in different zones, challenges between these zones becoming limited wars and the differing values of the missiles in different zones representing the different values of military weapons in different situations. A group of missiles may be allowed to count for more than the sum of their individual worth, as they then become the more valuable weapon system. And the sides may start the game asymmetrically, as would every real disarmament situation.

Games such as these simulate almost every aspect of war and disarmament—they include surprise attack, zonal inspection, limited war, escalation, weapon systems, and all the other paraphernalia of strategic analysis. And Pilisuk's proposal for the game constitutes a vast research program which will take many years to complete. To date, only a few results are available, but they are striking.

The object of all Prisoner's Dilemma games which simulate disarmament is to find a way of playing the game which will result in the opponent playing cooperatively either always or as often as possible. "I am still searching for that elusive model," writes Pilisuk, "but I am of the belief that whether the model found is strong, weak or worthless the work still demonstrates that a technology of moves towards trust, disarmament and peace can be compiled and that experimental data will provide a strong supplement to historical data." For a games researcher, these are strong words; most of the experts will not admit that their results have any direct relevance to international relations.

Why is Pilisuk so optimistic? Basically because he ran a series of the games and found a simple model for inducing cooperation. He then used an experimenter to play the game using the model. Pilisuk reports that the experimenter

> . . . used a strategy which acknowledged three
> variables which came out of earlier work—strong
> sensitivity to the performance of the other player,
> sustained unilateral overtures of trust, and abso-
> lute honesty in inspection. Precisely he showed
> at pay-off time just one less missile than his
> adversary had shown on the previous trial and
> he showed, at inspection, exactly what he was
> going to show at pay-off. Of the 16 players he
> opposed, 8 became doves, 6 ended as mug-
> wumps, and only 2 were hawks.

In other words, the success was based on small unilateral disarmament moves sustained over a period of time. There is now increasing evidence that this is a strategy which induces cooperation. And the evidence comes from quite disparate sources.

One such source is Charles Osgood, a psychologist at the University of Illinois. Years before Pilisuk invented his disarmament game, Professor Osgood had been singled out for special abuse by the strategists. Peering into the murky world of arms and strategy, Osgood—without ever working at the professional think tanks— had dared to publish a book called *An Alternative to War or Surrender*. The germ of his idea was GRIT—which stood for Graduated and Reciprocated Initiative in Tension Reduction. Reduced to its basics, this means that disarmament could be started if one side made a small, unilateral gesture of disarmament to reduce tension. If the other replied in similar vein, a second move of this type should be made. If the other side did not reply, the first should wait a little and then make its second move anyway. In time, Osgood argued, tension would be so reduced that the second side would respond.

The idea was castigated by strategists. GRIT was no alternative to war or surrender, they argued, but was surrender in the particular insidious form of "surrender by installments." But that GRIT could reduce tension was soon confirmed by an internation simulation.

The simulation was run by Wayman J. Crow in August 1962. It involved five countries. On one side was a major nuclear power, Omne, and its smaller nonnuclear ally, Ergo. On the other was Utro, another major nuclear power, with two nonnuclear smaller allies, Algo and Ingo. Ingo was the only country not a member of the International Organization.

Each of the countries was represented by three decision makers, and the chief decision maker of Omne was told to practice GRIT halfway through the game without telling any of his 14 colleagues. The experimenters measured world tension throughout the game by a content analysis of the written messages the decision makers used to communicate with one another.

As the game started, Omne deliberately tried to increase tension. It gave nuclear weapons to its ally, Ergo, and refused to discuss terms on which Ingo might be admitted to the International Organization. Then, as tension mounted, Omne introduced its first GRIT measure. It invited Ingo to attend meetings of the International Organization as a nonvoting member. It went on to spend money on a research program, the benefits of which were to be used exclusively by the three smaller powers. It curtailed its own arms buildup and then announced it would defend itself only with a small and invulnerable nuclear force.

The experimenters who were measuring world tension found that it went up when the first GRIT move was made. The unexpectedness of the move appeared to create hostility and suspicion. But tension did then relax, and the GRIT moves were eventually reciprocated by the other nations. By the end of the game, world tension was decisively lower than at the beginning of the game and much lower than immediately before GRIT had been tried.

A somewhat similar idea to GRIT comes from the world of economics. Its name—the "Cournot Multi-Stage Long-Sighted Game"—is even more dreadful than GRIT but is based on a mathematically more rigorous economic theory. Its adaptation to disarmament is due to Walter Isard and Tony E. Smith.

Consider the problem of two firms trying to sell the same goods in a market in which there is fixed demand. How do the firms determine their policies? This very real problem is well-known to economists who have found that this particular "economic system" has an equilibrium position, marked E on the diagram below. The maximum that could be achieved is actually somewhat higher than this and is represented by the dotted line marked "Welfare boundary." Obviously both firms would do better if they could move to point O, the optimum position. Yet each firm is individually more concerned about getting to either A or B, which will improve its own profits but not that of its competitor. As a result, they tend to stay in deadlock at point E.

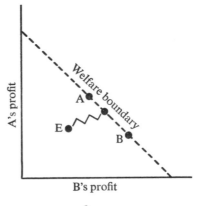

FIG. 3

Isard and Smith showed, again quite rigorously, that there is a solution to this problem as applied to disarmament. It is to take the course of small moves in turn, which is the jagged line joining E and O. This can be done by agreeing to only three rules. The first is that either side can make a move of only a small, predetermined size. The second is that the other side can veto any move. And the third is that the sides move alternately, and they take turns starting.

We now have a whole series of suggestive ideas: From psychology an idea called GRIT, subsequently confirmed by internation simulation. From games theory a strategy for cooperation which includes "sustained unilateral overtures of trust" and evidence that one player's moves influence those of his opponent. And from economics a result which suggests disarmament through small reciprocated steps. This, in turn, is also confirmed by a result I have not yet mentioned. Pilisuk's Michigan Disarmament game (previously described) involves 20 moves in which each side turns over up to two cards at a time to disarm or arm. This is the long version of the game. The short version is for both players to turn over as many cards as they want to at once. The games are structurally and logically identical. They are, however, psychologically different. And Pilisuk has found that the long game produces more cooperation—suggesting that disarmament is more easily reached through a series of small moves than through one big one.

Though it is satisfying to find a possible example of where theory suggests practical recommendations, this may not be the most important contribution of the disarmament games. These have produced what in the long term may be a far more significant result. It is that when subjects are shown the problem in the form of a game—displayed, for instance, as a Prisoner's Dilemma matrix— they are able to cooperate much more frequently. If they are shown the problem alone, with no matrix, they behave less cooperatively.

Similar results have been found in many different games, and they might be expected from common sense. A deeper understanding, a more penetrating analysis, certainly ought to lead to better mutual results. And consider Schelling's theory of tacit bargaining —by which people are able to make agreements with each other without communicating. Their ability to do this depends on their both identifying "prominence points"—noon as the time of day, heads instead of tails, or a crossroads as a meeting point. Now Schelling was not trying to inform people how to behave; he was merely articulating what people did, often subconsciously.

But by doing merely that, he must also influence behavior. Two people who have read Schelling's book are much more likely to reach a tacit bargain, because they have had the principle highlighted, than are two people who have not read the book (though I know of no experimental results to prove this easily testable theory). It follows that the very act of doing research on problems involving cooperative behavior is likely to produce more cooperation and agreement, providing the research becomes widely known. This result has important implications for people trying to prevent conflict turning to violence; it has even more important implications for those who seek ways of resolving conflicts after they have broken out.

Conflict Resolution

In the real world of the 1970s, there is need for other things than critiques of deterrence and sophisticated disarmament games. As I write, a score or so of nations are at war with one another; relationships between another ten or so have worsened to the point of imminent conflagration. What chance is there that a scientific probing of the dynamics of conflict will reveal ways of bringing these conflicts to a close?

Over the past decade, the *Journal of Conflict Resolution* has published the ideas of more than a hundred specialists in this field. For the most part, its articles have been as obscure as they are long, as confusing as they are enlightening. If the germ of some bold new idea for resolving conflict lies hidden in this literature, I have been unable to find it.

This may be the result of my own obtuseness, but at least some of the experts seem to be of the same opinion. Talking about the new field of conflict research, Professor Rapaport writes: "Very likely our whole repertoire of concepts relating to conflict will need to be radically revised, purged, refined, perhaps discarded, before we can develop systematic and fruitful methods of research in this area." This is the process which seems still to be going on, and which makes the field so impenetrable to an outside observer.

But there is one major piece of work which is both theoretically well-defined and which is being tried in practice. In this it is unique and on that score alone deserves inclusion in this book.

The unit doing this work is the Center for the Analysis of Conflict at University College, London. The models and theories from which it works derive primarily from its director, Dr. John Burton —previously an Australian diplomat and now one of the few conflict researchers with extensive diplomatic contacts throughout the world. His theories are tough and uncompromising.

First, Dr. Burton claims the international system can be studied only as the international system. Analogies with animal behavior, with human psychology, or with industrial disputes are useless because nation-states behave differently and uniquely. Second, national boundaries are geographical accidents which relate only poorly to a nation's activities. Trade, communication, and the movements of people occur across them all the time and they all tend to diminish the significance of the boundary. Third, nations behave as they want to, in ways which they judge best, and it is useless to try to impose artificial constraints on them; international law, for instance, will work only as far as it coincides with a nation's own desires—and if it chooses to break the law, it will. Hence Dr. Burton has little time for the League of Nations or the United Nations Security Council. He has even less time for ideas of world government—arguing rather that nations should be made smaller so that their peoples can participate more actively in politics.

Dr. Burton's theories of conflict are based on the mirror-image idea and on the fundamental assumption that no nation behaves aggressively—ever. Nations, he claims, are by their nature nonaggressive. But they often believe their enemies are aggressive. When Israel makes a preemptive strike against Egypt, it is because she fears Egyptian aggression. When she clings to the territory gained, it is not because she is aggressive but because she is saying to Egypt that there is now a bargaining position from which Egypt can learn to accept the fact of Israel's existence.

From all this a number of other ideas follow. For instance, history cannot be relied upon to tell us much about international conflict because it is selective—to analyze a conflict, every concept in the mind of each side must be considered. Hence the proper method of action is not to try to single out individual causes of conflict but to consider them in their entirety. And the means of resolving conflicts is to let participants reach their own agreements, with no outside coercion. To effect this the two sides must be brought into active and prolonged discussion so that they break down their mirror images of each other's position. "The impressive lesson," Dr. Burton writes of his attempts to do this, "was that in analysis and in resolution of conflict it was communication between the parties that was constructive and effective."

The experiments themselves involve actually getting two or three of the top spokesmen on each side to sit round a table in the company of political and social scientists. The latters' job is not to act as mediators but to help the participants in their own analysis of their conflict—by pointing out, for instance, social or political theories which may help in the analysis. By mid-1969 two full-scale "confrontations" had been held at the center in London (the countries involved have asked not to be identified). Each was started by a letter from the director to the heads of the governments concerned or their most senior representatives. This was followed by a visit from the London team to explain the approach and stress that it was not a "disarmament conference"—but an attempt at analysis which would help academics and possibly the participants. In both cases, the confrontations actually began while violence was still raging. Initially feelings ran high on each side and communication was extremely difficult. Each side—and there are often more than two in any complete analysis of a conflict—is allowed to express its own point of view at length before discussion begins.

It is still too early to assess the significance of these experiments. There are indications, however, that as the techniques of the experimenters improve, so does the chance of conflict resolution. But one should ask what evidence there is that the models and theories on which the idea is based are correct. Dr. Burton's ideas challenge so many of our traditional concepts that they seem to demand proof. I have already summarized the evidence for the mirror-image idea, and it is now well accepted. One other example will have to suffice.

The grouping of nations into bigger units of any kind runs counter to Dr. Burton's ideas. "Avoidance of military alliances," he told a conference of biologists in 1963, "may be a strategic policy more in accord both with political reality and with our academic knowledge of the nature of aggression than the traditional policies of alliances which consistently throughout history have ultimately produced the results they sought to avoid." When nations group together to defend themselves, do they really provoke the war they are trying to avoid? Some time after Dr. Burton's categorical assertion, Drs. J. David Singer and Melvin Small set out to test the idea.

They studied 112 alliances that had been set up in the period from 1815 to 1939 and sought to correlate them with subsequent wars. They found, for instance, that in seven wars in which Austria-Hungary had been involved, an alliance preceded each. An alliance preceded four of the five wars in which England was involved and six of the seven wars in which Russia was involved. Using the statistics more cleverly, they discovered that the longer a nation stayed in an alliance, the greater was the chance of a subsequent war. War was also positively correlated with the number of alliances containing major powers and with the number of defense pacts each major power had. "The chances of an allied nation staying out of an impending war during the years covered in this study," the scientists told a conference of peace researchers in 1963, "were not particularly good." On this point, at least, Dr. Burton's thesis seems to hold good.

It may be, however, that the thesis will not stand up to the test of time; other results may show it to be based on faulty premises. This will not necessarily destroy the validity of the "controlled communication" experiments which are still taking place. These have an obvious parallel to psychoanalysis—except that the national leaders talk to one another rather than to their analysts. In both types of analysis the ideas of "right" and "wrong" are eschewed, and the patients learn to see their behavior as a result of environmental stress. In both cases they work through their own problems in an effort to understand their situation better.

The practice of psychoanalysis, of course, is based on many different theories, each about as different from the next as it could be.

And since these theories were proposed, psychological tests have shown parts of all of them to be founded on faulty ideas. But as therapy, psychoanalysis is still useful. The same could be true of Dr. Burton's ideas.

Whether or not this will prove to be the case—for controlled communication or any other resolution technique—there is a psychological point which needs emphasizing. The rewards of this work may turn out to be indirect ones. "They may come not at all from a 'know-how' which will somehow enable us to 'manage' conflict," claims Professor Rapaport.

> They may come rather as a consequence of
> turning the attention of men away from the
> questions which now overwhelmingly occupy
> them—questions concerned with the acquisition
> of mastery over nature and (increasingly) over
> people—to questions related to understanding the
> dynamics of conflict, its cataclysmic aspects as
> well as the logical.

Rapaport's psychological point is a good one. But there is a philosophical one that cannot be ignored. The whole idea of looking scientifically at conflict implies a position of neutrality for the impartial, scientific observer. It implies that conflict is a process that can be objectively studied, that it is not caused by real but by perceived issues of what is right or wrong, and that the best thing to do about conflict is to stop it. This traditional liberal view of war and conflict is now being seriously challenged. The challenge comes from a sharply critical section of the peace research movement which argues that conflict can be a healthy way of achieving social change and that, in a world of hideous social injustice, it may literally be more "violent" to leave things as they are than to change them by force.

CHAPTER IX

Revolution and Change

The Violence of Neglect–Twilight Wars–Twilight Technologists–The Revolution in Peace Research–Disaster Research

"A recipe for change presupposes a cook."
Herman Schmid
Lecture to Conflict Research Society
London February 7, 1970

Most of this book has been concerned with the threat to our survival posed by future wars and our preoccupations with them. It remains to examine the other side of the coin: are there any types of war essential for our future survival?

The question is not so absurd as it may sound. If, as now seems undeniable, the human race has entered a period of crisis, we may have to make some tough decisions to survive. Relief organizations working in disaster areas are familiar enough with the problem. In a situation of catastrophe, emergency foods and drugs are given not to the dying but to the relatively strong. Where supplies are limited, they must be used to prevent the maximum number of deaths and not squandered on those for whom there is already no hope. Faced with a similar situation on a global scale, people may well decide to resort to violence to obtain the resources, food, and living space which they believe are being unjustly hoarded by their government or by other governments. In such a situation, who is to say that this would not be a "just war"?

The Violence of Neglect

To contemplate such possibilities requires tough thinking. It is a basic tenet of modern society that war, conflict, and violence are abhorrent, especially the latter. But our views on these things are neither static nor consistent. It is not so long since the Church condoned torture as a means of changing the minds of would-be heretics. Until quite recently, it was considered just to hang a man for stealing a sheep. And we still see no moral problem in offering a soldier the choice between certain death at the hands of a firing squad if he deserts and probable death at the hands of the enemy if he joins the attack.

Even less clear-cut are our attitudes toward less physical forms of violence. Though hanging is now abolished in most of civilized society, lifelong prison sentences are not. (In Dallas, Texas, on March 20, 1970, a man who stole about eighty dollars was sentenced to 1,000 years in prison.) These are held to be just punishments, as is the use of tear gas, water hoses, and truncheons when wielded by the police to quell demonstrations. When wielded by the demonstrators, however, they are called "violent methods" and condemned universally, sometimes even by those sympathetic to the cause of the demonstration. In short, our public declarations that all violence is evil and abhorrent are daily negated by the penal systems whose existence we condone. And they are profoundly qualified by our judgments as to which causes are just and which are not. Violence is the name we give to the other fellow's use of force.

To add to the confusion, we are only now beginning to distinguish between gross physical violence and what might be called "structural violence" or the "violence of neglect." Egil Fossum, a young peace researcher from Oslo, has called this "the silent violence that is generated by the social structure, taking its toll through hunger, sickness and humiliation and which can be seen in tables of life expectancy, infant mortality, caloric intake, epidemic diseases, etc." The results of our neglect of the underprivileged in every society, and of the underdeveloped regions in nearly every nation south of the equator, are every bit as violent as the actions of the thugs who beat bank cashiers to death in more "enlightened" regions.

Furthermore, we are willing to condone some forms of violence as one of the prices of modern society. It seems likely that any advanced country could reduce the number of people killed on the roads to near zero. But the costs are judged too high. In Britain

7,000 road deaths a year are allowed to occur for want of the political and financial resources needed to reduce them further. And the provision of "danger money" to those whose jobs involve physical risk is further evidence that some forms of structural violence are acceptable, if the price is right.

One of the great modifiers of our attitude to violence is geographical distance. Death from starvation is a violent way to die, and nobody lets anybody starve in their own living rooms. But every inhabitant of every advanced country does just that every day in a less direct way. When we vote for governments which are not prepared to spend more than a few per cent of their country's wealth on foreign aid—and no government is—we condemn to an early death people in South America, Africa, and Asia. It is in this vaguely defined area of remote and indirect violence that our beliefs about what can and what cannot be allowed are likely to change most.

Such a change is already being forced upon us by swift communications. On-the-spot reporting of the Biafran war and famine brought home a disaster whose impact would previously have been anesthetized by distance. Yet that was only one isolated instance in a sea of suffering. What was seen of Biafra on television was, in fact, symptomatic of life in much of the southern hemisphere. Furthermore, that scene is one due to be reenacted over nearly two-thirds of the earth's land mass in the decades to come—unless, that is, some new way is found of bringing home to the privileged few the extent of the crises now engulfing the underprivileged many.

Future generations, I predict, will look upon our global negligence in this regard as evidence of the profound moral decay of the twentieth century. They will judge us as we judged the "Inquisition civilizations" of the past—as a society guilty of condoning barbarism on an unimaginable scale. As Nero fiddled while Rome burned, so the strategists of civilized society planned for nuclear war while the unwatched countries of the Third World limped slowly and painfully along the road to starvation.

But it will be surprising if the present situation survives even to the end of the 1970s. The reason is not that the Third World will necessarily become more violent as it gets hungrier, poorer, and more overpopulated. But it will get more violent as it realizes that none of these fates is inevitable. The significance of the wind of change is that it carries with it the seeds of hope. And, perversely, it is hope which in a desperate situation breeds violence.

This already classic law of social science applies to conflict situations at every level of society. The master and his slave have a relationship which is full of latent conflict, but this is rarely expressed. Until such time as the slave realizes he is a slave, and that there is some hope of his achieving freedom, he does not think to protest. And only when he believes that his cries for help will be heard by others does he raise his voice in anger. That there is as little violence as there is in South Africa is because the apartheid regime takes good care to offer the oppressed majority no hope of change and no chance of contact with the outside world.

But elsewhere—in both hemispheres—the message is being carried home. The "revolution of rising expectations" is already upon us. In America, summer after summer black people, seeing for the first time the chance of equal status with whites, turn their city ghettos into fiercely burning ruins. Demonstrations are no longer symbolic gestures, for people have realized that it is possible to stop governments from building airports over their villages or filling their sports grounds with all-white Southern African sports teams. While these examples may seem trivial, the implications for international politics are grave indeed.

Speaking in Montreal on May 18, 1966, Robert McNamara produced some surprising statistics of violence. He claimed that during 1958–66 there had been 164 outbreaks of violence of international significance. Fifteen (9 per cent) were conventional conflicts, 76 (47 per cent) were long insurgencies, and 73 (43 per cent) were brief coups or revolts.

Even more revealing was an examination of the type of country in which these conflicts occurred. No less than 87 per cent of the "very poor" countries experienced internationally significant conflict during these years. For the poor and middle-income countries the corresponding figures were 69 per cent and 48 per cent. But only 1 of the 27 "rich" countries experienced a major internal strife. The poverty gap, McNamara later claimed, was a "seismic fissure, driving deep into the earth's sociological crust." It was bound to produce "thunderous earthquakes of violence if rich and poor countries alike do not move to meet the threat." McNamara's move, a few months later, from the Defense Department to the World Bank was an even more eloquent statement.

But the true meaning of poverty is more than lack of wealth—it is better defined as the inability to influence the events which affect one's life. The cause may be financial, physical, or political. Ted Gurr and his colleagues at Princeton have tried to measure political deprivation and to see how it correlates with violence and internal strife. In a study of 21 "Western" nations during 1961–65, they found that the death rate from internal strife was highest in Rhodesia and South Africa. During that period in Rhodesia the equivalent of more than 1,000 people per 100 million population were killed in internal violence. In South Africa the equivalent death rate was about 400 people per 100 million inhabitants.

From a complicated series of statistics, Gurr was able to deduce what many had long suspected. "The more discontented people are," he told a London symposium in 1970, "the less likely they are to resort to nonviolent protest and the more likely they are to rebel."

Such is the driving force behind the revolution of rising expectations. What are the rich nations doing about it? As in most of this book, we will take as our example the world's richest nation of all, the United States.

Twilight Wars

Senator William Fulbright does not mince his words when attacking United States foreign policy. "Without becoming militarist in the sense of committing themselves to the military virtues as standards of personal behavior," he writes, "the American people have nonetheless come to place great—and, in my opinion, excessive—faith in military solutions to political problems. Many Americans have come to regard our defense establishment as the heart and soul of our foreign policy." It is not then surprising that the threat of revolution in the Third World produced in the United States—a nation itself born of revolution—an instantaneous military response.

And it was a novel response. It did not take the RAND Corporation to work out that nuclear weapons and supersonic aircraft could do little to stem the rising tide of discontent south of the equator. Instead the Pentagon chose the weapons of counterinsurgency and openly began a study of means by which guerrilla uprisings, coups, and revolts could be quickly suppressed. Interpreting all these as Communist-led, if not actually Moscow-inspired, it saw no contradiction in studying the classic 1937 work on guerrilla warfare by the Chinese leader, Mao Tse-tung. The lessons from this and similar tracs were instilled not only into all senior U.S. Army officers but into many more military leaders from countries thought prone to internal disorder. These were the new "twilight soldiers," trained to squash the silent wars that seethed in the jungles and wastes of corrupt regimes.

The John F. Kennedy Center for Special Warfare at Fort Bragg in North Carolina was the counterinsurgency headquarters. There, on 140,000 acres of training ground, the U.S. Army taught survival, jungle fighting, and psychological warfare on a scale that escalated throughout the 1960s. Some 1,600 resident specialists served as instructors, organized into what now sounds like a nineteenth-century Ruritanian mockery of military affairs. The units at Fort Bragg included the First Radio Broadcasting and Leaflet Battalion; the First Loudspeaker Company; and even a Headquarters Company Propaganda Platoon—a unit which, according to the commanding officer, Colonel George M. Jones, boasted in 1960 a full complement of "scriptwriters, artists, illustrators, announcers, linguists and news writers." Special typewriters were developed and language courses offered in all the common languages as well as Vietnamese, Swahili, Arabic, Persian, Burmese, Lingala, Amharic, and Hindi-Urdu.

The training was tough as well as scholarly. The trainees visited mountain and cold weather schools and training sites in Alaska, Colorado, and Utah. They attended jungle warfare schools in the Canal Zone and Georgia. They went to underwater school at Key West in Florida and underwent special training with Navy frogmen in Virginia.

Although the Fort Bragg center was intended primarily for African and Latin American countries, another jungle warfare school—the "School of the Americas"—was in operation at Fort Gulick in the Canal Zone. This was created specifically for Latin American guerrilla graduates and by March 1965 had instructed no less than 15,500 Latin Americans in the fine art of counter-insurgency. Another school in Okinawa specialized in training for Southeast Asia, and a fourth at Bad Tölz in Germany for European and Middle Eastern countries. Mobile training teams operated in other likely countries such as Liberia and Mali.

By 1962 this activity had outgrown the control of the Central Intelligence Agency, whose brainchild it was. In that year it came under Army orders, and inevitably interservice rivalry soon broke out. The Marines were skeptical, claiming that what was taught was no more than what Marines did, had done in the past, and would continue to do in the future. The Air Force forged a school for Air Commandos as an offshoot of the Elgin Air Force Base in Florida and soon had 5,500 specially trained airmen at its fingertips. The Army's Special Forces had by 1966 risen to 12,000 or more. And even the Navy got in on the act by establishing its Sea-Air-Land teams known as "SEAL" units.

The tip-off on this frenzied activity came when President Kennedy first publicly embraced the counterinsurgency cause. Presenting the defense budget on March 28, 1961, he called for greater funds to "deal with guerrilla forces, insurrections and subversions." To ram the point home his special adviser on National Security Affairs, Walt Rostow, made it one of his first jobs to address a graduation ceremony at Fort Bragg. What he said there has become something of a seminal speech—as was clearly intended—which reflected counterinsurgency policy of the time. Rostow made it clear that change was to be expected and approved in the Third World—a region, he said, which was undergoing "the revolution of modernization." The U.S. Army was interested in the process, Rostow went on, because "communism is best understood as a disease in the transition to modernization." This remarkable insight, implying as it does that every developing country should follow the footsteps of the United States, carried with it the implication that all violent and unconstitutional change should be stamped out. "The best way to fight a guerrilla war," Rostow said, "is to prevent it from happening. And this can be done." To those who were intended to do it, Rostow offered a final encouragement:

> I salute you as I would a group of doctors, teachers, economic planners, agricultural experts, civil servants, or those others who are now leading the way in the whole southern half of the globe.

One of the places they led to, of course, was Vietnam—a country in which the American half of the war was for a long time fought only by the Special Forces, or "Green Berets." But by 1965 the futility of that policy had been finally established. Instead of handfuls of highly trained men quietly squashing a Communist-led revolution, the United States was flying in brigades of infantry, squadrons of B-52 aircraft from Strategic Air Command, and routing many of its aircraft carriers toward Southeast Asian waters. But failure in Vietnam did not daunt the counterinsurgency enthusiasts.

"U.S. Secret Army Fighting Reds by Red Methods," claimed *U.S. News and World Report* in April 12, 1965. "Spurred on by Communist aggression in Vietnam, the U.S. now is waging a new kind of warfare around the world, using 25,000 skilled Americans and spending 2 billion dollars a year. This elite 'secret army' is carrying on counter-insurgency in 50 nations in an effort to halt communist subversion and terror before it reaches the Vietnam stage." The article went on to mention the countries in which this new kind of war was being waged. They included Chile, Venezuela, Panama, Guatemala, Iran, Thailand, Algeria, Mali, Ethiopia, the Congo, and Colombia.

In his book, *The Weapons of World War III,* John S. Tompkins is more specific about these activities.

> More than 250 teams of Army, Navy and Air
> Force men are working on a variety of special
> projects ranging from engineering and medical
> help to training of local military and police units
> in counter-guerilla tactics. Venezuela, for example,
> has been able to improve substantially its control
> of guerilla and terrorist elements with U.S.-trained
> military and police units. In Peru, the Government
> has made good progress against guerilla
> concentrations with its U.S.-trained and -supported
> Army and Air Force. In Colombia, training and a
> few helicopters have aided the Army to
> re-establish Government control in the rural
> insurgent areas. The Bolivian Army is being
> trained and equipped to counter intermittent
> violence in the mines. A Guatemalan counterin-
> surgency force is being supported with weapons,
> vehicles, radios, and training. And our military
> assistance to Uruguay is oriented toward im-
> proving the small arms, ammunition, communica-
> tions, and transportation equipment of its security
> forces.

Enough has been said to illustrate the character of the American counterinsurgency plans. Their preoccupation with communism is clear enough, but we should stop to ask what implications they have for the peoples of the Third World? In what ways will they speed the process of modernization, halt oppression, reduce poverty, and feed the hungry?

There is abundant evidence that the policy is designed not so much to prevent change leading to communism but to preserve the status quo if there is any danger that communism may result from change. The distinction is an important one and cannot be brushed aside by saying that no change is better than violent change. Egil Fossum has made a special study of military coups in Latin America, of which there have been no less than 105 in the past 60 years. He concludes:

> . . . poverty will be more and more of a problem
> in the years to come and contribute significantly to

> the polarizing of the Latin American societies be-
> tween those accepting and those rejecting the
> existing social order. In such a situation, recourse
> to violence will be the only way to change govern-
> ments and bring about change . . . military coups
> can be conceived of as a functional equivalent to
> elections.

The suppression of unconstitutional change may well serve the best interests of the United States, but there are reasons to doubt that such a policy will serve the best interests of the peoples of Asia, Africa, and Latin America. Robert Heilbronner has put it more forcibly. "It must be said aloud," he writes, "that our present policy prefers the absence of development to the chance for Communism— which is to say that we prefer hunger and want and the existing inadequate assaults against the causes of hunger and want to any regime that declares its hostility to capitalism."

His charge is borne out by a smaller and less public facet of coun- terinsurgency plans. Where the situation calls for it, these forces have been called on not to suppress change but to induce it. The only situations so far where this treatment has been called for have been in countries where Communist or left-wing governments have already attained power. That these should be toppled, regardless of the effect on the country concerned, is also part of the United States "counter"insurgency program. As evidence one can cite the paper on guerrilla warfare that was circulated to all senior officers in the Pentagon in 1961. Unsigned, it read: "To turn the guerilla warfare coin over, we must find a way to overthrow a communist regime in power short of general war and even short of limited war."

The CIA's role in trying to overthrow many left-wing regimes has been remorselessly documented in recent years. Perhaps the unhap- piest example to date was in Guatemala in the 1950s.

In World War II that country found itself in the hands of an almost fascist regime. But in 1944 a revolution established Juan Arévalo as President, and he immediately began a reform program. Forced labor on banana plantations was abolished, unions were made legal, and attempts to modernize the economy were made. Seven years later Jacobo Arbenz was elected President, and he added to the program a much-needed series of land reforms. At that time some 2 per cent of the population owned 70 per cent of the land. And by far the biggest owner was the Boston-based United Fruit Company, from whom in 1954 the new President seized 234,- 000 acres of uncultivated land. As compensation, the company was offered $600,000 worth of bonds, the value they had attached to the land for tax purposes. United Fruit then filed a claim for nearly $16 million worth of compensation.

At this point the CIA began to intervene forcefully. It provided arms and encouragement for a right-wing exile government of Army forces then in Honduras. A plan for a military coup was laid, of which Eisenhower was later claimed to have said, "I am prepared to take any steps that are necessary to see that it succeeds." It did. Arbenz was overthrown, the new regime established, and the land restored to the United Fruit Company. The revolution, known as "Operation el Diablo," was neither bloodless nor cheap. United States planes were used to bomb Guatemala City, and the invasion is said to have cost the United States taxpayer more than $5 million. And in the next two years the United States spent some $90 million on Guatemalan aid, compared to the $600,000 it had spent in the previous 10.

Guatemala's subsequent history does not make happy reading. Between 5,000 and 8,000 suspected Communists were thrown into jail. Secret election ballots were eliminated and the vote taken away from what the new dictator, Castillo Armas, called the "illiterate masses"—some three-quarters of the country. In his book *The Winds of Revolution* Tad Szulc described Armas as a "political failure, a wastrel of American aid, a protector of corruption, and an unthinking defender of the pre-revolutionary *status quo*." Three years later Armas was assassinated, but United States interest in Guatemala remained unshaken.

Twilight Technologists

In the 15 years that have elapsed since the Guatemalan affair, priorities have changed. Gross physical intervention with the affairs of other countries has been supplemented by more sophisticated financial and technical approaches. The strings attached to foreign aid, for instance, have been found capable of pulling Third World governments in the directions which the United States prefers. Near to Vietnam the strings are particularly tough—at one time all the United States aid given to Thailand, for instance, was divided solely between counterinsurgency help and military assistance (60 per cent for the former, 40 per cent for the latter). And in his book *Intervention and Revolution,* Richard J. Barnet, co-director of the Institute for Policy Studies, claims that of the $62,238 million given in foreign aid over 1953–67, only $16,092 million was for economic development alone. All the rest was earmarked for use in connection with military assistance, counterinsurgency, or police action.

Spurred on by the problems of Vietnam, help has also been sought from the technologists. In short order, the Army established two new laboratories—the Limited Warfare Laboratory and the Electronic Warfare Quick Reaction Facility. The Advanced Projects Research Agency established Project AGILE under the heading of Remote Area Conflict. And from these and other units there emerged an unholy series of devices for killing, maiming, burning, poisoning, detecting, and brainwashing the luckless inhabitants of the developing nations. Small rifles were manufactured for small Asians, and the Special Purpose Individual Weapon promised, according to John S. Tompkins, to deliver "high velocity steel bullets, about an inch long, but only as thick as a pencil lead. The bullets are stabilized with tiny metal fins and, looking like little arrows, they are called 'flechettes.' " The scientific tests needed to develop such weapons—which involve firing them at goats—are not published in the open scientific literature.

The repellency of this technological nightmare is such that I am relieved not to have to describe it in further detail. For the idea that high military technology had anything really significant to offer to the problem of the Third World was stillborn. But what has proved significant is another form of scientific perversion with novel, limitless, and incalculable implications. This is the colonization of social scientists by the military establishment.

On December 4, 1964, the U.S. Army Special Operations Research Office issued a document describing the largest single social science research program ever devised anywhere in the world. In little more than a year, this plan had caused uproar throughout American universities, stimulated a congressional hearing, State Department censure, and a veto from the President of the United States. It ranks in importance with the famous Frisch-Peirls Memorandum on the atomic bomb and started with these already historic words:

> Project Camelot is a study whose objective is to
> determine the feasibility of developing a general
> social systems model which would make it possible
> to predict and influence politically significant
> aspects of social change in the developing nations
> of the world. . . . The project is conceived as a
> three to four year effort to be funded at around
> one and one-half million dollars annually. It is

> supported by the Army and the Department of
> Defense, and will be conducted with the co-
> operation of other agencies of the government. . . .
> The US Army has an important mission in the
> positive and constructive aspects of nation building
> as well as a responsibility to assist friendly govern-
> ments in dealing with active insurgency prob-
> lems. . . .

Camelot was to study the political situation in 13 Latin American countries, three Middle Eastern ones, four in the Far East, two in Europe, and one in Africa. The document quoted was sent to many distinguished social scientists, accompanied by an invitation to attend a four-week conference on the project, for which a fee of $2,000 was offered. But the Army made the mistake of extending invitations to some scientists whom it might have judged would not be sympathetic to the idea of "influencing" social change in the Third World. And so, in fairly short order, the document found its way into the hands of the Chilean press who condemned it as "brazen intervention" by a vast continental spy plan. It did not take long for the U.S. ambassador in Chile to make a formal complaint to the State Department about the impossible position which this hitherto unknown project had placed him in, and for high Defense and State Department officials to step in and cancel the whole fiasco some three months before it was due to begin.

And for a few months the fierce light of publicity illuminated the ugly specter of how the social scientist might replace the physical scientist as the brains behind future wars. But the illumination was fleeting, and only a few chose to pursue the implications of Project Camelot. One who did was Professor Kenneth Boulding. "The cloud of the 'Camelot' fiasco hangs heavily over the relations between Government and the social sciences," he wrote, "and foreshadows all too clearly the possible shape of things to come. It could well be that the kind of knowledge which would result from taking the social sciences seriously would turn out to be more threatening to traditional values and institutions even than the H bomb and bacteriological weapons."

But of course that prospect did not disappear just because Camelot had been canceled. Writes John S. Tompkins:

> Despite the flap over Project Camelot some other
> study projects are going ahead in more discreet
> hands. One called "Numismatics" is an analysis of
> the strategic and tactical factors underlying

military counter-insurgency operations. Another
called "Role" is studying the changing roles of
indigenous military establishments. "Resettle" is
probing the problems of agrarian colonization in
co-operation with the Peruvian Government. "Sim-
patico" is an effort in Colombia to analyze military
civic action programs and their effect on the
attitudes of people. "Secure" is a study of internal
security problems such as riot control. And it appears that a sixth study—whose title is classified—
is covering much of the same ground as Camelot
set out to do: ". . . to explore major sociological
and psychological vulnerabilities in selected
countries . . ."

After Camelot, much of the Defense Department's involvement
with social science disappeared from public view. It reappeared, un-
intentionally, in the summer of 1967 when members of the National
Academy of Science's Defense Science Board met to discuss what
social science research could be of much use to the DoD. Although
the resulting document, entitled "Report of the Panel on Defense
Social and Behavioral Sciences," was confidential, Professor Irving
Louis Horowitz performed a public service by describing it in an
article in *Trans-Action*. "What we have in this report," he wrote,
"is a collective statement by eminent social scientists, a statement
that can easily be read as the ominous conversion of social science
into a service industry of the Pentagon."

The report was wide-ranging. It recommended increased funds for
the study of Project 100,000—the plan to turn rehabilitated juvenile
delinquents into soldiers. It urged the expansion and testing of "techniques for the improvement of items which might assist in forecasting alliances, neutralities, hostile activities, etc., and for use in
tactical decision-making." And it recommended a wide range of
research in foreign areas which in effect added up to a plea for a
new and expanded Project Camelot. Finally, it addressed itself to
the problem of how more social scientists could be persuaded to
work for the military:

More high quality scientists could probably be
interested in DoD problems if DoD would more
frequently state its research needs in terms which
are meaningful to the investigator rather than to
the military. . . . Publicity concerning the distinguished behavioral scientists who have long-term

commitments to the DoD should be disseminated
as a way of reassuring younger scientists and
improving our research image.

In the light of such evidence, the fears of scientists quite outside
the military network seem amply confirmed. Not only is there a
theoretical possibility that social and psychological science will be
used to condition people for political ends, but the plans for doing
just that are being actively laid. "Psychology as the science of how
to manipulate man according to somebody's master plan," said Ma-
rie Jahoda, professor of social psychology at Sussex University in
the spring of 1969, "is the specter that haunts me when I look to
the future." The only qualification that needs to be added is that the
specter has already arrived.

The Revolution in
Peace Research

To most liberal thinkers the ideas behind the United States counterinsurgency plans described over the past few pages are politically
objectionable. The idea of peace research, on the other hand, is
wholly praiseworthy. And here lies an awful dilemma. Peace research—as it was originally conceived—was an attempt to use the
objective analysis of science to prevent organized, collective forms
of violence. That definition is also a good description of the U.S.
Department of Defense's motive for enlisting the help of social scientists in dealing with problems in the Third World. So it is not
surprising to find scientists writing in peace research journals ac-
knowledging that their research had been made possible by grants
from the Department of Defense. It was not long before the $64
million question was publicly raised: had peace research sold its
soul to the devil?

To understand the furious debate that has ensued within the peace
research movement, we have to go back to its origins. Peace research was conceived during the most frigid moments of the cold
war. At that time the issues were clear enough: if nuclear war could
not be prevented, global extinction seemed possible if not probable.
On any analysis, all other issues paled into irrelevance before this
one—a technology for stopping conflict had to be developed, and it
had to be developed quickly. Scientists peered into the family, into
industry, and into international behavior to try to glean lessons as

to how conflict could best be suppressed. Our knowledge of arbitration and mediation, and the principles behind them, grew more in a decade than it had in the previous centuries of neglect. All this was reflected by the title of the new journal launched to report the results of this discipline—the Journal of Conflict Resolution. And the papers it published carried through the implications of its title: they all tried to show how conflicts might be better understood and so more quickly terminated. Most of those who wrote such papers described themselves as conflict researchers. Originally, they were mostly American, not all of them too fussy about who paid for their research. Thus it was that in the late 1950s a U.S. Navy research station commissioned Project Michelson—the largest scientific investigation of deterrence theory ever launched.

At this time peace and conflict research were not very critically distinguished. Some of the impetus for peace research came from the United States, but there were also powerful pressures at work in Britain and Scandinavia. And unquestionably it was the social scientist, Professor Johan Galtung of Oslo University, who at the age of 28 turned European peace research into a thriving and forceful movement.

Galtung's restless intellectualism forced peace research into new avenues as every year went by. He set a breathtaking pace, editing (and sometimes writing the best part of) his own journal, the *Journal of Peace Research*. His own interests in sociology and in futurology were so broad, his enthusiasm so persuasive, and his capacity for travel so nearly limitless, that demand for people to write and speak about peace research in Europe soon exceeded supply. It was Galtung who made the subject respectable in Europe; and, inevitably, it was Galtung who was later to be charged with having sold the subject out to the reactionary forces of the establishment.

Inevitably, too, it was Galtung who first began to ask the fundamental questions about what peace research was trying to do and where it was aiming to go. Looking beyond the end of the cold war, and toward the growing restiveness of the Third World, it was Galtung who coined the term "negative peace" as the goal toward which most peace and conflict researchers were working. By this he meant that their concern was solely to establish a condition in which physical violence was absent. To Galtung, and soon to many others, this was not enough. To them peace meant something more positive, whose attainment should be the long-term goal of peace researchers.

Meanwhile, it was argued, there was plenty of need for anything which helped bring about a condition of negative peace. Time was short, the threat was real, and efforts still had to be made to find new ways of patching the well-worn tire of international relations. Only when this had been done should energy be expended in trying to change the tire completely.

While denying little of this, Galtung also pointed out that there were dangers in giving negative peace any kind of priority. If this were done, he claimed in 1967, peace research "could easily become research into the conditions of maintaining power, of freezing the *status quo,* of manipulating the underdog so that he does not take up arms against the top dog." Peace research, he concluded, "may easily become a conservative force in politics." Galtung was in a good position to judge, for only a few years before in Latin America, he had played a pivotal role in helping to topple and expose the DoD's Project Camelot.

Fundamental to the concept of negative peace, of course, is the idea that all conflict is bad. There is, on the contrary, a great deal of evidence that conflict has many positive functions—not the least of which is to bring two parties with different ideas into positive contact. In many ways, conflict is the stuff of which life is made, and Galtung was quick to point to the absurdities of any philosophy which tried to deny that conflict had any role to play in molding society. In 1969 he wrote:

> In political thinking conflicts are acknowledged
> but they are there to be done away with, and the
> methods are legion. One way is to do away with
> the antagonist. Several methods present them-
> selves. The more vulgar method is to eliminate
> him physically—perhaps by defining him as in-
> ferior, subhuman or a class enemy, so that he can
> be segregated, isolated, or even exterminated.
> There is the more refined, democratic way—by
> permitting him to organize himself as a party, but
> at the same time relegating him to a constant
> minority position so that he is eliminated culturally
> by being outvoted.

A more positive attitude, Galtung claimed, would be to bring conflict out into the open—by encouraging its study, by teaching conflictology in schools and making its management the responsibility of everyone. This was not a job that should be left any longer to elitist groups such as the military, industrial boards, the police, or administrators. "Conflict affects us all," he wrote, "so conflict management belongs to us all." And to rub the point home he drew an unforgettable analogy:

> It is not merely a question of "learning how to live with conflict." That is like the official Victorian attitude towards sex—something you must tolerate but not enjoy. In conflict, as in sex, toleration is not enough: you must like it, love it too. Both are the salt of life. They enrich our existence—if we have the courage and maturity to meet the challenge fully—and even joyfully.

But even before Galtung had written this, many of his most dire predictions about peace research had been fulfilled. The controversy reached crisis point when the International Peace Research Society declared the time had come to make a practical, rather than a theoretical, contribution. Accordingly, it chose to address its entire June 1968 conference to the question of Vietnam. And what resulted was a set of papers almost wholly from American academics as to how the Vietnam conflict could be brought most quickly to a close. As this was also the fervent desire of both the State and Defense Departments, the papers had much in common with that type of thinking.

They posed the question, for instance, of how best the Saigon regime could "establish its legitimacy in the eyes of the villager." The strategy of forcible "pacification" of hamlets was examined and one paper even analyzed the idea that legitimacy of the Saigon government might be established most quickly by increased bombing of those regions which did not regard Saigon as legitimate. Talking of the National Liberation Front, another author claimed that it, like "all revolutionary movements recruit from among previously criminal and/or other deviant groupings." And the introduction to the printed papers made it quite clear that they were addressed primarily to the formulators of United States policy in the hope of helping them solve their problems.

But if the content of these papers made this meeting of "peace" researchers somewhat extraordinary, so too did the interests of the contributors. They included, for instance, Ithiel de Sola Pool, a distinguished member of the Center for International Studies at the Massachusetts Institute of Technology. Now MIT is a modern technological university more financially committed than any other in the United States to the goals of military technology and arms development. It has also been intimately involved with the affairs of the CIA. Two years before the peace research conference, Pool had had this to say about the relationship between the CIA and social science:

> The CIA, as its name implies, should be the
> central social research organization to enable the
> federal government to understand the societies and
> cultures of the world. The fact that it uses as
> little social science as it does is deplorable. We
> should be demanding that they use us more.

The response to all this was immediate. The younger peace researchers, particularly from Scandinavia, saw in the Vietnam papers all that they wanted least to come out of peace research. The "young Turks"—as their elders fondly and somewhat patronizingly dubbed them—argued that there was nothing scientific about the Vietnam conference; it was, they said, merely a meeting of technologists dedicated to the goal of United States victory in Vietnam. And the asymmetry of the argument was proved by the fact that there were no papers about how the National Liberation Front could bring the war to a close most quickly. The point was well made.

It was made most eloquently in 1968 in an article by Herman Schmid from the University of Lund. Called "Peace Research and Politics," it relentlessly exposed all the logical inconsistencies of the idea of peace research and mercilessly attacked the "liberal" ideologies on which the discipline appeared to be based.

First, Schmid claimed, for there to be a scientific investigation of conflict, the scientist himself had to be neutral and his position had to be perfectly symmetrical to the two parties. The whole of conflict research was based on this idea, and it had indeed suggested improved ways of analyzing the East-West nuclear deadlock. But none of these techniques could be used to help analyze conflicts in which the two sides were not balanced—which meant almost every kind of conflict except that of all-out nuclear war. In short, Schmid concluded, "most formal conflict models can only be used for a type of conflict which is very infrequent."

A second problem was that "the peace researcher will have to ally himself with those who have power in the international system" if he is to be listened to. So the idea of a neutral, scientific attitude to most conflicts was an absurdity. The peace researchers Schmid was to write later, had either to "join one of the conflict parties and try to influence him, or join neither and be ignored by both."

Schmid's careful and elaborate analysis went on to question just what was meant by the term "peace" in peace research. He showed, as Galtung had, the dangers of negative peace but also questioned the doctrine of positive peace—which was, he said, a tautological, umbrella term under which any researcher could group all the things he valued most highly, such as integration, racial harmony, economic development, or population control. Such an activity was not research but politics.

Schmid did not advocate reform in the peace research movement but drastic change. The nub of his recommendation was that:

> Peace research . . . should formulate its problems, not in terms meaningful to international and supernational institutions, but in terms meaningful to suppressed and exploited groups and nations. It should explain not how manifest conflicts are brought under control, but how latent conflicts are manifested. It should explain not how integration is brought about, but how conflicts are polarized to a degree where the present international system is seriously challenged or even broken down.

By the time the International Peace Research Association met in Czechoslovakia in 1969, the "young Turks" had taken Schmid's paper to heart. Peace research, they thundered, was a technology of pacification which failed to recognize that revolution and wars of liberation might be needed to establish any kind of peaceful society. "This is the scientific insight," claimed another Scandinavian, Lars Dencik, "with which a new peace and conflict research, or revolution research, will confront the ideological blindfolds of traditional peace research."

What are we to make of this revolution in peace research? Can this strident new tone, openly advocating revolution research, be reconciled with the superficially more sympathetic and moderate aims of the early peace researchers? It seems unlikely.

Two parties to a conflict which have roughly balanced resources and political freedom have little to gain from war. If the older techniques of peace and conflict research can be used to stop the bloodshed, well and good. But this philosophy cannot be applied to all conflicts—least of all to the type of conflict, caused by repression and by political and social injustice, which seems likely to typify the decades to come. Here the traditional liberal view, of stamping out all violence at any cost, must be found wanting. The basic reason is that the violence already exists, concealed within the structure of the situation. If that structure can be changed by a quick and even violent revolutionary war, most people will be better off. And in places like South Africa, revolution may well be the only conceivable cure for a fatally diseased society.

But revolution is not something that can be lightly advocated. There are dangers. Should the revolution fail, savage reprisals may be made by the threatened government; and the conditions which led to the uprising are likely to worsen. On the other hand, successful revolutions can have their drawbacks too. Only too often those who were the underdogs establish themselves as top dogs, and the top dogs, if they are not exterminated, become bottom dogs. This is a zero-sum game in which the net gain is nil.

The dynamics of revolution, and its range of possible consequences, are almost unexplored territory. If this is the type of topic to be probed by the new revolution research, then I think the subject could prove of great value. But there are two reservations.

The first is that this new science, like all the sciences that went before it, could be misused. When the young Turks of peace research made their challenge, they charged that up to that time peace research had been no more than a "technology of pacification." It was a fair charge. A similar charge can be made of revolution research. What may come out of this activity may be no more than a "technology of revolution"—a technology which could easily be adopted and misused by groups who themselves have nothing to offer other than a lust for power. This, of course, is a danger attendant on any technology that seeks to improve the human condition.

The second reservation is more complex. The need for revolution research arises from recognition of the fact that structural violence already exists within many of today's societies. Where that violence is caused by exploitation and repression, revolution research may provide an answer. But there are many kinds of structural violence which are not caused by political injustice but which stem from the population explosion itself and the explosive rise of technology which accompanies it. Some examples will make the point clearer.

Disaster Research

Consider the following facts. In the past 100 years the human race has learned to travel 100 times faster than it could; it has increased its energy resources and its rate of population growth by 1,000 times; using computers, it has learned to handle data a million times faster; it has increased the power of its weapons by more than a million times; and it has learned to communicate 10 million times faster. In the face of such sensational advance, it is not surprising that society finds it difficult to keep pace, nor that these purely technical changes have generated a reservoir of social unease whose depth seems to have been seriously underestimated.

This book has been concerned with only one of these extravagant advances—the increase in our weapon power and its implications. For humanity as a whole, this technical advance remains the single most unwanted and threatening result of our technological age. But to some individuals, some families, some nations, there are more immediate problems. The starving have no need to worry about nuclear weapons. The overcrowded are not too concerned about the military space program. Those dying of the "disease of civilization" may actually see the hunt for future weapon systems as the irrelevancy which it is.

Science and technology are intimately involved with our future problems. Some have been directly caused by technical advance—chemical pollution is the most obvious example. Others have been indirectly caused. Even in the next decade, for example, we may expect famines to engulf as many as 100 million people at a time. The cause will have been medical techniques, some discovered as much as 50 years ago, which appeared to provide us with an efficient form of "death control." Yet other problems, such as aggression, poverty, and suppression, are as old as man himself and have no apparent relationship with technical advance. Yet of course they have. The nuclear weapon has turned aggression into global suicide; the wealth-producing potential of science and technology has shown that poverty need not be endured and that suppression is unnecessary in a world where there is potentially enough for everyone.

For these reasons, the technological explosion itself threatens our survival as immediately as do the military preoccupations which are its essential core. And if we are to devise any sensible set of solutions, we may have to attack the problem as a whole rather than single out the war explosion as a special case. This means examining everything from environmental degradation to biological warfare, from famine to overpopulation, from the effects of city living to the implications of automation.

Few scientists have tried to stare this alarming conglomeration of facts in the face. One who has is John Platt, associate director of the Institute of Mental Health at the University of Michigan. And he is concerned not only with the individual crises that appear to lie ahead, but with their cumulative effects on one another. What

would have happened, he asks, if the Cuban missile crisis had occurred on the same day as the East Coast power blackout? Or if
the hot line between Washington and Moscow had gone dead? His
conclusion is not encouraging:

> In the continued absence of better ways of
> heading off these multiple crises, our half-life (the
> time over which we have a 50:50 chance of surviv-
> ing) may be no longer than 10 or 20 years, but
> more like 5 to 10 years, or less. We may have even
> less than a 50:50 chance of living until 1980. . . .
> Anyone who feels more hopeful about getting past
> the nightmares of the 1970's has only to look be-
> yond them to the monsters of pollution and popu-
> lation rising up in the 1980's and 1990's. Whether
> we have 10 years or more like 20 or 30, unless we
> systematically find new large scale solutions, we
> are in the gravest danger of destroying our society,
> our world, and ourselves in any number of different
> ways well before the end of this century.

Such a warning cannot be lightly dismissed. But Dr. Platt points
to some cause for optimism. Things cannot go on as they have
for very much longer. For 50 years we have become so accustomed to measuring progress in terms of faster, heavier, higher,
and richer that it is almost impossible to visualize the process ever
stopping. Yet there are limits—limits set as much by the boundaries of technical possibility as by the finite size of the planet
earth. The latter, for instance, suggests it will be impossible ever
to cross the earth in any form of transport in much less than an
hour without some form of gravity control. We are not so far from
that limit today. In practical terms we may well settle for the supersonic aircraft as the ultimate need for earthly speed. In other areas
we may have already reached limits which it does not seem useful
to exceed. "We may never have," says Dr. Platt, "faster communications or more TV or larger weapons or a higher level of danger
than we have now."

If this is the case, mankind has reached a critical state. The
problem is to survive the transition through this area of criticality,
for things may turn out to be easier on the other side of it than
they are now. In other words, the crisis of crises now looming so
large may be a temporary affair. And to cross the chasm ahead we
may need a crash program of research for survival. What are the
fundamental issues that lie ahead?

The first problem we are familiar with: total annihilation from nuclear, chemical, or biological warfare, however caused. During the next five years, this is likely to be the only problem of this magnitude. And this situation may continue for up to 20 years. But after that—in the time period 20 to 50 years ahead—we must probably reckon that we will either have solved the problem or that there will be nobody left to solve it.

The second group of problems—of smaller magnitude—involve great destruction and physical, biological, or political change. Dr. Platt believes these will not threaten us in the next five years. But we shall see their effects in the period 5 to 20 years ahead in the form of "famines, ecological upsets, development failures, local wars and the rich-poor gap." In the period 20 to 50 years ahead lie unsolved questions about economic structure and political theory, population balance, world management, and universal education.

Even this does not complete the balance sheet. Three other groups of crises—each progressively smaller in their effect—can be foreseen. The first, producing "widespread almost unbearable tension," will come from racial conflict, the need for participation, rising expectations of the poor, and environmental degradation, all within the next five years. Transport, disease, and the loss of old cultures are likely to cause "large scale distress." And, on a less-serious level, problems of water supply and regional organization are likely to cause "tension producing responsive change," also within five years. So it goes on. And with a list as long and as serious as this, who can deny that somehow someone is going to have to do something about it?

A first reaction is that the problems are so numerous and so profound that any attempt to face them would require so much change as to be impossible. On this point, perhaps, we need not be too pessimistic. "Probably no human institution," writes Dr. Platt, "will continue unchanged for another 50 years, because they will all be changed by the crises if they are not changed in advance to prevent them." And if one tries to compare almost anything or anywhere with what it was like 10 years ago, one can see what Dr. Platt means.

Dr. Platt's solutions are very similar to the response of peace researchers to military technology. "Technology did not create human conflicts and inequities," he writes, "but it has made them unendurable. And where science and technology have expanded the problems in this way, it may be only more scientific under-standing and better technology that can carry us past them. The

cure for the pollution of rivers by detergents is the use of nonpol-
luting detergents." And so Dr. Platt goes on to call for crash programs of research involving every kind of specialist from lawyers to
biologists, from doctors to engineers. Addressing himself to the
question of who will commit himself to such a program and who
will organize it, he concludes:

> The task is clear. The task is huge. The time is
> horribly short. In the past we have had science
> for intellectual pleasure, and science for the con-
> trol of nature. We have had science for war.
> But today, the whole human experiment may
> hang on the question of how fast we now press
> the development of science for survival.

To me, Dr. Platt's suggestions—going far beyond the need for
revolution research—seem to be a minimum recipe for survival.
But whether even they are sufficient is another matter. They will
not be if—as begins to seem possible—technological society has
built into it a structural violence guaranteed to destroy it in the
end.

The Technology Explosion

"While we weren't watching we have
become dinosaurs again."
Professor George Wald
Chicago, March 20, 1970

Our nuclear journey has been a long one. It is time
now to weave the threads together and examine the nature of the
fabric that results. We must do so with the knowledge that this
has not been a simple story with a happy ending. It would have
been reassuring to learn that all the perils of military technology
will shortly be corrected by the combined efforts of our biologists,
peace and conflict researchers, and survival experts. I hope I have
said enough to show that this is both unlikely in practice and probably impossible in theory. But that does not leave us with only a
negative finding, with yet another doom-laden prediction of the
future. On the contrary, I believe it is a finding of quite extraordinary significance because it points up the essential routes that our
science and technology must follow in the future. For what we
have in the nuclear journey is a case history of the relationship
between science and the world. Its outcome has implications for
almost every important debate about our future that is now taking
place.

To recapitulate, we have seen how the invention of the bomb
led to a new way of life for our scientists and technologists. It
took them first into space and then into the oceans in the search
for greater security against the invention of their own making. We
have seen, too, something of the perils that lie ahead in the shape
of military technologies that wait to be invented—technologies that
are forcing the pace of unwanted discovery and application, technologies that fly in the face of our current concern with preserving
the natural environment against the ravages of economic growth
and earthly rape on which our advanced societies depend. We have

312

looked at the implications of all this for the "warfare states" in which we live. We have seen how technology has become warfare by other means, how the arms race has degenerated into a laboratory race against the unknown rather than an armaments race against foreign powers.

Within all this lies a familiar message that daily becomes more relevant: science and technology are immensely powerful instruments of cultural evolution. Our laboratories contain the seeds of social revolutions so overwhelming that, when they begin to sprout, we find ourselves quickly dwarfed by our own inventions. After 25 years of the technical arms race only now are we beginning to understand that it promises not to lessen the impact of the age-old problem of war, but rather to seal conflict into our society as a universal way of life that promises a universal way of death.

Recognizing this, of course, it is easy to assume that science and technology are simply being pointed in the wrong directions. If we used them instead to look at the other side of the coin, we should expect results of equal significance. Thus did our biologists and peace researchers begin to probe the technology of peace with great optimism. On historical precedent alone, they were right in assuming their results could be equally revolutionary. If science's relationship to the world were symmetrical in terms of good and evil, peace research—given even moderate backing and time to evolve its own equivalent of Einstein or Freud—should provide the answers that are so urgently needed.

To be sure, peace research has not yet had a fair hearing or time to reach its "takeoff" point. But the rumblings now being heard within the peace research movement should give us pause. They suggest, in effect, that the very idea of peace research may be based on a misconception so profound as to render the concept quite invalid. The implication is that the other side of the coin of military technology—the application of science to the study of peace—may be scientifically nonexistent. We are left with an asymmetry that penetrates right to the heart of our philosophical beliefs about the nature of the social universe we inhabit. The case history we have followed indicates that we should think twice before committing scientists to solving problems which the overzealous application of previous scientific advance has itself produced.

Unhappily, this trend is already well-advanced. We have realized that technological advance can be a mixed blessing and we have begun the slow process of trying to correct our worst excesses. From the chemical industries that have so nearly turned our en-

vironment into a wasteland of by-products have come antipollu-
tion programs in which new chemicals are produced to dissolve the
old. From the pesticide people have come studies into biological
control, by which it is hoped to use insects and microorganisms to
wage the chemical war previously fought by DDT, dieldrin, and
picloram. From those who, with the best will in the world, ultimately brought us the population explosion have come medical advances which promise to bring the birthrate once again into stable
relation with the death rate. All these efforts are aimed at technical
solutions to problems that were either previously unknown or were
insignificant until technology inflated them to obscene proportions.
They are all examples of "second-generation technology."

Peace research offers the supreme example—some might argue
even a parody—of the problems of second-generation technology.
For at first sight, no applied science would seem more deserving
of our support than one devoted to peace. When the peace researchers turned their attention to the practical problems of Vietnam, they did so with the best of intentions. Yet what they had
to say looked more like strategic analysis than peace research.

One was left wondering whether a logical, rational, or scientific
approach could ever make a useful contribution to this kind of
problem. After all, United States policy makers would argue, and
perhaps rightly, that there was nothing unscientific, irrational, or
illogical in the analysis that led them into Vietnam in the first place.
On the contrary the social science backing behind the policies of
counterinsurgency was extensive indeed.

If peace research is to be assessed on its Vietnam performance,
it would have to be found not only wanting but also dangerous—
dangerous in that it has provided a military establishment with
suggestions of alternative ways to pursue already-established policies. If peace research is symptomatic of second-generation technology as a whole, we have a clear warning of how easily things
can go wrong. As much was really clear from the time technologists first turned their attention to the urban problem in the United
States. Reasoning (correctly) that all the worst city riots occurred
only during the long, hot summers, they came up with a truly remarkable recommendation: that air conditioning be installed in all
slum property in all big cities. Whether the idea was serious or
merely facetious, it illustrates well how counterintuitive a technical
approach to a serious problem can become. The distressing thing
is that the logic that leads to this type of solution is as difficult to
fault as is the logic that leads to the concept of mutual deterrence.

But it is the preoccupation with logic which allows us to forget that deterrence is, as Theodore Roszak has put it, "nothing but an exquisitely rationalized social commitment to genocide."

With the example of peace research firmly in mind, our current tribulations appear more real than ever. What began in 1945 as a nuclear explosion has turned into a technology explosion, fragments from which have lodged themselves deep within society. An unthinking obsession with manipulation, with the ordering of our lives and our environment with the products of science and technology, threatens our future in a dozen different ways. We have poisoned, in some cases irreversibly, the earth and the sea, the sky and the land. A once-pleasant countryside has been turned into a concrete wilderness which yearly becomes less capable of supporting the ever-increasing population which depends on it. Our social critics take it in turns to argue that it is the pesticides or the motor car or nuclear power or new biological discoveries or our decaying cities that will soon make man as extinct as any of his Pleistocene precursors. They may each be right.

In the face of such attack, it helps little to quibble about inaccuracies here or exaggerations there. So far our chosen solution to all these problems is to exhort those who have perpetrated them to do something to clear up the mess. If peace research is a good model of the fate of this approach, then we can already predict that the offspring of this type of marriage of convenience will be sterile. In other words, the focusing of scientific attention on our gargantuan technology-inspired problems may be no more than the involuntary spasm of a society conditioned to seek all progress through the blindfold of technological advance.

It seems, in fact, as though we need much more radical solutions. To find them I believe we shall have to go back to our original motives for jumping on the bandwagon of scientific progress, and ask whether they were really inspired by a vision of future society that is any longer either meaningful or desirable.

The counter-culture of the young, of course, has already done just that and reached its perhaps too-hasty conclusion. Yet, as Theodore Roszak has argued so brilliantly in his *The Making of a Counter-Culture*, the dissident young do deserve to win any encounter with the defenders of technocracy:

> For the orthodox culture they confront is fatally
> and contagiously diseased. The prime symptom
> of that disease is the shadow of thermonuclear

annihilation beneath which we cower. The counter-culture takes its stand against the background
of this absolute evil, an evil which is not defined
by the sheer fact of the bomb, but by the total
ethos of the bomb, in which our politics, our
public morality, our economic life, our intellectual
endeavor are now embedded with a wealth of
ingenious rationalization. We are a civilization
sunk in an unshakable commitment to genocide,
gambling madly with the universal extermination
of our species. And how viciously we ravish our
sense of humanity to pretend, even for a day,
that such horror can be accepted as "normal,"
as "necessary"! Whenever we feel inclined to
qualify, to modify, to offer a cautious "yes . . .
but" to the protests of the young, let us return
to this fact as the decisive measure of the technocracy's essential criminality: the extent to
which it insists, in the name of progress, in the
name of reason, that the unthinkable become
thinkable and the intolerable become tolerable.

In this view the counter-culture is no longer alone. Over the past
couple of years, one university after another has begun to question
its role as a center of scientific research and to ask instead what
that research promises for our future. At conference after conference, a concern has been expressed both that science is leading us
into dangerous and materialistic wastelands and that more science
will never make them more fertile. At Chicago, on March 20, 1969,
George Wald, Nobel Laureate and professor of biology at Harvard,
received a standing ovation for a speech which epitomizes this
new attitude to science.

Drawing gently on his biological experience to cast matters into
perspective, Professor Wald told of the ancient revolution which
the mammals worked on the now-extinct dinosaurs and other rep-
tiles. "While we weren't watching," he said, "we have become dinosaurs again. . . . This time it's going to be a do-it-yourself extinction. And we've got power enough to drag all the rest of life along
with us."

But he drew some comfort from the fact that we were biologically still mammals which cared for their young ("Chinese kids
have mothers, Russian kids have mothers, I think even Viet Cong
kids have mothers"). This meant, he said, that those engaged in
working for the worst aspects of the technocracy had a pull of

conscience with their offspring: "I have a message for all the defense contractors and subcontractors, and the people working for them, and the generals and the admirals, and all the rest of them. That message is: clear it with the kids. If you haven't kids of your own to clear it with, clear it with the other people's kids. If you can clear it with them, if they'll buy it, I'll buy it too."

In the same simple style, Professor Wald went on to outline his program, starting with Vietnam. "Please don't think me frivolous," he said. "I've thought about little else for a long, long time. I'll tell you where I come out. I'll tell you how I think we get out of Vietnam. In ships."

When it came to sorting out the other ramifications of undesirable technology, the professor did not seek help from cost-effectiveness studies, from strategic loopholes, trip-wire philosophies, disarmament inspection schemes, or even peace research. "As our children go," he said, "so goes humanity." His program boiled down to this:

> When we have made a better world for children,
> we will have the best world for grownups, too.
> You may think that's an impractical program.
> It's just as practical as it can be. It's the most
> practical one I know. Are ABM's good for chil-
> dren? You tell me. Are nuclear weapons good
> for children? Are supersonic transports good for
> children? Are more cars on the road good for
> children? You tell me.

Professor Wald's directness, even his sentiment, should not be judged solely for its eloquence. Gentle as his words may seem, naive as they may sound, they constitute a frontal attack on a worldwide system of belief—a belief that science and technology must in the end turn out to be good for us, and therefore for our children. We should not be deceived as to the nature of the commitment that is being challenged.

For 300 years science and technology have grown faster than any other human activity. In the process they performed myriad functions. They freed men from primitive superstitions which for centuries had crippled both mind and body. They showed the world that astronomers knew more of the universe than the Church, thus liberating the human intellect for an exploration whose boundaries had previously been sharply limited by religious belief, and the scientific mind began, as Paul Goodman has put it, "a wandering dialogue with the unknown."

The wonders it revealed poured forth practical benefit. New technology created wealth, the Industrial Revolution, and—it was falsely argued—a chance for men to straighten their backs from the plough and examine a world in which there was time for other things than working and sleeping. As traditional religion waned, so did the world unconsciously learn to put its faith in technical progress. It had discovered a system which would in time explain everything, make everything possible. If this was ever in doubt before the bomb, it never was after it. No one needed conversion to a faith which from a few pounds of gray metal could liberate a mushroom cloud of death reaching to the heavens themselves. This was a spiritual experience, more profound than anything the Christian saints of other millennia could conjure up. A new religion was born.

That religion is now under attack because it has been found more powerful than even those who believe in it would wish. Just as the Protestants rejected Rome for its autocracy, so today's dissidents attack technology for the self-perpetuating power it seems to generate. Today, they argue, it is the weapons that make the policies, the computers that govern the people.

They also point, with unerring accuracy, to another similarity. By the sixteenth century medieval logic had progressed to a point of hopeless introspection. In its efforts to support the papacy it proceeded to ever more curious exercises of the mind bound neither by relevance to the real world nor by empirical checks which might have revealed its absurdity. There is little difference, today's critics argue, between a culture that gives its best minds over to the job of estimating how many angels can fit on a pinhead, and one that devotes its primary intellectual thrust to detailed calculations of the exact effects of a nuclear holocaust. Both are bound for extinction, the latter for one of its own making.

It was in 1510 that Luther went to Rome to discover the extent of the cultural and moral scandal that permeated the established Church. Seven years later he nailed his theses to the cathedral door and the Reformation began. Who will nail his theses to the laboratory door, and when, is not yet clear. But anyone who is worried by the war explosion will read the small print very carefully. They may find there a recipe for change which has equal relevance for East and for West, for north and for south—for capitalists and for communists, for developed and for underdeveloped.

The ingredients for this recipe have yet to be itemized. They will consist of much more than palatable doses of corrective medicine, and they will surely stem from a vigorous reassessment of the type of technological world which will allow the human race to continue its existence not just for decades or centuries but for millennia. We should be quite clear that the models of the future which we are pursuing now will not allow that. Quite apart from the increasing chance of nuclear annihilation, our current fixations with perpetual economic growth, with the mining of the earth's dwindling natural resources, with feeding ever-increasing populations and maintaining the gap between the rich and the poor all ensure that the war explosion—in one form or another—will bring the great experiment of human evolution to an abrupt close.

While I cannot predict what new wisdom the scientific theses in the making will embrace, I suspect they will find some inspiration from the most ambitious claim ever made by the peace researchers. They will turn the attention of men to new goals and away from questions, to quote Professor Rapaport once again, "which now overwhelmingly occupy them—questions concerned with the acquisition of mastery over nature and (increasingly) over people." In doing so they will have to reinterpret an eighteenth-century definition of social morality which defines as acceptable any action by the individual providing it could be repeated throughout society without ill effect. The golden law of technology, I predict, will turn out to be somewhat similar: the science and technology of the future will have to be valid for all men for all time. Thus defined it can be used neither for the technological rape of the planet earth nor for the manipulation of people. In this way we may yet be able to avoid the predictions of the war explosion and all the possible causes of it which we have so far been able to envisage.

Sources

Introduction: The War Explosion

Blackett, P. M. S. "The Ever-widening Gap." Address at University of Chicago symposium on "The Social Control of Science and Its Applications" (March 20, 1969)

Borgstrom, Georg. "The World Food Crisis" in *Futures* (June 1969)

Getting, Ivan A. "Halting the Inflationary Spiral of Death" in *Air Force/Space Digest* (April 1963)

Ozbekhan, Hasan. "The Role of Goals and Planning in the Solution of the World Food Problem" in Jungk, Robert, and Galtung, Johan (eds.), *Mankind 2000*. Boston: Universitetsforlaget, 1969

Revelle, Roger. "Population" in *Science Journal* (October 1967)

Taylor, Wallis. "Our World, A.D. 2000" in *New Scientist* (July 17, 1969)

United Nations. *World Population Prospects*. New York: United Nations, 1966

von Suttner, Bertha. *Memoiren*. Berlin: Deutsche Verlags Anstalt, 1909

Worsley, Peter. *The Third World*. 2nd ed. Chicago: University of Chicago Press, 1970

Chapter I: The Nuclear Future

Barnaby, C. F. "The Gas Centrifuge Project" in *Science Journal* (August 1969)

Barnaby, C. F. and others. *The Nuclear Future*. London: The Fabian Society, 1969

Barnaby, C. F. (ed). *Preventing the Spread of Nuclear Weapons*. New York: Humanities, 1969

Beaton, L. "Nuclear Proliferation" in *Science Journal* (December 1967)

Brown, Neville. "Blows to Non-proliferation" in *New Scientist* (February 6, 1969)

Brown, Neville. "Nuclear Matchmaking across the Channel" in *New Scientist* (June 19, 1969)

Brown, Ronald. "A Laser Trigger for H-Bombs?" in *New Scientist* (February 6, 1969)

Calder, Nigel (ed). *Unless Peace Comes*. New York: Viking, 1968

Calder, *Unless Peace Comes* (see above)

Cockroft, Sir John, "The Perils of Nuclear Proliferation" in Nigel *Scientist* (September 1961)

Dyson, Freeman J. "The Neutron Bomb" in *Bulletin of the Atomic*

Eggertson, Paul. "The Dilemma of Human Reliability" in *Psychiatry* (August 1968)

Emelyanov, V. S. "Nuclear Reactors Will Spread" in C. F. Barnaby, *Preventing the Spread of Nuclear Weapons* (see above)

Fink, Daniel J. "Strategic Warfare" in *Science and Technology* (October 1968)

Galtung, J., and Jungk, R. (eds). *Mankind 2000*. Boston: Universitetsforlaget, 1969

Glasstone, S. (ed). *The Effects of Nuclear Weapons*. Washington, D.C.: U.S. Department of Defense and Atomic Energy Commission, 1957 and 1962

Hachiya, M. *Hiroshima Diary*. Chapel Hill: University of North Carolina Press, 1955

Halperin, Morton M. "After Vietnam: Security and Intervention in Asia" in *Journal of International Affairs* (Vol. 2, 1968)

Holifield, Chet. "Hearings before the Subcommittee on Military Operations, Committee on Government Operations, Civil Defense" (March 1960); "Civil Defense—1961" (August 1961)

Holifield, Chet. "Hearings before the Special Subcommittee on Radiation, Joint Committee on Atomic Energy Fallout from Nuclear Weapons Tests" (May 1969); "Biological and Environmental Effects on Nuclear War" (June 1959)

Institute for Strategic Studies. *The Military Balance 1969–1970*. London: The Institute of Strategic Studies, 1969

James, Francis. "In China's Wild West" in *The Observer* (June 15, 1969)

Lapp, Ralph. *Kill and Overkill*. London: Weidenfeld and Nicolson, 1962

Lapp, Ralph. *The Weapons Culture*. New York: Norton, 1968

Novick, Sheldon. "Basement H-Bombs" in *Environment* (December 1968)

Phelps, J. B., et al. *Accidental War: Some Dangers in the 1960s*. Ohio: Mershon National Security Program, Ohio State University, 1960

Prawitz, J. "Safeguards and Related Arms Control Problems" in C. F. Barnaby, *Preventing the Spread of Nuclear Weapons* (see above)

Raser, John R. "The Failure of Fail-Safe" in *Trans-action* (January 1969)

Sidel, V. W., Geiger, J. J., and Lown, B. "The Medical Consequences of Thermonuclear War: II, The Physician's Role in the Postattack Period" in *New England Journal of Medicine* (Vol. 266, 1962, pp. 1137–45)

Stone, Peter. "How Cheap Is It to Make the Bomb?" in *The Statist* (October 8, 1965)

Stonier, Tom. *Nuclear Disaster*. Harmondsworth: Penguin Books, 1964

Storr, Anthony. *Human Aggression*. New York: Atheneum, 1968

Tinbergen, N. "On War and Peace in Animals and Man" in *Science* (June 28, 1968)

United Nations. "Effects of the Possible Use of Nuclear Weapons and the Security and Economic Implication for States of the Acquisition and Further Development of These Weapons." New York: United Nations, 1967

Yahuda, Michael B. "China's Nuclear Option" in *Bulletin of the Atomic Scientists* (February 1969)

Zuckerman, Sir Solly. "Judgment and Control in Modern Warfare" in *Foreign Affairs* (January 1962)

Zuckerman, Sir Solly. *Scientists and War*. New York: International Publications Service, 1970

Chapter II: Missiles and the Moon

Air Force Magazine Editors. Space Weapons. New York: Praeger, 1959

Bloomfield, Lincoln P. (ed.). *Outer Space: Prospects for Man and Society*. New York: Praeger, 1968

Brennan, D. G. *Arms and Arms Control in Outer Space* in Lincoln P. Bloomfield, *Outer Space* (see above)

Brown, Ron. "Bringing STD to the Military" in *New Scientist* (June 12, 1969)

Butz, J. S. "MOL: The Technical Promise and Prospects" in *Air Force/Space Digest* (October 1965)

Clarke, Arthur C. *Man and Space*. New York: Life Science Library, 1968

Clemens, Walter C. "Outer Space and Arms Control" in *Bulletin of the Atomic Scientists* (November 1967)

Cole, Dandridge M. "Response to the Panama Hypothesis" in *Astronautics* (June 1961)

Dornberger, Walter (see Witze, Claude)

Downs, Eldon W. (ed.). *The U.S. Air Force in Space*. New York: Praeger, 1966

Freitag, R. F. "After Apollo—the Space Station, Shuttle and Tug" in *Science Journal* (August 1970)

Freitag, R. F. "Navigational Satellites" in *Science Journal* (December 1965)

Frye, Alton. "Breaking the Cold War Stalemate" in *Air Force/Space Digest* (July 1962)

Gatland, Kenneth W. "Espionage from Orbit" in *Flight International* (April 10, April 17, 1969)

Gatland, Kenneth W. "New Tasks for Spy Satellites" in *New Scientist* (August 15, 1968)

Gavin, James M. *War and Peace in the Space Age*. New York: Harpers, 1958

Glines, C. V. "DOD: NASA's Silent Partner" in *Armed Forces Management* (May 1969)

Golovine, M. N. *Conflict in Space*. London: Temple Press, 1962

Graham, John. "One Step Nearer to Safeguard" in *Financial Times* (August 8, 1969)

Gunston, W. T. "The Controversial ABM" in *Science Journal* (July 1969)

Institute for Strategic Studies. *Strategic Survey 1969*. London: ISS, 1970

Kalkstein, Marvin. "Anti-ABM" in *Trans-Action* (June 1969)

Kennan, Erlend A., and Harvey, Edmund H. *Mission to the Moon*. New York: William Morrow, 1969

Klass, Philip J. "Value of Bombardment Satellites Debated" in *Aviation Week* (July 11, 1960)

Leary, Frank. "Antisatellite Defense" in *Space/Aeronautics* (June 1969)

Leavitt, William. "MOL: Evolution of a Decision" in *Air Force/Space Digest* (October 1965)

Levy, Lillian (ed.). *Space: Its Impact on Man and Society*. New York: W. W. Norton, 1965

Mandelbaum, Leonard. "Apollo: How the United States Decided to Go to the Moon" in *Science* (February 14, 1969)

Rathjens, George W. "The Dynamics of the Arms Race" in *Scientific American* (April 1969)

"Reusable Space Shuttle Effort Gains Momentum" in *Aviation Week & Space Technology* (October 27, 1969)

Schriever, Bernard A. "Does the Military Have a Role in Space?" in Lillian Levy (ed.) *Space: Its Impact on Man and Society* (see above)

Schwartz, Leonard E. "Manned Orbiting Laboratory" in *International Affairs* (January 1967)

Shapiro, Sidney. "Manned Space Stations" in *Science Journal* (February 1969)

Shepherd, Colston E. "A Space Patroller for the RAF" in *New Scientist* (September 13, 1962)

Smart, Ian. *Advanced Strategic Missiles: A Short Guide*. London: ISS, Adelphi Paper 63, 1970

Sternglass, Ernest J. "Can the Infants Survive?" in *Bulletin of the Atomic Scientists* (June 1969)

Sternglass, Ernest J. "Infant Mortality and Nuclear Tests" in *Bulletin of the Atomic Scientists* (April 1969)

Syvertson, C. A. "Aircraft without Wings" in *Science Journal* (December 1968)

Van Dyke, Vernon. *Pride and Power: The Rationale of the Space Program*. Urbana: University of Illinois Press, 1964

Wiesner, Jerome B. "The Cold War Is Dead but the Arms Race Rumbles On" in *Bulletin of the Atomic Scientists* (June 1967)

Wiesner, Jerome B., Chayes, Abram (eds.). *ABM: An Evaluation of the Decision to Deploy an Antiballistic Missile System*. New York: Harper and Row, 1969

Witze, Claude (interview with Walter Dornberger). "Let's Get Operational in Space" in *Air Force/Space Digest* (October 1965)

Yates, Sidney R. "Showdown on the ABM" in *Bulletin of the Atomic Scientists* (March 1969)

Young, Hugo, Silcock, Bryan, and Dunn, Peter. *Journey to Tranquillity.* New York: Doubleday, 1970

Zuckerman Sir Solly. "Judgment and Control in Modern Warfare" in *Foreign Affairs* (January 1962)

Chapter III: Military Control of the Oceans

Austin, Carl F. "Rock Site: A Way into the Sea" in *Sea Frontiers* (November–December 1967)

Bascom, Willard. "Techology and the Ocean" in *Scientific American* (September 1969)

Beverton, R. J. H. "NERC Policy on Submersibles" in *Science Journal* (August 1969, p. 28)

Bond, George. "New Horizons under the Sea" (mimeograph)

Bulban, Erwin J. "Navy Studies Deterrent Force for 1980s" in *Aviation Week & Space Technology* (June 8, 1964)

"Deep Ocean Sub–Sea Floor Military Bases of the 70's" in *Ocean Science News* (January 18, 1968)

"Effective Use of the Sea." *Report of the Panel on Oceanography of the President's Science Advisory Committee.* Washington, D.C.: U.S. Government Printing Office, June 1966

"From Dead Reckoning to Pinpoint Navigation" in *Science Horizons* (November 1969)

Frosch, Robert. *House of Representatives Report Number 999*

Gulland, J. A. "The Ocean Reservoir" in *Science Journal* (May 1968)

Haines, R. G. "Eyes and Ears on the Nuclear Patrol" in *New Scientist* (August 28, 1969)

Hawkes, Nigel. "UK Submersible Finds No Users" in *Science Journal* (June 1969)

Hersh, Seymour M. "An Arms Race on the Sea Bed?" in *War/Peace Report* (August–September 1968)

Holt, S. J. "The Food Resources of the Ocean" in *Scientific American* (September 1969)

Institute for Strategic Studies. *The Military Balance 1969–70.* London: The Institute for Strategic Studies, 1969

Laird, Melvin R. *Defense Report: Statement before the Senate Armed Services Committee* (Department of Defense mimeograph, March 19, 1969)

Leary, Frank. "Search for Subs" in *Space/Aeronautics* (September 1965)

Leary, Frank. "Who's Winning the Undersea War?" in *Space/Aeronautics* (February 1969)

Leydon, John K. "The ONR Oceanographic Program" in *Naval Research Reviews* (April 1967)

Loftas, Tony. *The Last Resource: Man's Exploitation of the Oceans.* Chicago: Regnery, 1970.

Marine Research Fiscal Year 1968. "A Catalog of Unclassified Marine Research Activities Sponsored During FY 1968 by Federal and Non-federal Organizations" (July 1969, p. 79)

Marine Science Affairs. "A Year of Plans and Progress, 1968," and "A Year of Broadened Participation, 1969," the second and third reports of the President to the Congress on Marine Resources and Engineering Development. Washington, D.C.: U.S. Government Printing Office.

Marvin, J. R., and Weyl, F. J. "The Summer Study" in *Naval Research Reviews* (August 1966)

Mero, John L. *The Mineral Resources of the Sea.* New York: American Elsevier, 1965

Niblock, Robert W. (ed). "Special Report on Oceanology" in *Technology Week* (September 26, 1966)

"ONR London: The Navy's International Scientific Exchange" in *Naval Research Reviews* (March 1967)

Opitz, Albert G. "From Science, Sea Power?" in *U.S. Naval Institute Proceedings* (October 1960)

Palmer, H. D. "Seamounts Will Act as Platforms" in *Undersea Technology* (August 1965)

Pardo, Arvid. "Control of the Seabed" in *Foreign Affairs* (October 1968)

Park, Ford. "Deep-sea Vehicles" in *International Science and Technology* (March 1965)

Pell, Claiborne. "The Sea Grant College" in *Navy* (May 1966)

Rechnitzer, Andreas. Quoted in Irwin Stambler, *The Battle for Inner Space.* New York: St. Martin's Press, 1962, p. 64

Rechnitzer, Andreas. "Underwater Exploration" in *Science Journal* (October 1965)

Scientific American. "The Ocean" (special issue, September 1969)

Siekevitz, Philip, and Sussman, Alfred. "Oceanography Prostituted by the Military" in *BioScience* (July 1969)

SIPRI (Stockholm International Peace Research Institute). "Submarine-launched Ballistic Missiles" in *SIPRI Yearbook of World Armaments and Disarmament* (New York: Humanities Press, 1969)

Spilhaus, Athelstan. "Man in the Sea" in *Science* (September 4, 1964)

"Submersible Fleet Needs More Use" in *Undersea Technology* (April 1969)

Towards a Better Use of the Oceans. Stockholm: Stockholm International Peace Research Institute (SIPRI), 1968

Valery, Nick. "A Policy for Ocean Industry" in *Science Journal* (December 1967)

Waters, O. D. "Oceanography's Role in Defense" in *Defense Industry Bulletin* (February 1968)

Chapter IV: The Environment Wreckers

Alland, Alexander, Jr. "War and Defense: An Anthropological Perspective" in *Bulletin of the Atomic Scientists* (June 1968)

Boffey, Philip M. "Nerve Gas: Dugway Accident Linked to Utah Sheep Kill" in *Science* (December 27, 1968)

Boucher, G., Ryall, A., and Jones, A. E. in *Journal of Geophysical Research* (74, 3808, 1969)

Briggs, J. C. "The Sea-level Panama Canal: Potential Biological Catastrophe" in *BioScience* (pp. 79–84, 1969)

Brodine, Virginia. "Six Questions for Australians" in *Environment* (April 1969)

Brodine, Virginia. "The Secret Weapons" in *Environment* (June 1969)

Carter, Luther J. "Earthquakes and Nuclear Tests: Playing the Odds on Amchitka" in *Science* (August 22, 1969)

Clarke, Robin. "Nuclear Engineering: A Mixed Blessing" in *Science Journal* (June, 1969, p. 6)

Clarke, Robin. *The Silent Weapons.* New York: David McKay, 1968.

Commoner, Barry. "The Myth of Omnipotence" in *Environment* (March 1969)

Eberhart, Jonathan. "To Pump or Un-pump" (report on waste disposal at Rocky Mountain Arsenal) in *Science News* (May 4, 1968)

Eggington, Joyce. "Unborn Die Years after A-Blast" in *The Observer* (July 6, 1969)

Emiliani, C., Harrison, Christopher G. A., and Swanson, Mary. "Underground Nuclear Explosions and the Control of Earthquakes" in *Science* (September 19, 1969)

Foley, Charles. "The Drops of Death That Fell from the Sky" in *The Observer* (April 5, 1970)

Goffman, John, and Tamplin, Arthur. *Hearings before Sub-committee on Air and Water Pollution* (November 18, 1969)

Gruchow, Nancy. "Project Sanguine Short-Circuited" in *Science* (November 14, 1969)

Kotsch, William J. "Weather Control and National Strategy" in *U.S. Naval Institute Proceedings* (July 1960)

Landry, John. "The Case for Plowshare" in *Oak Ridge National Laboratory Review* (Winter 1969)

Lovell, Sir Bernard. "The Pollution of Space" in *Bulletin of the Atomic Scientists* (December 1968)

MacDonald, Gordon J. F. "Weather Modification" in *Science Journal* (January 1968)

Martell, E. A. "Plowing a Nuclear Furrow" in *Environment* (April 1969)

Meselson, M., and Perry Robinson, J. P. "The Status of Tear Gas and Other Sensory Irritants in Chemical Warfare." Paper given to Pugwash Biological Warfare Study Group at Marianske Lazne, Czechoslovakia (May 22–23, 1969)

Miskel, J. A. "Release of Radioactivity from Nuclear Cratering Experiments," UCRL-14778, Lawrence Radiation Laboratory, University of California (August 26, 1966)

Nelson, Bryce. "Herbicides: Order on 2,4,5,-T Issued at Unusually High Level" in *Science* (November 21, 1969)

Pakiser, L. C., et al. "Earthquake Prediction and Control" in *Science* (December 19, 1969)

Pfeiffer, E. W. "Ecological Effects of the Vietnam War" in *Science Journal* (February 1969)

Phillips, John. "Tsunamis" in *Science Journal* (December 1967)

SIPRI. *The Problem of Chemical and Biological Warfare* (Volumes I–VI). Stockholm: SIPRI, 1970

Sternglass, Ernest J. "Can the Infants Survive?" in *Bulletin of the Atomic Scientists* (June 1969)

Sternglass, Ernest J. "Has Nuclear Testing Caused Infant Deaths?" in *New Scientist* (July 24, 1969)

Tamplin, Arthur R. "Fetal and Infant Mortality and the Environment" in *Bulletin of the Atomic Scientists* (December 1969)

Tschirley, F. H. "An Assessment of Ecologic Consequences of the Defoliation Program in Vietnam." Agricultural Research Service, USDA (April 12, 1968)

Tucker, Anthony. "Man-made Earthquakes" in *The Guardian* (April 24, 1969)

United Nations Group of Consultant Experts. *Chemical and Bacteriological (Biological) Weapons and the Effects of Their Possible Use.* New York: United Nations, 1969

United Nations Scientific Committee. *Report of the United Nations Scientific Committee on the Effects of Atomic Radiation.* New York: United Nations, 1958, 1962

"U.S. Navy Wiring Wisconsin for Doomsday" in *Halifax Chronicle-Herald* (October 21, 1969)

Whiteside, Thomas. "A Reporter at Large: Defoliation" in *New Yorker* (February 7, 1970)

WHO Group of Consultants. *Health Aspects of Chemical and Biological Weapons.* Geneva: World Health Organization, 1970

Chapter V: Science in the Warfare State

Blackett, P. M. S. "Memorandum to the Select Committee on Science and Technology" in *Nature* (September 14, 1968)

Boffey, Philip M. "Nixon and NSF: Politics Block Appointment of Long as Director" in *Science* (April 18, 1969)

Burhop, Eric, and Moon, P. B. "Atomic Survey," London: Atomic Scientists Association, 1946

Clarke, Robin. "Sponsored Research and Universities" in *Science Journal* (January 1969)

Defense Estimates 1969–70. London: HMSO, 1969

Farrington, Benjamin. *Science in Antiquity* (2d ed.) New York: Oxford University Press, 1969

Federal Funds for Research, Development and Other Scientific Activities Fiscal Years 1966, 1967 and 1968. Washington, D.C.: U.S. Government Printing Office, 1967

Federal Support to Universities and Colleges, Fiscal Years 1963–66. Washington, D.C.: U.S. Government Printing Office, 1967

Foster, John S. "The Leading Edge of National Security" in *International Science and Technology* (October 1968)

Galbraith, John Kenneth. *How to Control the Military*. New York: Signet (The New American Library), 1969

Garwin, Richard L. "Strengthening Military Technology" in *International Science and Technology* (October 1968)

Goldwater, Barry. Address quoted in *Science* (May 16, 1969)

Hamilton, Andrew. "Basic Research: Congress on Prowl" in *Science* (November 14, 1969)

Kidd, Charles V. *American Universities and Federal Research*. Cambridge, Mass.: Harvard University Press, 1959

Klass, Philip J. "New Radar Telescope to Map Ionosphere" in *Aviation Week & Space Technology* (April 19, 1963; see also note on same subject on page 63 of the issue dated October 13, 1969)

Langer, Elinor. "Nuclear Stockpile" in *Science* (May 8, 1964)

Leitenberg, Milton. "Scientific Research and Strategic Weapons Development." Paper delivered at Pugwash Conference at Marianske Lazne, Czechoslovakia (May 10, 1969)

LeMay, Curtis E., with Smith, Dale C. *America Is in Danger*. New York: Funk & Wagnalls, 1968

Long, Franklin A. "Strategic Balance and the ABM" in *Bulletin of the Atomic Scientists* (December 1968)

McCarthy, Eugene J. "The Power of the Pentagon" in *Saturday Review* (December 21, 1968)

"The Military-Industrial Complex" in *Newsweek* (June 9, 1969)

Miller, J. P. Presidential Address before the Association of Graduate Schools, San Francisco, October 21, 1968

The National Security State. Quoted in *Congressional Record* (November 6, 1969, F9417 *et seq.*)

Orlans, H. "The Impact of the Federal Government on Higher Education" in L. C. Deighton, et al. (eds), *The Encyclopedia of Education*. New York: Macmillan, 1969

Price, Don K. *The Scientific Estate*. Cambridge, Mass.: Harvard University Press, 1965

Price, William J., Ashley, William G., and Martino, Joseph P. *Relating the Accomplishments of AFOSR to the Needs of the Air Force*. Arlington, Virginia: Air Force Office of Scientific Research, 66—2423

Price, William J. *The Role of AFOSR in AFOSR Research*. Arlington, Virginia: Air Force Office of Scientific Research, 67—0300

Rabinowitch, Eugene. "Responsibility of Scientists in Our Age" in *Bulletin of the Atomic Scientists* (November 1969)

Rivkin, Steven R. *Technology Unbound*. Oxford: Pergamon Press, 1969

Rothschild, J. H. *Tomorrow's Weapons*. New York: McGraw-Hill, 1964

Second Report from the Select Committee on Science and Technology: Defense Research. London: HMSO, 1969

SIPRI Yearbook on World Armaments and Disarmament 1968–69. New York: Humanities Press, 1969

Statistics of Science and Technology. London: HMSO, 1967 and 1968

Teller, Edward. "Essay on Nuclear Weapons Research Management Policies" in *Aviation Week & Space Technology* (April 22, 1963)

Thomson, Murray. "Militarism 1969" in *Peace Research Reviews* (Vol. 2, No. 5, October 1968)

Warner cartoon published in *Punch* (7, 53, 58 and 59, 1842)

World Military Expenditures, 1966–67 (Research Report 68–52). Washington, D.C.: U.S. Arms Control and Disarmament Agency, December 1968

York, Herbert F. "Military Technology and National Security" in *Scientific American* (August 1969)

Chapter VI: The Psychology of Aggression

American Anthropological Association. "War: The Anthropology of Armed Conflict and Aggression" in *Natural History,* December 1, 1967

Andreski, Stanislav. "Origins of War" in J. D. Carthy and F. S. Ebling (eds.). *The Natural History of Aggression* (see below)

Ardrey, Robert. *African Genesis.* New York: Atheneum, 1961

Burton, John W. "Conflict as a Function of Change" in *Conflict and Society,* edited by Anthony De Reuck and Julie Knight. London: Churchill, 1966

Burton, John. "The Nature of Aggression as Revealed in the Atomic Age" in Carthy and Ebling (eds.), *The Natural History of Aggression*

Carthy, J. D., and Ebling, F. J. (eds). *The Natural History of Aggression.* London: Academic Press, 1964

Dicks, M. V. "Intra-personal Conflict and the Authoritarian Character" in Anthony De Reuck and Julia Knight (eds.), *Conflict in Society.* London: Churchill, 1966.

Eckhardt, William. "Psychology of War and Peace" in *Journal of Human Relations* (XVI, 2, 2d Quarter, 1968)

Freedman, D. G. "The Origins of Social Behaviour" in *Science Journal* (November 1967)

Freud, Sigmund. *Civilization and Its Discontents.* London: Hogarth Press, 1930

Gardner, Robert, and Reider, Karl G. *Gardens of War.* New York: Random House, 1969

Gorer, Geoffrey. "Man Has No 'Killer' Instinct" in M. F. A. Montagu, *Man and Aggression* (see below)

Hass, Ernst. "Common Opponent Sought . . . and Found?" in *Bulletin of the Atomic Scientists* (November 1968)

Hill, Denis. "Aggression and Mental Illness" in Carthy and Ebling (eds.), *The Natural History of Aggression*

Hoagland, Hudson. "Technology, Adaptation, and Evolution" in *Bulletin of the Atomic Scientists* (January 1969)

Kuo, Zing Yang. "Genesis of the Cat's Response to the Rat" in R. C. Birney, et al., *Instinct.* Princeton: Van Nostrand, 1961

Leach, Edmund. "Don't Say 'Boo' to a Goose" in M. F. A. Montagu (ed.), *Man and Aggression*

Leyhausen, Paul. "Man as a Social Animal" in *Science Journal* (October 1969)

Leyhausen, Paul. "The Sane Community: A Density Problem?" in *Discovery* (September 1965)

Lorenz, Konrad. *On Aggression.* New York: Harcourt, Brace & World, 1966

Mathews, L. Harrison. "Overt Fighting in Mammals" in Carthy and Ebling (eds.), *The Natural History of Aggression*

Montagu, M. F. Ashley (ed.). *Man and Aggression.* New York: Oxford University Press, 1968

Morris, Desmond. *The Naked Ape.* New York: McGraw-Hill, 1968

Olds, James. "Emotional Centres in the Brain" in *Science Journal* (May 1967)

Radcliffe-Brown, A. R. *Structure and Function in Primitive Society.* London: Cohen and West, 1952

Russell, Claire and W. M. S. *Violence, Monkeys and Man.* London: Macmillan, 1968

Scott, J. P. "That Old-Time Aggression" in M. F. A. Montagu, *Man and Aggression*

Storr, Anthony. *Human Aggression.* New York: Atheneum, 1968

Storr, Anthony. "Possible Substitutes for War" in Carthy and Ebling (eds.) *The Natural History of Aggression*

Tinbergen, M. "On War and Peace in Animals and Man" in *Science* (June 28, 1968)

Zuckerman, Sir Solly. *The Social Life of Monkeys and Apes.* London: Kegan Paul, Trench, Trubner, 1932

Chapter VII: The Natural History of War

Alcock, N. Z., and Lowe, Keith. "The Vietnam War as a Richardson Process" in *Journal of Peace Research* (No. 2, 1969)

Boulding, Kenneth E. "A Data-Collecting Network for the Sociosphere" in *Impact of Science on Society* (April–June 1968)

Boulding, Kenneth E. "The Future of the Social Sciences" in *Science Journal* (September 1965)

Boulding, Kenneth E. "National Images and International Systems" in *Journal of Conflict Resolution* (June 1959)

Broch, Tom, and Galtung, Johan. "Belligerence among the Primitives" in *Journal of Peace Research* (No. 1, 1966)

Brody, Richard A. "Some Systemic Effects of the Spread of Nuclear Weapons Technology: A Study through Simulation of a Multi-nuclear Future" in *Journal of Conflict Resolution* (December 1963)

Bronfenbrenner, Urie. "The Mirror Image in Soviet-American Relations: A Social Psychologist's Report" in *Journal of Social Issues* (17, 3, 1961)

Crow, Wayman J., and Raser, John R. "A Simulation Study of Deterrence Theories" in *Proceedings of the International Peace Research Inaugural Conference*. Assen: Royal Van Garcum 1966

Denton, Frank H., and Phillips, Warren. "Some Patterns in the History of Violence" in *Journal of Conflict Resolution* (June 1968)

Eckhardt, William, and White, Ralph K. "A Test of the Mirror-image Hypothesis: Kennedy and Khrushchev" in *Journal of Conflict Resolution* (September 1967)

Friberg, Mats, and Jonsson, Dan. "A Simple War and Armament Game" in *Journal of Peace Research* (No. 3, 1963)

Galtung, Johan. "Secession as a World Tendency: A Proposal" (paper delivered at 19th Pugwash Conference on Science and World Affairs, Sochi, U.S.S.R., October 22–27, 1969)

Greaves, Fielding L. *Military Review* (December 1962)

Guetzkow, Harold. "Some Correspondences between Simulations and Realities in International Relations" in Morton A. Kaplan (ed.), *New Approaches to International Relations* New York: St. Martin's Press, 1968

Guetzkow, H., Alger, C. F., Brody, R. A., Noel, R. C., and Snyder, R. C. *Simulation in International Relations*. Englewood Cliffs, N.J.: Prentice-Hall, 1963

Haas, Michael. "Societal Approaches to the Study of War" in *Journal of Peace Research* (No. 4, 1965)

Hermann, Charles, and Margaret. "An Attempt to Simulate the Outbreak of World War I" in *American Political Science Review* (June 1967)

Hermann, Charles, and Margaret. "On the Possible Use of Historical Data for Validation Study of Inter-Nation Simulation." Northwestern University: 1962 (prepared under contract to U.S. Naval Ordnance Test Station)

Holsti, Ole R. "The Belief System and National Images: A Case Study" in *Journal of Conflict Resolution* (September 1962)

Holsti, Ole R., and North, Robert C. "The History of Human Conflict" in Elton B. McNeil (ed.), *The Nature of Human Conflict*. Englewood Cliffs, N.J.: Prentice-Hall, 1965

Klingberg, Frank L. "Predicting the Termination of War: Battle Casualties and Population Losses" in *Journal of Conflict Resolution* (June 1966)

Kybal, Dalimil. "Science and Technology in the 1970s" in *NATO's Fifteen Nations* (February–March 1969)

North, Robert C., Brody, Richard A., and Holsti, Ole R. "Some Empirical Data on the Conflict Spiral" in *Peace Research Society* (*International*) Papers (I, 1964)

Rapaport, Anatol, and Richardson, Lewis F. "Richardson's Mathematical Theory of War" in *Journal of Conflict Resolution* (September 1957)

Richardson, L. F. *Arms and Insecurity*. Pittsburgh: Boxwood Press, 1960

Richardson, L. F. "Could an Arms Race End without Fighting?" in *Nature* (September 29, 1951)

Richardson, Lewis F. *Statistics of Deadly Quarrels*. Pittsburgh: Box-wood Press, 1960

Rutherford, Brent M. "Psychopathology, Decision-making, and Political Involvement" in *Journal of Conflict Resolution* (December 1966)

Smoker, Paul. "The Arms Race: A Wave Model" in *Peace Research Society (International) Papers* (IV, 1966)

Smoker, Paul. "Fear in the Arms Race: A Mathematical Study" in *Journal of Peace Research* (No. 1, 1964)

Smoker, Paul. "Trade, Defence and the Richardson Theory of Arms Races: A Seven-Nation Study" in *Journal of Peace Research* (No. 2, 1965)

Sorokin, Pitirim. *Social and Cultural Dynamics*. Totowa, N.J.: Bed-minster Press, 1941 (repr. 1962)

Tchijevsky, A. L. "Physical Factors of the Historical Process" in *Journal of Cycle Research* (Vol. 5, No. 4, 1956)

Voevodsky, John. "Quantitative Behavior of Warring Nations" in *The Journal of Psychology* (72, 1969 pp. 269–292)

Wheeler, Raymond H. "Wheeler's Indexes of War" in *Journal of Cycle Research* (Vol. 10, No. 4, 1960)

Wheeler, Raymond H. "The Effect of Climate on Human Behavior in History" in *Transactions of the Kansas Academy of Science* (Vol. 46, 1943)

White, R. K. "Mirror Images in the East-West Conflict" (address delivered at American Psychological Association Convention, September 4, 1961)

Wilson, Andrew. *The Bomb and the Computer*. New York: Delacorte, 1969

Wood, David. *Conflict in the Twentieth Century*. London: Institute for Strategic Studies, Adelphi Paper 48, 1968

Wright, Quincey. *A Study of War* (2d ed.). Chicago and London: University of Chicago Press, 1965

Chapter VIII: The Science of Conflict

Bullough, Vern L. "The Roman Empire vs. Persia: A Study of Successful Deterrence" in *Journal of Conflict Resolution* (March 1963)

Burton, John W. *Conflict and Communication*. London: MacMillan, 1969

Burton, J. W. "The Nature of Aggression as Revealed in the Atomic Age" in J. D. Carthy and F. J. Ebling (eds.), *The Natural History of Aggression*. London: Academic Press, 1964

Clarke, Robin. "How They Brought the Good News: Critical Role for Pugwash in Paris Peace Talks" in *Science Journal* (January 1969)

Crow, Wayman J. "A Study of Strategic Doctrines Using the Internation Simulation" in *Journal of Conflict Resolution* (September 1963)

De Reuck, Anthony, and Knight, Julie (eds.). *Conflict in Society*. London: Churchill, 1966

Deutsch, Morton, and Krauss, Robert M. "Studies of Interpersonal Bargaining" in *Journal of Conflict Resolution* (March 1962)

Henkin, Louis (ed.). *Arms Control: Issues for the Public*. Englewood Cliffs, N.J.: Prentice-Hall, 1961

Isard, Walter, and Smith, Tony E. A. "Practical Application of Game Theoretical Approaches to Arms Reduction" in *Peace Research Society (International)* (IV, 1965)

Kahn, Herman. *On Thermonuclear War*. Princeton: Princeton University Press, 1961

Levine, Robert A. "Arms Agreement: A Model of Stalemate" in *Journal of Conflict Resolution* (December 1962)

Milburn, Thomas W. "The Intellectual History of a Research Program" in Dean G. Gruitt, and Richard C. Snyder (eds.), *Theory and Research on the Causes of War*. Englewood Cliffs, N.J.: Prentice-Hall, 1969

Milburn, Thomas W. "What Constitutes Effective Deterrence" in *Journal of Conflict Resolution* (June 1959)

Naroll, Raoul. "Deterrence in History" in Dean G. Pruitt and Richard C. Snyder (eds.). *Theory and Research on the Causes of War*. Englewood Cliffs, N.J.: Prentice-Hall, 1969.

Neild, Robert. "What Has Happened to Disarmament." David Davies Memorial Institute of International Studies. Annual Memorial Lecture, 1968

Newman, James R. "Thermonuclear War" in *Scientific American* (March 1961)

Osgood, Charles E. *An Alternative to War or Surrender*. Urbana: University of Illinois Press, 1962

Pilisuk, Marc. "Timing and Integrity of Inspection in Arms Reduction Games" in *Peace Research Society (International) Papers* (V, 1966)

Pilisuk, M., and Rapaport, A. "A Non-Zero Sum Game Model of Some Disarmament Problems" in *Peace Research Society (International) Papers* (I, 1964)

Pilisuk, M., and Rapaport, A. "Step-wise Disarmament and Sudden Destruction in a Two-Person Game: A Research Tool" in *Journal of Conflict Resolution* (March 1964)

Pitman, George R. "A Calculus of Military Stability" in *Journal of Peace Research* (No. 4, 1966)

Pruitt, Dean G., and Snyder, Richard C. (eds.). *Theory and Research on the Causes of War*. Englewood Cliffs, N.J.: Prentice-Hall, 1969

Rapaport, Anatol. "Formal Games as Probing Tools for Investigating Behavior Motivated by Trust and Suspicion" in *Journal of Conflict Resolution* (September 1963)

Rapaport, Anatol. "Games Which Simulate Deterrence and Disarmament" in *Peace Research Reviews* (August 1967)

Rapaport, Anatol. *Strategy and Conscience*. New York and London: Harper and Row, 1964

Raser, John R. "Deterrence Research: Past Progress and Future Needs" in *Journal of Peace Research* (No. 4, 1966)

Schelling, Thomas C. *Arms and Influence*. New Haven, Conn.: Yale University Press, 1966

Schelling, Thomas C. *The Strategy of Conflict.* Cambridge, Mass.: Harvard University Press, 1960

Singer, J. David, and Small, Melvin. "National Alliance Commitments and War Involvement 1815–1945" in *Peace Research Society (International) Papers* (V, 1966)

SIPRI Yearbook of World Armaments and Disarmament 1968/69. Part II, section 2A: Nuclear Weapon Testing Programmes, 1945–68. London: Duckworth, 1970

"Vietnam: Some Basic Issues and Alternatives." *Peace Research Society (International) Papers* (X, 1968)

Chapter IX: Revolution and Change

Barnet, Richard J. *Intervention and Resolution.* Cleveland, Ohio: World Publishing Company, 1968

Boulding, Kenneth E. "Dare We Take the Social Sciences Seriously?" in *American Psychologist* (November 1967)

Dencik, Lars. "Peace Research: Pacification or Revolution?" *(Proceedings of IPRA Third General Conference.* Assen, 1970)

Fossum, Egil. "Factors Influencing the Occurrence of Military Coups D'Etat in Latin America" in *Journal of Peace Research* (3, 1967)

Fossum, Egil. "Some Comments on the Possible Contribution of the Military to the Peaceful Development of the Poor Countries" in *Bulletin of Peace Proposals* (Vol. 1, No. 1, 1970)

Galtung, Johan. "Conflict as a Way of Life" in *New Society* (October 16, 1969)

Galtung, Johan. "Peace Research: Science or Politics in Disguise?" PRIO publication 23–6 (Oslo, 1967)

Gurr, Ted. Seminar at Peace Research Center (London: February 25, 1970)

Hagan, Roger. "Counter-Insurgency and the New Foreign Relations" in *The Correspondent* (Autumn 1964)

Heilbronner, Robert. "Counterrevolutionary America" in *Commentary* (April 1967)

Horowitz, Irving Louis. "Social Science Yogis and Military Commissars" in *Trans-Action* (May 1968)

Horowitz, Irving Louis (ed.). *The Rise and Fall of Project Camelot.* Cambridge, Mass.: MIT Press, 1967

Jones, Colonel George M. "Commander's Report on Fort Bragg Special Warfare Center" in *Army Navy Air Force Journal* (July 30, 1960)

"Man Gaoled for 1000 Years." *The Times* (March 21, 1970)

Platt, John. "What We Must Do" in *Science* (November 28, 1969)

Pool, Ithiel de Sola. "The Necessity for Social Scientists Doing Research for Governments" in *Background* (August 1966)

Schmid, Herman. "Peace Research and Politics" in *Journal of Peace Research* (3, 1968)

Schmid, Herman. "Peace Research as a Technology for Pacification." *Proceedings of IPRA Third General Conference.* Assen, 1970

Szulc, Tad. *The Winds of Revolution.* New York: Praeger, 1965

Tompkins, John S. *The Weapons of World War III: The Long Road Back from the Bomb.* New York: Doubleday, 1966

Epilogue: The Technology Explosion

Ellul, J. *The Technological Society.* New York: Knopf, 1964

Goodman, Paul. "Can Technology Be Humane?" in *New York Review of Books* (1970)

Morison, Robert S. "Science and Social Attitudes" in *Science* (July 11, 1969)

Price, Don K. "Purists and Politicians" in *Science* (January 3, 1969)

Roszak, Theodore (ed.). *The Dissenting Academy.* New York: Pantheon, 1968

Roszak, Theodore. *The Making of a Counter-Culture.* New York: Doubleday, 1969.

Tishler, Max. "The Siege of the House of Reason" in *Science* (October 10, 1969)

Wald, George. Address at MIT (March 4, 1969)

Wald, George. "America's My Home. Not My Business, My Home." Address given at University of Chicago symposium, "The Social Control of Science and Its Applications" in *Bulletin of the Atomic Scientists* (May 1969)

About the Author

Robin Clarke has been editor of the British scientific magazines Discovery *and* Science Journal, *as well as BBC broadcaster on "Scientific Discovery." He is the author of* The Silent Weapons, *published in 1968.*